MATERIALS AND LOGISTICS MANAGEMENT

MATERIALS AND LOGISTICS MANAGEMENT

Prof. K. Shridhara Bhat
B.E. (Mech), PG DIM, MBA, F.I.I.M.M.
Managing Director,
Akshaya Management Consultancy Services,
Bengaluru - 560 085,
Karnataka, India.

Himalaya Publishing House

MUMBAI • NEW DELHI • NAGPUR • BENGALURU • HYDERABAD • CHENNAI • PUNE • LUCKNOW • AHMEDABAD • ERNAKULAM • BHUBANESWAR • INDORE • KOLKATA • GUWAHATI

First Edition : 2009
Reprint : 2013

Published by : Mrs. Meena Pandey for **Himalaya Publishing House Pvt. Ltd.,** "Ramdoot", Dr. Bhalerao Marg, Girgaon, **Mumbai - 400 004.** Phone: 022-23860170/23863863, Fax: 022-23877178
E-mail: himpub@vsnl.com; Website: www.himpub.com

Branch Offices :

New Delhi : "Pooja Apartments", 4-B, Murari Lal Street, Ansari Road, Darya Ganj, New Delhi - 110 002. Phone: 011-23270392, 23278631; Fax: 011-23256286

Nagpur : Kundanlal Chandak Industrial Estate, Ghat Road, Nagpur - 440 018. Phone: 0712-2738731, 3296733; Telefax: 0712-2721215

Bengaluru : No. 16/1 (Old 12/1), 1st Floor, Next to Hotel Highlands, Madhava Nagar, Race Course Road, Bengaluru - 560 001. Phone: 080-32919385; Telefax: 080-22286611

Hyderabad : No. 3-4-184, Lingampally, Besides Raghavendra Swamy Matham, Kachiguda, Hyderabad - 500 027. Phone: 040-27560041, 27550139; Mobile: 09390905282

Chennai : No. 8/2, 2nd Madley Street, Ground Floor, T. Nagar, Chennai - 600 017. Mobile: 09345345055

Pune : First Floor, "Laksha" Apartment, No. 527, Mehunpura, Shaniwarpeth (Near Prabhat Theatre), Pune - 411 030. Phone: 020-24496323/24496333; Mobile: 09370579333

Lucknow : House No 731, Shekhupura Colony, Near B.D. Convent School, Aliganj, Lucknow - 226 022. Mobile: 09307501549

Ahmedabad : 114, "SHAIL", 1st Floor, Opp. Madhu Sudan House, C.G. Road, Navrang Pura, Ahmedabad - 380 009. Phone: 079-26560126; Mobile: 09377088847

Ernakulam : 39/176 (New No: 60/251) 1st Floor, Karikkamuri Road, Ernakulam, Kochi - 682011, Phone: 0484-2378012, 2378016; Mobile: 09344199799

Bhubaneswar : 5 Station Square, Bhubaneswar - 751 001 (Odisha). Phone: 0674-2532129, Mobile: 09338746007

Indore : Kesardeep Avenue Extension, 73, Narayan Bagh, Flat No. 302, IIIrd Floor, Near Humpty Dumpty School, Indore - 452 007 (M.P.). Mobile: 09301386468

Kolkata : 108/4, Beliaghata Main Road, Near ID Hospital, Opp. SBI Bank, Kolkata - 700 010, Phone: 033-32449649, Mobile: 09883055590, 07439040301

Guwahati : House No. 15, Behind Pragjyotish College, Near Sharma Printing Press, P.O. Bharalumukh, Guwahati - 781009, (Assam). Mobile: 09883055590, 09883055536

DTP by : Page Designers, Bengaluru.

Printed at : M/s. Seven Hills Printers, Hyderabad. On behalf of HPH.

PREFACE

Materials constitute a major input to the manufacture of both consumer durable and non-durable products. Therefore, management of materials become crucial for most organizations to be successful in their business. Since the cost of purchasing, storing, preserving, moving and shipping of materials account for over half of the product's cost, the focus of materials management will be on reducing both *cost of materials* and *cost on materials*, adding value to the products and improving profitability for the organization.

Logistics and the closely related concept of Supply Chain Management are essential corner stones of competitive strategy, increased market share and shareholder value for most organizations. Logistics management comprises both inbound logistics (concerned with flow of materials and components from the suppliers to the production system) and outbound logistics (distribution of the product in the channel of distribution, finally to the end user) Inbound logistics is also known as materials management. Since both materials management and logistics management are integral parts of supply chain management which has become a strategic area in modern business, it is most relevant that a subject titled "Materials and Logistics Management" has been introduced as a compulsory subject for MBA programme of Pune University.

This book is organized into 14 chapters, giving the basic concepts and techniques of materials management, logistics management and supply chain management. The salient features of this book includes box illustrations, tables, exhibits, snapshots and case studies which help students to understand the concepts, techniques and their practical applications.

I thank Sri Niraj Pandey and Sri Anuj Pandey of Himalaya Publishing House for publishing this book. I also thank Sri Surendra of Himalaya Publishing House, Pune branch who motivated me to author this book. Neverthless, I thank Sri B.S.Madhu and Kum.Divya for their timely effort in completing the DTP work and coverpage design.

I thank my family members, friends and well wishers for their encouragement and support in this task.

I invite readers, especially faculty members who teach this subject to offer their constructive suggestions to improve the quality of the contents of this book because in my opinion continuous improvement of quality in the most important asset of any another.

K. SHRIDHARA BHAT
No.680, 'Akshaya', 1 'C' Main,
Kempegowda Layout, 3rd Block,
3rd Phase, Banashankari III Stage
Bangalore - 560 085. Ph : (080) 26694761
Email : sbhat680@yahoo.com

CONTENTS

CHAPTER 1 : INTRODUCTION TO MATERIALS MANAGEMENT 1 - 15

Evolution of Materials Management, Importance of Materials in Manufacturing organisations, Importance of Materials Management, Definitions of Materials Management, Objectives of Materials Management, Functions of Materials Management, Scope of Materials Management, Challenges of Materials Management, Materials Management Organisation, Materials Management Concepts, Interfaces Of Materials Management with Other Functions, Modern Trends in Materials Management, Review Questions

CHAPTER 2 : INTRODUCTION TO LOGISTICS MANAGEMENT 16 - 34

What is Logistics?, What is Logistics Management?, Scope and importance of Logistics Management, Development of Logistics, Need for Logistics Management, Logistical Activities, Role of Logistics in Supply Chain Management, The Role of Logistics in The Economy, The Role of Logistics in The Organisation, Logistics Costs, Total Cost Concept, Integrated Logistics Management, Review Questions

CHAPTER 3 : LOGISTICS PLANNING AND STRATEGY 35 - 57

The Hierarchy of Planning, Logistics Planning, The Changing Logistics Environment, Logistics Strategies, Formulating Logistical Strategy, Logistics Oursourcing, Review Questions

CHAPTER 4 : INTRODUCTION TO SUPPLY CHAIN MANAGEMENT 58 - 94

Overview of Supply Chain Management, Nature and Scope of Supply Chain Management, A Model of Supply Chain Management, Supply Chain Drivers, A Framework for Structuring Supply Chain Drivers, Evolution of Supply Chain Management, Importance of Logistics/Supply Chain Management, Third Party/ Contract Logistics Services, Review Questions

CHAPTER 5 : DEMAND FORECASTING 95 - 108

Need of Demand Forecasting, Forecasting Time Horizons, Types of Forecasts, Features common to all forecasts, Objectives of Demand Forecasting, Steps in The Forecasting Process, Overview of Qualitative Methods, Overview of Quantitative Methods, Monitoring and Controlling Forecasts, Solved Problems, Review Questions

CHAPTER 6 : MATERIALS PLANNING AND CONTROL 109 - 123

What is Materials Planning?, Materials Budgeting, Materials Control, Organising for Materials Control, Review Questions

CHAPTER 7 : INVENTORY MANAGEMENT 124 - 160

Nature and Importance of Inventory, Classification of Inventories, Functions of Inventory, Inventory Costs, Inventory Decisions, Importance of Inventory Management, Inventory Control Systems, Inventory control systems for Independent-Demand Items, Inventory Control of Dependent Demand Items, Solved Problems, Review Questions

CHAPTER 8 : MATERIALS REQUIREMENT PLANNING 161 - 196

Resources Requirement Planning, Materials Requirement Planning (MRP or MRP-I or mrp), Manufacturing Resource Planning or MRP-II, General Overview of MRP (Materials Requirement Planning), Operation of the MRP System, Definitions of Terms Used in MRP System, The MRP Computational Procedure, Manufacturing Resource Planning (MRP II), Enterprise Resource Planning, Just-In-Time Systems (JIT), Solved Problems, Review Questions

CHAPTER 9 : PURCHASING MANAGEMENT 197 - 235

Functions of Purchasing Department, Purchase Parameters, The Transition to Supply Management, Major Developments in Supply Management, Supply Chains, Classification of Purchasing Goods, Purchasing Cycle, Purchasing Systems, Purchasing Methods, Purchasing Organisations, Forms of Purchasing Organisations, Purchasing Policy and Procedures, Purchasing Management Process, Make or Buy Decisions, Global Sourcing, Costs Associated with Global Sourcing, Review Questions

CHAPTER 10 : VENDOR DEVELOPMENT 236 - 256

Need for Vendor Development, Levels of Vendor Assessment, Vendor Evaluation and Selection Process, Key Supplier Evaluation Criteria, Choosing the Suppliers, Vendor Evaluation and Vendor Rating, Vendor Evaluation, Vendor Rating (or Supplier-Evaluation) Plans, Managing Supplier Relationships, Solved Problems, Review Questions

CHAPTER 11 : STORES MANAGEMENT 257 - 278

Objectives of Stores Management, Functions of StoreKeeping, Planning for StoreKeeping, Location of Stores, Stores Organisation, Layout of Stores, Storage System , Measurement of Stores Efficiency, Stores Management Functions, Standardisation and Simplification in Stores Management, Review Questions

CHAPTER 12 : STANDARDISATION AND CODIFICATION 279 - 294

Classification and Codification, Standardisation, Two Areas of Standardisation, Organising Standardisation Program, Simplification, Specification, Kinds and Sources of Industrial Standards, Variety Reduction, Benefits of Variety control, Review Questions

CHAPTER 13 : VALUE ANALYSIS/VALUE ENGINEERING **295 - 314**

Value Analysis (or Value Engineering), Objectives of Value Analysis, Areas of Application of Value Analysis, Steps in Carrying out a Value Analysis Exercise, Techniques of Value Analysis, Review Questions

CHAPTER 14 : MATERIALS HANDLING **315 - 332**

Functions of Materials Handling, Scope of Materials Handling, Importance of Materials Handling, Objectives of Materials Handling, Materials Handling Principles, Materials Handling Costs, Factors Influencing Materials Handling System, Organisation for Materials Handling, Unit Load Concept, Flow Pattern, Problems in Materials Handling, Factors Affecting selection of Materials Handling Equipments, Types of Materials Handling Systems, Selection and Design of Handling System, Types of Materials Handling Equipments, Miscellaneous Handling Equipments, Evaluation of Materials Handling Performance, Efficiency in Handling Materials, Relationship Between Plant Layout and Materials Handling, Safety in Materials Handling, Review Questions

ANNEXURES **333 - 348**

REFERENCES **349**

INDEX **351 - 357**

CHAPTER 1 INTRODUCTION TO MATERIALS MANAGEMENT

The efficiency of any manufacturing organisation depends on the availability of component parts and materials in the proper quantity, quality, price, range and time. Failure in any of these areas increases costs and decreases profit as certainly as outmoded production methods or ineffective selling techniques. This simple but obvious point has only recently come to be properly understood. This book presents the principles, methods and strategies that represent the modern approach to materials management in all sectors of the economy.

In analysing business operations, the phrase *"Value-added concept"* is often used to characterise the difference between the cost of component materials and the selling price of the finished product. This difference in value represents the unique contribution of each organisation to the production process. Many companies produce component parts and materials for other firms manufacturing specialised products demanded by the customers. On an average, a manufacturing firm buys slightly more than half of the rupee value of its sales. In other words, the value added is typically less than 50 per cent of its sales. Conversely, the average company purchases materials valued at more than half of what it sells. Therefore, a firm's profit is to a large extent determined by how effectively it procures and manages these materials.

The organisational approach known as **materials management** has gained validity in recent years. Production and operations managers found it necessary to develop an **organised body of knowledge** related to planning, acquisition and utilisation of materials in the process of production and it has resulted in the discipline known as **"materials management".** All activities involved in bringing materials into and through the plant are combined under one head known as **"materials manager".** By giving the materials manager overall authority, responsibility is centralised to assure that the **overall cost** of materials is kept at the lowest possible level. The basic rationale for this organisational change is to overcome the problems of conflicting objectives. *For example*, purchase department's concern to ensure continuous supply of component materials may conflict with the inventory control department's objective to minimise inventory levels or the objective of shipping in full car load lots.

Today organisations view procurement as a professional activity including activities involved in obtaining materials at minimum cost, transporting them and providing storage and moving toward the production process. It also includes economic analysis of supply (*i.e.*, purchase economics), demand and prices and the assessment of international events that affect materials.

➤ EVOLUTION OF MATERIALS MANAGEMENT

Historically, the five 'M's of manufacturing firms *viz.*, Men, Materials, Machines, Money and Methods have shifted their positions from time to time in their relative importance. In the early days of industrialization, the focus was on men (labour) as they were the main source of productive power. Over a period of time, the emphasis shifted towards machines, which became the main source of industrial power after the Industrial Revolution. As the methods of production became more and more complex due to the increased customer demand for sophisticated products of high quality, there was greater need of efficient management to manage the complex production systems.

In the early 1920s, purchasing and maintaining stock of materials was the responsibility of purchasing managers or "chief controllers of purchasing and stores" in many industries. During and immediately after World War II the focus shifted on various functions associated with materials such as purchasing, receiving, inspecting, storing, preserving, handling, issuing, accounting, transporting and disposing surplus and obsolete materials. These functions grouped under one common head known as materials manager and the department responsible for all these activities came to be known as "materials management department". But the head of materials management department performed a staff function to support the production department and had to report to the production head (director of production) in the organizational hierarchy.

The oil crisis of the 1970's changed the priorities of industries all over the world. The exorbitant hike in oil prices and the heavy budget allocations on oil made the industries to control their expenditure on the inputs, mainly materials of all kinds because of the large scope to reduce the expenses on materials. Since the beginning of 20th century, materials have been getting more and more attention and will continue to do so in the future also. Now a days material has become an important and inevitable input of a production system since the **cost of materials** and **cost on materials** (cost incurred in purchasing and storing the materials) put together account for 50 to 85% of the production cost depending on the nature of the product and the type of the production system.

Modern manufacturing organisations adopted systems approach to management, which resulted in the integrated materials management concept. All functions related to materials such as materials planning, purchasing, storing and inventory control were integrated under materials management function. The position of the head of the integrated materials management department was elevated to be on par with heads of other functional areas *viz.* production, finance and human resources.

➤ IMPORTANCE OF MATERIALS IN MANUFACTURING ORGANISATIONS

Materials are any commodities used directly or indirectly in producing a product or service such as **raw materials, component parts, assemblies and supplies.** In the manufacturing organisations, the important inputs are referred to as 5 Ms *viz.*, Men (Labour), Machines, Money, Materials and Methods. The relative importance among these five Ms have shifted from time to time. In the beginning of industrialisation the focus was on machines, men (labour) and methods, but from around 1970 onwards the emphasis is on materials. Material is an important and inevitable input of a production system since the **cost of materials** and **cost on materials** (cost incurred in purchasing and storing the materials) put together account for 50 to 85% of the production cost depending on the nature of the product and the type of the production system.

➤ IMPORTANCE OF MATERIALS MANAGEMENT

Management of materials in most organisations is crucial to their success because the cost of purchasing, storing, moving and shipping materials account for over half of the product's cost. Improving productivity is a crucial factor in facing the challenge of competition and this involves driving down the cost of all aspects of business activities. Since there is maximum scope of cost reduction in the area of materials, doing the job of efficient and effective management of materials is seen as the key to higher productivity. Production and operations managers are working hard to develop a better way of managing materials so that on-time deliveries, quality and costs are improved and firms can survive in an increasingly competitive world. Reasons for significance of managing materials in an organisation are :

(i) The amount of money spent on materials is higher than other inputs put together (*i.e.,* machinery, labour, energy etc.).

(ii) Materials offer considerable scope for reducing costs and improving profits.

(iii) Since material is treated as a major part of current assets, improving return on investment depends on the effective utilisation of materials and keeping down the capital invested in the form of **inventory** of materials (which is treated as current assets).

(iv) Materials add **value** to the product.

(v) Quality of finished product depends on the quality of materials used to produce them.

(vi) Materials management encompasses areas such as purchasing, storing, inventory control, material handling, transportation and shipping etc.

(vii) There is need for procurement and preservation of scarce materials for future use.

(viii) There is increasing demand for ensuring safety of environment by using bio-degradable and less toxic materials which do not cause any health hazard.

(ix) The efficiency of a firm depends upon the availability of **right materials in right quantity**, at the **right time,** at the **right price** from the **right source of supply** (vendor).

(x) Materials are life blood of development of humanity.

➤ DEFINITIONS OF MATERIALS MANAGEMENT

Materials management has been defined in several ways. Some of the important definitions are as follows:

(i) Materials management is the "management of the flow of materials into an organisation to the point, where, those materials are converted into the firm's end product(s)."
(Bailey and Farmer)

(ii) Materials management is the "process by which an organisation is supplied with goods and services that it needs when the material is either consumed or incorporated into some product. The executives who engage in materials management, are concerned with three basic activities *viz.,* buying, storage of materials and movement". (Ammer)

(iii) Materials management is "a confederacy of traditional materials activities bound by a common idea – the idea of an integrated management approach to planning, acquisition,

conversion, flow and distribution of production materials from the raw materials stage to the finished product stage". (Lee and Dobler)

(iv) Materials management is "the grouping of management functions related to the complete cycle of **materials flow,** from the purchase and internal control of production materials to the planning and control of work-in-process to the warehousing, shipping and distribution of the finished product. It differs from **materials control** in that the latter term, traditionally is limited to the internal control of production materials".

(American Production and Inventory Control Society)

The key words in this definition are **materials flow** – in order for raw materials to be converted into a finished product, materials must flow through a production or manufacturing process.

(v) Materials management is "the function responsible for the coordination of planning, sourcing, purchasing, moving, storing, preserving and controlling materials in an optimum manner so as to provide a pre-determined service to the customer at a minimum cost".

(P. Goplakrishnan and M. Sundaresan)

(vi) Materials management is "an organisational concept in which a single manager has authority and responsibility for all activities, principally concerned with the flow of materials into an organisation. It includes purchasing, production planning and scheduling, incoming traffic, inventory control, receiving and stores".

(National Association of Purchasing Management, USA)

(vii) Materials management is "a total concept involving an organisational structure unifying into a single responsibility, the systematic flow and control of materials from identification of the need through delivery to customers.

Included within this concept are the material functions of planning, scheduling, purchasing, storing, moving and distributing. These are logically represented by the disciplines of production and inventory control, purchasing and physical distribution.

The objective of materials management is to contribute to increased profitability by coordinated achievement of least materials cost. This is done through optimising capital investment, capacity and personnel, consistent with the appropriate customer service level".

(International Federation of Purchasing and Materials Management)

Other simple definitions are as below :

(i) Materials management deals with planning, executing and controlling the flow of materials in relation to changes in variables like demand, prices, availability, quality, delivery schedules etc.

(ii) Materials management encompasses all activities concerned with the materials except those directly connected with designing and manufacturing the product.

(iii) Materials management is a basic function of the business that adds value directly to the product itself.

(iv) Materials management is the process of management which coordinates, supervises and executes tasks associated with flow of materials to, through and out of an organisation.

(v) Materials management consists of planning, directing, coordinating and controlling those activities which are concerned with materials and inventory requirements from the point of their inception to their introduction into the manufacturing process.

It begins with the determination of quality and quantity of materials and ends with the issue of materials to production to meet customer's demand as per schedule and at the lowest cost.

➤ OBJECTIVES OF MATERIALS MANAGEMENT

The objectives of materials management are generally classified into two categories :

(i) **Primary** objectives or **direct** objectives which contribute to the achievement of some of the firm's overall objectives.

(ii) **Secondary** objectives or **indirect** objectives which arise due to materials department assisting some other department in the organisation.

These objectives are discussed below :

Primary Objectives : These are concerned with achieving : *(i)* low prices, *(ii)* high inventory turn over (*i.e.,* as low inventory as possible), *(iii)* low cost acquisition and possession, *(iv)* continuity of supply, *(v)* consistency of quality, *(vi)* low payroll cost, *(vii)* cordial relations with suppliers, *(viii)* development of personnel and *(ix)* maintenance of good records.

These objectives are briefly discussed in the following paragraphs.

(i) **Low Prices :** Objective of purchasing materials at the least possible price is important because it helps in reducing the production costs and improves profits. This objective applies to all purchases including raw materials, parts, components, assemblies which are bought and services as well as transportation.

(ii) **High Inventory Turnover:** The inventory turn over is the ratio of cost of goods sold to cost of average inventory held in the organisation over a period of one year.

$$i.e., \text{ Inventory turn over ratio} = \frac{\text{Cost of goods sold}}{\text{Cost of average inventory held}}$$

When average inventory is low, the capital tied up in inventory is low and this will increase the inventory turnover ratio. This in turn increases the efficiency of utilisation of the firm's capital and improves the return-on-investment (ROI).

(iii) **Low Cost Acquisition and Possession :** Efficient receiving, handling and storing of materials result in low acquisition and possession costs. The cost of ordering and carrying inventory can be reduced to the minimum by optimising the order quantities per order.

(iv) **Continuity of Supply :** If continuity of supply of materials is not maintained, shortage of materials may cause idling of machines and labour and also stoppage of production. This will result in increase in production costs, increase in expediting and transportation costs and so on. In continuous production and mass production systems, continuity of supply is extremely important because of automation in production processes and lack of flexibility in the production process.

(v) **Consistency of Quality :** Quality of raw materials, components, parts, assemblies which make up the product very much determines the quality of the end product. Purchase managers should ensure **quality at the source** *i.e.,* quality should be maintained by the suppliers.

(vi) **Low Payroll Costs :** This objectives is concerned with keeping the pay-roll costs low in all activities coming under the purview of materials management (*i.e.,* material planning, purchasing, storing, material handling, shipping etc.) and also keeping the idle time in the

production departments at the minimum level by avoiding shortage of materials. Lowering pay roll costs adds to profitability.

(vii) **Cordial Supplier Relations :** Maintaining cordial relationship with suppliers will be helpful in getting prompt supplies from suppliers at reasonable prices at the right time, and it builds mutual trust and confidence between the firm and its suppliers. In such situations the customers are more likely to place orders with the firms having reliable suppliers. Also, the firm can have flexibility and can respond better to its customer's needs of changes in product design, purchase quantity, improvement in quality and changes in delivery schedules, which require the cooperation of suppliers.

(viii) **Development of Personnel :** The materials managers must develop the executives and employees in their departments by training them adequately to acquire the necessary knowledge and skills for efficient functioning in the their area of operations. This will create potential leaders among the subordinates and will be helpful in smooth succession without disputing the efficient functioning of the departments.

(ix) **Maintenance of Good Records :** Since employees of the purchasing department may have the tendency to favour the suppliers and accept grafts for doing favours to them, it is necessary to maintain good records of all transactions such as quotations, tenders, comparative statements, management approvals for placing orders, purchase order copies, invoices, inspection reports, payment of bills etc. Good record keeping helps to remove the onus of suspicion from honest employees who have to work in an environment which may be associated with corruption, favouritism etc.

Secondary Objectives : These are indirect objectives which may be achieved by contribution of materials management activities helping other departments to achieve their primary objectives. Some of the important secondary objectives are : *(i)* reciprocity, *(ii)* new materials and products, *(iii)* economic make-or-buy decisions, *(iv)* promotion of standardisation, *(v)* product improvement, *(vi)* good inter departmental relations, *(vii)* accurate economic forecasts.

These secondary objectives are discussed in the following paragraphs:

(i) **Reciprocity :** Reciprocity means reciprocal relationships of a firm with its customers. This means a firm buys as much materials as possible from its customers. *(i.e.,* customers become suppliers wherever possible). A firm buying some items (say raw materials) from a supplier firm will try to sell its products to the same supplier *For example,* a furniture manufacturer may try to sell his products to the supplier firm which supplies raw materials (*i.e.,* steel sheets) to his firm.

(ii) **New Materials and Products :** The purchase department can help the product development and R & D departments by giving them information about latest developments taking place in materials and components being supplied by the suppliers. This will help R & D engineers and product development engineers to adopt latest technology materials and components in their designs.

(iii) **Economic Make-or-Buy :** The purchase manager can furnish valuable information regarding outside sources of supply to the committee of managers responsible for make-or-buy decisions.

(iv) **Standardisation :** The purchase department can coordinate with the standards department of the firm in the field of standardisation, simplification and variety reduction which will bring substantial cost reduction.

(v) **Product Improvement :** The purchase department can assist the engineering or product design department in its primary objective of product improvement. The purchase department can suggest economic sources of supply for raw materials and components which can help design engineers to incorporate changes in product design effecting cost reductions without affecting product quality.

(vi) **Inter-departmental Relationships :** All other departments in a firm need the help of materials management department to purchase their requirement of materials, machinery, equipments, suppliers, stationery items, tools, furnitures, office equipments and so on. Hence, mutual cooperation and good interdepartmental relationships between materials management department and other departments are essential for the smooth functioning of any organisation.

(vii) **Economic Forecasts :** Materials management department has the responsibility of forecasting the future prices, costs and general business activity (booms and recessions in a business cycle). Purchase managers translate these general economic forecasts into specific forecasts for purchased materials. They are familiar with the market and general business conditions through their day-to-day contacts with suppliers.

Box 1.1 shows the objectives of materials management in a summarised form.

BOX 1.1 : Summary of Objectives of Materials Management

(i) Lower prices for materials and equipments purchased.
(ii) Higher inventory turnover-ratio.
(iii) Continuity of supply of materials.
(iv) Reduced procurement lead time.
(v) Reduced transportation costs.
(vi) Less duplication of efforts.
(vii) Reduced obsolescence of materials
(viii) Improved vendor relationship.
(ix) Better records and information regarding materials and suppliers.
(x) Better inter-departmental cooperation.
(xi) Development of personnel in materials management field.
(xii) Improvement of overall productivity of the firm.

➤ FUNCTIONS OF MATERIALS MANAGEMENT

Materials management functions accomplish the main objective of making available materials and services of **right quality** in the **right quantity** at the **right time** from the **right source** at the **right price.**

The major functions of materials management are :

(i) Material planning and budgeting, *(ii)* Procurement of materials, *(iii)* Storage of materials, *(iv)* Issue of materials, *(v)* Inventory control, *(vi)* Vendor development, *(vii)* Vendor evaluation and vendor rating, *(viii)* Material accounting, *(ix)* Materials handling and transportation, *(x)* Disposal of scrap, *(xi)* Traffic management, *(xii)* Logistics management, *(xiii)* Purchase analysis and research, *(xiv)* Supply chain management.

➢ SCOPE OF MATERIALS MANAGEMENT

Basically materials management span of activities are :

(i) **Planning :** What is needed, how much, where and when, to fulfill the objectives of the organisation. Scheduling of purchase of materials is a detailed time phased plan.

(ii) **Procuring :** the raw materials, parts, components or subassemblies to meet the schedules on time from the required sources.

(iii) **Controlling :** the follow up or tracking to ensure that the plans and schedules are adhered to, expediting, record keeping, data collection and information feed back-all facilitate controlling.

(iv) **Storing :** receiving, incoming inspection, and storing and issuing of the raw materials, component parts, sub-assemblies and work in-process required by the manufacturing function. Also, it includes storage and handling of the finished goods and office supplies.

(v) **Handling :** movement, packaging, transfer and delivery of materials involved from incoming receipt to final distribution of finished products.

(vi) **Distribution :** of the finished goods, warehousing, packing and shipping to customer.

(vii) **Transportation and Traffic Control :** routing standards, carrier selections, commodity rates, consolidation and dispatching shipments.

Exhibit 1.1 illustrates the grouping of all functions concerned with the flow of materials from planning for procurement to ultimate delivery to customers.

EXHIBIT 1.1 : Materials Management Concept

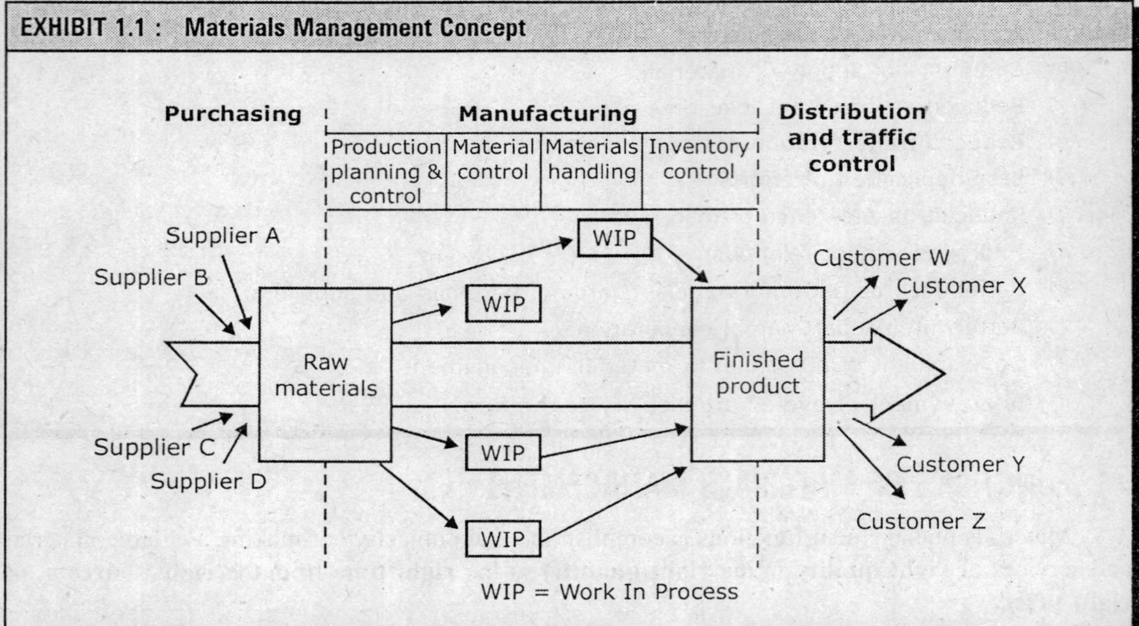

Phases in Materials Management : There are four principal phases of the materials management function.

Phase 1. Planning : The basic planning elements are plans for capacity or production levels and required inventory levels. Integral to these plans is the sales forecast for the products. The detailed time sequenced plan called the schedule meets the sales forecast and inventory requirements.

Phase 2. Material Utilisation : This is concerned with the efficiency of the flow of materials through the plant as finished goods.

Phase 3. Physical : This involves the physical storing, receiving, and issuing of materials and physical checking of inventory of raw materials work-in-process and finished goods and record keeping.

Phase 4. Control or Follow Up : This includes the information feed back and corrective action generated by this information monitoring the production rates, schedules, plant loads, dispatching, expediting and resultant follow up.

➢ CHALLENGES OF MATERIALS MANAGEMENT

The challenges of materials management are :

1. Scarce capital for investing in material inventory.
2. Difficulty in forecasting demand accurately.
3. Increasing cost of land and storage space.
4. Selection of appropriate vendors
5. Optimising purchasing quantity of materials.
6. Diversification of product lines.
7. Optimising time and quantity of demand for products.
8. Managing information.

➢ MATERIALS MANAGEMENT ORGANISATION

Materials management is treated as an important area of management like production, marketing, finance and human resources management. The materials manager directly reports to the chief executive officer (CEO). In enterprises where the cost of materials is a major part of the cost of production, materials management is not considered as a sub function of production, but considered as equal to production management. But in small or medium scale industries the materials management function is considered as a part of production management function. It is considered as a *service* function or supporting function to production.

Exhibit 1.2 : Organisation Structure of Materials Management Department

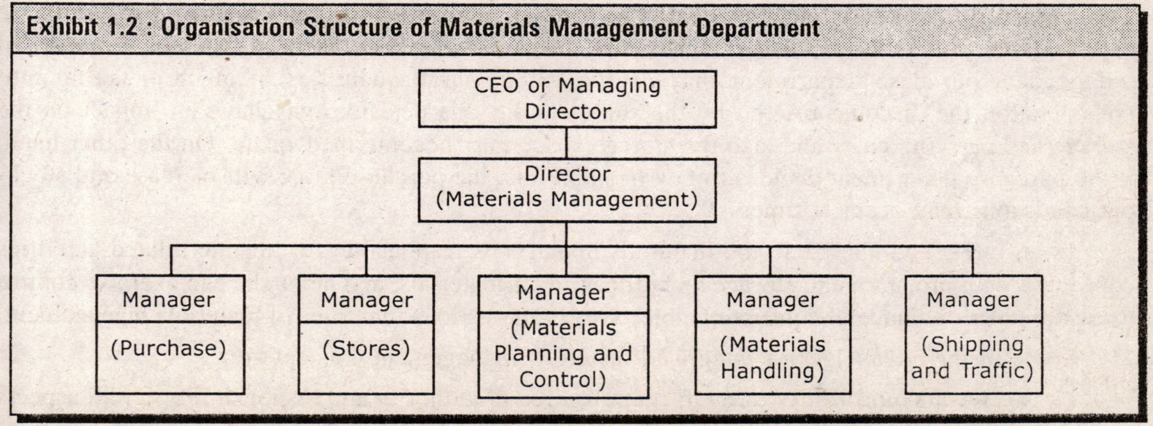

➢ MATERIALS MANAGEMENT CONCEPTS

In majority of the industries, input materials constitute about 50 to 60 per cent of the sales turnover achieved through sales of finished products. A major part of the fixed capital in manufacturing firms is in plant and machinery and a substantial part of the working capital is in raw materials, component parts and supplies. All these have been acquired through the purchase function which is one of the functions of materials management. Because of this importance of materials management, it is worth-while to discuss two concepts of materials management namely: *(i)* **Profit-centre concept** and *(ii)* **Integrated concept.**

Profit-centre Concept: Purchasing which is a part of materials management is responsible to buy materials of the **right quality**, in the **right quantity**, at the **right time**, at the **right price**, from the **right source** with the delivery at the **right place**. This objective must be achieved with a minimum investment in inventory by balancing the risk of stock-out and production stoppage, the cost of forward and buying and the economics of quantity purchases. Another objective is the maintenance of adequate quality of bought-out materials. Also, the other objectives are: **avoidance of duplication, waste and obsolescence** with respect to various items purchased etc. Thus the purchasing manager has the objective of sustaining the company's competitive position by reducing costs and ensuring quality of materials.

To achieve the above objectives, purchasing (and hence materials management) can be viewed as a "**profit centre**". Any stock-out and the resulting loss of production is treated as a loss. The reduction in price of bought-out material by right sourcing is considered as a profit. Any saving due to avoidance of wastage and obsolescence adds to profit. Reduction of inventories without affecting production adds to profit by reducing inventory carrying costs. Since materials department is considered as a spending department (*i.e.*, cost centre), every rupee saved on purchasing is a rupee earned (*i.e.*, profit). For instance, many Japanese companies have the slogan "**we live by sales, but make our profit from materials**".

Material managers can significantly contribute to the profitability of their firms by implementing scientific techniques which can result in decreased working capital, less cash outflow and hence increased profit or reduced costs. For instance, material managers can effectively contribute to import substitution and save valuable foreign exchange for the country.

Integrated Concept: Materials management involves various functions such as materials planning, purchasing, receiving, storing, controlling inventory, and disposal of surplus and scrap. These functions are interrelated and cannot be handled independently. For instance, if the purchase department operates independently, it may take decisions which are sub optimal. *For example*, an independent purchase department may decide to buy large quantities of an item taking into consideration the discount offered by the supplier. But this decision may have an impact on the storage and carrying costs and also the storage space may become inadequate. On the other hand, if the purchase department decides to buy in small lots, the purchase price will increase and stock-out conditions may occur at times.

In an integrated approach, the materials manager is responsible for all interrelated activities concerned with procurement, storage and utilisation of materials, and he or she can exercise control to ensure proper balance of conflicting objectives of the various functions of materials management.

Some of the advantages of integrated materials management concept are:

(i) **Better accountability** through centralisation of authority and responsibility for all aspects of materials function.

(ii) **Better coordination** between materials management department and user departments.

(iii) **Better performance** due to better communication and coordination between materials planning, purchasing, stores and inventory control departments — all of which are integrated organisationally under materials management department/division.

(iv) **Use of electronic data processing (EDP)** By centralising the materials function, all information regarding materials can be centralised under one materials management information system (MMIS). This facilitates collection, collation and analysis of data leading to better decisions.

Systems Approach to Materials Management

The integrated concepts of materials management views various functions of materials management such as materials planning, purchasing, storing and inventory control as interdependent functions which are integrated under materials management function. This concept is extended to view materials management as a **sub-system** of a larger productive system.

A **system** may be defined as any group of interrelated parts or components which function together to achieve some stated or predetermined goals. A large productive system is viewed as a social system as well as a technical system having many divisions/departments each of which is a sub-system of the total productive system. For instance, a productive system has four distinct and essential parts, namely *(i)* **input** *(ii)* **conversion process** *(iii)* **output** and *(iv)* **control**. The output is connected to the input through a feed back loop to facilitate control and to take corrective measures when needed to achieve the desired goals.

A business organisation or a productive system is regarded as an open system (not a closed loop system) because it does not operate independently of its environment and also it is affected by external environmental factors (variables).

When a systems concept is used as a frame-work for managing materials (one of the major inputs), it can be observed that materials management not only interacts with its external environment but also interacts with other components of the system.

Since materials management involves an integrated process of materials flow, into, through and out of an organisation (*i.e.*, productive system), it can be viewed as having two kinds of interfaces – *(i)* **internal** and *(ii)* **external**.

The **internal interfaces** include market forecasting, production, finance, inventory control, inspection and quality control, materials handling, traffic and physical distribution logistics and the material flow process.

The **external interfaces** include customers (or consumers) and suppliers/other companies.

The systems approach to materials management has the following benefits:

(i) Reliable and accurate performance to achieve the desired results.

(ii) Strict adherence to plans and schedules (*i.e.*, by effective utilisation of resources such as materials, machines, labour and finance).

(iii) Timely and optimum procurement of materials.

(iv) Optimum inventory turn-over ratio.

(v) Good vendor – vendee relations (supplier partnerships).

(vi) Optimum supply and physical distribution logistics.

(vii) Control of overall costs of materials.

(*viii*) Coordination of various materials management functions.

(*ix*) Elimination/minimisation of duplication of functions related to materials management.

(*x*) Resolution of conflicts through centralised authority and responsibility for materials.

➢ INTERFACES OF MATERIALS MANAGEMENT WITH OTHER FUNCTIONS

Since materials management is concerned with flow of materials into, through and out of an organisation, we can view the interface of materials management with other functions as (*i*) **internal interfaces** and (*ii*) **external interfaces**

The internal interfaces include (*a*) demand forecasting (*b*) production (*c*) finance (*d*) inventory control (*e*) quality control (*f*) materials handling (*g*) traffic and physical distribution logistics and (*h*) material flow processes.

The external interfaces include (*a*) with customers/consumers and (*b*) with suppliers/other organisations

Both internal and external interfaces are briefly discussed in the following paragraphs:

1. Internal Interfaces

(*a*) **Demand forecasting:** Forecasting is defined as estimating the future demand for products and services and the resources necessary to produce these outputs. Sales forecasts or demand forecasts are the foundation for the planning of production and in-turn planning of inputs for production *viz.*, materials, machine capacity, manpower, finance *etc.*

(*b*) **Production:** Materials is one of the major inputs for the production processes that are required to be carried out to produce the outputs (goods and services) demanded by customers. Continuous, uninterrupted flow of materials at all stages of production processes is very important to minimise the production cycle time and also for better utilization of all productive resources such as machines, equipments and labour.

(*c*) **Finance:** Organisations incur costs both for acquiring the required materials (*i.e.*, cost of materials) and for ordering and holding the materials (cost on materials) to make the materials available for the production centres as and when required for the production processes. Infact substantial money (capital) can be tied up in the form of inventory. Therefore to reduce costs and to make better use of capital (money) inventory control techniques are employed.

(*d*) **Inventory control:** Inventory control aims at optimizing the total inventory costs, which consists of (*a*) ordering costs and (*b*) inventory carrying costs. Inventory control techniques determine the quantity to be ordered and when the order is to be placed on the supplier so as to ensure that materials are made available to production when required and at the same time keeping inventories as low as possible and stock-out situations as few as possible.

(*e*) **Quality control:** Inspection and control of quality of incoming materials is crucial in materials management even though these are not functions of materials management. Incoming materials are inspected to check both for quantity and quality of materials supplied by vendors. Quality of the product very much depends on the quality of raw materials, parts and components used to build the product. *Quality at source* is an important concept of quality management.

(*f*) **Materials Handling:** Handling materials right from the receiving or transit stores to the holding stores and then to the production centres is an integral part of materials management and its interface with production management. Materials management ensures efficient and effective materials handling keeping the handling cost at the minimum possible level and at the same time keeping the materials movement time as short as possible.

(g) **Traffic and Physical distribution logistics:** Materials management is responsible for packing and dispatching of finished goods to the customers or the channel members for distribution to retail outlets. Physical distribution logistics or outbound logistics is concerned with outbound transportation of finished goods in the distribution channel using the cost effective mode of transportation and locating the warehouses in suitable location so as to minimize the total transportation and warehousing costs without affecting customer service level desired.

(h) **Materials Flow process:** In a production system, materials flow right from the receiving point to the dispatch of finished goods, The distance through which the materials flow in the production system and the time taken for the movement through various stages of production together with intermittent storages constitute the production cycle. The materials flow should be smooth and uninterrupted in order to keep the materials handling costs low and to keep the production cycle short.

Materials management aims at achieving these objectives by managing both materials flow and information flow (to facilitate timely decisions)

2. External Interfaces

(a) **Consumers/customers:** Materials management's interface with customers/consumers is not direct but through the company's marketing, which handles customer demands. As customer's requirements and expectations change over time, existing products may become obsolete, and new products may have to be developed. These new products may require new raw materials and components, new processing materials and machinery *etc.*, which in –turn affects materials management functions. In case of industrial products where customer demands for spare parts have to be met urgently, direct contact between materials management and the customers may reduce the delay in supply of spare parts.

(b) **Suppliers/other firms:** Materials management more directly interfaces with suppliers as compared with customers. Co-operation with suppliers is to have good long-term supplier relationships to ensure steady supply of materials from suppliers. Materials management should keep close liason with suppliers and other organisations seeking trade relationships. Materials management must promote healthy relationships with suppliers by objective assessment and rating of suppliers on a rational basis.

➤ MODERN TRENDS IN MATERIALS MANAGEMENT

Studying flow of materials – the acquisition, storage, movement and processing of raw materials, components, assemblies – is a good way to understand manufacturing. Also, services such as retailing, warehousing and transportation companies can be viewed as systems of material flows. In these systems, all organisational functions are greatly affected by the planning and control of the materials system.

Supply Chain Management : A **supply chain** refers to the way materials flow through different organisations starting with basic raw materials and ending with finished products delivered to the ultimate customer. It consists of a sequence of suppliers, warehouses, operations, and retail outlets.

Supply chains form complex networks involving many companies and materials co-ordination of all companies involved in a supply chain (including effective communication) is crucial to providing high quality finished products in a timely manner at the lowest possible cost. The most relevant aspects of supply chain management involve all management functions related to the flow of materials from the company's direct suppliers to its direct customers including purchasing, warehousing, inspection, production, materials handling and shipping and distribution.

Materials management and **logistics management** are two alternative names sometimes used to refer to **supply-chain management** *within a single firm.* Some organisations have centralised their diverse materials management functions under one department headed by a **materials manager** or **supply chain manager or director-materials management.**

Four important activities in materials management or supply-chain management, are purchasing, logistics, warehousing and expediting.

Logistics management is the management (*i.e.,* the planning, execution and control) of all factors that affect the materials flow and the information about it, seen from the perspective of customer requirements, for the purpose of achieving high delivery reliability, a high degree of delivery completeness and a short delivery time.

Logistics management function involves short-term materials planning, the supply of raw materials and other purchased goods, internal transportation, storage and physical distribution. It is some times also referred to as materials management and/or **integrated business logistics.**

Exhibit 1.3 illustrates relationship between supply chain management and materials management.

EXHIBIT 1.3 : Supply Chain Management in Manufacturing

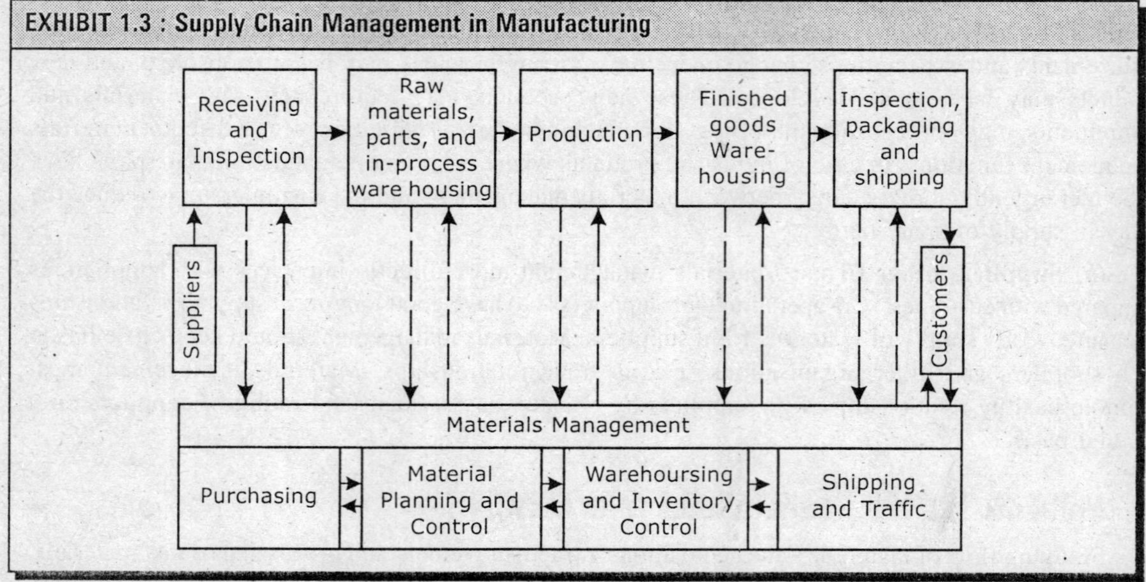

Supply chain management is a systems approach to viewing the supply channel and distribution channel as a whole rather than a set of fragmented parts. It differs from traditional approaches on inventory control and focuses on management of inventory through the entire supply chain. Successful supply chain management relies on forming strategic partnerships with trading partners along the supply chain.

Supply chain management should be considered as a logical extension of the logistics concepts.

In order to be able to manage costs throughout the supply chain, effective and cooperative supplier relationships are required. Hence, purchasing and supply management (including supplier management) can be viewed as an integrated part of supply chain management which encompasses both the logistics and the purchasing and supply function.

➤ REVIEW QUESTIONS

1. Define the term "materials management".
2. State the importance of materials management.
3. State the primary and secondary objectives of materials management.
4. Mention some key functions of materials management.
5. Discuss the scope of materials management.
6. Explain briefly the various phases of a materials management department.
7. Mention the challenges of materials management today.
8. Explain with an organisational chart, the organisational structure of materials management.
9. Discuss the "profit-centre concept" and the "integrated concept" of materials management.
10. Explain what is meant by "systems approach to materials management".
11. List the benefits of systems approach to materials management.
12. Discuss the modern trends in materials management.
13. Discuss the evolution of materials management.
14. Discuss the interfaces of materials management with other functions of an organisation.

❖ ❖ ❖ ❖

CHAPTER 2

INTRODUCTION TO LOGISTICS MANAGEMENT

Logistics is concerned with getting products and services where they are needed and when they are desired. In a modern society, most of the customers and consumers take excellent logistics service as granted and tend to notice logistics only when there is a problem, *for example*, non availability of goods and services they need very badly. When consumers go to the retail stores, they expect products to be available in good condition, *for example,* fresh fruits, meat, vegetables and the like. It is difficult to visualise accomplishing any manufacturing and marketing activity efficiently and effectively without logistical support. Logistics is a broad, far-reaching function, having a great impact on the standard of living of a modern society.

To understand some of the implications of logistics activity to consumers, we may consider the following:

(i) The difficulty of consumers in shopping for food, clothing and other items in one place (super bazaar or retail shop) if logistical systems do not bring all these items together in one place.

(ii) The problem in locating the proper size or style of an item (say shoes or ready made garments) if logistical systems fail to provide a wide product-mix, colours, sizes and styles through the assortment process.

(iii) The frustration for consumers when they go to a store to purchase an advertised item and find out that the item has not arrived at the store yet.

The issues mentioned above illustrate how logistics affects many facets of the daily lives of consumers and the impact it has on individuals and the society.

Logistics involves the integration of information, transportation, inventory, warehousing, materials handling and packaging. The operating responsibility of logistics is the geographical positioning of raw materials, work-in-process, and finished goods inventories where required at the lowest cost possible. Logistical process facilitates the flow of materials from suppliers to the manufacturing firms and the distribution of finished products through marketing channels to consumers. The complexity of logistics increases with the number of industrial manufacturers, suppliers, and the channel intermediaries such as wholesalers, distributors and retailers within a nation. The complexity of logistics becomes awesome when we consider business on a global basis, having global manufacturers, global suppliers and global consumers.

➤ WHAT IS LOGISTICS?

Logistics is defined as the process of anticipating customer needs and wants, acquiring the capital, materials, people, technologies, and information necessary to meet those needs and wants, optimising the goods or service — providing network to customer requests and utilising the network to fulfil customer requests in a timely manner.

Box 2.1 lists the various perspectives of the definitions of logistics.

Box 2.1 : Definitions of Logistics

Perspective	Definition
(i) Inventory	Management of materials in motion and at rest.
(ii) Customer	Getting the right product to the right customer, in the right quantity, at the right time and at the right cost. (referred to as the seven 'r's of logistics.
(iii) Dictionary	The branch of military science having to do with processing, maintaining and transporting materials, personnel and facilities.
(iv) International Society of Logistics	The art and science of management, engineering and the technical activities concerned with requirements, design and supplying and maintaining resources to support objectives, plans and operations.
(v) Utility/value	Providing time and place utility/value of materials and products in support of organisational objectives.
(vi) Council of Logistics Management	That part of the supply chain process that plans, implements and controls the efficient and effective flow and storage of goods, services and related information from point of origin to point of consumption in order to meet customer requirements.
(vii) Component Support	Supply management for the plant (inbound logistics) and distribution management for the firm's customers (outbound logistics).
(viii) Functional Management	Determination of materials requirement, purchasing, transportation, inventory management, warehousing, materials handling, industrial purchasing, facility location analysis, distribution, return goods handling, information management, customer service, and all other activities concerned with supporting the internal customer (manufacturing) with materials and the external customer (retailer) with products.
(ix) Common Culture	Handling the details of an activity.

Types of Logistics

Logistics should be viewed as a part of management and has four subdivisions:

(i) **Business Logistics:** It is the part of the supply chain process that plans, implements and controls the efficient flow and storage of goods, services, and related information from point of origin to point of use or consumption in order to meet customer requirements.

(ii) **Military Logistics**: The design and integration of all aspects of support for the operational capability of the military forces and their equipment to ensure readiness, reliability and efficiency.

(iii) **Event Logistics**: The network of activities, facilities and personnel required to organise, schedule and deploy the resources for an event to take place and to efficiently withdraw after the event.

(iv) **Service Logistics**: The acquisition, scheduling and management of the facilities/assets, personnel and materials to support and sustain a service operation or business.

➤ WHAT IS LOGISTICS MANAGEMENT?

Traditionally, organisations have divided the responsibility for materials management among three departments: *(i)* purchasing, *(ii)* production, planning and control and *(iii)* distribution. This form of organisation is defined to as a ***segmented structure***, having a manager for each of these three departments who reports to a different person. Because of the tremendous amount of co-ordination needed in the segmented structure, many firms have restructured to centralise most materials management tasks in one department and elevate its manager to a higher level in the hierarchy of managers in the organisation. Such a form of organisation is referred to as an ***integrated structure*** and the unified new department is called ***materials management*** or ***logistics management*** department. This approach brings to gather all the tasks related to flow of materials from the purchase of raw materials to the distribution of finished products and recognises that the various materials management tasks are all part of the same supply-chain management activity.

Logistics management is the process of planning, implementing, and controlling the efficient, effective flow and storage of goods, services, and related information from point of origin to point of consumption for the purpose of conforming to customer requirements.

The definition reflects the need for total movement from point of material procurement to location of finished product distribution. It also includes the flow of materials and services in both the manufacturing and service sectors (such as the government, hospitals, banks, wholesalers and retailers). In addition, the ultimate disposal, recycling and reuse of the products need to be considered because logistics management is becoming more and more responsible for removing packaging materials once a product is delivered, and removing old equipment and disposing of the same.

Because of the various diverse functions coming under the purview of logistics management, it is also known by several other names such as the following: *(i)* Business logistics, *(ii)* Channel management, *(iii)* Distribution management, *(iv)* Industrial logistics, *(v)* Physical distribution management, *(vi)* Supply management, *(vii)* Materials management, *(viii)* Quick-response system, *(ix)* Logistical management and *(x)* Supply-chain management.

➤ SCOPE AND IMPORTANCE OF LOGISTICS MANAGEMENT

Logistics is not confined to manufacturing operations alone. It is relevant to all types of enterprises including organisations such as government departments, institutions such as hospitals, universities, and service organisations such as banks, financial service institutions, wholesalers and retailers and the like.

Some of the activities encompassed under logistics umbrella are illustrated in *Exhibit 2.1.*

Exhibit 2.1 : Components of Logistics Management

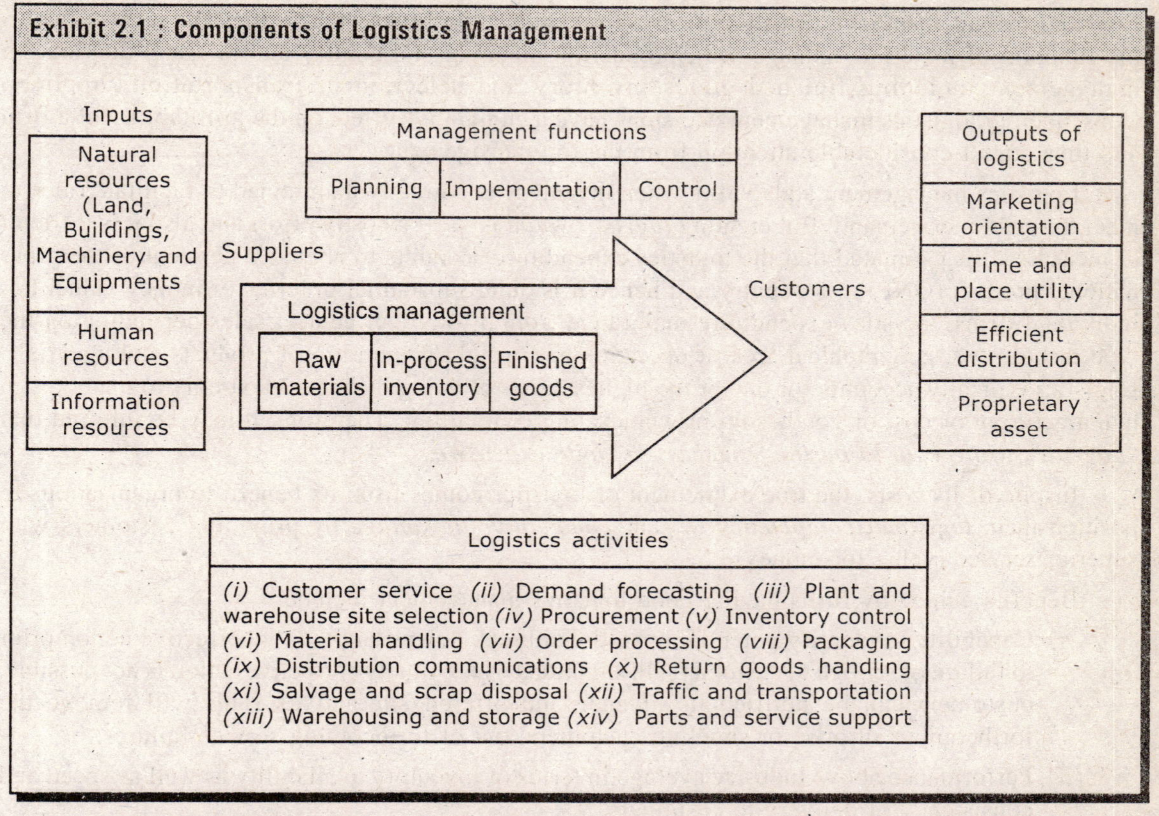

Logistics is dependent on inputs such as natural resources (raw materials), human, financial and information resources. The raw materials supplied by suppliers are converted into in-process inventory and then into finished goods by logistics management. Management functions such as planning, implementation and control provide the framework for logistics activities. The outputs of the logistics system are competitive advantage through time and place utility, efficient transportation of finished goods to the customer and providing a logistics service mix, making logistics a proprietary asset to the organisation. Efficient and effective performance of the logistics activities listed in *Exhibit 2.1* will result in the desired outputs.

In a manufacturing organisation having an integrated structure, activities such as purchasing, production planning and control, warehousing, and inventory control are centralised under materials management department and distribution of finished goods is done by marketing department.

Although many activities and decisions are integrated under materials under management, considerable amount of cross-functional co-ordination is required. *For example*, marketing typically does the forecasts for demand and processes the incoming customer orders. Production planning and control uses this information to plan work force schedules and work priorities. At the same time, marketing needs information regarding current production schedules and production capacity so as to process incoming customer orders in order to make realistic delivery promises. After receipt of brought-out materials sent by suppliers or finished goods shipped to customers, the information regarding the same must be made available to accounts department for making payments to suppliers or billing customers. All these cross-functional co-ordination requires an efficient information system.

Logistics management includes all these cross-functional co-ordination activities and it co-ordinates the function of materials management, production planning and control and physical distribution management including finished goods inventory and selection of transportation suppliers. Consequently logistics management decisions have a cumulative effect on the profitability of a firm and thus attract considerable attention from the top management.

Logistics management adds **value** when inventory is correctly maintained to facilitate sales to meet the customer demand. But creating *logistics value* is itself a costly effort and also it is difficult to measure. It is estimated that the logistics expenditure accounts to about 10 per cent of the gross national product (GNP) of a country and hence it is quite substantial in terms of money value. For individual firms, logistics expenditure may range from 5 to 35 per cent of sales depending on the type of business, geographical area of operation and weight/value ratio of products and materials. Logistics typically accounts for one of the highest costs of doing business, next only to materials in manufacturing or cost of goods sold in wholesaling or retailing. Therefore, it may be inferred that "*Logistics while vital to business success, is quite expensive.*"

Inspite of its costs, the true excitement of logistics comes from its benefit to organisations to position their ***logistical competency*** to gain *competitive advantage* by providing customers with superior service (value for money).

Benefits gained by firms having good logistics management include:

(i) Capability to identify potential operational break downs and taking corrective action prior to failure of service to customers. In situations where timely corrective action is not possible, customers can be notified in advance and offered alternatives. This will remove the forthcoming surprise or shock to customers, out of forthcoming service failures.

(ii) Performance above industry average in terms of inventory availability as well as speed and consistency of delivery to customers.

(iii) Capability to monitor logistical performance on a real-time basis through efficient information systems.

(iv) High delivery performance (near perfect orders).

(v) Commitment to continuous improvement.

(vi) Firms having world-class logistical competency can become attractive suppliers and ideal business partners.

Logistical management includes the design and administration of systems to control the flow of material, work-in-process and finished goods inventory to support business unit strategy. Its overall goal is to achieve a targeted level of customer service at the lowest possible total cost. Logistics managers are responsible for planning and administration of detailed and complex work involved in logistics management.

Logistical Competency: Logistical competency is a relative assessment of a firm's capability to offer competitively superior customer service at the lowest possible total cost. A company seeking differentiation on the basis of logistical competency, outperforms its competitors in all facets of operations. This means that logistical performance is focused to support any or all manufacturing and marketing requirements in such a manner that exploits delivery capability. The strategy is to provide superior service at a total cost below industry average. The characteristics of firms having superior logistics performance or competency are: *(i)* alternative logistical capabilities, *(ii)* emphasis on flexibility, *(iii)* time-based performance, *(iv)* operational control and *(v)* commitment to perfect customer service performance.

Firms seeking *strategic positioning* focus on how to compute on the basis of four processes essential to success. These processes are: *(i)* creation of customer value, *(ii)* planning, *(iii)* control and *(iv)* succession generation. A firm must perform all these processes for long-term survival and growth. Expectations regarding logistical competency directly depend on a firm's strategic positioning. All firms must perform logistics to achieve their primary business goals. Logistics competency must be proactively used to gain competitive advantage. Creation of customer value is essential to gain and retain a loyal customer base. Logistics is one of several competencies required to create customer value. Logistics must be managed as a core competency of the firm seeking creation of superior customer value.

The Logistical Mission: Logistics of a firm is an integrated effort aimed at helping to create customer value at the lowest cost. Logistics exists to satisfy customer requirements through relevant manufacturing and marketing operations. Logistics managers seek to achieve the desired quality of customer service through state-of-the-art operating competency.

The level of logistics service depends on the amount of resources a firm is willing to commit. The limiting factor for resources is economics and not technology. *For example*,

(i) A dedicated inventory can be maintained in a warehouse close to a major customer.

(ii) A fleet of trucks can be held in a constant state of readiness for quick delivery.

(iii) Dedicated communications can be maintained on a real-time basis between the customer firm and a supplier's logistical operation, to facilitate order entry.

(iv) A product or a component can be delivered within minutes of identifying a customer requirement by means of a high-state of logistical readiness.

But such high level of customer service would be extremely costly and not necessary to support most marketing and manufacturing operations. Hence, logistical service must be viewed as a balance of **service priority** and **cost**. The cost-benefit impact of logistical failure is directly related to the importance of service performance to the customer involved. The more significant the service failure impact upon the customer, the greater the priority placed on logistical performance.

Basic logistics service is measured in terms of the following factors: *(i) Availability*, *(ii) Operational performance* and *(iii) Service reliability* which are briefly discussed below:

(i) **Availability** means having inventory to consistently meet customer requirements of materials and products. High inventory availability does not necessarily mean high investment in inventory. Technology enables new ways to achieve high inventory availability without having high capital investment in inventory.

(ii) **Operational performance** is concerned with elapsed time from order receipt to delivery. It involves delivery *speed* and *consistency*. Even though many customers want fast delivery, they also emphasise consistency of fast delivery. To achieve smooth operation, customer firms seek first consistency of service and then delivery speed. Also, a firm's operational performance is viewed in terms of *flexibility i.e.*, how flexible it is in accommodating unusual and unexpected requests from its customers. Operational performance is also concerned with how a firm handles all aspects of customer needs including service failure on a day to day basis.

(iii) **Service reliability** is concerned with the quality attributes of logistics. The key to quality is accurate measurement of availability and operational performance. To achieve service reliability, the measures to assess inventory availability and operational performance must

be identified. If the management is committed to continuous improvement, the firm's logistics performance can also continuously meet its customer expectations. Logistics quality can only be achieved by careful planning supported by training, comprehensive measurement and continuous improvement. Service performance can be improved by establishing goals on a selective basis, since some products are more critical than others because of their importance to the customer and their relative profit contribution. It must be related that customers are different and that services must be matched to accommodate unique preferences and purchase potential of customers.

➤ DEVELOPMENT OF LOGISTICS

Even though logistics activity had been associated with the earliest forms of organised trade, it began to gain attention in the early 1900s as an area of study, in the distribution of farm products in the US, as a way to support the organisation's business strategy and as a way of providing *time* and *place utility*.

Further logistics contributed towards the Allied Victory in World War II and began to receive more recognition and emphasis. Military logistics provides the ability to efficiently and effectively distribute and store supplies and personnel which are the key factors in the success of armed forces of any country in the war. According to Peter Drucker, a noted business expert, a management consultant and an author of many books on management, "*Logistics is one of the last frontiers of opportunity for organisations working to improve their corporate efficiency.*"

Further to the application of logistics in military operations, deregulation of the transportation industry in the late 1970s and early 1980s provided more options to organisations regarding the modes of transportation they use and also increased the competition within and between transportation modes. Consequently, transport carriers became more creative, flexible, customer oriented and competitive for their survival and growth. As a result shippers now have more transportation options and they are in a position to negotiate on rate, terms and service and buy the best transportation services.

➤ NEED FOR LOGISTICS MANAGEMENT

Today's organisations worldwide need logistics management more than ever because of the following: *(1)* **Competitive Pressures** *(2)* **Information Technology** *(3)* **Channel Power** and *(4)* **Profit Leverage**.

These are discussed briefly in the following paragraphs.

1. Competitive Pressures: During the 1970s, logistics received more attention as a major cost driver to offset the effect of rising interest rates and increasing energy costs. In addition the logistics costs became more critical for many multinational companies because of globalisation of their business. These developments affected logistics primarily in two ways:

(i) The growth of world-class competitors which has pressurised organisations to differentiate themselves and their product offerings. Logistics enable domestic firms to provide more reliable and responsive service to customers in the local markets than overseas competitors.

(ii) As firms increasingly buy and sell off-shore, the supply chain between the manufacturing firm and its supplier and customer firms becomes longer, costlier and more complex. Hence in such situations, excellent logistics is necessary to take advantage of global opportunities.

Another factor strongly contributing to the increased emphasis and importance of logistics is he growing need for cost control to enable firms to compete better. The most important way to mprove a company's profitability is through cost reduction and cost control. Cost reduction is rated as the most important issue for firms followed by issues such as quality and customer service.

2. Information Technology: With the explosion of information technology, organisations gained the ability to better monitor transaction intensive activities such as ordering, transportation movement) and storage of goods and materials. Computerised quantitative models along with nformation technology increased the ability to manage material flows and to optimise inventory evels and movements. *For example*, systems such as material requirement planning (MRP I), listribution resource planning (DRP) and just-in-time (JIT) allowed firms to link many activities such as order processing, inventory management, forecasting and production scheduling. Many irms developed growing interest in logistics because of factors such as: *(i)* advancements in nformation systems technology, *(ii)* higher emphasis on customer service, *(iii)* growing recognition of the systems approach and *(iv)* total cost concept.

Profit leverage arising out of the application of logistics resulted in the realisation that logistics can be used as a *strategic weapon* in competing in the market place.

3. Channel Power: The channel power shifted from manufacturers to wholesalers, distributors and retailers. This has had a great impact on logistics. In major consumer good industries, when competition increases, many suppliers and manufacturers are forced out of competition and a few eading competitors remain in the market. Those who remain are highly competitive and are able to offer very high quality products. In the views of consumers, all of the leading brands are substitute for each other and lower brand loyalty decreases the manufacturer's power which in turn increases the retailer's power. Ultimately sales of consumer products are determined by what is in stock, and not by what particular brand offered to the customers.

4. Profit Leverage: Any amount of money saved in logistics costs has a greater impact on the organisation's profitability than a similar increase in sales revenue. Any savings in logistics costs directly adds to the company's profit. To achieve same amount of profit through sales, a firm has to put more effort and increase sales revenue considerably because profit earned through sales is only a small per cent of sales revenue. Hence, a rupee saved in logistics is a rupee increase in the company's profit. Therefore, we can infer that logistics cost savings have much more leverage than an increase in sales.

LOGISTICAL ACTIVITIES

Logistics managers are responsible for the following activities: *(i)* Traffic and transportation, *(ii)* Materials handling, *(iii)* Warehousing and storage, *(iv)* Inventory control, *(v)* Industrial packaging, *(vi)* Order fulfilment, *(vii)* Demand forecasting, *(viii)* Plant and warehouse site location, *(ix)* Production planning, *(x)* Return goods handling, *(xi)* Purchasing, *(xii)* Parts and service support, *(xiii)* Customer service levels and *(xiv)* Salvage and scrap disposal.

These activities are briefly discussed in the following paragraphs:

(i) **Transportation**: In a logistics system, the major focus is upon the physical movement or flow of goods or upon the network that moves the product. This network is composed of transportation agencies. The logistics manager selects the mode or modes of transportation used in moving the raw materials and finished goods.

(ii) **Storage**: It involves warehousing and inventory management which are closely related activities. A direct relationship exists between transportation and the level of inventory and the number of warehouses required. Storage and transportation have a trade-off relationship between them. Firms which have slow means of transport need more warehousing space to keep higher inventory levels as compared to those using faster transport.

(iii) **Packaging**: The type of transportation selected affects the packaging requirements both for moving a finished product to the market and for the inbound materials. Industrial packaging should be such that it protects the goods from damage during transportation especially through road, rail or ocean shipping.

(iv) **Materials handling**: Material handling is crucial for efficient warehouse operation. Logistics managers are responsible for movement of goods into a warehouse, storing them and moving the goods from storage to packing and shipping areas and for onward transportation to customers.

(v) **Order fulfilment**: Order fulfilment consists activities involved with completing customer orders. Logistics ensures that the delivery lead time is reduced to the minimum in order to complete customer orders in time.

(vi) **Inventory forecasting**: Accurate forecasting of inventory requirements and materials and parts are essential for effective inventory control, especially in firms using a just-in-time (JIT) or material requirement planning (MRP) approach to control inventory.

(vii) **Production planning**: It is closely related to forecasting in terms of effective inventory control. Once the forecast is developed and the current inventory on hand and usage rate are assessed, production planning managers can determine the units to be produced to meet market demand. Production planning is integrated into logistics.

(viii) **Purchasing**: Purchasing or procurement is included in logistics because the transportation cost relates directly to location of the supplier sources. In terms of transportation and inventory costs, the quantities purchased would also affect logistics cost.

(ix) **Customer service**: Customer service levels in many ways glue together other logistics areas. Decisions about inventory, transportation and warehousing relate to customer service requirements. Logistics plays an extremely important role in ensuring that the customer gets the right product at the right place and at the right time. Logistics decisions about product availability and inventory lead time are critical to customer service.

(x) **Site location**: A change in the location of a manufacturing plant or a warehouse could alter time and place relationships between plants and markets or between supply points and plants. Such location changes will affect transportation cost and service, customer service, inventory requirements *etc.* Hence, transportation cost is frequently a very decisive factor in deciding on a location of a plant or a warehouse.

➤ ROLE OF LOGISTICS IN THE SUPPLY CHAIN MANAGEMENT

A ***supply chain*** refers to the way that materials flow through different organisations, starting with raw materials and ending with finished products delivered to the ultimate consumer.

Supply chain management can be viewed as a pipeline or conduit for efficient and effective flow of products/materials, services, information and money from supplier's suppliers through the various intermediate organisations out to the customer's customers. *Exhibit 2.2* illustrates this view of supply chain management.

Exhibit 2.2 : Logistics Supply Chain

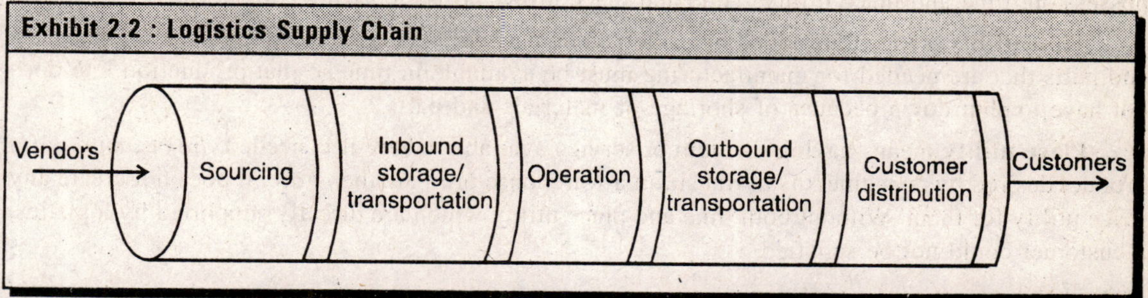

Supply chain management represents a logical extension of the logistics concept. It is also known as *demand chain management, demand flow management, value chain management, value networks,* and *synchronisation management*. The terms *supply chain, demand chain, value chain* or *value network* — all used as synonyms. The generic value chain is illustrated in *Exhibit 2.3*.

Exhibit 2.3 : Generic Value Chain

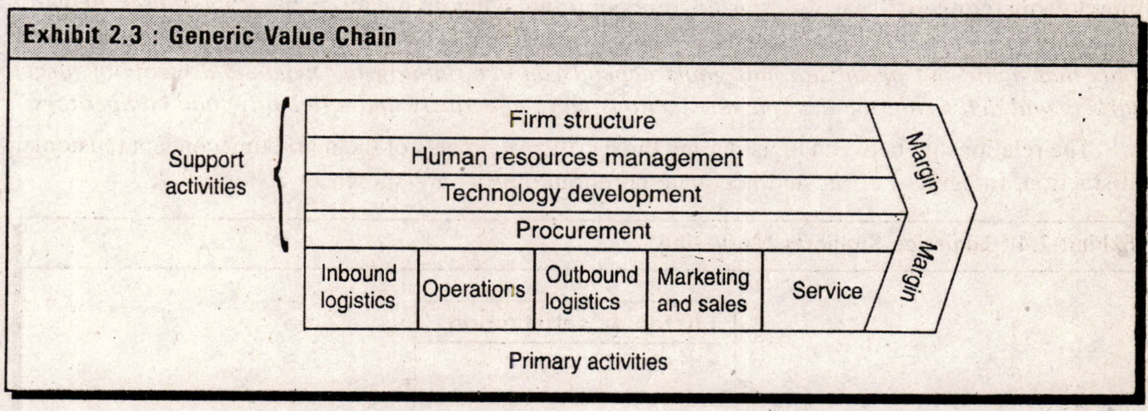

As can be seen in the value chain illustration, inbound and outbound logistics are important primary components of the value chain, that is contributing ***"value"*** to the firm's customers and thereby making the firm financially viable. The ***outbound logistics*** involves physical distribution of finished goods (usually higher in value than raw materials). This means the finished goods inventory, warehousing, materials handling and packaging costs are higher than their raw material components. Hence the impact of transportation selection is more significant. The ***inbound logistics*** involves transportation of raw materials and component parts from suppliers to the firm, inventory requirements, warehousing, packaging and materials handling.

Logistics management added inbound logistics to the outbound logistics of physical distribution.

➤ THE ROLE OF LOGISTICS IN THE ECONOMY

Logistics plays a key role in the economy in two ways: *(i)* Logistics is one of the major expenditures for businesses, thereby affecting and being affected by other economic activities *(ii)* Logistics supports the movement and flow of many economic transactions and it is an important activity in facilitating the sale of virtually all goods and services.

Logistics adds value by creating *time utility* and *place utility*. Utility represents the value or usefulness that an item or service has in fulfilling a want or need. Four types of utility are: form, possession, time and place utility. Time and place utility are supported by logistics.

Time utility is the value added by having an item ***when*** it is needed. *For example*, all materials and parts that are needed for manufacturing must be available in time so that production line does not have to shut down because of shortage of materials and parts.

Place utility means having the item or service available ***where*** it is needed. *For example*, if a product desired by consumers is in transit, in a warehouse or in another store, it does not create any place utility for them. Without both time and place utility which are directly supported by logistics, a customer could not be satisfied.

➤ THE ROLE OF LOGISTICS IN THE ORGANISATION

In recent years, effective logistics management has been recognised as a key opportunity for the improvement of both the profitability and competitiveness of organisations.

Because of the importance of ***"customer service"*** many organisations which were adopting "**marketing concept**" earlier, started re-examining what it meant to be ***"customer driven"*** organisation. The marketing concept is defined as a "*marketing management philosophy which holds that achieving organisational goals depends on determining the needs and wants of target markets and delivering the desired satisfactions more effectively and efficiently than competitors.*"

The relationship between logistics and three critical elements of the marketing concept (customer satisfaction, integrated effort and adequate corporate profit) are shown in *Exhibit 2.4*.

Exhibit 2.4 : Logistics Supports Marketing

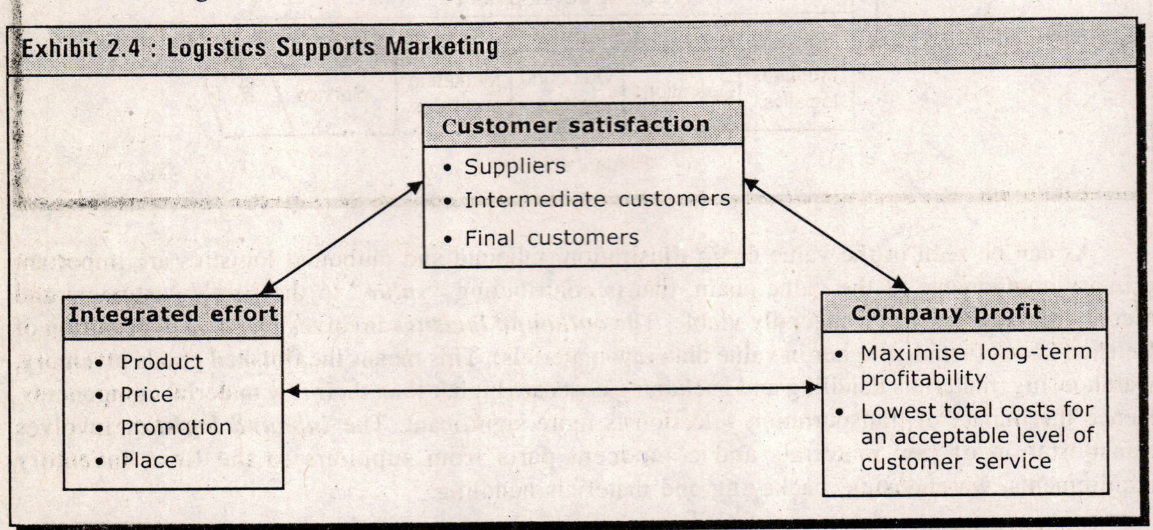

Logistics plays a key role in each of these three elements of the marketing concept.

The four P's of the marketing mix require that for a firm to be successful, the marketing effort must integrate the ideas of having the right product, at the right price promoted with right promotion mix and available in the right place. Logistics has a major role, especially in getting the product to the right place at the right time. Availability of a product or service for the customer when and where it is needed ensures customer satisfaction due to time and place utilities.

Exhibit 2.5 illustrates the relationship between "marketing mix" elements and logistics.

Place (or distribution) is the key element of the marketing mix with which logistics interfaces directly. Expenditures involved in distribution, support the levels of customer service provided by the organisation. This includes **on-time delivery**, **high order filling rates**, **consistent transit times**, and similar issues.

Exhibit 2.5 : Cost-trade offs required in marketing and logistics

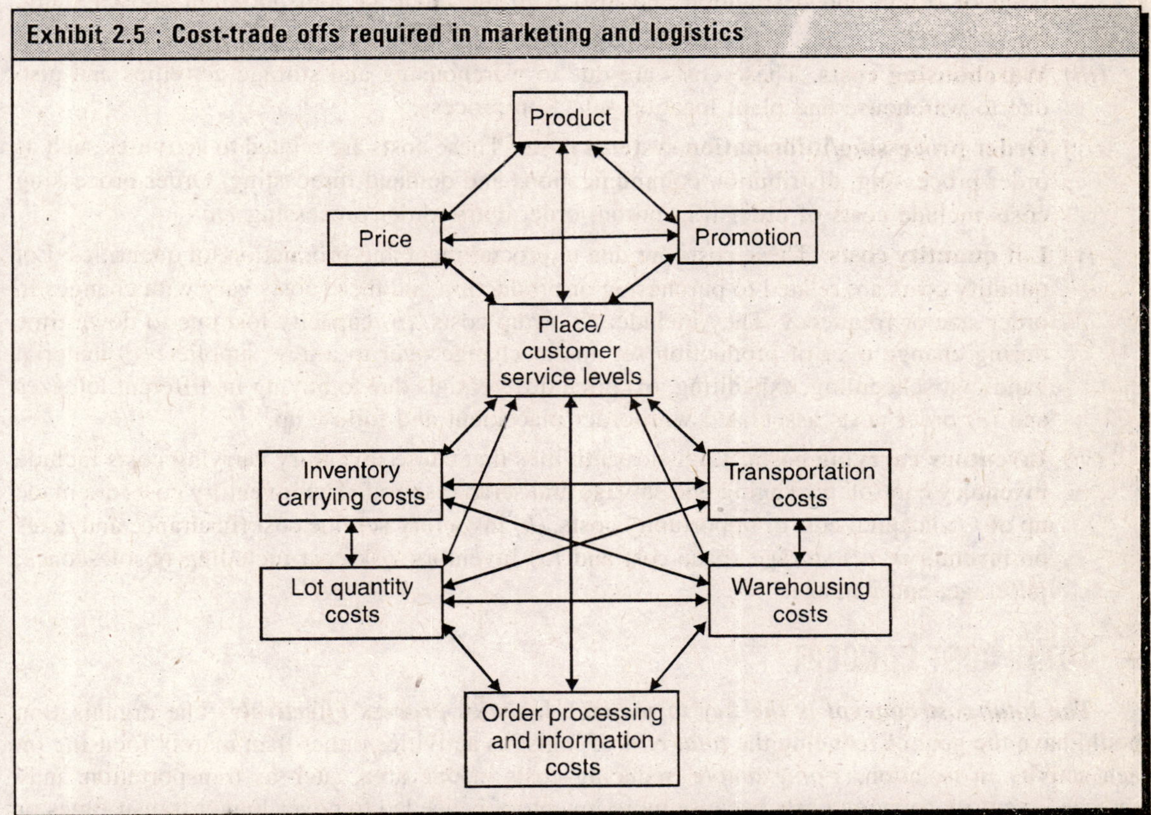

Customer services is an output of the logistics system and is a key way to gain competitive advantage. An organisation can adjust customer service levels to meet what level of service is desired by the customer and what the customer is willing to pay for. The ***total cost concept*** is used to accomplish the cost trade-off analysis in marketing and logistics interface. This concept of "total cost" is the key to effectively managing logistics processes. The ultimate goal of the organisation is to reduce the total cost of logistics activities. The effort to reduce costs in one area, such as transportation, may increase inventory carrying costs as more inventory is required to cover longer transit times or to balance against greater uncertainty in transit times.

➤ LOGISTICS COSTS

Logistics costs are created by logistics activities such as customer service, transportation, warehousing, order processing and information, lot quantity and inventory carrying, which are discussed in the following paragraphs:

(i) **Customer service level***:* The key cost trade-off resulting from varying levels of customer service is the cost of lost sales. Expenses for customer service support includes the costs of order fulfilment, parts and service support and costs of return goods handling.

(ii) **Transportation costs***:* These costs are determined by the activity of transporting goods. Costs vary considerably with volume of shipment, weight of shipment, distance between point of origin and destination and also with the mode of transportation chosen (land, ocean or air).

(iii) **Warehousing costs***:* These costs are due to warehousing and storage activities and also due to warehouse and plant location selection process.

(iv) **Order processing/information systems costs***:* These costs are related to activities such as order processing, distribution communications and demand forecasting. Order processing costs include costs of order transmittal, order entry, order processing *etc.*

(v) **Lot quantity costs***:* These costs are due to procurement and production lot quantities. Lot quantity costs are related to purchasing or production and these costs vary with changes in order size or frequency. They include: *(a)* setup costs, *(b)* capacity lost due to down time during change over of production set ups or change over to a new supplier, *(c)* material handling, scheduling, expediting, *(d)* price differentials due to buying in different lot sizes and *(e)* order costs associated with order placement and follow up.

(vi) **Inventory carrying costs***:* Logistics activities that cause inventory carrying costs include inventory control, packaging and salvage and scrap disposal. The inventory costs are made up of *:* *(a)* capital cost or opportunity costs, *(b)* inventory service cost (insurance and taxes on inventory), *(c)* storage space cost and *(d)* inventory risk cost including obsolescence, pilferage, and damage.

➤ TOTAL COST CONCEPT

The total cost concept is the key to manage logistics process effectively. The organisation should have the goal of reducing the ***total cost*** of logistics activities rather than merely focusing on each activity in isolation. *For example,* reducing costs in one area, such as transportation, may increase inventory carrying costs because more inventory is needed to cover longer transit times or to balance against greater uncertainity in transit times.

Exhibit 2.6 shows six major cost categories with which management should be concerned while making decisions regarding logistics activities which drive these major cost categories. These six major cost categories comprise the fourteen key logistics activities listed below:

(i) Customer service

(ii) Demand forecasting

(iii) Inventory management

(iv) Logistics communications

(v) Materials handling

(vi) Order processing

(vii) Packaging

(viii) Parts and service support

(ix) Plant and warehouse site selection

(x) Procurement

(xi) Return goods handling

(xii) Reverse logistics

(xiii) Traffic and transportation

(xiv) Warehousing and storage

Exhibit 2.6 : Total Cost Concept

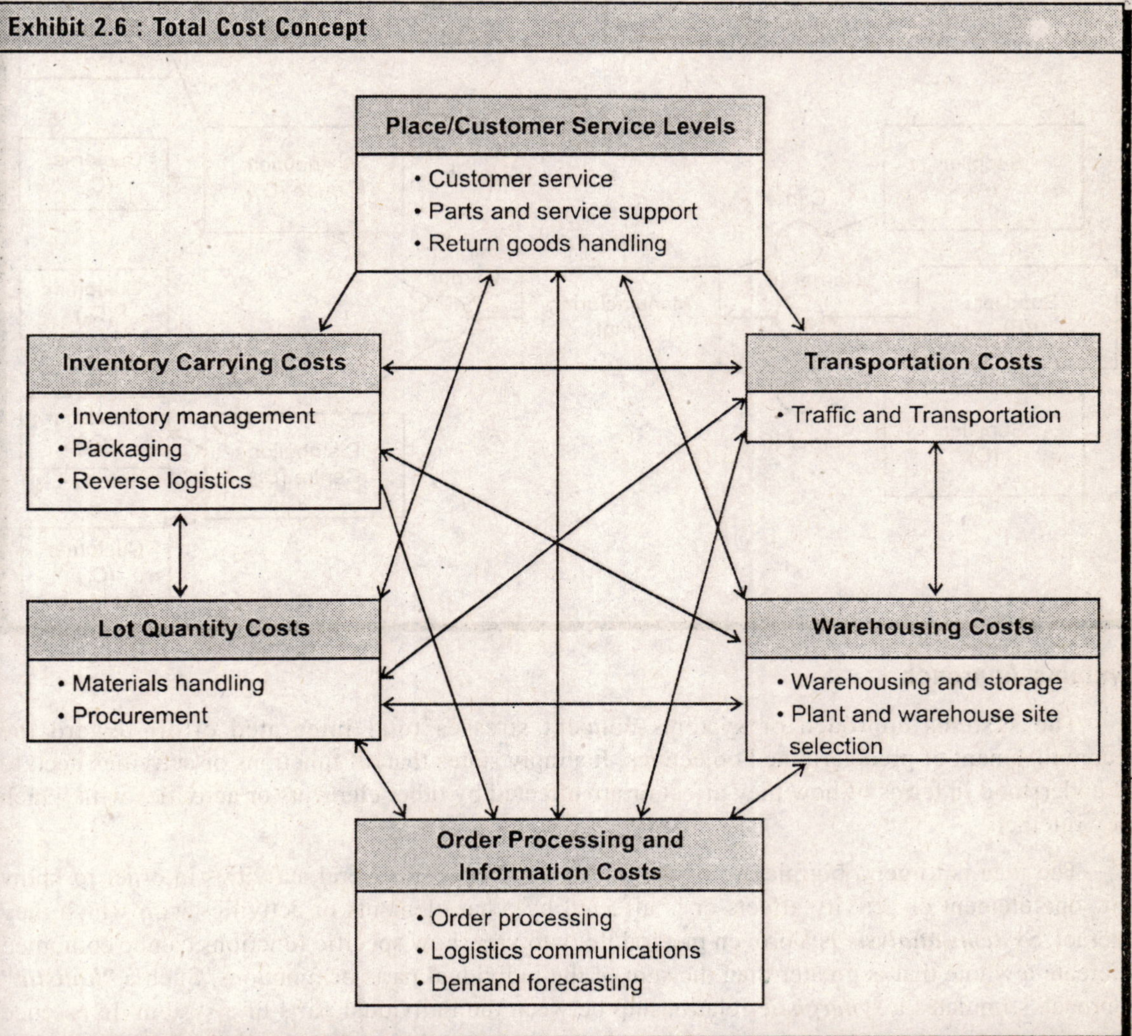

➤ INTEGRATED LOGISTICS MANAGEMENT

Logistics management involves managing the movement of raw materials and components from source of supply to the manufacturing plant, and the movement of the finished goods from the manufacturing plant to warehouses, or to retailers or to the final consumer. To manage the entire supply chain *i.e.,* from source of raw materials to the final consumer, efficiently and effectively, managers need to develop a systems approach in logistics management. Logistics is in itself, a system, it is a network of related activities with the purpose of managing the orderly flow of material and personnel within the logistics channel. *Exhibit 2.7* illustrates a simplified example of the network of relationships to be managed by logistics in a channel of distribution.

Exhibit 2.7 : Distribution Channel Managed by Logistics

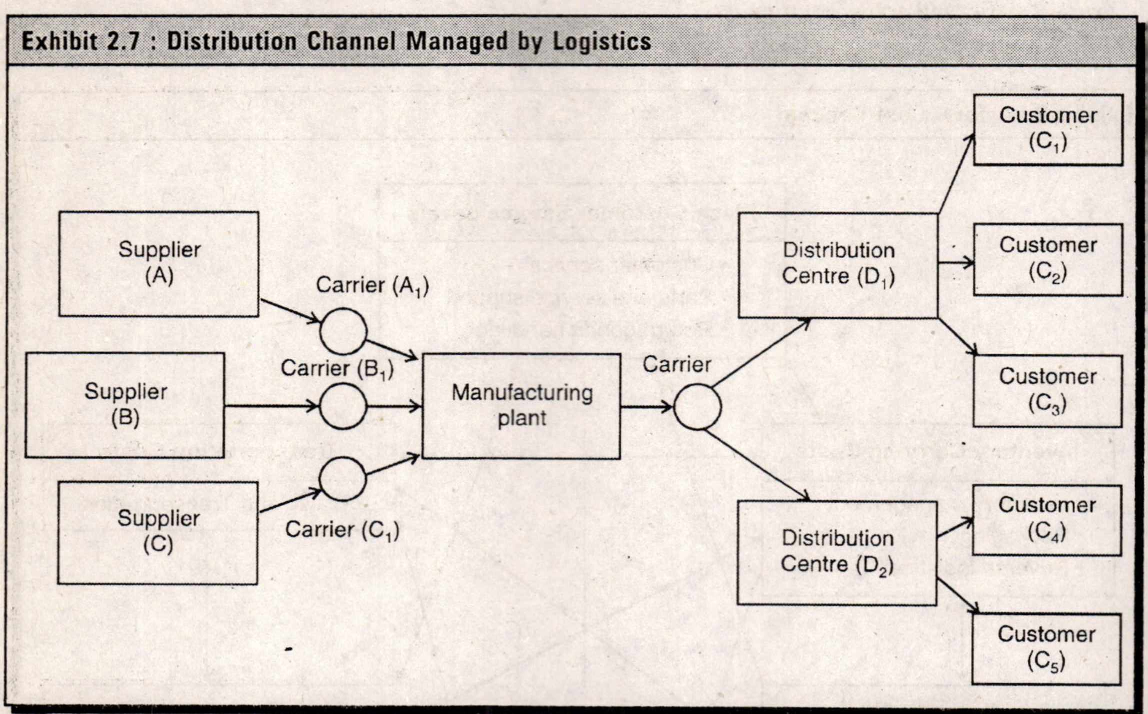

Systems Approach

The systems approach or systems concept stresses total integrated effort toward the accomplishment of predetermined objectives. It simply states that all functions or activities need to be understood in terms of how they affect or are affected by other elements or activities with which they interact.

The idea is to get a big picture of the interaction between several activities in order to know how one element or activity affects or is affected by other elements or activities with which they interact. ***Systems analysis*** is a proven methodology to view how specific functions can be combined to create a whole that is greater than the sum of the individual parts or functions. Such a ***"holistic"*** approach stimulates a ***synergistic*** relationship between the individual parts of a system. In essence it means the sum, or outcome of a series of activities is greater than its individual parts. *For example*, eventhough it is desirable to have high inventory levels in order to improve fulfillment of customer orders, high inventory levels increase storage costs as well as the risk of obsolescence. Hence, it is necessary to trade-off those unfavourable factors with the favourable aspects of a decision before deciding what levels of inventory to be carried? Sub-optimisation often occurs when the impact of decisions on the larger system, such as the firm or the distribution channel is not considered. That means, eventhough the individual activities in that system appear to be operating well, the total system may however perform poorly. Hence, the systems must be viewed as a whole in order to understand the opportunities for improvement and the implications of those opportunities.

Integrated Logistics

Integrated logistics integrates the activities such as physical distribution, materials management, logistics engineering, business logistics, logistics management, distribution management and even supply chain management. Even though all these activities vary from one another, they share one key ingredient; ***the concept of a continuous, uninterrupted flow of the product.*** All logistics activities must work together to move the product smoothly through the channel of distribution to the final customer.

Integrated logistics is a ***service - oriented process***. It involves actions which help movement of the product from the source of raw material to the final customer. In doing so, it supports marketing and production is selling and producing the products. Even if the advertising campaign is very effective, or the sales force is very efficient, without integrated logistics, marketing can not fill customer orders. Likewise, production lines will become idle if integrated logistics fails to transport raw materials and components from the source to the plant. Also, even if production produces goods in time, if the same can not be moved to a market efficiently and effectively, it does not serve any purpose. Hence, integrated logistics, marketing and production must intervene and how well they coordinate determines how well customers are served.

When managers use a systems orientation, they focus their attention to the interaction of all parts of the system. These parts of the system are referred to as ***components***. Each component has a specific function to perform toward facilitating system objectives.

The Integrated Logistics Model

Integrated logistics is defined as "*the process of anticipating customer needs and wants, acquiring the capital, materials, people, technologies and information necessary to meet those needs, optimising the goods or service – producing a network to fulfil customer requests and utilising the network to fulfil customer requirements in a timely way*".

The conceptualisation of integrated logistics model is illustrated in the shaded area of *Exhibit 2.8.*

Exhibit 2.8 : Logistical Integration

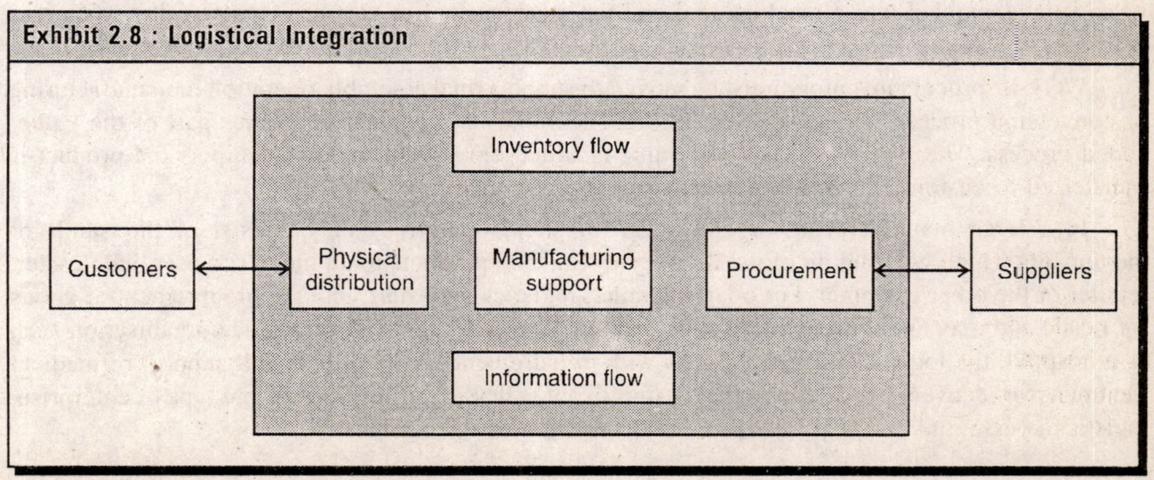

Logistics is viewed as the competency which links an enterprise with its customers and suppliers. Information from and about customers flow through the enterprise in the form of sales activity, forecasts and orders. The information is refined into specific manufacturing and purchasing plans. As products and materials are procured, a value-added inventory flow is initiated which ultimately results in transfer of ownership of finished products to customers.

The logistics process is viewed ***in terms of*** two interrelated efforts – ***inventory flow*** and ***information flow***.

Before discussing these two types of flows in greater detail, two observations are made:

(i) Viewing internal operations (shown in shaded area of *Exhibit 2.8*) in isolation in order to elaborate the basic importance of integrating all functions and work involved in logistics. But such integration alone will not ensure that the firm will achieve its performance goals. In today's competitive business environment, firms must integrate their customers and suppliers also in order to be fully effective. This extension, through external integration is referred to as ***supply chain management*** and detailed discussion of the same is beyond the scope of this both.

(ii) The basic process illustrated in *Exhibit 2.8* is not restricted to manufacturing firms and for - profit businesses alone. There is a need to integrate requirements and operations in all businesses including public sector organisations. *For example*, wholesaling or retailing firms link physical distribution and purchasing since traditional manufacturing is not required. However, the whole-salers and retailers must complete the logistics value added process.

The internal operations of a firm namely ***inventory flow***, ***physical distribution***, ***manufacturing support***, ***procurement*** and ***information flow*** are briefly discussed in the following section.

1. Inventory Flow : The movement and storage of materials and finished products are concerned with the operational management of logistics. The starting point of logistical operations is the initial shipment of a material or component part from a supplier and the logistical operation ends when a manufactured or processed product is delivered to a customer.

Right from the point of purchase of a material or component, the logistical process adds value by moving inventory ***when*** and ***where*** needed. Generally, a material gains value at each step of its conversion into a finished inventory. *For example*, an individual machine component has greater value when it is assembled into a machine tool and the machine tool in turn has greater value when it is delivered to a buyer.

Work-in-process inventory must be moved to support final assembly operation in manufacturing or conversion process. The cost of each component and its movement becomes part of the value-added process. The final or meaningful value is added only when the ownership of the product is transferred to customers ***when*** and ***where*** specified by them.

In a large manufacturing organisation, logistical operations may consist of thousands of movements which will end up in the delivery of finished products to an industrial user, wholesaler, retailer or the other customer. For a large retailer, logistics may start with the procurement of goods for resale and may end with delivery to or pick up from consumers. For a service organisation such as a hospital, the logistics operation starts with procurement and ends with full support of medical treatment for recovery of patients. What is significant is that regardless of size and type of enterprise, logistics is essential and requires continuous attention of management.

2. Logistical Operations : To understand better, logistical operations are divided into three areas: *(a)* physical distribution, *(b)* manufacturing support and *(c)* procurement. These are briefly discussed below:

(a) ***Physical distribution*** is concerned with movement of a finished product to a customer who is the final destination of the marketing channel. The channel participant's marketing effort is vital in ensuring the availability of the product to the customers. Efficient delivery of an assortment of products ***when*** and ***where*** needed is crucial for the success of marketing effort. It is through the physical distribution process that the time and space of customer service become an integral part of marketing. Thus, physical distribution acts as a link between a marketing channel and its customers. One common feature of all physical distribution systems is that they link manufacturers, wholesalers, and retailers into the marketing channels that provide product availability as an integral aspect of the overall marketing process.

(b) ***Manufacturing Support :*** Manufacturing support focuses on managing work-in-process inventory as it flows through the stages of manufacturing. The primary logistical responsibility in manufacturing is to participate in formulation of a ***master production schedule*** (MPS) and to arrange for timely availability of materials, component parts and work-in-process inventory. Manufacturing support's overall concern is not ***how*** production occurs but rather ***what***, ***when*** and ***where*** products will be manufactured. But the difference between physical distribution and manufacturing support is that while physical distribution attempts to service the desires of customer by accommodating the uncertainty in customer demand, manufacturing support controls the supply of requirements for the manufacturing process. Hence, it is useful to separate manufacturing support from ***outbound*** (physical distribution) and ***inbound*** (procurement) activities from the view point of overall logistical planning.

(c) ***Procurement :*** Procurement is concerned with purchasing and arranging inbound movement of materials, parts and/or finished inventory from suppliers to manufacturing and assembly plants, warehouses or retail stores. The acquisition process is called ***purchasing*** in manufacturing organisations, in government organisations it is called ***procurement*** and in retailing and wholesaling it is called ***buying***. All these three terms namely ***purchasing***, ***procurement*** and ***buying*** are referred to as ***inbound logistics***.

Within a typical enterprise, the three areas of logistics *viz.*, procurement, manufacturing support and physical distribution overlap. The prime concern of an integrated logistical process is to coordinate overall value – added inventory movement. The three areas combine to provide integrated management of materials, semi-finished goods and finished products moving between locations, supply sources and customers of the enterprise. In this, logistics is concerned with strategic management of total movement and storage.

Box 2.2 lists the specific operating concerns of procurement, manufacturing support and physical distribution in overall logistics.

3. Information Flow : Information flow identifies specific locations within a logistical system that have requirements of information. Information also integrates the three operating areas *viz.*, *(i)* ***physical distribution***, *(ii)* ***manufacturing support*** and *(iii)* ***procurement***. The primary objective of developing and specifying information requirements is to plan and execute logistical operations. Within individual logistics areas, information regarding size of order, available inventory and urgency of movement has to be shared. Information requirements arise simultaneously when the actual work is performed in physical distribution, manufacturing support and procurement. Whereas these areas contain the actual logistics work, information facilitates coordination of planning and control in day to day operations. Lack of accurate information will result in wastage of effort involved in the logistical system.

Box 2.2 : Specific Operating Concerns of Physical Distribution, Manufacturing Support and Procurement in Overall Logistics

1. **Physical Distribution :** *Activities related to providing customer service: (i)* Receiving customer orders and processing them, *(ii)* Deploying inventories, *(iii)* Storage and handling, *(iv)* Outbound transportation within a channel of distribution includes the responsibility to coordinate with marketing planning in such areas as pricing, promotion support, customer service levels, delivery standards, handling return merchandise and life cycle support. The pricing objective is to assist in revenue generation by providing strategically desired customer service at the lowest total cost.
2. **Manufacturing Support :** *Activities related to planning, scheduling and supporting manufacturing operations*: Requires master schedule planning and performing activities such as: *(i)* Storing semi-finished inventory, *(ii)* handling, *(iii)* transportation and *(iv)* time phasing of components. Includes responsibility for storage of inventory at manufacturing plants and maximum flexibility in the coordination between manufacturing and physical distribution operations.
3. **Procurement :** *Activities related to obtaining products and materials from outside suppliers.* Requires performing: *(i)* resource planning, *(ii)* supply sourcing, negotiation, *(iii)* order placement, *(iv)* inbound transportation, *(v)* receiving and inspection, *(vi)* storage and handling and *(vii)* quality assurance. Includes the responsibility to coordinate with suppliers in such areas as scheduling, supply continuity, hedging; and speculation as well as research to find new sources of supply. The primary objective of procurement is to support manufacturing or resellers by providing timely purchasing at the lowest total cost.

➤ REVIEW QUESTIONS

1. Define the terms logistics and logistics management.
2. What are the various types of logistics?
3. Briefly discuss the various functions coming under the purview of logistics management.
4. Discuss the scope and importance of logistics management.
5. What is meant by logistical competency?
6. Explain the factors by which logistics service is measured.
7. Explain the need for logistics management.
8. Trace the development of logistics.
9. Briefly explain the various activities for which logistics managers are responsible.
10. Discuss the role of logistics in the supply chain management.
11. What is meant by a "value chain"?
12. Discuss the role of logistics in the economy.
13. Discuss the role of logistics in the organisation.
14. Discuss the various elements of logistics costs.
15. What is "Integrated Logistics"? Describe the integrated model.

CHAPTER 3

LOGISTICS PLANNING AND STRATEGY

The logistics environment is constantly changing because of changes taking place in markets, competitors, suppliers and technology. In order to develop or refine the strategy of an enterprise to match this changing environment, a systematic planning is necessary to formally include the relevant considerations and effectively evaluate the alternatives.

In a constantly changing logistics environment, even for established industries, a firm's markets, demands, costs and service requirements change rapidly in response to customer and competitive behaviour. In response to these changes, firms often face the following questions:

(i) How many distribution centres should be used and where should they be located?

(ii) What are the trade-offs between inventory and service, for each distribution centre?

(iii) What types of transportation equipments should be used and how should transport vehicles be routed? and

(iv) Should a material-handling technology be applied in the firm's distribution centre?

Such questions are characterised as complex and data intensive. The complexity is due to a number of factors influencing the total logistics costs and the number of potential alternatives available to logistics managers. A large amount of information is required to evaluate logistics alternatives. *For example*, information regarding possible service alternatives, cost characteristics and operating technologies are required for analysis before evaluating alternative logistics strategies.

Since logistics planning and strategy are valuable contributors to an organisation's strategic planning process and strategy, it may be relevant to discuss key elements of the ***strategic planning process*** and also how to develop a ***logistics strategic plan. Strategic planning*** process is concerned with identifying and evaluating resource acquisition options for sustaining and enhancing the company's competitive position over the long term.

Strategy is defined as a plan, method or a series of manoeuvres for obtaining a specific goal or result. Strategy is also defined as *"a set of dynamic, integrated decisions that must be taken in order to position a business in its complex environment"*. Strategy represents the overall action or approach to be taken to achieve the firm's goals and objectives.

Because the strategic planning process exists to support an organisation's strategy, it is necessary to understand the overall concept of organisational strategy before discussing logistics strategy. The **corporate mission statement** is the overriding objective of the organisation which serves to guide the organisation's strategy, activities and goals.

Why Corporate Strategy is Important to Logistics?

A clear understanding of corporate strategy by logistics managers will enable them to take decisions that are in the best interest of the organisation. The logistics strategy must be based on the corporate strategy and the knowledge of the corporate strategy will help the logistics personnel to know how to value various alternatives in making decisions about trade-off between logistics costs and customer service. *For example,* if the objective is to achieve differentiation by offering fast, reliable deliveries (*i.e.,* making the trade-off of cost versus delivery reliability), logistics managers would choose road transport over rail transport. If low cost is the primary objective, the choice would be rail transport to deliver products to customer. If logistics managers do not understand corporate strategy, they will not be able to make decisions consistent with the corporate decisions affecting the company as a whole. Hence a logistics plan must be developed so as to execute a logistics strategy and monitor progress.

➤ THE HIERARCHY OF PLANNING

For any organisation, planning is essential for its survival and growth in its business. While planning, management should take into consideration the overall mission (corporate mission statement) of the organisation and develop specific action plans to enable the organisation to move in the right (desired) direction. Because of the rapidly changing (dynamic) business environment, managers need to anticipate changes and equip their organisations to best incorporate, respond to and take advantage of such changes. Managers should be proactive rather than being reactive in a crisis mode and should be able to move forward in achieving their firm's mission.

Organisational planning is usually carried out in a hierarchy: *(a)* Strategic planning, *(b)* Tactical planning and *(c)* Operational planning. **Strategic planning** is done at the highest level of management for a long term and the resulting plan is known as **strategic plan**. The planning horizon for strategic planning may vary from 5 to 10 years. It is less detailed and its focus is on competition, resources and stake holders. It integrates the corporate and the supply chain. The strategic plans usually include projected revenues and expenses, lines of business, anticipated relative share of the market, and sales and profits from existing business lines.

Tactical planning is done at the middle management level and generally having a planning horizon of one to five years. The resulting plan is a medium range plan called a **tactical plan**. Tactical plans are often more specific than strategic plans in terms of product lines and may be broken down into detailed quarterly revenues and expenses. Tactical plans usually include a capital expenditure plan which indicates firm's annual investment in new plant and equipment and other capital assets. Issues such as building warehouses, purchasing material handling or transportation equipments and other major expenditure to support the **logistic infrastructure** are addressed as part of the capital expenditure plan in tactical plans.

Operational planning is carried out in more detail on yearly basis, broken down to quarterly or monthly plans. The resulting plan is called operating plan which breaks down revenues, expenses and associated cash flows and activity by month for a one year period. The detailed operating plan guides the activities at the junior management level and facilitates monitoring of actual performance by comparing it with planned performance. Production scheduling and material purchases are based on the operating plan. A firm can use its operating plan to anticipate its logistics needs from warehouse capacity to shipping. It permits logistics to anticipate its labour costs and to negotiate contracts with third party logistics providers.

Relationship Between Logistics Strategy and Corporate Strategy

Logistics strategic planning can be defined as: *"A unified, comprehensive and integrated planning process to achieve competitive advantage through increased value and customer service, which result in superior customer satisfaction, by anticipating future demand for logistics services and managing the resources of the entire supply chain. This planning is done within the context of the overall corporate goals and plan."*

Since logistics strategic planning is a complex process, it require a clear understanding of how the different elements and activities of logistics interact in terms of trade-offs and the total cost to the organisation. Logistics strategy can be best formulated only by understanding the corporate strategy. Majority of logistics managers believed that the logistics plan was critical to the firm's corporate strategic plan. But many firms focus more on marketing or manufacturing planning rather than on logistics strategic planning and logistics planning is less commonly used in many organisations.

Logistics can contribute to and support an organisation's strategic planning process in a number of ways. Six specific ways that show how logistics supports corporate strategy in **Intel** are as follows:

(i) Increased planning capability and reduced inventory as a result of reliable delivery time.

(ii) Increased profit margin and improved customer service

(iii) Reduced inventory levels through shorter cycle time

(iv) Increased marketing advantage from consistent, shorter order cycles

(v) Uninterrupted supply of in-bound materials

(vi) Reduced total costs by incorporating logistics into the corporate planning process.

The benefits of logistics support to corporate strategic planning are:

(i) Operating improvements, *e.g.*, lower inventory and shorter lead times.

(ii) Strategic advantage, *e.g.*, lower total cost and improved customer service.

The Organisational Planning Process

The logistics planning depends on corporate strategic planning which directs the logistics plan. The corporate logistic planning considers the following environments:

(i) Legal and political environment.

(ii) Technological environment

(iii) Economic and social environment and

(iv) Overall competitive environment.

Exhibit 3.1 illustrates the influence of environment in organisational planning.

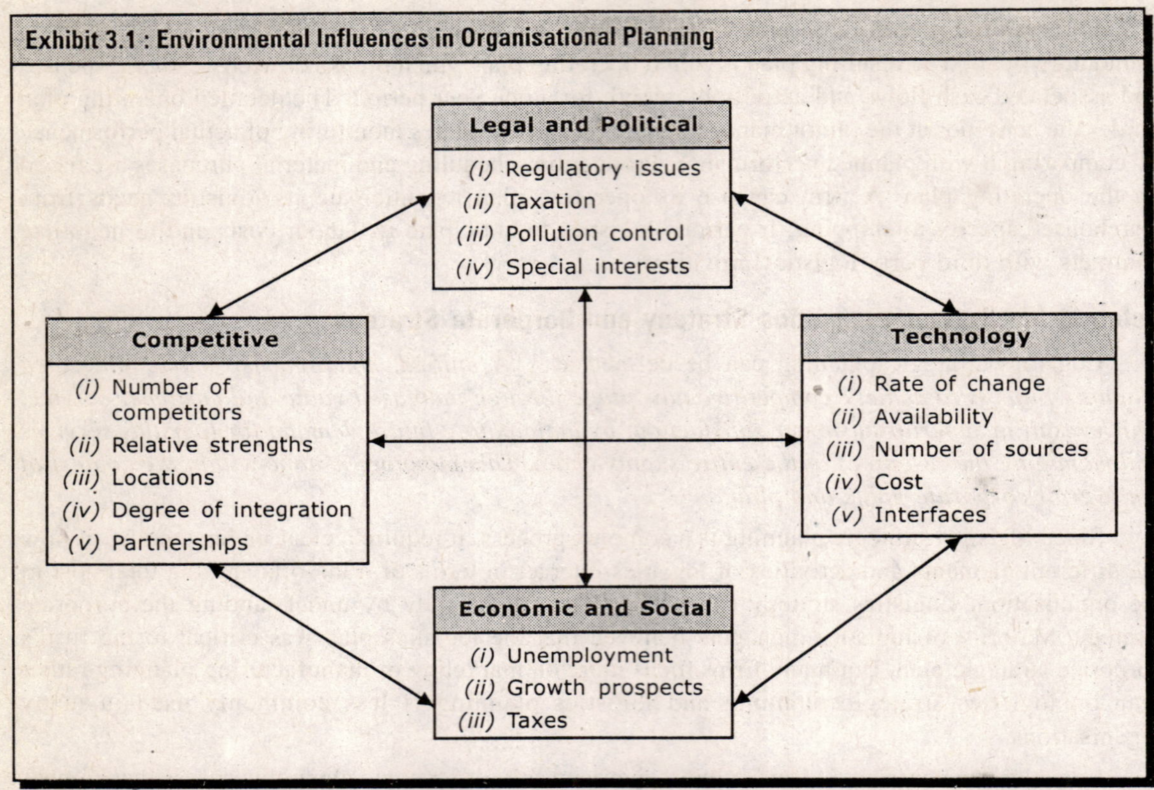

Since these four environments interact with one another, the effects of each environment upon the others make the assessment of environment, a complicated task.

Based on the forecasted trends in the environmental factors and the projected inflation and economic growth rates, the corporate strategic planning is carried out.

The corporate strategic planning process has the following major steps:

(i) Evaluation of consumer and/or industrial customer needs

(ii) Identification of possible target markets

(iii) Evaluation of target markets

(iv) Selection of target markets

(v) Formulation of channel objectives and channel strategy

(vi) Identification and evaluation of channel structure alternatives

(vii) Selection of the channel structure and

(viii) Development of the strategic logistics plan.

The starting point for the logistics function to participate in the corporate strategic planning is step number five *i.e., **"formulation of channel objective and channel strategy"***.

The logistics function has a major role to play in the channel of distribution in terms of many logistics activities performed and also as an interface with channel members who support the channel of distribution of the organisation.

Once the channel objectives and strategy are determined, the next step is to identify channel alternatives. Identifying channel alternatives has become more complicated due to: *(i)* participation in partnering, *(ii)* outsourcing and *(iii)* supply chain management.

The issues to be considered in formulating channel alternatives are:

(i) desired consistency and speed of delivery

(ii) information flows

(iii) the degree of control desired and

(iv) the cost of service.

Next, the channel structure holding the most promise in terms of meeting organisational objectives should be analysed in depth. The factors to be considered are: *(i)* operating costs, *(ii)* investment required, *(iii)* degree of control, *(iv)* flexibility and *(v)* the ability to meet channel objectives.

The Strategic Logistics Plan

Strategic logistics plan depends on a number of inputs from various functional areas. They are: *(i)* ***marketing***, *(ii)* ***manufacturing***, *(iii)* ***finance/accounting*** and *(iv)* ***logistics***. These are briefly discussed in the following paragraphs:

Marketing is closely related to logistics and hence provides the key inputs to logistics. Marketing provides information about product/service offerings, pricing, and promotion for each channel. This information includes: *(i)* Sales volume by month, *(ii)* type of customer, *(iii)* regional area, *(iv)* product introductions and deletions, *(v)* customer and *(vi)* geographical area.

Also logistics function must be aware of specific policies related to key customers and be able to support.

Customer service policies are critical to logistics strategy. Logistics must participate with the organisation's management in setting such policies to ensure that they are *feasible* and *economical*. Customer service policies should include the following information by type of customer and region:

(i) Order placement methods, *(ii)* Order entry, *(iii)* Target cycle, *(iv)* Order cycle variability, *(v)* Desired fill-rate or in-stock levels.

Also, customer service policies should be related to *product substitution*, *expediting*, *transhipment*, and *customer pickup*.

Manufacturing provides some key informations to logistics strategic plan. These are: *(i)* locations of current and planned production facilities and *(ii)* planned volume and product mix for each location.

When the same product is produced at multiple locations, logistics can decide how to serve each market most efficiently.

Finance/accounting provides forecasts of costs related to inflation rates and growth assumption to project future costs. It provides the cost data required to perform cost trade-off analysis. Also it is responsible for capital budgeting which determines the availability of capital for improving logistics equipments and infrastructure.

Logistics provide data and analysis related to the existing logistics network to the other functions, including current storage and distribution facilities owned and rented, both at manufacturing locations and in the field, equipment capacity and capabilities at each location, and current transportation arrangements between various channel members. The costs associated with these activities and the various channels used and proposed, must be identified by logistics. Evaluation and solution of channel members are critical aspects of this process.

Evaluation and Selection of Channel Members

Channel members help the management of the firm to implement the logistics plan. Alternatives regarding choice of carriers, warehouses and other logistics service providers must be developed. The selection of channels members is done by judging them according to predetermined criteria to meet objectives. These criteria include reliability, consistency, geographical coverage, variety of service offerings, use of information technology and cost.

Ongoing Channel Evaluation and Improvement

Regular monitoring and reporting of actual performance results of channel members are necessary to keep performance on track.

The expected level of performance is taken as basis for comparison. Some of the measures of performance of both logistics function and external channel members are: *(i)* on time delivery, *(ii)* response speed for emergencies, *(iii)* delivery time variability and *(iv)* response to customer inquiries. If the channel performance is not satisfactory, the management has three options: *(i)* whether to continue to work with existing channel members toward improvement, *(ii)* replace the intermediary with one providing similar services and *(iii)* restructure the channel of distribution.

Developing a Strategic Logistics Plan : The requirements of a strategic logistics plan are:

(i) a thorough grasp and support of corporate strategy and supporting marketing plans in order to optimise cost-service trade-offs

(ii) thorough understanding of the customers' view regarding the importance of various customer service elements and the performance of the firm compared with its competitors.

(iii) A knowledge of the cost and profitability of channel alternatives.

The focus of the strategic logistics planning process should be on determining required customer service levels. External and internal market research can be used to obtain the information regarding the required customer service levels. Logistics audit also helps in obtaining this information.

Logistics Audit : The logistics audit should be conducted on a routine basis and it involves a review of how logistics is performing with respect to its objectives. The logistics audit complements and supports the strategic planning process. This is done as follows:

(i) By linking logistics strategies and objectives to corporate strategies and objectives.

(ii) By identifying key measures of logistics performance.

(iii) By comparing customer perceptions of logistics performance with key measurements and objectives.

(iv) By comparing actual performance with desired performance and analysing gaps in actual performance.

(v) By analysing trade-offs among desired performance levels on key result areas.

(vi) By designing systems to reflect key goals and objective and

(vii) Identifying expected performance and continually monitoring results.

Logistics audit is formally conducted over a year to help align the efforts of the logistics function and to focus the strategic planning process.

The logistics audit process starts with the formation of a logistics audit team. This team comprises those involved in managing or performing logistics activities such as warehousing, customer service, and traffic and also those who use logistics service, (such as corporate function, management information systems, finance/accounting and also the external customers). The other members of the logistics audit team could be representatives from manufacturing, sales and key customers.

Developing Logistics Strategy : To develop the logistics strategy, the managers should understand their organisation's overall strategy and the key trade-offs in the organisation. The primary goal of logistics is to support the organisation's customer service goals efficiently and effectively. To do this, the logistics function and the organisation's management must find answer to the following questions:

(i) What do customers desire in terms of service levels and capabilities?

(ii) How is the competition performing in terms of customer service?

(iii) How is the organisation performing at present compared to the competition in those areas which the customers perceive as important.

Logistics costs also are important aspects of analysing alternative logistics service offering. The first two questions can be answered by a marketing and logistics audit of the external environment. The third question can be answered by conducting an internal audit in conjunction with customer service.

The Logistics Plan : Once the logistics strategy has been formulated, a logistics plan must be developed to support that strategy. The logistics plan includes the specific activities required to be undertaken by the logistics function to achieve its objectives. The logistics decisions are made in a hierarchical manner as illustrated in *Exhibit 3.2.*

Exhibit 3.2 : Logistics Decisions in a Hierarchy

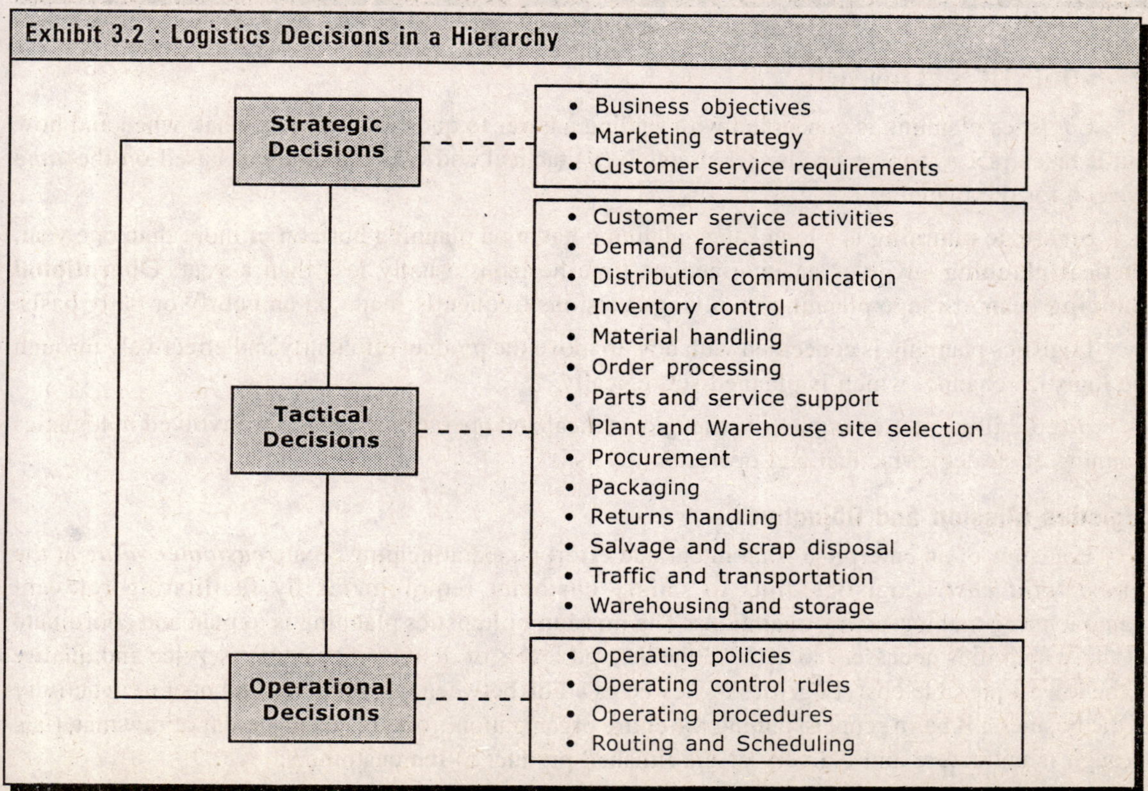

The logistics plan covers a variety of issues and requires inputs from people participating in each of the logistics activities. *Box 3.1* illustrates the outline of a logistics strategic plan.

Box 3.1 : Outline of Logistics Plan

(i) Logistics Mission
(ii) Key Issues and objectives
  (a) Customer service performance (b) Information systems
  (c) Human resource requirement (d) Supplier relationships
  (e) Outsourcing
(iii) Comparison with previous plan performance
(iv) Internal analysis (current position)
  (a) Organisation (b) Human resources
  (c) Transportation (d) Relations with internal customers
  (e) Quality (f) Service
(v) External/situational analysis
  (a) Competitor logistics performance (b) Trends
  (c) Public, private and contract warehouses (d) Public, private and contract carriage
(vi) Five year vision
(vii) Action plan vision
(viii) Implementation issues
(ix) Other critical issues

➢ LOGISTICS PLANNING

Logistics planning is concerned with finding answer to questions such as what, when and how and it takes place at three levels: *(i)* strategic *(ii)* tactical and *(iii)* operational, based on the *time horizon* for the planning.

Strategic planning is a long-range planning having a planning horizon of more than one year. **Tactical planning** involves an intermediate time horizon, usually less than a year. **Operational planning** is short-range planning involving decisions frequently made on an hourly or daily basis.

Logistics planning is concerned with how to move the product efficiently and effectively through the logistics channel which is planned strategically.

Box 3.2 illustrates examples of strategic, tactical and operational decisions involved in logistics planning at strategic, tactical and operation levels.

Logistics Mission and Objectives

Logistics of an enterprise is an integrated effort aimed at helping create ***customer value*** at the ***lowest total cost***. Logistics aims to satisfy customer requirements by facilitating relevant manufacturing and marketing operations. The **mission** of logistics planning is to plan and coordinate all those activities necessary to achieve the desired levels of delivered customer service and quality at the lowest possible cost. Logistics is viewed as a link between market place and operating activity of the business. It has a scope spanning the entire organization from the management of raw materials through manufacture and delivery of the finished product to the customers.

Box 3.2 : Examples of Decisions Made in Strategic, Tactical and Operational Planning Levels in Logistics Planning

Decision Area	Level of Decision		
	Strategic	Tactical	Operational
(i) Facility location	Number, size, and location of warehouses, manufacturing plants and terminals	–	–
(ii) Inventories	Stocking locations and policies for inventory control	Safety stock levels	Reordering quantities and timing
(iii) Transportation	Selection of mode of transport	Seasonal leasing of transport vehicles	Routing and despatching of transport vehicles
(iv) Order processing	Order entry, transmittal and processing system design	–	Order processing and back-order filling
(v) Customer service	Establishing standards for customer orders	Setting priority rules to customers.	Expediting deliveries
(vi) Warehousing	Selection of material handling equipments and design of stores layout	Seasonal space choices and utilisation of private space	Order picking and stocking
(vii) Purchasing	Development of supplier-buyer relationship	Vendor selection, forward buying, contracting.	Releasing orders and expediting supplies

Logistics Mission Statement

The mission statement provides a foundation upon which a company develops objectives, strategies, plans and tactics. It defines the basic purpose of an organisation and identifies the parameters under which the firm will operate. Like corporate mission statements, logistics mission statements too will provide direction for developing business strategies.

An example of a typical logistics mission statement is given below:

"Logistics has the potential to become the next governing element of strategy as an inventive way of creating value for customers, an immediate source of savings, an important discipline on marketing and a critical extension of product flexibility."

Typically, mission statements will contain eight key components and it is applicable to logistics mission statement also.

The key components are:

(i) Targeted customers and markets

(ii) Principal products and services

(iii) Geographical domain

(iv) Core technologies

(v) Survival, growth and profitability

(vi) Company philosophy (basic priorities of the firm)

(vii) Company self-concept (strengths and weaknesses relative to its competitors)

(viii) Desired public image (*i.e.*, firm's social responsibility).

Firms need a clear statement of purpose in order to develop the best combination of activities that must be carried out in their day-to-day operations. In summary, the logistics mission statement is an important document to guide the planning, implementation and control of the logistics activities of a firm.

Logistical Objectives

There are six different operational objectives which must be achieved by the firm in terms of logistical system design and management. These operational objectives which primarily determine the logistical performance include : *(i) rapid response, (ii) minimum variance, (iii) minimum inventory, (iv) movement consolidation, (v) quality and (vi) life-cycle support*. Each of these objective is briefly discussed.

(i) **Rapid Response :** This objective is concerned with a firm's ability to satisfy customer service requirements in time. Because of information technology, it has become possible to increase the capability to postpone logistical operations to the latest possible time and then accomplish rapid delivery of required inventory. This enables the firm to eliminate excessive inventories which otherwise would have been held in anticipation of customer demand. Rapid response capability emphasises responding to customer demand on a shipment-to-shipment basis.

(ii) **Minimum Variance :** Any unexpected event which disrupts the performance of a system is termed as ***variance***. Any aspect of logistical operation may cause variance. *For example,* delays in expected time of customer order receipt, unexpected disruptions in manufacturing, damaged goods arriving at a customer's premises, or delivery of goods to a wrong location – all result in a time variance in operations which must be resolved. Variance may occur in both internal and external operations. Traditionally variances are accommodated by using safety stock inventory using high-cost premium transportation. Such practices have now been replaced by using information technology to achieve positives logistics control. By minimizing variances, logistical productivity can be improved by economising on costs of operations. Thus the basic objective of overall logistical performance is to ***minimise variance***.

(iii) **Minimum Inventory :** This inventory involves commitment of assets and relative turn velocity. The total commitment is the financial value of inventory deployed throughout the logistical system. The "turn velocity" involves the rate of inventory usage over time (*i.e.*, inventory turn over ratio). Effective utilisation of assets devoted to inventory is reflected in terms of high inventory turn rates together with availability of inventory. The objective is to reduce inventory deployed to the lowest level consistent with customer service goals so that the overall total logistics cost is kept at the lowest level. The operational defects in a system do not become apparent until inventories are reduced to their lowest possible level. Eventhough the concept of zero inventory is popular with managers, it must be remembered that inventory can and does facilitate some benefits in a logistical system such as improved return on investment due to economies of scale in manufacturing or procurement. Hence the objective should be to reduce and manage inventory to the lowest possible level and at the same time achieving desired operating objectives.

(iv) **Movement Consolidation :** Transportation cost is one of the most significant logistical costs. It is directly linked to the nature of the product, size of shipment and distance transported. Premium service logistical systems use high-speed small-shipment transportation which is typically a high cost transportation. Therefore it is desirable to achieve ***movement consolidation*** to reduce transportation cost. Generally, the larger the overall shipment and the longer the distance it is transported, the lower the transportation cost per unit. Hence, the size of overall shipment can be increased by consolidation of small shipments for transportation.

(v) **Quality :** Total quality management (TQM) has become a major commitment throughout all facets of industry. Hence logistics also seeks to contribute to ***continuous quality improvement***. Logistics can add value by avoiding defects in products and by keeping customer service promises. Logistical costs once incurred, cannot be reversed. But when quality fails the logistical performance needs to be reversed and then repeated (*i.e.,* return of defective materials to suppliers, or return of defective products to manufactures and then replacement of the same). Hence in order to avoid the costs of returns and replacements, logistics must perform to the required quality standards. The logistics managers face the challenge of achieving zero defect logistical performance, performing logistical operations across a vast geographical area and performing them ***right the first time***. Thus logistics is a significant part of developing and maintaining ***continuous improvement*** **of** ***total quality***.

(vi) **Life-cycle Support :** Many products are sold with some guarantee that the products will perform as advertised over a specific period. In such cases, if defects are observed in the products sold, product recall becomes necessary and the normal value added inventory flows toward customers must be reversed. Also product recall may become necessary due to rigid quality standards, product expiry dates and responsibility for hazardous consequences of product use. Further, increasing number of laws prohibiting waste disposal and need for recycling waste or scrap materials (such as glass bottles, plastic containers, packaging materials etc.) will necessitate ***reverse logistics***. Hence, reverse logistical requirements have become part of sound logistical strategy. This kind of customer service support logistics extended over the entire life-cycle of a product is known as **"life-cycle support"**. The commitment to life-cycle support constitutes a versatile and demanding operational requirement and the largest costs of logistical operations. Hence the support capabilities of a logistical system must be carefully designed. As a result of world-wide attention to environmental concerns, the reverse logistical competence requires the capacity to recycle ingredients and packaging materials. In other words, life-cycle support means ***"cradle-to-cradle"*** logistical support.

➢ THE CHANGING LOGISTICS ENVIRONMENT

Business environments change constantly. As the ***competitive environment*** of business continues to change, bringing with it new complexities and concerns for management generally, these changes have significant impact on the design and management of a logistics system. Logistics managers must implement significant modifications to the logistics systems managed by them on a quick response basis. Four forces drive business environment change: ***the market, competition, technological evolution*** **and** ***government regulation***. These four factors cause companies to adjust their logistics strategies and tactics on a continuous basis. Infact, of the many strategic issues that business organisations confront today perhaps the most challenging are in the area of logistics. The most pressing challenges at present are:

(i) The customer service explosion

(ii) Time compression

(iii) Globalisation of industry

(iv) Organisational integration

These challenges are briefly discussed in the following paragraphs:

(i) **The Customer Service Explosion :** Customer in today's market is more demanding, not just of product quality, but also of quality service.

In today's "commodity" markets, customer perceives little technical difference between competitive offers (product differentiation) and hence there is a need for the creation of differential advantage through added value. ***Customer service*** is one prime source to create thin added value. "*Customer service is defined as a process for providing significant value added benefits to the supply chain in a cost-effective way*". Customer service may also be defined as the constant provision of ***time*** and ***place utility***. It involves on-time delivery and after-sales-support. Its role is to enhance "value-in-use" meaning that the product becomes worth more to the customer because service has added value to the core product. While the core product of competitive firms do not have significant differences, a firm can add value to its core product by significantly differentiating its total offer (*i.e.*, core product plus the service package) from that of its competitors.

Companies giving high priority for their ***logistics performance*** can achieve recognition for ***service excellence*** and thus establish a differential advantage over their competition (Xerox, DMW and Dell computers are some of the examples of such companies). Such competitive advantage can be achieved through service resulting from a combination of strategy for service, the development of appropriate delivery systems and total commitment from all the employees of the company-right from the Chief Executive down to the lowest level employee.

Service excellence can only be achieved through a closely integrated ***logistics strategy***. The ability to become a world-class supplier depends upon the effectiveness of the firm's operating systems, the presentation of its products, the creation of its images and the influencing of customer perceptions. In this context, managing the logistics of service delivery on a consistent basis becomes the crucial source of differential advantage.

(ii) **Time Compression :** *Time* has become a key issue in management today because of the following reasons:

(a) Product life cycles are shorter than ever.

(b) Industrial customers and distributors require just-in-time deliveries.

(c) End users are more willing to accept a substitute product if their choice is not readily available.

(d) New product introduction to the market should be done in the minimum possible lead time.

In addition to all these initiatives which are necessary for a business to survive, the issue of the problem of **extended logistics lead times** is given more importance along with the concern with the process of creating and managing innovation.

The scope of logistics lead-time management includes a number of complex activities that must be managed in order to gain and retain customers. These activities are related to decisions taken on the sourcing and procurement of materials and components through the manufacturing and assembly process to the final distribution and after sales service/support.

Logistics is basically concerned with the provision of ***"availability"*** of materials to the manufacturing units and the finished products to the customers. To carryout this logistics function (both in-bound and out-bound logistics) it is necessary to integrate the marketing and manufacturing planning functions. Because of extended supply and distribution "pipelines", there is limited coordination of supply decisions with the changing requirements of the market place resulting in restricted visibility that purchasing and manufacturing have of final market demand. Hence a new and different approach to the management of lead time is required to establish enduring competitive advantage by ensuring timely response to volatile market demand.

(iii) **Globalisation of Industry :** In the current era of globalisation, changes in customers' expectations or geographical locations continually transform the nature of markets and in turn, generate constraints that modify the flows of goods within companies.

Technological break-through and emerging markets open up new ways of reorganising, adapting and optimising the flow of raw materials, semifinished goods, products, spare parts and recycle materials. In the global business, materials and components are sourced world wide, manufacturing is outsourced off shore and finished products are sold in many different countries perhaps with local customisation. Therefore, for global companies, the management of logistics process has become an issue of central concern. The global company is compelled to seek to achieve competitive advantage by identifying global markets for its products/services and then developing a manufacturing and logistics strategy to support its marketing strategy.

(iv) **Organizational Integration :** In traditional organisations functional departments such as materials management, production, marketing etc., function rather independently without system approach and integration among various functions. But in today's competitive environment, to achieve a position of sustainable competitive advantage, organisations have to dispense with the out moded functional organisational structures and instead have managers who are broad-based integrators and are oriented towards the achievement of market place success based upon managing processes and people that deliver service. *For example,* materials management must be integrated with production management which in turn must be integrated with marketing management. Hence, knowledge of systems theory and behavioural science will be a key prerequisite for managers of today. Also the managers need to be market-oriented with a sharp focus upon customer service as the primary source of competitive advantage.

➢ LOGISTICS STRATEGIES

The corporate strategy drives the functional strategies namely manufacturing, marketing, finance and logistics strategies. Selecting a good logistics strategy requires much of the same creative processes required for developing a good corporate strategy. Innovative logistics strategies can provide competitive advantages to the firm.

Three ***major objectives*** of a logistics strategy are *(i)* ***cost reduction***, *(ii)* ***capital reduction*** *and (iii)* ***service improvement***.

Cost reduction strategy aims at minimising the variable costs associated with movement and storage. Alternative courses of action such as choosing among different warehouse locations or selecting among alternative modes of transport are evaluated to formulate the best strategy for cost reduction. Services levels are not varied while the minimum cost alternatives are being explored, keeping profit maximisation as the prime goal.

Capital reduction strategy is directed toward minimising the level of investment in the logistics system. This strategy has the motive of maximising return on logistics assets. Some of the examples of this strategy are:

(i) Shipping direct to customers to avoid warehousing.

(ii) Choosing public warehouses instead of private warehouses.

(iii) Selecting just-in-time supply approach rather than keeping inventory and

(iv) Using third-party providers of logistics services.

Eventhough higher variable costs are incurred in these strategies as compared to strategies requiring a higher level of investment, the return-on-investment may be higher.

Exhibit 3.3 : Flow of Logistics Planning

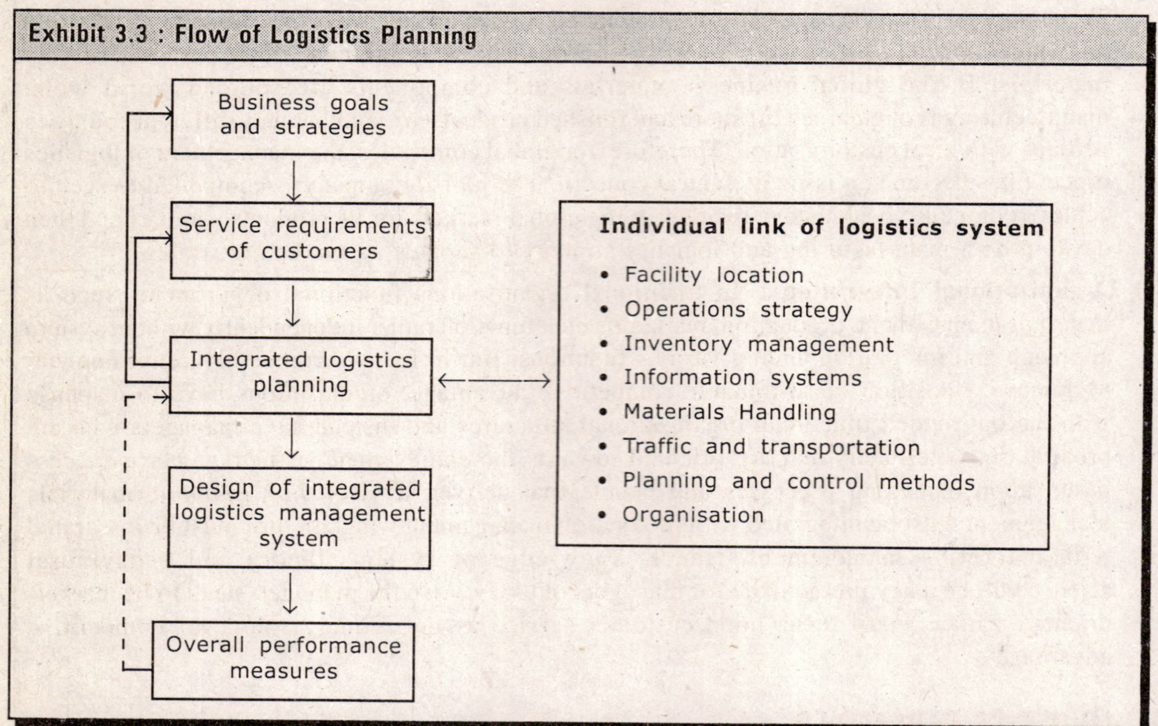

Service improvement strategies recognise the relationship between revenues and the level of logistics service provided. Although costs increase rapidly with increased levels of logistics customer service, the higher revenues may offset the higher costs. The service strategy is developed taking into consideration the service provided by the competition.

A ***proactive*** logistics strategy usually begins with the determination of business goals and customer service requirements. Proactive strategies are referred to as ***"attack"*** strategies to meet competition. The design of the logistics system is derived from these attack strategies. Each link in the logistics system in planned and balanced with each other in an integrated logistics planning process, which is illustrated in *Exhibit 3.3*.

Generic Logistics Strategies

Logistics activities are performed by manufactures, wholesalers and retailers; but they often are organised differently. Manufactures may use any one of the following three organisational strategies:

(i) Process-based strategy, *(ii) Market-based strategy,* *(iii) Channel-based strategy*

Process-based strategy is concerned with the management of a broad group of logistics activities as a value added chain. This strategy emphasises the achievement of efficiency from managing the activities of purchasing, manufacturing, scheduling and physical distribution as an integrated system.

Market-based strategy is concerned with the management of small group of logistics activities across multi division business or across multiple business units. Market-based strategy results in a logistics organisation that seeks *(i)* to make joint product shipments to customers on behalf of different business or product groups and *(ii)* to facilitate sales and logistical coordination by a single order-invoice.

Channel-based strategy focuses on the management of logistics activities performed jointly in combination with dealers and distributors. The channel orientation focuses on external control.

Wholesalers carryout traditional whole-saling functions such as transportation and storage and they offer a number of value-added services including light manufacturing and assembly, pricing, order processing, inventory management, logistics system design and development of promotion materials.

Retailers have direct contact with end users and face high level of competition. Hence they place more emphasis on inventory, warehousing and customer activities than manufacturers. Because rapid response is critical due to low margins, retailers request direct deliveries to the retail stores from manufactures. They also purchase many logistics services from third party logistics providers rather than performing those activities themselves.

Triangle of Logistics Decision Making

Four problem areas involved in logistics planning are: *(i)* customer services levels, *(ii)* facility location decisions, *(iii)* inventory decisions and *(iv)* transportation decisions.

The three logistics decision areas are illustrated in *Exhibit 3.4*.

Exhibit 3.4 : The Triangle of Logistics Decision Making

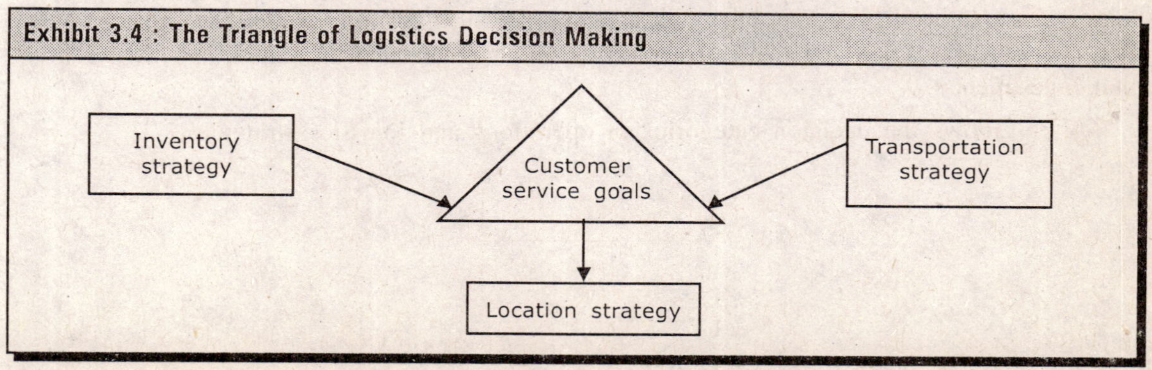

The desired customer service level is a resultant of the strategies formulated in other three areas *viz.*, facility location decisions, inventory decisions and transportation decisions which are interrelated and which have great impact on the design of the logistics system.

Relationship Between Operations Strategy and Logistics Strategy

Operations and logistics strategy is a multidimensional concept that embraces all the critical operations and logistics activities of the firm, providing it with a sense of unity, direction and purpose.

Operations and logistics strategy has the following characteristics:

(i) is a coherent, unifying and integrative pattern of decisions

(ii) determines and reveals the purpose of operations and logistics of the firm (in terms of the firm's long-term objectives, action programs and resource allocation priorities)

(iii) attempts to support or achieve long-term sustainable advantage for the firm by responding properly to the opportunities and threats existing in the environment of the firm.

Twelve decision categories involved in a comprehensive operations and logistics strategy are:

(i) Structure of facilities networks.

(ii) Choice of operations process technology.

(iii) Choice of logistics process technology.

(iv) Vertical integration of the supply chain.

(v) Work force.

(vi) Operations planning and control.

(vii) Distribution planning and control.

(viii) Quality management.

(ix) Transportation policy.

(x) Customer service policy.

(xi) Organisational infrastructure.

(xii) Sourcing.

The above twelve decision categories can be further classified into two general categories: *(i)* ***structural*** and *(ii)* ***infrastructural*** decisions. The structural decisions have long-time impact and are irreversible in nature. The infrastructural decisions deal with non-structural features of the operations and logistics system. They comprise of procedures, control systems and organisational alternatives of various activities. Infrastructural decisions are tactical in nature and involve less capital investments.

*Box 3.3 s*hows the decision categories in operations and logistics strategies.

Box 3.3 : Decision Categories in Operations and Logistics Strategy

***(I)* Structural Decisions :**	
Major decision categories	**Issues/Decisions**
(i) Facilities Network	Supply chain structure, Number of echelons and for each echelon. • number of facilities • facility size • facility location • facility focus **Links between facilities** • information flows • sourcing patterns
(ii) Operations process technology	• Equipment • Degree of automation • Investment timing
(iii) Logistic process technology	• Warehousing/transportation technology, extent of information technology.
(iv) Vertical integration	• Degree of integration • Direction (forward, backward) • Balance of capacity
***(II)* Infrastructure Decisions :**	
Major decision categories	**Issues/Decisions**
(i) Work force	• Training/recruiting • Payment system • Job security
(ii) Operations planning and control	• Degree of centralisation/decentralisation • Computerisation • Inventory levels • Location of inventory
(iii) Distribution planning and control	• Degree of centralisation/decentralisation • Distribution channel selection • Inventory level • Location of inventories
(vi) Quality	• Quality improvement programs • Quality control standards • Quality measurements
(v) Transportation policy	• Modes of transportation • Logistic alliances • Out sourcing/sub contracting
(vi) Customer- service policy	• Frequency of delivery • Ordering methods • Pricing policies
(vii) Organization	• Structure • Reporting relationships • Support groups • Performance measures
(viii) Sourcing	• Purchasing • Selection of suppliers • Offshare sourcing.

➢ FORMULATING LOGISTICAL STRATEGY

Logistics planning problem is viewed as a network of ***links*** and ***nodes***. The links of the network represent the movement of goods between various inventory storage points such as retail stores, warehouses, factories or vendors which are referred to as nodes. Any pair of nodes may be connected by several links to represent alternate forms of transportation service, different routes and different products. Nodes represent points where the flow of inventory is stopped temporarily-*for example,* at a warehouse before the products are moved on to retail store or on to a final customer. The move-store activities for inventories represent only a part of the total logistics system. There is a network of information flows in addition to the network of inventory flows. The sources of information include sales revenues, product costs, inventory levels, warehouse utilisation, forecasts, transportation rates and the like. Links in the information network consists of the mail or electronic methods for transmitting information from one geographical location to another geographical location or from one node to another node. Nodes are the various points of data collection and data processing. *For example,* a clerk who handles order processing or prepares bills of lading or a computer that updates inventory records are referred to as nodes.

The information network is similar to the product flow or inventory flow network (*i.e.,* both consist of links and nodes). But the major difference between these two networks is that product mainly flows "down" the distribution channel (toward final consumer) whereas information usually flows "up" the channel (towards sources of raw materials). These two networks namely product flow network and information flow network are combined to form a logistics network. These networks are dependent on each other. Designing of these networks each separately can lead to a suboptimal design of the entire logistics system. Hence the logistics system has to be designed as a combined system of product flow and information flows networks-viewing the logistics system as a whole rather than by its parts.

Logistics planning thus becomes a problem of designing the logistics system. The logistics system network has to be constructed as a configuration of manufacturing plants/factories, warehouses, retail outlets, deployed inventories, transportation services and information processing systems that will result in an optimal balance between the revenues resulting from the level of customer service established by the network design and the costs associated with the design and operation of the network.

Exhibit 3.5 shows the nodes and links in a logistics system.

Guidelines for Strategy Formulation

The various guidelines for formulation of logistics strategy are:

(i) When to plan the logistics network.

(ii) Appraisal and audit of logistics network in five key areas of demand, customer service, product characteristics, logistics costs and pricing policy.

(iii) Total cost concept.

(iv) Differentiated distribution concept.

(v) Mixed strategy concept.

(vi) The principle of postponement.

(vii) The concept of consolidation.

(viii) Standardisation in production and reduction of product variety.

Exhibit 3.5 : Nodes and Links in Logistics Systems

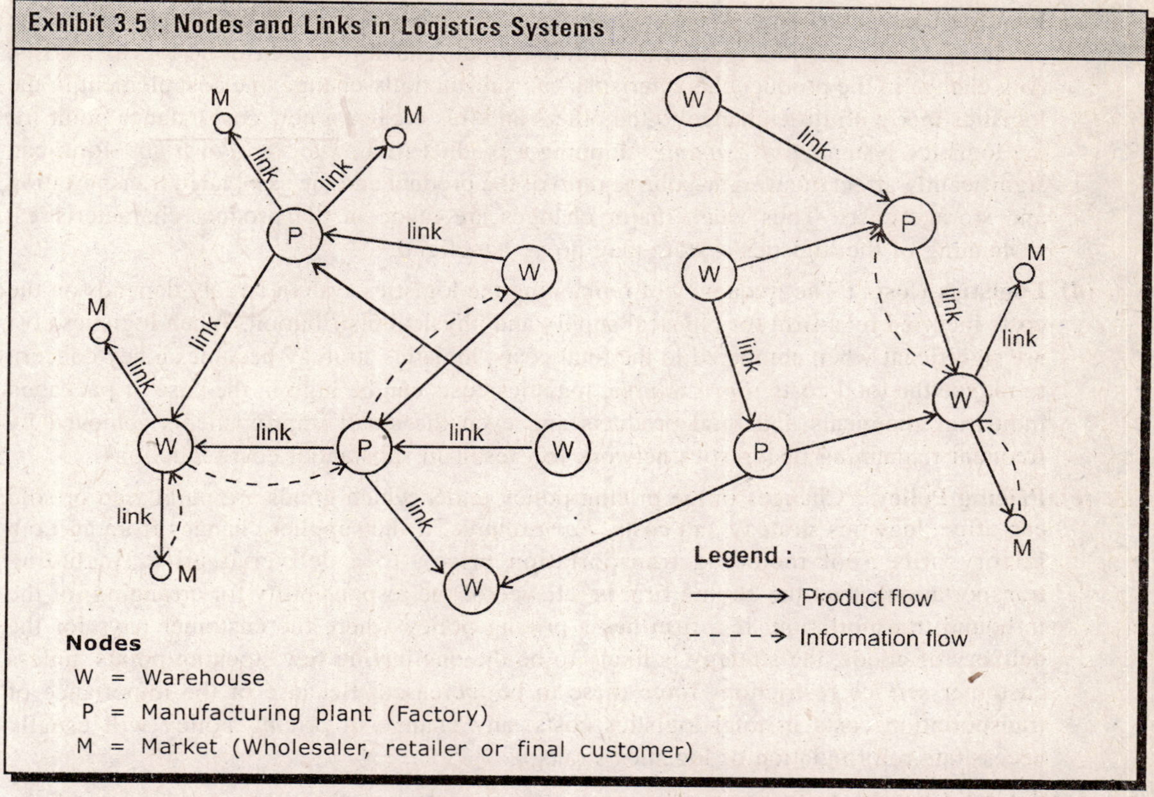

These guidelines are briefly discussed in the following paragraphs:

(i) **When to Plan :** The first consideration in logistics planning process is "when the network should be planned" or planned again. If no logistics system currently exists (as in the case of a new firm) there arises a need for planning a new logistics network. In cases where a logistics network already exists, a decision must be made to modify the existing network if necessary.

(ii) **Appraisal and Audit of Logistics Network :** General guide lines for network appraisal and audit can be offered in the five key areas of demand, customer service, product characteristics, logistics cost and pricing policy.

(a) **Demand :** The logistics network configuration is greatly influenced by the level of demand and its geographical dispersion. Substantial shifts in demand patterns may require location of new plants or warehouses in areas where demand is growing. On the contrary, facilities in slow growth areas or declining markets need to be closed.

(b) **Customer Service :** Broadly, customer service includes inventory availability, speed of delivery and speed and accuracy of filling orders. The costs associated with these factors increase as the customer service level is raised. Distribution costs will be highly sensitive to the level of customer service the firm wishes to provide. When service levels have to be changed due to competition, revision of policies or change in customer service goals of the firm, logistics strategy has to be reformulated.

(c) **Product Characteristics :** Product characteristics such as weight, volume and value of the product and also the risk associated with the product tend to increase the logistics costs. Any change in the product characteristics can substantially change one cost element in the logistics mix with little change to the others and this creates a new cost balance point for the logistics system. *For example,* shipping a product in a *"knocked down kit"* form can significantly affect the weight-volume ratio of the product and the associated transportation and storage costs. Thus when major changes are made in the product characteristics, replanning of the logistics system may prove beneficial.

(d) **Logistics Costs :** The frequency of replanning the logistics system largely depends on the costs incurred by a firm for physical supply and physical distribution. When logistics cost are significant when compared to the total costs, logistics strategy becomes a key concern to reduce the total costs. *For example,* logistics costs can be high in the case of packaged industrial chemicals and food products and even the small improvements achieved by frequent replanning of logistics network can result in substantial cost reductions.

(e) **Pricing Policy :** Changes in the pricing policy under which goods are purchased or sold can affect logistics strategy and costs. *For example,* if the supplier changes from an f.o.b factory price (not including transportation price), to a delivered price (including transportation), then the buying firm is relieved of the responsibility for arranging for the in-bound transportation. If a firm has a pricing policy where the customer pays for the delivery of goods, the strategy is likely to be the one having few stocking points, unless customer service restrictions force these to be increased. Because of the importance of transportation costs in total logistics costs, any change in pricing policy will usually necessitate reformulation of logistics strategy.

(iii) **Total Cost Concept :** Trade-off analysis which is central to the scope and design of the logistics system, leads to the ***total cost concept***. Cost trade-off recognises that reducing total logistics costs and/or improving customer service frequently occurs by trading off one activity centre against another. *For example,* shifting the mode of transport from rail to truck (road) may result in lower inventory costs (because of faster and more reliable service) which offsets the higher cost of transportation by truck. This conflict is managed by balancing the activities so that they are collectively optimised. *Exhibit 3.6* shows the conflict between transportation and inventory costs as a result of changing the mode of transportation from rail to truck and to air. The direct cost of the transport service and the indirect cost effect on inventory levels are in conflict with each other. The best economic choice occurs at the point where the sum of both costs is the lowest as indicated by the dotted line in the *Exhibit 3.6*.

The logistics network should incorporate most of the potential cost conflicts relevant to logistics. The total cost concept is the trade-off of all costs that are in cost-conflict with each other and that can affect the outcome of a particular logistics decision.

(iv) **Differentiated Distribution Concept :** The fundamental principle for logistics planning states that "**not all products should be provided the same level of customer service**". Because of different service requirements, different product characteristics and different sales volumes among multiple products distributed by a firm, multiple distribution strategies should be provided within the product line. Hence, products are broadly classified as high, medium and low sales volume items and different stocking levels are applied to each group. This principle may also be applied to inventory locations.

An improved strategy might be to differentiate those products which should move through the warehouse from those which should be shipped directly to customers from plant, vendors or other source points. Those customers ordering in high-volume quantities should be served direct, while other customers would be served from warehouses. Also fast-moving products should be stored in the field warehouses with the most forward locations in the distribution channel and the medium-volume items should be stored in few regional locations. The slow-moving items should be located only at centralised stocking points such as warehouses at manufacturing plants.

Exhibit 3.6 : Cost Conflict Between Transportation and Inventory Costs

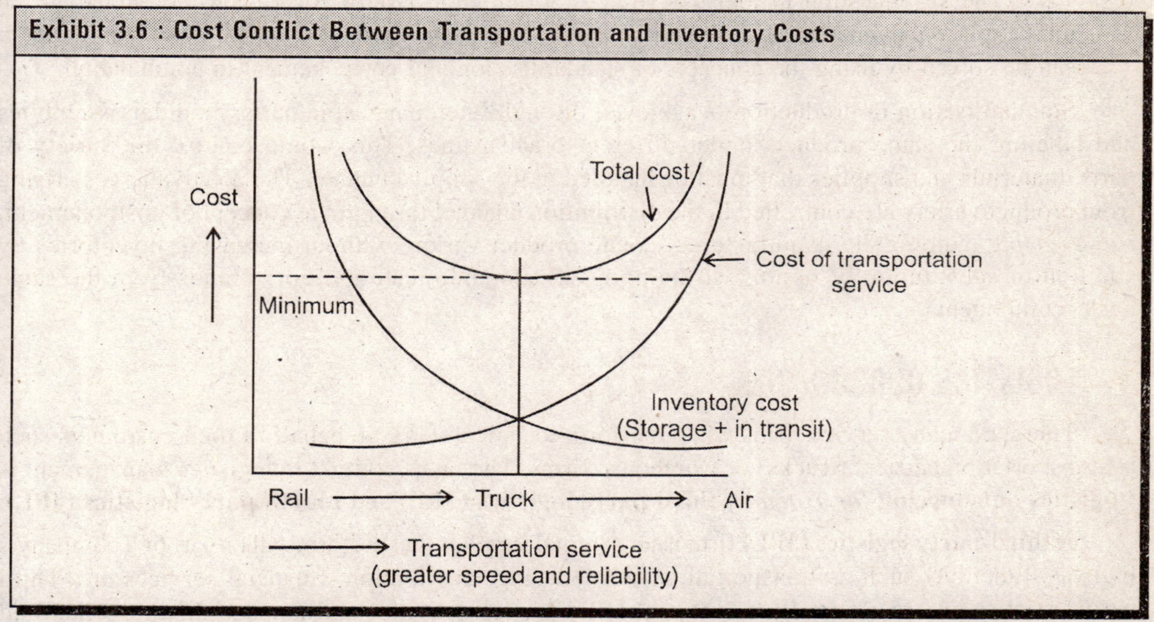

(v) **Mixed Strategy Concept :** This concept is stated as below:

"A mixed distribution strategy will have lower costs than a pure or single distribution strategy".

A single strategy may benefit from economies of scale and simplicity of administration. It has an economic disadvantage when the product line varies substantially in terms of volumes, weight, order size, sales volume and customer-service requirements. A mixed strategy establishes an optimal strategy for separate product groups and often has lower costs than a single strategy for all product groups.

(vi) **The Principle of Postponement :** This principle is stated ad below:

"The time of shipment and the location of the final product processing in the distribution of a product should be delayed until a customer order is received". This principle involves *(a)* ***time post-ponement*** *i.e.,* avoiding shipping goods in anticipation of when demand will occur and *(b)* ***form-postponement*** *i.e.,* avoiding creating the form of the final product in anticipation of that form.

(vii) **The Concept of Consolidation :** Consolidation implies creating large shipments from small ones. It is a powerful economical force in strategic logistics planning. *For example,* customer orders arriving at a warehouse might be combined with orders received later. This would

increase the size of the average shipment, thereby lowering the average per-unit shipping costs. Cost benefit of order consolidation must be balanced with potentially reduced customer service resulting from longer delivery time.

In general, the concept of consolidation will be most useful in logistics strategy formulation when quantities shipped are small. The smaller the shipment size, the greater the benefit of consolidation.

(viii) **Standardisation :** Increase in product varieties can increase inventories and decrease shipment sizes. The key question in logistics strategy formulation is how to provide the variety in the market place that customers desire without significantly increasing logistics costs. This problem can be solved by using the concepts of standardisation and postponement in combination.

Standardisation in production is achieved through interchangeable parts, modular assemblies and labeling the same products under different brand names. This would control the variety of parts, materials and supplies that must be handled in the supply channel. The disadvantages arising from product variety are controlled in the distribution channel through the concept of postponement. *For example,* automobile manufacturers create product variety without increasing inventories by addition or substitution of options at the point of sale and create multiple brands from the same basic components.

➤ LOGISTICS OURSOURCING

There are many service firms which perform logistical work on behalf of their customers such as transportation carriers (trucks) or warehouse firms. The modern trend in logistics management is **Logistics outsourcing** *for example,* **third party logistics (3PL)** and **fourth party logistics (4PL)**.

A **third-party logistics (3PL)** firm is an external supplier that performs all or part of a company's logistics functions such as transportation, warehousing, distribution, financial services etc. Third party logistics provider firms integrate multiple logistics activities and manage them together and also provide "solutions" to logistics/supply chain problems. Nowadays, to meet the increased set of functions ranging from e-procurement to reverse logistics, organisations have been outsourcing their activities to various logistics service providers (referred to as third party logistics service provider or simply as a third party). **Fourth-party Logistics** (4PL) is an emerging trend in supply chain management in which a customer firm out-sources the entire set of logistics and supply chain activities to a single logistics provider firm which will act as a single point of contact for all their vendors, service providers and customers with regard to any logistics need in order to provide an overall maximum benefit. A fourth party logistics (4PL) is a supply chain integrator that assembles and manages the resources, capabilities and technology of its own organisation with those of complementary service providers to deliver a comprehensive supply chain solution. The third party or fourth party logistics providers must be willing to accept reasonable managerial direction and control from their customers and the contracting firm's (*i.e.,* customer firm) management remains responsible for successful performance of the required logistical activities.

➤ REVIEW QUESTIONS

1. What is strategic planning?
2. Why corporate strategy is important to logistics?

3. Discuss the three levels in the hierarchy of planning in organisational planning.
4. What is meant by "Logistics Strategy"?
5. What is strategic logistics plan?
6. Discuss the relationship between Logistics strategy and Corporate strategy.
7. Discuss the influence of environment in organisational planning.
8. Discuss the steps involved in córporate strategic planning.
9. Discuss the influence of inputs from various functional areas on the strategic logistics plan.
10. Discuss the requirements of strategic logistics planning.
11. What is logistical audit? How is it done?
12. Explain how a logistics strategy is developed?
13. List the logistics decisions made in strategic, tactical and operational levels in an organisation.
14. Give an outline of a logistics plan.
15. What is logistics planning?
16. What is meant by logistics mission statement?
17. "There are six operational objectives which must be achieved by the firm in terms of logistical system design and management". Elaborate.
18. "In fact of the many strategic issues that business organisations confront today, perhaps the most challenging are in the area of logistics". Discuss these challenges.
19. Discuss the various kinds of logistics strategies.
20. Discuss the relationship between operations strategy and logistics strategy.
21. Explain how a logistics strategy is formulated?
22. What is meant by logistics oursourcing.
23. Distinguish between third-party logistics and fourth-party logistics.

❖ ❖ ❖ ❖

INTRODUCTION TO SUPPLY CHAIN MANAGEMENT

Supply Chain Management is an essential aspect of business today. The idea is to apply a total systems approach to managing the entire flow of information, materials and services from raw materials suppliers through factories and warehouses to the end customers.

Consider how materials might flow from a company's suppliers, through the company's operations and then on to its customers. An increasingly popular perspective today is to view the flow of materials from suppliers all the way to customers as a *system* to be managed. This perspective is commonly referred to as ***supply chain management***.

What is a Supply Chain?

In its broadest sense, a ***supply chain*** refers to the way that materials flow through different organisations, starting with raw materials and ending with finished products delivered to the ultimate consumer.

A supply chain is a sequence of suppliers, transporters, warehouses, manufacturers, wholesalers/distributors, retail outlets and final customers. Different companies may have different supply chains due to the nature of their operations and whether they are primarily a manufacturing operation or a service operation. *Exhibit 4.1a* illustrates a typical supply chain for a manufacturing organisation and *Exhibit 4.1b* illustrates a typical supply chain for a service organisation.

Exhibit 4.1a : Supply Chain for a Manufacturing Organisation

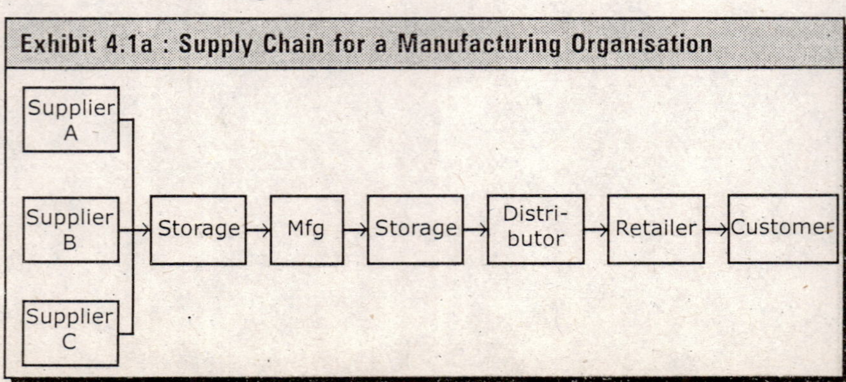

Exhibit 4.1b : Supply Chain for a Service Organisation

Supplier A
Supplier B
Storage
Service
Customer

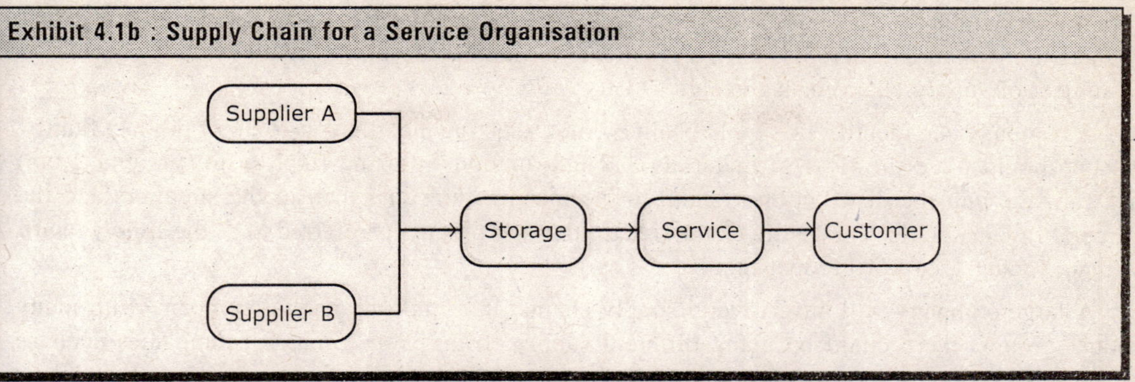

Exhibit 4.2 : Stages of a Detergent Supply

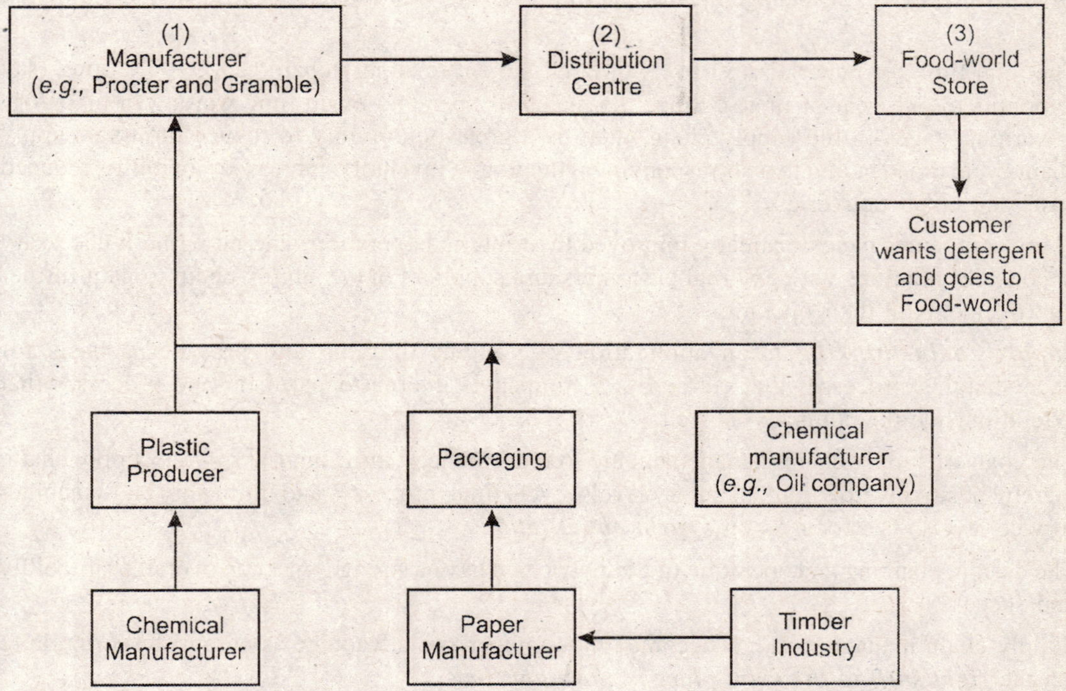

(1)
Manufacturer
(e.g., Procter and Gramble)
(2)
Distribution
Centre
(3)
Food-world
Store
Customer
wants detergent
and goes to
Food-world
Plastic
Producer
Packaging
Chemical
manufacturer
(e.g., Oil company)
Chemical
Manufacturer
Paper
Manufacturer
Timber
Industry

A company can identify its supply chain by first selecting a particular product group or product family. Then it should trace the flow of materials and information from the final customer (end users) backward through the distribution system, to the manufacturer and then to the suppliers and the source of raw materials. This entire chain of activities and processes is known as the ***supply chain*** for that product groupchain

A large company will have several supply chains. In a multi-divisional company with many product groups, there could be many different supply chains. *For example,* large companies such as

Procter and Gamble or General Electric may use 50 to 100 different supply chains to bring their products to the market. There has been a great deal of interest recently in industry and academic in the subject of supply chain management.

A company can identify its supply chain by first selecting a particular group of product family. Then it should trace the flow of materials and information from the final customer (end users) backward through the distribution system, to the manufacturer and then to the suppliers and the source of raw materials. This entire chain of activities and process is referred to as the ***supply chain*** for that product group or product family.

A large company will have several supply chains. In a multi-divisional company with many product groups, there could be many different supply chains. *For example,* companies such as General electric or Procter and Gamble may use 50 to 100 different supply chains to bring their products to the market. *Exhibit 4.2* illustrates the stages of a detergent supply chain.

Importance of Supply Chain Management

Of late, supply chain management is gaining growing importance because of the following reasons:

(i) The total time for materials to travels through the entire supply chain can be quite long (say 6 months to one year or more). Since the materials spend so much time waiting in inventory at various stages in the supply chain, there is a great opportunity to reduce the total supply chain cycle time leading to a corresponding reduction in inventory, increased flexibility, reduced costs and better deliveries.

(ii) Many companies have drastically improved their internal operations and now find it necessary to consider relations with external customers and suppliers in the supply chain to gain further improvements in their operations.

(iii) ***Supply chain thinking*** is an application of systems thinking and provides a basis for understanding processes that cut across a company's internal department and processes that extend outside the company as well.

(iv) The goals of supply chain management are to reduce uncertainty and risks in the supply chain, thereby positively affecting inventory levels, cycle time, processes and ultimately end-customer service levels. The focus is on ***system optimisation***.

(v) The design, planning and operation of a supply chain have a strong impact on overall profitability and success.

(vi) Supply-chain management has become a hot competitive advantage as companies struggle to get the ***right stuff to the right place at the right time***.

(vii) All the "Total quality Management", "Just-in-Time system", "Reengineering", "Team work" and "Delighting the Customers" depends on the relationships with suppliers and distributors who are part of the supply chain.

(viii) Supply chain management includes transportation vendors, suppliers, distributors, banks, credit and cash transfers, bills payable and receivable, warehousing and inventory levels, order fulfillment and sharing customer, forecasting and production information.

(ix) As firms strive to increase their competitiveness via product customisation, high quality, cost reductions and speed-to-market, they place added emphasis on supply chain management.

(x) Supply chain management builds a chain of suppliers that focus on both waste and maximising value to the ultimate customer. The key to effective supply chain management is to make suppliers "partners" in the firm's strategy to satisfy the ever-changing market place.

Box 4.1 lists various definitions of supply chain management

Box 4.1 : What is Supply Chain Management?

1. "Supply chain management is the **integration** of the various activities encompassed by the supply chain through improved supply chain relationships to achieve a sustainable competitive advantage".

   [The **supply chain** encompasses all activities associated with the flow and transformation of goods from the raw materials stage (*e.g.,* extraction) through to end users, as well as the associated information flows. Materials and information flow both up and down the supply chain.

   The supply chain includes systems management, operations and assembly, purchasing, production scheduling, order processing, inventory management, transportation, warehousing, and customer service.

   Supply chains are essentially a series of linked suppliers and customers, every customer is in turn a supplier to the next downstream organisations until a finished product reaches the ultimate end user]. — Robert Monczka, Robert Trent, Robert Handfield.

2. "Supply chain management is defined as the systematic, strategic coordination of the traditional business functions and the tactics across these business functions within a particular company and across business within the supply chain, for the purposes of improving the long-term performance of the individual companies and the supply chain as a whole".

   — Ronald H. Ballou

3. "Supply chain management is a set of approaches utilised to efficiently integrate suppliers, manufacturers, warehouses and stores, so that merchandise is produced and distributed at the right quantities, to the right locations, and at the right time, in order to minimise system-wide costs while satisfying customer service level requirements"

   — David Simchi - Levi, Philip Kaminsky, Edith Simchi -Levi

4. "Supply chain Management (SCM) is the integration and management of supply chain organisations and activities through cooperative organisational relationships, effective business processes and high levels of information sharing to create high performing value systems that provide member organisations a sustainable competitive advantage".

   — Robert B Hand field, Ernest L. Nichols. Jr.

5. "Supply chain management is a collaborative based strategy to link cross enterprises business operations to achieve a shared vision of market opportunity. It is a comprehensive arrangement that can span from raw material sourcing to end customer purchase".

   — Donald J. Bower sox

6. "Supply chain management is a collection of actions required to coordinate and manage all activities necessary to bring a product to market, including processing raw materials, producing goods, transporting and distributing those goods and managing the selling process".

   — Jules Abend

7. "Supply chain management is the ability to get closer to the customer". — Marty Weil

8. "Supply chain management encompasses the planning and management of all activities involved in sourcing and procurement, conversion and all logistics management activities. It also includes coordination and collaboration with channel partners, intermediaries, third party service providers and customers. In essence SCM integrates supply and demand management within and across companies". — Council of Logistics Management, USA.

9. "Supply chain management is the process of planning, implementing and controlling the operations of the supply chain with the purpose to satisfy customer requirements as efficiently

as possible. Supply chain management spans all movement and storage of raw materials, work-in-process inventory and finished goods from point-of-origin to point-of-consumption.

10. "Supply chain management is an integrating function with primary responsibility for linking major business functions and business processes within and across companies into a cohesive and high performing business model. It includes all of logistics management activities as well manufacturing operations and derives coordination of processes and activities with and across marketing, sales, product design, finance and information technology".

What is Integrated Supply Chain Management?

"Integrated supply chain management is a proven business strategy that has gained wide acceptance in recent year due to increasing customer demands for quality, delivery and speed. New and radical ways of communicating, coupled with cost reduction and more interdependent supplier, provider and customer relationships, have contributed to the emergence of an integrated supply chain approach".

Relevance of Supply Chain Management to TQM

Distribution or logistics or supply chain management has become a hot competitive advantage as companies struggle to get the right stuff to the right place at the right time. It is the cumbersome process by which companies move materials, parts and products to customers. Hard pressed to knock out competitors on quality or price, companies are trying to gain an edge through their ability to deliver the right stuff in the right amount at the right time. Logistics, a long unsung, operations – intensive area, has suddenly become very strategic.

All the TQM, JIT system, reengineering and teamwork and delighting the customers depends on the relationship with suppliers and distributors who are part of the supply chain.

Exhibit 4.3 : The Supply Chain

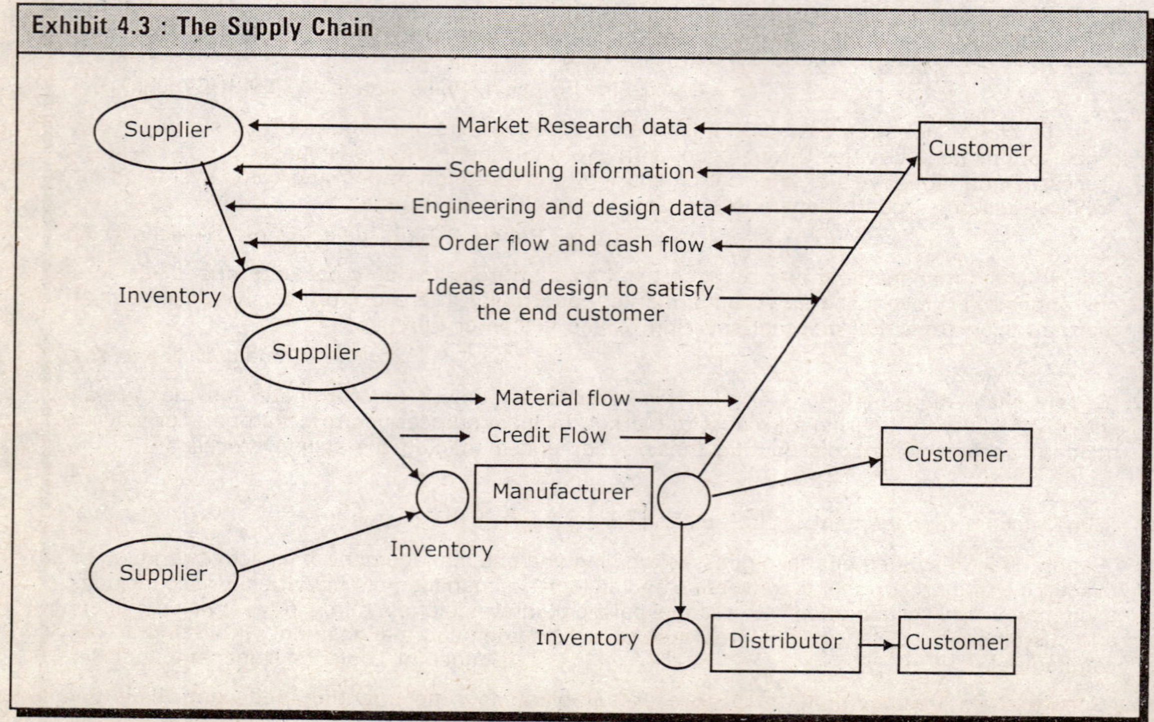

As *Exhibit 4.3* suggests, the supply-chain management includes determining :

(i) transportation vendors

(ii) credit and cash transfers

(iii) suppliers

(iv) distributors and banks

(v) accounts payable and receivables

(vi) warehousing and inventory levels

(vii) order fulfillment and

(viii) sharing customer, forecasting and production/information.

The idea is to build a chain of suppliers that focus on both waste and maximising value to the ultimate customer.

As firms strive to increase their competitiveness via product customisation, high quality, cost reductions and speed-to-market, they place added emphasis on the supply chain. The key to effective supply-chain management is to make the suppliers "partners" in the firm's strategy to satisfy an ever-changing market place.

➤ OVERVIEW OF SUPPLY CHAIN MANAGEMENT

How is inventory created? : A basic purpose of supply-chain management is to control inventory by managing the flow of materials. ***Inventory*** is a stock of materials used to satisfy customer demand or support the production of goods or services. In a manufacturing organisation, there is an inward flow of input materials such as raw materials (steel *for example*), component parts, office supplies and consummables to facilitate the manufacturing process (conversion or transformation process). The rate of production depends on the demand (customer orders) for the finished goods. Another possible outward flow is that of scrap generated in the conversion process and defective products produced and rejected. Together, the rate of input and output flows determine the level of usable inventory (cushion against stock out of input materials). Firms use total quality management to reduce defective materials, the larger the scrap flows, the larger will be the input flow of materials required for a given level of output. Inventories may be held in the form of raw materials and bought out components, work-in-process (WIP) and finished goods.

Managing the flow of material is common to organisations in every segment of the economy : manufacturers, wholesalers, retailers, government departments, hospitals, educational institutions and the like. In a manufacturing firm, raw materials pass through one or more processes, which transform them into various levels of WIP inventory. Final processing of this inventory yields finished goods inventory, which may be held at the firm, the distribution centre, warehouse owned by the manufacturer or wholesaler and at retail locations. Typically, the manufacturers may spend 60 to 70 percent of the total sales revenue on purchased materials and services. A typical service provider may spend 30 to 40 percent of total revenue on purchased materials and services. Nowadays, companies are relying more than ever on suppliers from around the world. Because materials comprise such a large component of sales revenue, companies can reap large profits with a small percentage reduction in the cost of materials. That is one reason why supply-chain management is becoming a key competitive weapon.

Materials Management : One area of operations and logistics playing a major role in supply chain management is that of materials management, which is concerned with decisions about purchasing materials and services, inventories, production levels, staffing patterns, schedules and distribution, either directly or indirectly.

Traditionally, organisations have divided the responsibility for materials management among three departments : purchasing, production control and distribution. This approach requires a tremendous amount of co-ordination to achieve a competitive supply system, since each of these departments report to different heads. Hence, many firms have restructured to centralise most materials management tasks in one department called ***materials management department***, although the name *logistics management* is also used sometimes. This approach brings together all tasks related to flow of materials, from the purchase of raw materials to the distribution of finished products or services.

Purchasing is usually responsible for working with suppliers to ensure the desired inward flow of materials and services. Purchasing may also be responsible for inventories of raw materials and components. Production control is responsible for determining production volumes and scheduling the machines and labour directly responsible for transformation process. Distribution is normally responsible for the outward flow of materials from the firm to its customers. It also may be responsible for finished goods inventories and selection of transportation suppliers. Materials management then is responsible for co-ordinating the efforts of purchasing and distribution. Consequently materials management decisions have a major cumulative effect on the profitability of a firm and thus attract considerable managerial attention.

Supply Chains : A supply chain consists of all stages involved, directly or indirectly, in fulfilling a customer's request. It not only includes the manufacturer and suppliers, but also transporters, warehouses, retailers and customers themselves. Within a manufacturing organisation, the supply chain includes functions such as new product development, marketing, operations, distribution, finance and customer service.

A supply chain is dynamic and involves the constant flow of information, product and funds between different stages. Each stage of the supply chain performs different processes and interacts with other stages of the supply chain. The primary purpose of the existence of any supply chain is to satisfy customer needs; in the process of generating profits for itself. Supply chain activities begin with a customer order and end when a satisfied customer has paid for his or her purchase. It is not necessary that only one player is involved at each stage of the supply chain. A manufacturer may receive material from several suppliers and then supply to several distributors. Therefore, most supply chains are actually networks and may be called as ***supply networks*** or ***supply webs*** to describe the structure of supply chains.

A typical supply chain may involve the following stages :

- Customers
- Retailers
- Wholesalers/distributors
- Manufacturers and
- Component/raw material suppliers.

Objective of a Supply Chain : The objectives are :

(i) To maximise the overall value generated. The *value* a supply chain generates is the difference between what the final product is worth to the customer and the effort the supply chain expends in filling the customer's request.

(ii) To achieve maximum *supply chain profitability.* Supply chain profitability is the total profit to be shared across all supply chain stages.

(iii) To reduce the supply chain costs to the minimum possible level.

Supply chain management involves the management of flows between and among stages in a supply chain to maximise total profitability.

Decision Phases in a Supply Chain

The three decision phases in a supply chain are :

(i) Supply chain strategy or design

(ii) Supply chain planning and

(iii) Supply chain operation.

These three phases are briefly described in the following section.

(i) **Supply Chain Strategy or Design :** The company decides how to structure the supply chain during this phase. The chain's configuration and the processes each stage will perform are decided. Strategic or long-range decisions made by companies include *(i)* The location and capacities of production and warehousing facilities, *(ii)* Products to be manufactured or stored at various locations, *(iii)* Modes of transportation to be made available along different shipping legs and *(iv)* Type of information system to be utilised. The company's strategic objectives must be supported by its supply chain configuration. For instance, a company's decisions regarding the location and capacity of its manufacturing facilities, warehouses and supply sources are all supply chain design or strategic decisions. Since these decisions are made for the long term, they are very expensive to be changed in the short term. Hence companies need to take into account uncertainty in anticipated market conditions over the next few year before they make supply chain design decisions.

(ii) **Supply Chain Planning :** In this phase, companies define a set of operating policies that govern short-term operations. The configuration of supply chain determined in the previous phase establishes constraints within which planning must be carried out. The planning phase starts with a forecast for the coming year of demand in different markets. Supply chain planning includes decisions regarding the following.

   (i) Which market to be served from which locations

   (ii) The planned build up of inventories

   (iii) The subcontracting of manufacturing

   (iv) The replenishment and inventory policies to be followed.

   (v) Policies regarding back up locations in case of a stock out and

   (vi) The timing and size of marketing promotions

Planning establishes parameters within which a supply chain will function over a specified period of time. However it must be ensured that planning decisions consider the uncertainty in demand, exchange rates and competition over the planning horizon.

(iii) **Supply Chain Operations :** During this phase, companies make decisions for the time horizon (weekly or daily) regarding individual customer orders. At this stage. The supply chain configuration is fixed and the planning policies already defined. The supply chain operation aims at implementing the operating policies in the best possible manner. Various activities involved in this phase are : *(i)* Allocating individual orders to inventory or production, *(ii)* Setting dates for fulfilling orders, *(iii)* Generating pick lists at a ware house, *(iv)* Allocating an order to a particular shipping mode or shipment. *(v)* Getting delivery schedules of trucks and *(vi)* Placing replenishment orders. Because operational decisions are made in the short term, there is often less uncertainty about demand information.

The design, planning and operation of a supply chain strongly affect the overall profitability and success of a firm.

Process View of a Supply Chain

Two different ways to view the process performed in a supply chain are.

1. Cycle view   2. The push-pull view

1. **Cycle View :** According to this view, the processes in a supply chain are divided into a series of cycles, each performed at the interface between two successive stages of a supply chain. All supply chain processes can be broken down into the following four process cycles:

   (a) **Customer order cycle**, *(b)* **Replenishment cycle**, *(c)* **Manufacturing cycle** and *(d)* **Procurement cycle**.

   Each cycle occurs at the interface between two successive stages of the supply chain. *Exhibit 4.4* illustrates the four cycles and five supply chain stages

Exhibit 4.4. Supply Chain Process Cycles

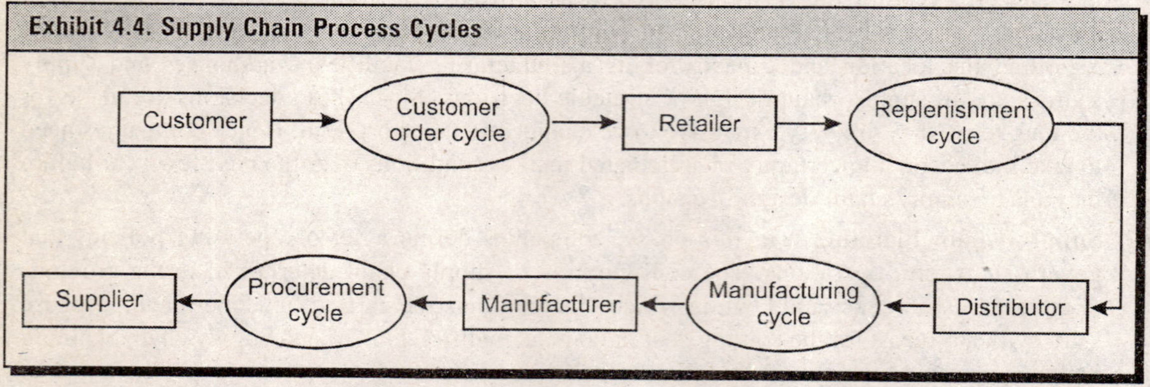

The four process cycle in the supply chain are briefly discussed in the following section:

(i) **Customer Order Cycle :** This occurs at the customer/retailer interface and include **customer arrival, customer order entry, customer order fulfillments and customer order receiving.**

Customer arrival refers to the customers visiting the location (supermarket or retail store) where he or she has access to his or her choices and make a decision regarding what to buy, how much to buy and so on.

Customer order entry refers to customers telling the retailer what products they want to buy and the retailer allocating those products to customers.

Customer order fulfillment refers to process by which the customer order is filled and sent to the customer.

Customer order receiving refers to the process by which customer receives what he has ordered and takes ownership of the products ordered.

(ii) **Replenishment Cycle :** This occurs at the retailer/distributor interface and includes all processes involved in replenishing inventory of the retailer. The processes involved in the replenishment cycle include: **Retail order trigger, Retailer order entry, Retail order fulfillment** and **Retailer order receiving**.

Retail Order Trigger : As and when the retailer fills customer order, inventory is depleted which must be replenished to meet future demand. The retailer devises a replenishment or ordering policy which triggers an order on the distributor so as to maximise profitability by balancing product availability and cost.

Retail Order Entry: The retailer places the order with the distributor or manufacturer. The purpose of the retail order entry process is to ensure that an order is entered accurately and conveyed quickly to all supply chain processes affected by the order.

Retail Order Fulfillment: This is a process by which retail order is filled by the distributor or manufacturer. The objective is to get the replenishment order to the retailer on time while minimising costs.

Retail Order Receiving : When the replenishment order arrives at a retailer, the retailer must receive it physically, update all inventory records and settle all product from distributor to the retailer as well as information and financial flows. This process helps to update inventories and displays quickly at the lowest possible cost.

(iii) **Manufacturing Cycle :** This occurs at the distributor/manufacturer interface and includes all processes involved in replenishing distributor (or retailer) inventory. The process involved in the manufacturing cycle include *(a)* Order arrival from the distributor, retailer or customer *(b)* Production scheduling, *(c)* Manufacturing and shipping and *(d)* Receiving at the distributor, retailer or customer.

(iv) **Procurement Cycle :** This occurs at the manufacturer/supplier interface and includes all processes necessary to ensure that materials are available for carrying out manufacturing as per the schedule. The manufacturer orders components from suppliers to replenish inventories. Component orders are based on the production schedule.

2. **Push/Pull View of Supply Chain Process :** All processes in the supply chain fall into one of two categories: *(i)* **Push processes** and *(ii)* **Pull processes**. In pull processes, execution is initiated in response to a customer order. In push processes, execution is in anticipation of customer order. At the time of execution of a pull process, demand is known with certainty whereas at the time of execution of a push process demand is not known but forecasted.

A push/pull view of the supply chain is useful when considering strategic decisions relating to supply chain design. This view facilitates a more global consideration of supply chain processes as they relate to a customer order. Pull processes may be regarded as ***reactive processes*** because they react to customer demand. Push processes may be regarded as ***speculative processes*** because they respond to forecast (speculative) demand rather than actual demand.

The **push/pull boundary** in a supply chain helps to separate, push processes from pull processes. *For example,* in a computer manufacturing company manufacturing personal computers, the beginning of assembly process represents the push/pull boundary. All processes carried out prior to assembly are push processes and all processes carried out after and including assembly are pull processes because they are initiated in response to a customer order.

Exhibits 4.5 illustrates the push/pull processes for a supply chain of a computer manufacturing company

Exhibit 4.5 : Push/pull Processes for a Personal Computer Manufacturing Company's Supply Chain

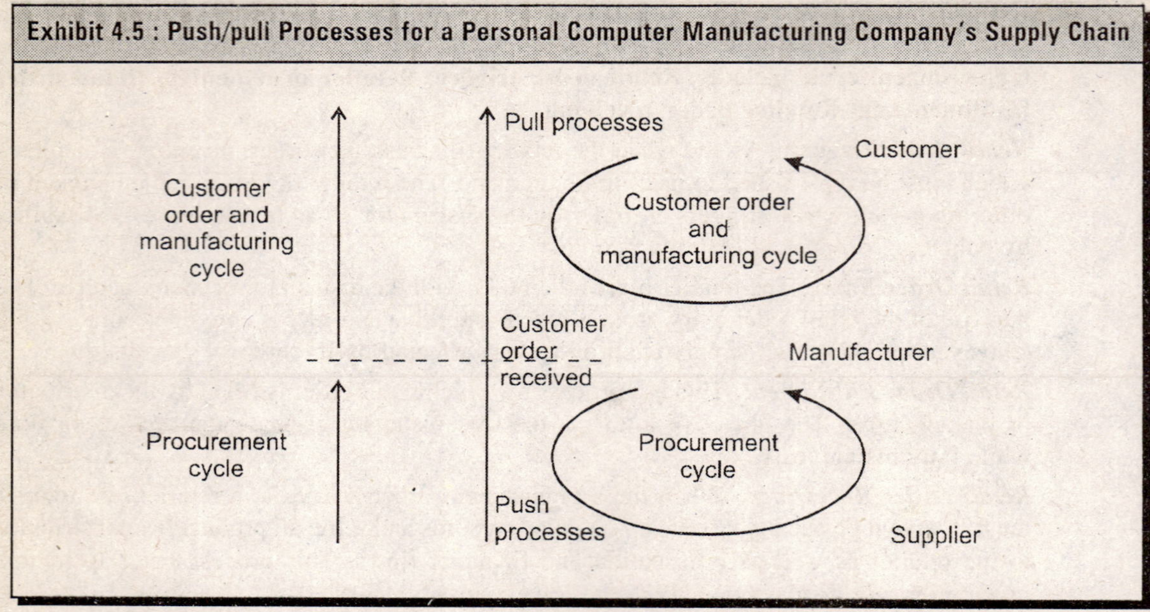

➤ NATURE AND SCOPE OF SUPPLY CHAIN MANAGEMENT

Three important activities involved in supply-chain management are *(i)* **purchasing**, *(ii)* **logistics**, *(iii)* **warehousing** and **expediting**. These activities form the framework for studying the nature and scope of supply chain management.

1. Purchasing

Purchasing is responsible for obtaining the materials, parts and supplies needed to produce a product or provide a service. In manufacturing, more than 60 percent of the cost of finished goods comes from purchased parts and materials. In wholesaling and retailing, the inventories of purchased materials sometimes exceed 90 percent. The importance of purchasing is not only just the cost of goods purchased, but also the quality of goods and services and the timing of deliveries of goods and services, both of which can have significant impact on operations.

Purchasing Interfaces : Purchasing is the link between the organisation and its suppliers. It exchanges information with suppliers and functional areas. *Exhibit 4.6* shows the interface of purchasing with other functional areas of the firm.

Operating units constitute the main source of requests for purchased materials and close co-operation between these units and the purchasing department is vital if quality, quantity and delivery goals are to be met. The purchasing department may require the assistance of the *legal* department in contract negotiations, in drawing up bid specifications for non-routine purchases and to help interpret legislation on pricing, product liability and contracts with suppliers.

Accounting is responsible for handling payments to suppliers, data processing is handled by the accounts departments which keeps inventory records, checks invoices and monitors vendor performance.

Design **and** ***engineering*** usually prepare material specifications which must be communicated to purchasing. Also, design and purchasing people may work closely to determine whether changes in specifications, design or materials can reduce the cost of purchased items.

Exhibit 4.6 : Purchasing Interfaces with Functional Areas of the Firm and with Suppliers

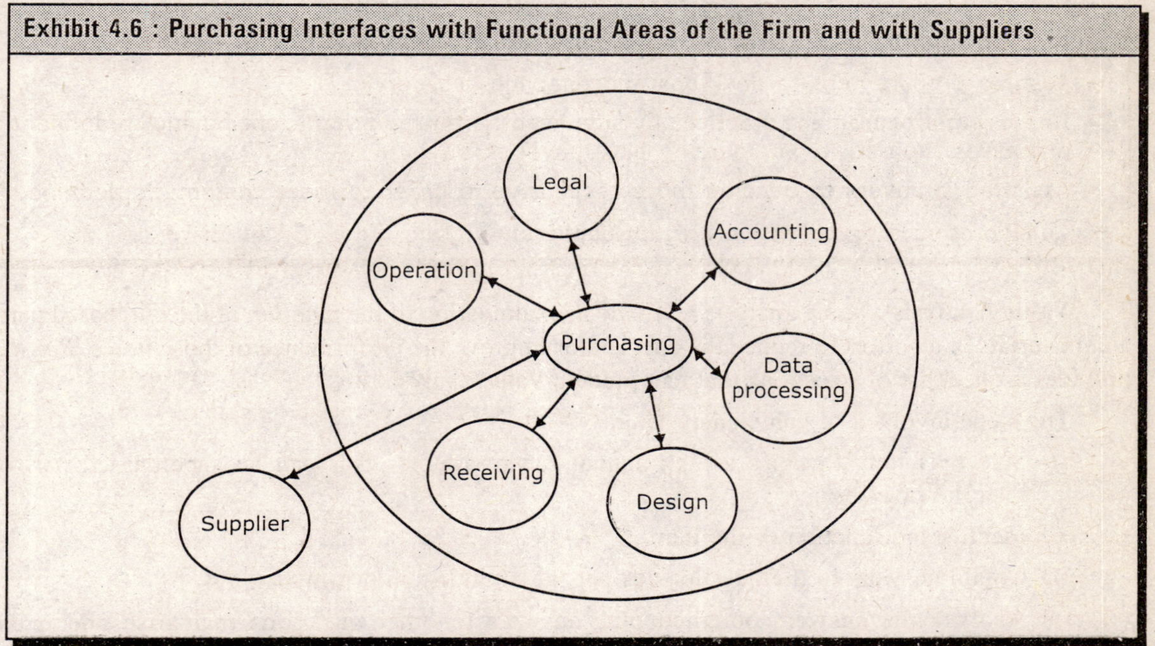

Receiving checks incoming shipments of purchased items to determine whether quality, quantity and timing objectives have been met and moves the goods to temporary storage. Purchasing must be notified when shipments are delayed, accounting must be notified when shipments are received so that payments can be made.

Suppliers *or* ***vendors*** work closely with purchasing to learn what materials will be purchased and what kinds of specifications will be required in terms of quality, quantity and deliveries. Purchasing must rate vendors on cost, reliability and so on. Good supplier relations can pay dividends on rush orders and changes and vendors provide a good source of information on product and material improvements.

The Purchasing Cycle : The purchasing cycle begins with a request from within the organisation to purchase material, equipment, supplies or other items from outside the organisation and the cycle ends when the purchasing is notified that a shipment has been received in satisfactory condition. The main steps in the purchasing cycle are :

(i) Purchasing receives the requisition

(ii) Purchasing selects a supplier

(iii) Purchasing places the order with the vendor

(iv) Monitoring orders and

(v) Receiving orders.

Box 4.2 lists the key challenges facing purchasing managers today.

Box 4.2 : Key Challenges Facing Purchasing Managers Today

Key challenges facing purchasing managers and executives today include the following:

- Reducing overheads and costs associated with purchasing.
- Reducing the cycle time for purchasing.
- Pushing procurement to desktops and enabling self-service.
- Improving procurement practices by significantly reducing inefficient buying, redundant processes, non-strategic sourcing and maverick buying.
- Assisting suppliers to become more responsive in order to meet customer's demand.
- Collaborating more effectively with suppliers.

Value Analysis : Value analysis refers to an examination of the *function* of the purchased parts and materials in an effort to reduce the cost and/or improve the performance of those items. *Box 4.3* provides a checklist of questions that can guide a value analysis.

The steps involved in value analysis are :

(i) Select an item that has a high annual rupee volume. This can be a purchased part or material or a service.

(ii) Identify the function of the item.

(iii) Obtain answers to the questions as per the checklist shown in *Box 4.3*.

(iv) Analyse the answers obtained plus answers to other questions that arise and make recommendations.

Box 4.3 : Checklist of Questions for Value Analysis

(a) Is the item necessary, does it add value or can it be eliminated?

(b) Are there alternative sources for the item?

(c) Can the item be provided internally?

(d) What are the advantages of the present arrangement?

(e) What are the disadvantages of the present arrangement?

(f) Could another part, material or service be used instead?

(g) Can specifications be made less stringent to save cost or time?

(h) Can two or more parts be combined?

(i) Can more (less) processing be done on the item to save on cost?

(j) Do suppliers/providers have suggestions for improvements?

(k) Do employees have suggestions for improvements?

(l) Can packaging be improved or made less costly?

Outsourcing : Outsourcing refers to buying goods or services from outside sources instead of making the goods or providing the services within the firm. The reasons for outsourcing are :

(i) Outside source can provide materials, parts or services better, cheaper or more efficiently (if they are large-scale producers having economy of scale).

(ii) Expertise and knowledge of outside sources.

(iii) A supplier may hold a patent on a necessary part/component.

(iv) To have the advantage of flexibility.

(v) When companies downsize and narrow their focus on core activities.

The risks of outsourcing are loss of control, greater dependency on suppliers and not possessing the ability to perform in-house.

Box 4.4 lists the top reasons for outsourcing

Box 4.4 : The Top Ten Reasons for Outsourcing

(i) Improve Company Focus

(ii) Access to World-Class Capabilities

(iii) Accelerate Re-engineering Benefits

(iv) Share Risks

(v) Free Resources of Other Purposes

(vi) Make Capital Funds Available

(vii) Cash Infusion

(viii) Reduce and Control Operating Costs

(ix) Resource not available Internally

(x) Function Difficult to Manage or Out of Control.

Factors to be taken into account by a company in deciding whether to outsource are:

(i) Cost to do it in-house versus cost to buy, including start-up costs versus cost to outsource.

(ii) Stability of demand and possible seasonality.

(iii) Quality available from suppliers compared with a firm's own quality capabilities.

(iv) The desires to maintain close control over operations.

(v) Idle capacity available within the organisation.

(vi) Lead times for each alternative.

(vii) Who has patents, expertise and so on.

(viii) Stability of technology and

(ix) The degree to which the necessary operations are consistent with or in conflict with current operations.

JIT Purchasing : Just-in-time manufacturing techniques requires just-in-time purchasing. The easy part of JIT purchasing include having to deal with fewer suppliers and forming long-term relationships with suppliers who emphasise co-operative spirit than low price. On-time delivery is usually the primary need of JIT manufacturers, followed by small lot sizes.

Suppliers

Good suppliers are a vital link in the supply chain. Late deliveries of parts or materials or missing or defective items can disrupt production schedules, increase inventory costs and cause late deliveries of end products.

Choosing Suppliers : When choosing suppliers, the key considerations are:

(i) Quality of the products or services and

(ii) On-time delivery.

There are many other factors to be taken into account while choosing the suppliers. *Box 4.5* lists some of those factors and questions that need to be addressed.

The importance of each factor often differs from company to company and even with a company from one product or service to another. Consequently, a manager must decide what weight to assign to each factor for each product or service and use those weights in selecting a supplier.

Box 4.5 : Choosing a Supplier

Factors to be considered	Questions to be answered
(i) Lead times and on-time delivery	• What lead times can the supplier provide? • What procedure does the supplier have for assuring on-time deliveries? • What procedures does the supplier have for documenting and correcting delivery problems? • Are there procedures?
(ii) Quality and Quality Assurance	• What procedures does the supplier have for quality control and quality assurance? • Are problems and corrective actions for quality documented? • Are investigations conducted to determine and correct the causes of non-conforming materials?
(iii) Flexibility	• How flexible is the supplier in handling changes in quantity, delivery schedules and product or service changes?
(iv) Location	• Is the supplier located nearby?
(v) Price	• Are prices reasonable given the entire package the supplier will provide? • Is the supplier willing to negotiate prices? • Is the supplier willing to engage in a joint effort to reduce costs (and prices)?
(vi) Product or service changes	• How much advance notifications does the supplier give when changes are made in products or services? • How financially stable is the supplier?
(viii) Other accounts	• Is the supplier heavily dependent on other buyer (s), causing the risk of giving priority to another buyer's needs over ours?

Evaluating Sources of Supply (Vendor Analysis)

Vendor analysis is the process of evaluating the sources of supply in terms of price, quality, reputation and service. The main factors a company takes into account when it selects a vendor are:

(i) **Price :** This is the most obvious factor, along with any discounts offered, although it may not be the most important.

(ii) **Quality :** A company may be willing to spend more money to obtain high quality.

(iii) **Services :** Special services such as replacement of defective items, instruction in the use of equipment, repair of equipment and the like can be key factors in selecting one supplier over another.

(iv) **Location :** Location of the supplier can have impact on shipping time, transportation costs and response time for rush orders or emergency service. Local buying can create goodwill in the community by helping the local economy.

(v) **Inventory Policy of Supplier :** If a supplier maintains an inventory policy of keeping spare parts on hand, this could be helpful in case of an emergency equipment break down.

(vi) **Flexibility :** The willingness and ability of a supplier to respond to changes in demand and to accept design changes could be important considerations.

Supplier Audits : Periodic audits of suppliers are helpful in getting current information on supplier's production capabilities, quality and delivery problems and so on. If the audit reveals problem areas, a buyer can address these before they result in serious problems. Some of the factors covered by a supplier audit are management style, quality assurance, materials management, design process used, process improvement policies and procedures for corrective action and follow-up.

Supplier's audits are also an important first step in the supplier certification program.

Supplier Certification : Supplier certification is a detailed examination of the policies and capabilities of a supplier. The certification process verifies that a supplier meets or exceeds the requirements of a buyer. This is particularly important when buyers are seeking to establish long-term relationship with suppliers. Certified suppliers are sometimes referred to as *world class* suppliers. Buyers can eliminate much or all of the inspection and testing of goods delivered by certified suppliers. For certification suppliers, some companies rely on standard industry certifications such as ISO 9000, which is perhaps the most widely used international certification.

Supplier Partnerships : Nowadays, companies have become increasingly aware of the importance of building good relationships with their suppliers. In the past, many firms regarded their suppliers as adversaries and dealt with them on that basis. Japanese firms have been very successful in building good relationships with their suppliers and getting numerous benefits from good supplier relations, including supplier flexibility in terms of accepting changes in delivery schedules, quality and quantities. Moreover, suppliers can often help identify problems and offer suggestions for solving them.

Many Japanese firms rely on one or a few suppliers to handle their needs while many US firms deal with numerous suppliers. Of late, the US firms have also moved in the direction of reducing the number of suppliers.

Keeping good relations with suppliers helps in maintaining a competitive edge. Many companies are adopting a view of suppliers as partners. This viewpoint stresses a stable relationship with relatively few reliable suppliers who can provide high-quality supplies, maintain precise delivery schedules and remain flexible relative to changes in productive specifications and delivery schedules. *Box 4.6* gives a comparison of contrasting views of suppliers.

Box 4.6 : Comparison of the Contrasting View of Suppliers

Aspect	Partner	Adversary
Number of suppliers	One or a few	Many, play off one against the others
Length of relationship	Long term	May be brief
	Low price	Moderately important, Major consideration
Reliability	High	May not be high
Openness	High	Low
Quality	Insured of the source, vendor certified	Buyer inspects, may be unreliable
Volume of business	High	May be low due to many suppliers
Location	Proximity may be stressed for short lead times and services	Widely dispersed
Flexibility	Relatively high	Relatively low

Suppliers can be a source of ideas that contribute to the competitiveness of an organisation. Nine areas in which potential ideas from suppliers could lead to improved competitiveness are :

(i) Reduce the cost of making the purchase

(ii) Reduce transportation costs

(iii) Reduce production costs

(iv) Improve product quality

(v) Improve product design

(vi) Reduce the time it takes to get the product to the market

(vii) Improve customer satisfaction

(viii) Reduce inventory costs and

(ix) Introduce new products or processes.

Some of the obstacles to supplier partnerships are :

(i) Because many of the benefits go to the buyer, suppliers may be hesistant to enter into such partnerships.

(ii) Suppliers may have to increase their investment in equipment which might put a strain on cash flow and

(iii) The cultures of the buyer and supplier might be quite different and not lend themselves to such an arrangement.

2. Logistics

Logistics refers to the movement of materials within a production facility, the shipment of incoming materials from suppliers and the shipment of outgoing products to customers. Materials include all the physical items used in the production process such as raw materials, parts, components, consummable supplies, fuel, equipments, tools, office supplies and so on.

Movement Within a Facility : The activities involved in the movement of materials within a production facility are :

(i) Removing materials from incoming vehicles and placing them on the receiving dock.

(ii) Moving materials from the receiving dock to inspections.

(iii) Moving materials from inspection to the warehouse and storing them until needed.

(iv) Retrieving materials from the warehouses and delivering them to production operations when needed.

(v) Moving materials between production operations.

(vi) Moving finished products from final assembly and storing them in the finished goods warehouse.

(vii) Retrieving finished goods from the finished goods warehouse and delivering them to packaging and shipping departments.

(viii) Moving packaged finished goods to the shipping dock and

(ix) Loading finished goods into outgoing vehicles at the shipping dock.

Movement of materials must be coordinated to arrive at the appropriate destinations at appropriate times. Workers and supervisors must take care so that items are not lost, stolen or damaged during movement.

Incoming and Outgoing Shipments : Overseeing the shipment of incoming and outgoing goods comes under the heading of ***traffic management***. This function handles schedules and decisions on shipping methods and times, taking into account costs of various alternatives, government regulations, the needs of the organisation relative to quantities and timing and external factors such as potential shipping delays or disruptions (such as highway construction, metallising the roads, trucker's strikes etc.).

Computer tracking of shipments (using global positioning systems) often helps to maintain knowledge of the current status of shipments as well as to provide other up-to-date information on costs and schedules.

Evaluating Shipping Alternatives

A situation that arises frequently in some businesses is making a choice between quicker (but more expensive) shipping alternatives such as overnight and slower but cheaper alternatives. In some instances, there is an overriding factor present that justifies sending a shipment by the quickest means possible, so there is little or no choice involved. However, in many instances, urgency is not the primary consideration, so there is a choice. The decision in such cases often focusses on the cost savings of slower alternatives versus the increased holding costs that would result from using the slower alternatives.

Innovations in Logistics

New developments are continually affecting logistics. Piggy back rail shipments, truck trailers on ships and other unique shipping methods are examples of hybrids that have resulted in great freight savings. Lighter weight shipping containers, unitised loads, consolidated shipments, deregulation of the trucking and airfreight industries and fluctuating fuel costs are examples of developments that are affecting logistics today. Computers facilitate availability of up-to-date information on the status of each shipment. Also, in complicated distribution problems, the computers can be used to plan better networks of shipping methods.

3. Warehousing and Expediting

Warehousing is the management of materials while they are in storage. It includes storing, dispersing, ordering and accounting for all materials and finished goods from the beginning to the end of the production process.

Warehousing operation deals with materials that directly support operations. The first problems that must be addressed are when to place an order. Orders are placed and shipments eventually appear in the receiving department, usually by either truck or rail road cars (railway wagons).

Contemporary Developments in Warehousing

Bar Coding : Bar codes are patterns of alternating wide and narrow black lines and white spaces and numbers and symbols that are seen on everyday products at supermarkets and retail stores. The bar codes (or the universal product codes) are read by scanning devices that use the information for a variety of purposes, such as recording prices and quantities, printing sales receipts and updating inventory records.

Bar codes are also useful in manufacturing and distribution. In distribution, companies can keep track of items in warehouses and enroute to customers. Managers can instantaneously determine the location of any item in the system and its status. (*for example,* enroute to customer, delivered to customer). In manufacturing, bar codes track the progress of jobs just before each operation and specific processing instructions for each job can be provided to operators. They are also used to update inventory records, monitor quality losses and monitor productivity.

Employee bar codes can be used to track employee attendance and location. Bar codes can be used for automatic sorting and packing of items as they move down a conveyor line.

Bar codes provide companies with high ability to monitor and control items in manufacturing and distribution by providing accurate, up-to-date information on quantity, quality, location and other data. This enables managers to realise significant improvements in productivity and effectiveness and to provide outstanding levels of customer service.

Electronic Data Interchange : Electronic data interchange (EDI) is the direct transmission of inter-organisation transactions, notices, debit or credit memos and the like. Benefits of such systems are:

(i) Increased productivity

(ii) Elimination of paper work

(iii) Lead time and inventory reduction

(iv) Facilitation of just-in-time systems

(v) Electronic transfer of funds

(vi) Improved control of operations

(vii) Reduction in clerical work and

(viii) Increased accuracy.

The use of EDI linkages with other organisations can be part of a strategy to achieve a competitive advantage by leveraging logistics performance. EDI is used in retail industries involving electronic communication between retailers and vendors. This approach is based on scanning bar codes and transmitting that information to vendors. This helps to create a just-in-time replenishment system that is keyed to customer buying patterns. EDI also known as "quick response", reduces the dependency on forecasts and the ability to achieve a closer match between supply and demand. It also helps to save inventory carrying costs.

Distribution Requirement Planning : Distribution requirement planning (DRP) is a system for inventory management and distribution planning. It extends the concepts of materials requirements planning (MRP I) to multi-echelon warehouse inventories, starting with demand at the end of the channel and working that back through the warehouse system to obtain time-phased replenishment schedule for moving inventories through the warehouses network. DRP is used to plan and coordinate transportation, warehousing, workers, equipment and financial flows.

JIT Deliveries : JIT systems often require frequent deliveries of small shipments that can make a tremendous burden on the delivery system in several respects:

(i) The increased traffic that results. Instead of one large delivery per week, a company switching to JIT may require many smaller loads every day.

(ii) There is a likely increase in transportation costs per unit. There is often a fixed cost per delivery and the fact that only a partial load is delivered does not change that fixed cost.

(iii) Any strike of transport services or postal services affect the delivery schedules causing disruption of the JIT-based companies.

Because of the above factors, it is necessary to carefully weigh the costs and benefits of using frequent, small deliveries and select a lot size that balances all relevant costs.

➢ A MODEL OF SUPPLY CHAIN MANAGEMENT

Supply chain management is the systematic, strategic co-ordination of the traditional business functions and the tactics across these business functions within a particular firm and across businesses within the supply chain, for the purposes of improving the long-term performance of the individual firms and the supply chain as a whole.

A *supply chain* encompasses all activities associated with flow and transformation of goods from the raw material stage (right from extraction) through to the end user, as well as the associated information flows. There exists flow of materials and information both up and down the supply chain. Supply chain management integrates all the activities in the supply chain through improved supply chain relationships, to achieve a sustainable competitive advantage.

Exhibit 4.7 shows the supply chain management model. Supply chain management coordinates the product flows across functions and across firms to achieve **competitive advantage** and **probability** for individual firms in the supply chain and the members of the supply chain collectively.

Business logistics and supply chain management promote the same mission and practically they are inseparable. Both have the mission of ***"getting the right goods or services to the right place, at right time and in the desired condition, while making the highest contribution to the firm"***.

Supply chain management may be viewed as having a broad scope which includes integrated business logistics management. Logistics may be viewed as a **subset** of supply chain management (SCM in short) whereas SCM considers additional issues beyond those of product flow. *For example,* SCM consider **manufacturing quality** and **product pricing**.

Exhibit 4.7 : A Model of Supply Chain Management

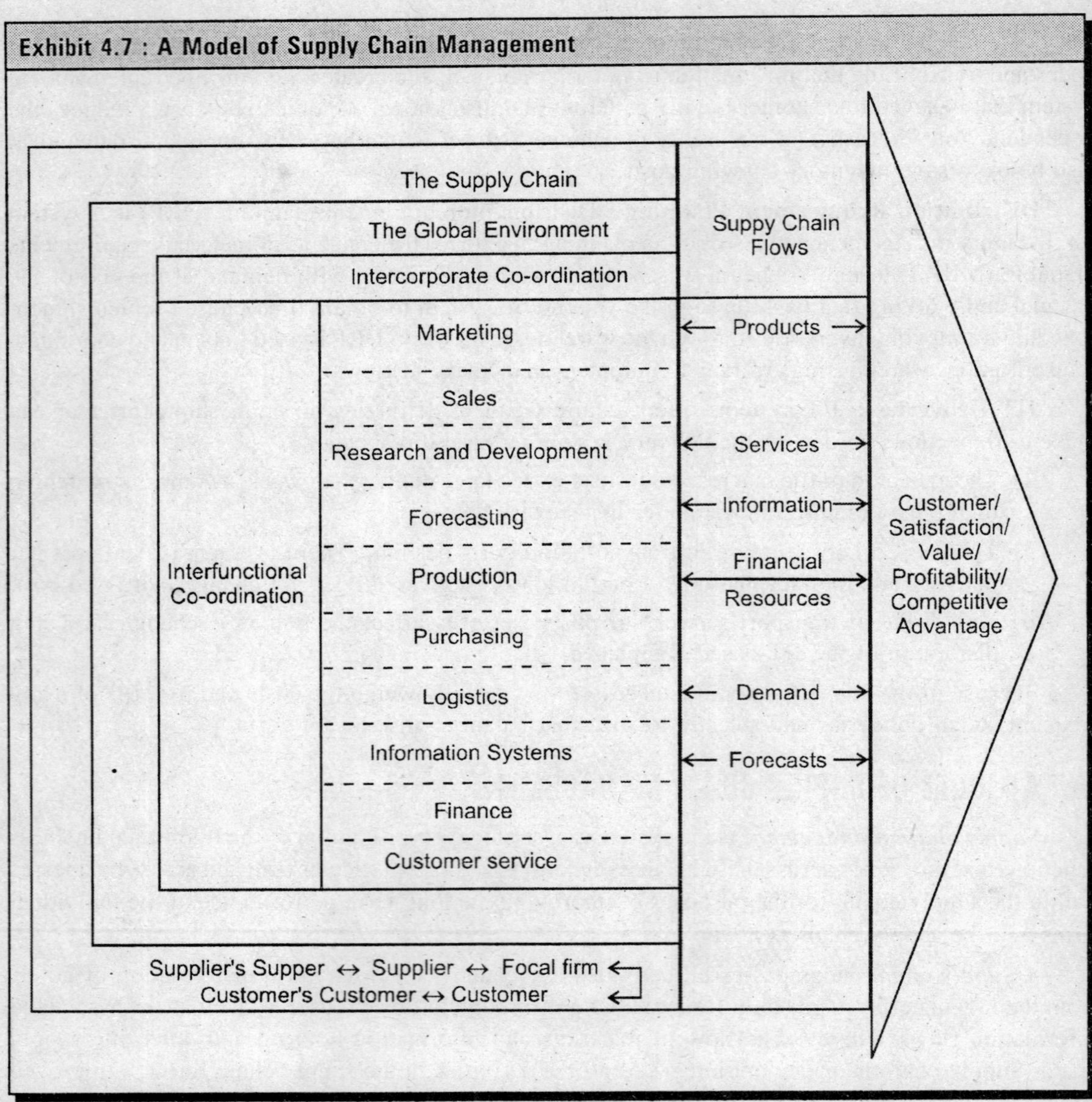

However broad the scope of SCM is, many firms in reality, do not practice this ideal. Many firms, which practice supply chain integration limit their scope to one tier upstream and one tier downstream. The focus seems to be concerned with the creation of seamless processes within their own firms and applying modern information technologies to improve the quality of information and speed of its exchange among members of the channel. It may be noted that it is difficult to draw a demarcation or a boundary between business logistics management and SCM. The focus will be on managing the product and service flows most efficiently and effectively through integration of and coordination with other channel members and service providers to improve the performance of the supply chain.

Business Logistics/Supply Chain Management Activities

Business logistics/supply chain management process comprises various activities (activity mix) that vary from firm to firm depending on a firm's specific organisational structure. It also depends on the management's perception of what constitutes the supply chain for its business and how important the individual activities to its operations. *Box 4.7* shows the important activities that take place along the supply chain these activities are divided into key activities and support activities.

Box 4.7 : Activities Along the Supply Chain

(A) Key Activities

1. Customer service standards cooperate with marketing to:

(a) Determine customer needs and wants for logistics customer service

(b) Determine customer response to service and

(c) Set customer service levels

2. Transportation

(a) Selection of mode and transport service

(b) Consolidation of freight

(c) Renting of carrier

(d) Scheduling transport vehicles

(e) Selection of equipment

(f) Processing claims and

(g) Rate auditing

3. Inventory management

(a) Inventory policies for raw materials and finished goods

(b) Short term sale fore-casting

(c) Product mix at warehouses

(d) Number, size and location of warehouses

(e) Push, pull and just-in-time strategies

4. Information flow and order processing

(a) Sales order-inventory interface procedures

(b) Methods for transmitting order information

(c) Ordering rules

5.Support Activities

1. Warehousing

(a) Determination of storage space

(b) Stock layout and dock design

(c) Warehouse configuration

(d) Stock placement

2. Material handling

(a) Selection of handling equipments

(b) Equipment replacement policies

(c) Order-picking procedures

(d) Stock storage and retrieval

3. **Purchasing**
   (a) Selection of sources of supply
   (b) Determination of purchase timing and
   (c) Determination of purchase quantities
4. **Packing design for**
   (a) Handling
   (b) Storage and
   (c) Protection from loss and damage
5. **Cooperation with production/operations for**
   (a)Specifying aggregate quantities
   (b)Sequencing and timing of production output and
   (c)Scheduling supplies for production/operations
6. **Information maintenance**
   (a) Collection, storage and manipulation of information
   (b) Analysis of data
   (c) Establishing control procedures

Difference Between Logistics Management and Supply Chain Management

A dictionary definition or meaning of the term *'logistics'* is " the branch of military science concerned with procuring, maintaining and transporting materials, personnel and facilities". The council of logistics management (CLM) defines logistics as "*that part of the supply chain process that plans, implements and controls the efficient, effective flow and storage of goods, services and related information from the point of origin to the print of consumption in order to meet customer requirements*".

The *logistics concept* began to appear in the business related literature in the 1960s under the label of ***physical distribution*** which had focus on outbound side of the ***logistics system***. Later, the business or commercial sector approach to logistics developed into **inbound logistics** (materials management to support manufacturing or operations) and **outbound logistics** (physical distribution of finished goods to support marketing) during the 1970s and 1980s. Then in the 1990s, logistics began to be viewed in the context of a ***supply or demand chain*** that linked all of the organisations from the vendor's vendor to the customer's customer. ***Supply chain management*** (SCM) is a term that has emerged in recent years that captures the essence of ***integrated logistics*** and even goes beyond it. SCM emphasises the ***logistics interactions*** that take place ***among*** the functions of marketing, logistics and production within a firm and those interactions that take place between separate firms within the product-flow channel. Supply chain management requires collaborative, coordinated flow of materials and goods through the logistics systems of all the organisations in the network.

Although functions such as physical distribution, materials management, industrial logistics, channel management etc., have been brought under the purview of logistics management, broadening the scope for logistics, implementation of logistics management is generally confined to the activities under the control of the firm's management. In otherwords, it would be difficult to implement logistics beyond a firm's own enterprise boundaries or even beyond its own internal logistics function.

On the other hand, supply chain management encompasses all activities in the supply chain associated with the flow and transformation of goods from raw materials stage (say extraction) through production to the end user as well as the associated information flows both up and down the supply chain. Thus supply chain management is viewed as the systematic, strategic coordination of the traditional business functions and the tactics across these business functions within a particular firm and across other businesses within the supply chain, with the objective of improving the long-term performance of the individual firms and the supply chain as a whole.

➤ SUPPLY CHAIN DRIVERS

For any firm to be successful, its **supply chain strategy** and **competitive strategy** must have a **strategic fit**. *i.e.*, both supply chain and competitive strategies should have the same goal. Strategic fit requires consistency between the priorities of the customers that the competitive strategy is designed to satisfy and the capabilities that the supply chain aims to build. In otherwords, strategic fit requires that a firm achieve the balance between responsiveness and efficiency in its supply chain which best meets the needs of the company's competitive strategy.

To understand how a firm can improve supply chain performance in terms of its responsiveness and efficiency, we need to examine the drivers of supply chain performance namely *(i)* Production, *(ii)* Inventory, *(iii)* Transportation, *(iv)* Facility location and *(v)* Information. These drivers of supply chain are discussed in the following paragraphs:

(i) **Production :** The performance of the supply chain is very much dependent on production *i.e.,* what is produced, how it is produced (the manufacturing process used) and when it has to be produced.

(ii) **Inventory :** All raw materials, work-in-progress and finished goods within a supply chain are referred to as inventory. Any change in inventory policies can greatly affect the efficiency and responsiveness of the supply chain. Decisions such as how much to store and where to store (in the firm's premises or warehouses or at the retailer's premises). *For example,* a retailer can quickly meet a customer demand by keeping a large inventory of an item, but it will increase the retailer's cost, thereby affecting its efficiency eventhough responsiveness has increased. On the contrary, reducing inventory will increase the retailer's efficiency but will affect its responsiveness.

(iii) **Transportation :** Inventory has be moved from point to point in the supply chain using transportation facilities taking the form of many combinations of modes (multimodal) and routes, each having its own performance characteristics. The responsiveness and efficiency of the supply chain is significantly affected by the choice of transportation modes and routes (affecting the speed and cost of transportation). Hence decisions regarding issues related to how to move a product from one location to another and by what mode of transportation are usually trade-off decisions. It is necessary to evaluate economies on one hand and the desired level of customer satisfaction on the other.

(iv) **Facility Location :** Facilities are the places in the supply chain network where inventory is stored, parts are fabricated and assembled into finished goods. Decisions regarding the location of the facilities (plant), their capacity and the flexibility of the facilities have a major impact on the performance of the supply chain. *For example,* an automobile firm

can locate its spare parts distributors and service centres close to customers to increase responsiveness at the cost of efficiency. On the contrary, fewer spare parts distributors and service centres may increase the efficiency of the supply chain network at the cost of its responsiveness.

(v) **Information :** Information consists of data and analysis regarding inventory, facilities (location, capacities etc.) transportation and customers throughout the supply chain. Information affects each of the other driver and hence is the biggest driver of supply chain performance. Information is helpful in making the supply more efficient and responsive at the same time. *For example,* information regarding customer demand patterns results in more accurate forecast of demand, which in turn will enable a firm to produce the required quantity of the product at the right time to meet customer demand. This makes the supply chain more responsive and yet efficient.

Exhibit 4.8 illustrates the supply chain decision-making framework indicating the role of supply chain drivers.

Exhibit 4.8 : Supply Chain Decision-Making Frame Work

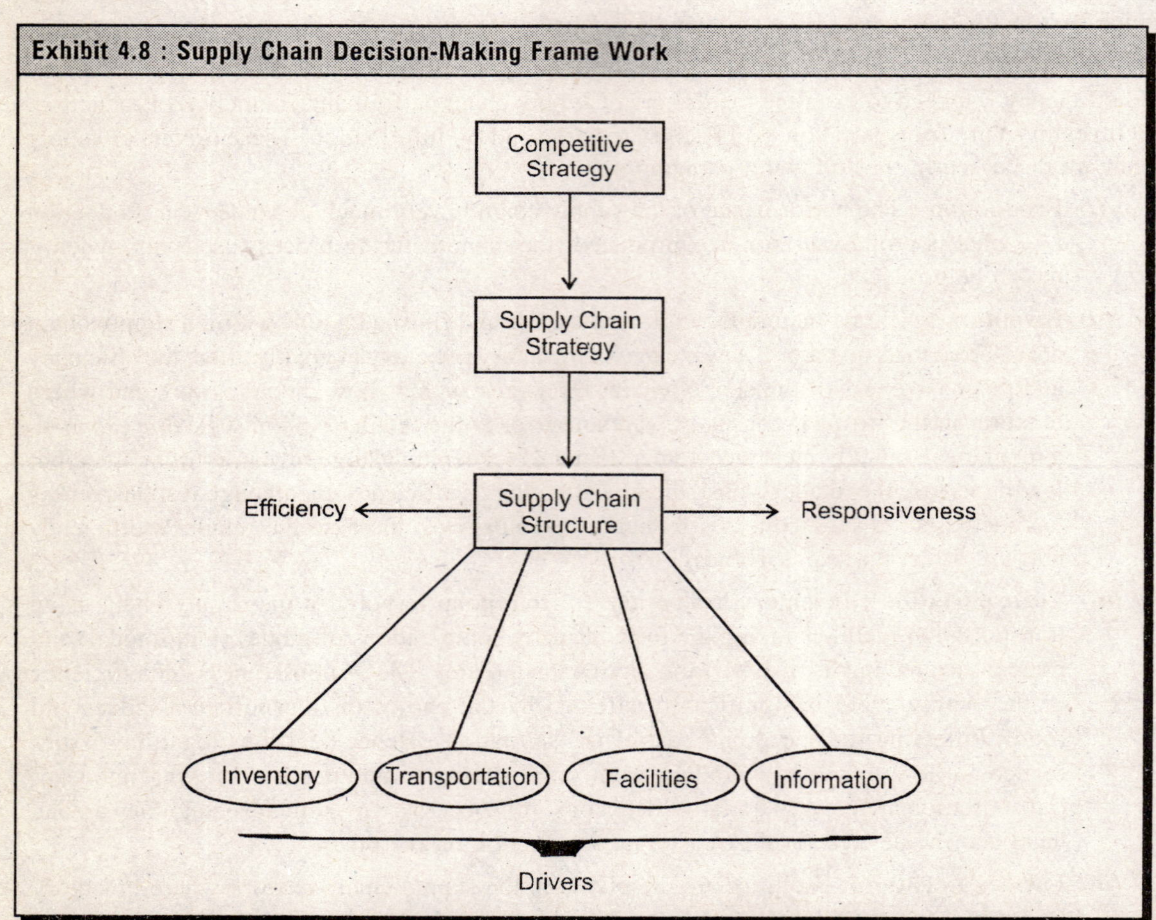

➤ A FRAMEWORK FOR STRUCTURING SUPPLY CHAIN DRIVERS

Global competition in the past decade has forced companies to optimise supply chain performance to serve as a critical lever for sustainable competitive advantage. Supply chain strategy aims to strike a **balance between responsiveness and efficiency** that results in strategic fit with the competitive strategy of the company. The supply chain drivers *viz.*, inventory, transportation, facilities and information are used to reach the goal of achieving the strategic fit. Supply chain managers must make a trade-off between efficiency and responsiveness for each of the supply chain drivers. The combined effect of these four drivers then determines the responsiveness and efficiency of the entire supply chain.

Most companies first make a decision regarding their competitive strategy and then decide their supply chain strategy. The supply chain strategy determines how the supply chain should perform with respect to efficiency and responsiveness. The supply chain must then use the supply chain drivers to reach the performance level determined by the supply chain strategy.

The role of the supply chain drivers in the supply chain and how they re used by supply chain managers to drive supply chain performance are discussed in the following section:

(i) Role of Inventory in the Supply Chain

Inventory occurs in a supply chain because of the mismatch between supply and demand. Inventory plays an important role in the supply chain to increase the amount of demand that can be satisfied by having the product ready and available when the customer wants it. Also inventory plays a significant role in reducing the cost of the product by exploiting any economics of scale that may exist during both production and distribution.

Inventory exists throughout the supply chain in various forms, from raw materials to work-in-process to finished goods that suppliers, manufacturers, distributors and retailers hold. Inventory is a major source of cost in a supply chain and its impact on responsiveness is significant. The location and quantity of inventory can vary the responsiveness to a great extent. Inventory also has a significant impact on the material flow in a supply chain. The time that elapses between the point at which material enters the supply chain to the point at which it exits is referred to as **material flow time**. Inventory also affects **through-put** which is the rate at which sales to the end consumer occur. According to Little's law, inventory is the product of flow time 'T' and through-put 'R' (*i.e.*, I = RT). This means inventory and flow time are synonymous in a supply chain. Because reduced flow time can be a great advantage in a supply chain, the amount of inventory needed should be reduced without increasing cost or reducing responsiveness.

Inventory has a significant role in the ability of a supply chain to support a firm's competitive strategy. A firm can use inventory to achieve high level of responsiveness (a competitive advantage) by locating large amount of inventory close to the market (customers). On the other hand, a firm can reduce cost by reducing inventory through centralised stocking. This strategy will support a firm's competitive strategy as a low-cost producer. The inventory drives the trade-off between responsiveness that results from high inventory and the efficiency that results from low inventory.

The major inventory related decisions to be made by supply chain managers to create more responsive and more efficient supply chains effectively are:

(a) **Cycle Inventory Decision :** Cycle inventory is the average amount of inventory used to satisfy demand between receipt of supplier shipments. The size of cycle inventory is the result of the production or purchase lot size. When firms produce or purchase in large lots to exploit economies

of scale in the production, transportation or purchasing process, cycle inventory increases along with an increase in carrying costs. A retailer must take cycle inventory decisions regarding how much to order for replenishment and how often to place these orders. Supply chain managers face the basic trade-offs between the cost of holding larger lots of inventory and the cost of ordering product frequently.

Another inventory related decision is determining **how much safety inventory to hold**. Safety inventory is the inventory which is held to meet the excess demand when demand exceeds expectation (or estimation). Safety inventory is needed to counter uncertainty in demand and in delivery lead time. Determining an appropriate amount of safety inventory involves making a trade-off between the costs of having too much inventory and the costs of losing sales due to stock-out (*i.e.*, not having enough inventory).

When the demand for a product is seasonal, seasonal inventory may have to be built up to counter predictable variability in demand affected by **seasonality**. The decision to build seasonal inventory or not depends on the ability of a firm to change the rate of its production system to adjust to a period of high demand without incurring large costs. The basic trade-off supply chain managers face in determining how much seasonal inventory to build is between the cost of carrying additional seasonal inventory and the cost of having a more flexible production rate.

The overall trade-off involved in inventory decisions is between responsiveness and efficiency. Increasing the inventory usually makes the supply chain more responsive to the customer while at the same time the cost increases thereby decreasing the efficiency of the supply chain. The supply chain manager must determine the optimal level of inventory for reaching the level of responsiveness and efficiency targeted by the firm's competitive strategy.

(ii) Role of Transportation in the Supply Chain

Transportation is concerned with the movement of the product between different stages in a supply chain. Like inventory, transportation too has a great impact on both responsiveness and efficiency of the supply chain. The speed of transportation (*i.e.*, time taken to move the material between two points *i.e.*, source and destination) depends on the mode of transportation and the quantity (volume and weight) of the product being transported. Also the type of transportation a firm uses affects the inventory and facility locations (*i.e.*, plants and warehouses) in the supply chain. Increasing speed of transportation through use of faster modes of transportation increases the firm's responsiveness but at the same time decreases transportation efficiency because of higher costs of transportation.

Transportation has a major role to play in a firm's competitive strategy when the firm is considering the target customer's needs it intends to satisfy. If the firm's target customer demands a very high level of responsiveness and if the customer is willing to pay premium price for that kind of responsiveness, then the firm can use transportation as a driver for making the supply chain more responsive. If the firm's target customers seek low prices for the products, then the firm having a competitive strategy of low cost production can use cheaper transportation modes to reduce the cost at the expense of responsiveness.

Both inventory and transportation may be used by a firm to increase its responsiveness or efficiency. The optimal decision would be to find the right balance between the two.

The key components of transportation that must be analysed when designing and operating a supply chain are:

(i) Mode of transportation-air, truck, rail, ship, pipeline etc.

(ii) Route and network selection.

(iii) Own transportation or outsourced transportation.

The overall trade-off for transportation is between the **cost** of transportation of a given product (**efficiency**) and the **speed** with which that product is transported (**responsiveness**).

(iii) The Role of Facilities (Manufacturing and Warehousing) in the Supply Chain

The facilities are concerned with **where** of the supply chain, while inventory is **what** is being transported along the supply chain and transportation is **how** it is moved. Facilities are the locations to or from which the inventory is moved (facilities include manufacturing plants and warehouses).

The supply chain performance in terms of responsiveness and efficiency is greatly influenced by facilities and their capacities to perform their functions. *For example,* efficiency increases when a firm manufactures a product in large quantities in one location (manufacturing plant) thereby gaining economies of scale. But the responsiveness decreases because of the distance involved in transporting the product to the customers located far from the facility. On the contrary, locating facilities close to customers increases the number of facilities needed and consequently increases costs and decreases efficiency.

Decisions regarding number of facilities and their locations play a crucial role in the design of supply chain. The various components of facilities decisions a firm must analyse are *(a)* **location,** *(b)* **capacity**, *(c)* **manufacturing processes**, *(d)* **warehousing methodology** (stock-keeping unit storage, job lot storage and cross docking).

The overall trade-off between responsiveness and efficiency involves facilities decisions having trade-offs between the cost of the number, location and type of facilities (efficiency) and the degree of responsiveness these facilities provide the customers of the firm.

(iv) Role of Information in the Supply Chain

Information eventhough not having a physical presence, deeply affects every part of the supply chain in many ways:

(a) Information connects various stages of the supply chain and allows them to coordinate their actions and provides many benefits of maximising total supply chain profitability.

(b) Information plays a crucial role in day-to-day operations of each stage in a supply chain. *For example,* a production scheduling system uses information on demand to create a schedule that allows the manufacturing plant to produce the right products in the right time to meet the demand.

Importance of information as a driver of supply chain performance has grown recently because of the developments in information technology.

Firms have increased the use of information to become more responsive and efficient. However, information also has a level at which trade-off between efficiency and responsiveness must take place.

Another key decision regarding information is **what information is most valuable in reducing cost and improving responsiveness within a supply chain**. This decision varies depending on the structure of the supply chain and the market segments served.

The key components of information within a supply chain which a firm must analyse to increase efficiency and improve responsiveness within its supply chain are:

(a) **Push Versus Pull Phase in the Supply Chain :** Push systems require information in the form of material requirements planning (MRP) systems to implement the master production schedule and to create schedules for suppliers with part types, quantities and delivery dates. Pull systems require information on actual demand to be transmitted quickly throughout the supply chain to facilitate production and distribution of parts and products that reflect the real demand accurately.

(b) **Co-ordination and Information Sharing :** Supply chain coordination is necessary for all the different stages of a supply chain to work toward the objective of maximising total supply chain profitability. Sharing of relevant information is necessary between different stages of the supply chain to accomplish this objective. *For example,* in a pull system, the manufacture must share demand and production information with the supplier who should produce the right parts in the right time and supply the same.

(c) **Forecasting and Aggregate Planning :** Managers must use sophisticated techniques to estimate future demand (*i.e.,* forecasts) or market conditions frequently with reasonable accuracy. Aggregate planning transforms forecasts into plans or activity to meet the projected demand. The aggregate plan becomes an important piece of information to be shared within the supply chain.

(d) **Enabling Technologies :** Many technologies are used to share and analyse information in the supply chain. Managers must decide which technologies to be used and how these technologies will be integrated into their firms and their supply chain partners. Some of these technologies include *(a)* Electronic data interchange (EDI), *(b)* The internet, *(c)* Enterprise resource planning (ERP) and *(d)* Supply chain software.

The fundamental trade-offs with the information driver is between responsiveness and efficiency. There are many information systems which increase both responsiveness and efficiency. However managers need to make the trade-off between the cost of information and the responsiveness that information creates in the supply chain.

Obstacles to Achieving Strategic Fit

To achieve strategic fit, a firm should be able to find a balance between responsiveness and efficiency of its supply chain along the responsiveness spectrum which best matches with the type of demand targeted by it. Over the years, the supply chain environment has changed considerably and the firms have been facing many obstacles that have created difficulty for the firms to achieve the ideal balance between responsiveness and efficiency. However, these obstacles have afforded firms increased opportunities for improving their supply chain management. A thorough understanding of the impact of these obstacles is critical for the firm's ability to achieve maximum profitability from its supply chain.

These obstacles are:

(a) **Increasing Variety of Products :** Manufacturers have resorted to **mass customisation** to meet the customer's demand for more customised products which has increased the variety of products in the market. *For example,* a customer can order a custom personal computer, built from a large number of configurations. Because of customer's demand for custom-made products to exactly meet their needs, market segments have become increasingly fragmented. The complexity of a supply chain increases by the increase in product variety, because of increasing

difficulty in forecasting and meeting demand. Increased variety tends to increase uncertainty which in turn results in higher cost and lower responsiveness within the supply chain.

(b) **Decreasing Product Life Cycles :** Because of the fast developments in product design and processing technologies, the product life cycle of products has been shrinking fast. This makes the job of achieving strategic fit more difficult because the entire supply chain is under pressure to constantly adapt to manufacture and deliver new products together with facing the problem of coping up with uncertainty of demand for these products. Increased uncertainty and reduced opportunity has put additional pressure on supply chains to coordinate and create a good match between supply and demand.

(c) **Highly Demanding Customers :** Nowadays customers have become highly demanding in terms of delivery lead times, cost and product performance. This has made it difficult for companies to force through any price increases without losing market share. Today's customers demand faster fulfillment, better quality and better performing products for the same price they paid years ago. Therefore, supply chains must perform better day by day in order to maintain or retain their business.

(d) **Fragmentation of Supply Chain Ownership :** Over the past several decades, companies have reduced their **vertical integration**. They have been **outsourcing** many non-core functions so that they develop their own core-competencies that provide them competitive advantage. The supply chain has a new ownership structure that has made the task of managing the supply chain more difficult.

As a result the supply chain is more difficult to coordinate. This problem would result in the reduction of overall supply chain profitability because of each stage working only to maximise its own profits.

(e) **Globalisation :** Over the past few decades, many countries who have become members of World Trade Organisation have liberalised their trade restrictions resulting in a spurt in global trade. This has opened up avenues for global sourcing and global markets resulting in global supply chains. Firms having global supply chains have been benefited by sourcing from global supplier base thereby achieving economies in their purchases. But global supply chains also cause added stress to the supply chain partners because of the increased distance between them, making coordination much more difficult.

Also, globalisation has increased competition because of the absence of protection to domestic firms in a country. The domestic firms have to compete with multinational companies to get their market share in the global market. This competitive situation makes supply chain performance a key to maintaining and growing sales while also putting more pressure on supply chains to make their trade-offs more precisely.

(f) **Difficulty in Executing New Strategies :** Once a good supply chain strategy is formulated, executing the same becomes more challenging. While many firms may have equally competent supply chain strategies, the firm which is better than others in executing its strategy would become more successful. Skillful execution of a strategy can be as important as the strategy itself.

All the obstacles discussed in this section are making it more difficult for the firms to achieve a proper balance between responsiveness and efficiency in their supply chain and therefore to achieve strategic fit. But these obstacles also provide tremendous opportunities to the firms in terms of untapped improvement within their supply chains. Therefore, now days, supply chain management is becoming a crucial factor in the success or failure of any firm and especially a global firm.

➢ EVOLUTION OF SUPPLY CHAIN MANAGEMENT

Eventhough the reference to supply chain management can be traced to the 1980s, the supply chain management concept captured the attention of senior level management in many organisations only in the 1990s. The power and potential impact of supply chain approach to make a firm globally more competent and to help increase the firms market share and its share-holder value were recognised by the top management of many firms.

The era of physical, distribution management started in the 1960s and the focus was on the outbound side of the firm's logistics system. Effective management of physical distribution function became an important issue. The activities focused in physical distribution management were *(i)* **inventory management**, *(ii)* **transportation**, *(iii)* **warehousing**, *(iv)* **order communications** and *(v)* **utilisation of the cubic capacity of the entire system**.

During the early 1970s, the focus shifted on the systems concept and ***total systems cost***. The systems relationship among transportation, inventory requirements, warehousing, exterior packaging and materials handling were recognised. *For example,* the mode of transportation selected has an impact on inventory warehousing, packaging, customer service and materials handling costs. Total cost of physical distribution system was lowered by evaluating alternate combinations of transport carriers, number and size of warehouses, location of plants and warehouses, inventory levels etc. *For example,* a low-cost transportation alternative could lead to higher inventory, packaging, warehousing and materials handling costs, offsetting the low transportation cost and leading to higher physical distribution system cost. Conversely a higher-cost alternative which is faster could lower those costs and perhaps could result in lower total cost of physical distribution.

Initially the focus was upon physical distribution of the finished goods (*i.e.,* outbound logistics) because of the higher value of finished goods which meant that their inventory, warehousing, materials handling and packaging costs were relatively higher than their raw materials (*i.e.,* inputs). Hence marketing managers were more concerned with the impact of transport selection on the physical distribution costs of finished goods.

In the 1980s, the logists or integrated logistics management concept began to be used in many organisations. Logistics, to start with added inbound logistics (*i.e.,* raw materials transportation form supply points and raw materials storage) to outbound logistics of physical distribution. Because of global sourcing of materials and suppliers for inbound system, the need for coordination with the outbound logistics system became critical for success of logistics systems. *Exhibit 4.9* illustrates the business logistics in a manufacturing organisation.

During the 1990s, the concept of supply chain management came into vogue and has now become the focal point for improving the global market place. **Supply chain management can be viewed as a conduit for the efficient and effective flow of products/materials, services, information and money from the supplier's suppliers through the various intermediaries (companies) to the customer's customers or the ultimate consumer**. The logistics supply chain is illustrated in *Exhibit 4.9* and *4.10.*

Exhibit 4.9 : A View of Business Logistics in a Manufacturing Firm

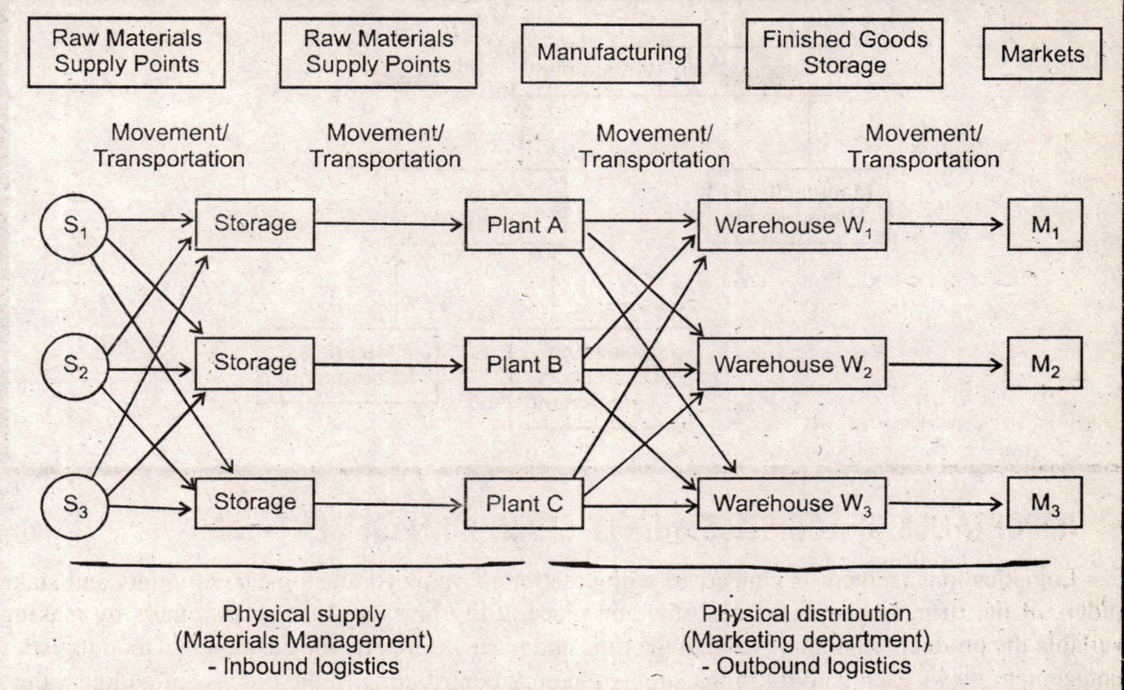

Raw Materials Supply Points
Raw Materials Supply Points
Manufacturing
Finished Goods Storage
Markets
Movement/ Transportation
Movement/ Transportation
Movement/ Transportation
Movement/ Transportation
S1
S2
S3
Storage
Storage
Storage
Plant A
Plant B
Plant C
Warehouse W1
Warehouse W2
Warehouse W3
M1
M2
M3
Physical supply (Materials Management) - Inbound logistics
Physical distribution (Marketing department) - Outbound logistics

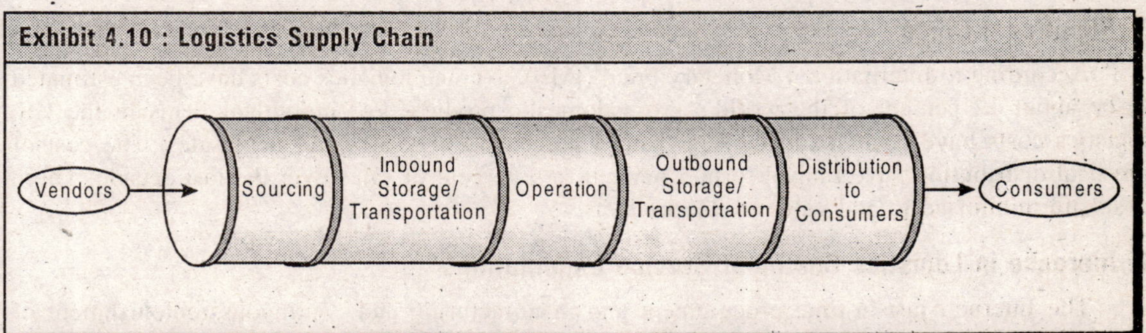

Exhibit 4.10 : Logistics Supply Chain

Vendors
Sourcing
Inbound Storage/ Transportation
Operation
Outbound Storage/ Transportation
Distribution to Consumers
Consumers

Traditionally, materials management is responsible for the consistent supplier relationship (referred to as **supplier partnership**) where as the marketing management or the sales and physical distribution management is responsible for the effective **customer relationship**.

Logistics management integrates materials management and sales and distribution management. Supply chain management integrates manufacturing management with logistics management. *Exhibit 4.11* illustrates the above relations among materials management, sales and distribution management, manufacturing management, logistics management and supply chain management.

Exhibit 4.11 : Relationship between Supply Chain Management and Other Areas of Management

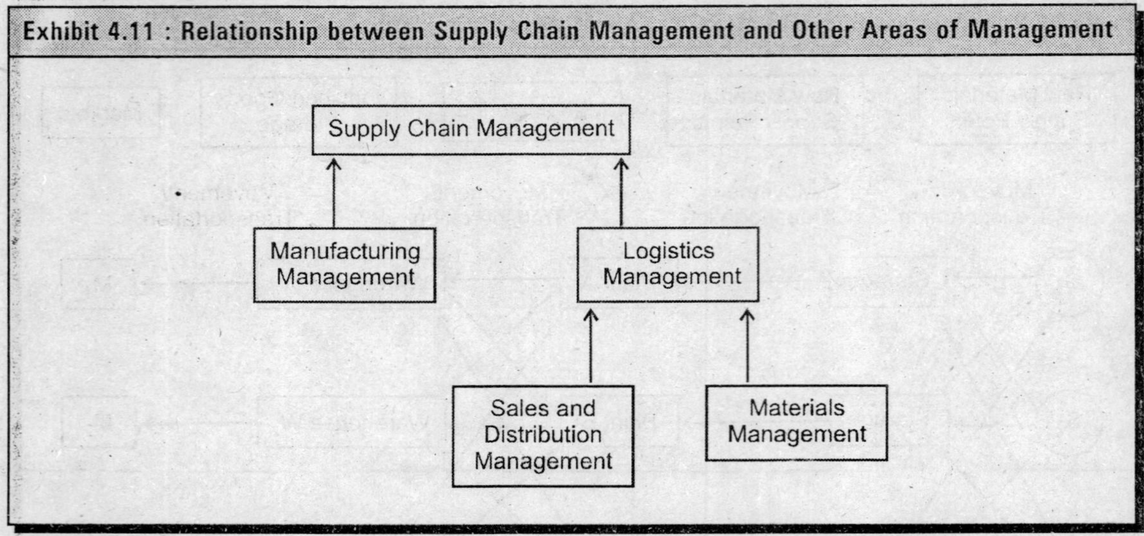

IMPORTANCE OF LOGISTICS/SUPPLY CHAIN MANAGEMENT

Logistics management is concerned with creation of value for customers, suppliers and stake holders of the firm. Logistics creates time and place utility or value for the customers by making available the products customers need at the time and place desired by the customers. Good logistics management views each activity in the supply chain as contributing to the process of adding value. The various reasons for increasing the importance of logistics as a value adding process are:

1. Significant Costs

According to International Monetary Fund (IMF), average logistics costs have been estimated to be about 12 percent of the world's gross domestic product. For individual firms in the US, logistics costs have been found to vary from 4 percent to over 30 percent of sales. The cost of physical distribution have ranged form 7 percent to 9 percent of sales over the last decade. These costs are minimised to add value to the products.

2. Increase in Logistics Customer Service Expectations

The Internet, just-in-time procurement and manufacturing and continuous replenishment of inventories have all made it possible for customers to expect rapid processing of their requests, quick delivery and product availability. The present world-class competitors have average order cycle times (the time between placement of an order and its receipt) of 7 to 8 days and a service rate of 90 to 95 percent. The **word-class logistics performance** for domestic companies consist of the following:

(i) Error rates of less than one per 100^{0} orders shipped.

(ii) Logistics cost lesser than 5 percent of sales.

(iii) Inventory turnover ratio of 20 or more for finished goods.

(iv) Total order cycle time of 5 working days.

(vi) Transportation cost of one percent of sales revenue or less.

3. Lengthening of Supply and Distribution Lines with Greater Complexity

In the present era of globalisation, firms are developing global strategies by designing their products for a global market and producing them wherever the cost of raw materials, components and labours are low. Alternatively firms produce locally and sell globally. Because of these trends, supply and distribution lines are stretched as compared to that in domestic business. This trend has occurred because global firms seek to cut costs or expand markets in order to compete successfully in global markets.

Globalisations of industries depend heavily on logistics performance and cost because firms take a global view of their operations. Because transportation costs account for a larger part of the total costs structure, logistics assumes greater importance within the firm. *For example,* when a multinational company seeks foreign suppliers for the raw materials and components or foreign location to assemble the product, the emphasis is on to increase profit. But while the material and labour costs are reduced, logistics costs are likely to increase due to increased transportation and inventory costs. The trade-off may lead to higher profit by reducing materials, labour and overhead costs eventhough logistics and tariff expenses increase. While outsourcing adds value by reducing costs, careful management of logistics costs and product-flow times in the supply chain is crucial for the firm to achieve higher overall profits.

Economic benefit of outsourcing is illustrated is *Exhibit 4.12* below:

Exhibit 4.12 : Economic Benefits of Oursourcing

Domestic Sources	Foreign Sources
Profit	Profit
Marketing	Marketing
Logistics	Logistics
Overhead	Tariffs
Materials	Overhead
Labour	Materials
	Labour

4. Importance of Logistics/Supply Chain to Competitive Strategy of the Firm

Firms compete based on a strategy of differentiating their product offerings from those of their competitors. Since logistics/supply chain has significant effect on a firm's costs and the supply-chain decisions affect the level of customer service, the firm can use logistics/supply chain decisions to penetrate new markets, to increase market share and to increase profits. Thus, good logistics/supply chain management can generate sales, not just reduce costs. *For example,* Wal-Mart has used logistics as the core of its competitive strategy to occupy the top position among merchandise retailers.

5. Logistics/Supply Chain Adds Significant Customer Value

For successful marketing, a firm must be able to ensure that its product is made available to its customers at the right time and at the right place. Eventhough a firm incurs costs in moving the product toward the customer or in making an inventory available in time, it creates value to the customer (*i.e.,* time value and place value). This value is as good as the value created by producing a quality product or by lowering the price.

Generally, a firm creates four types of value in its products or services, namely ***form value, time value, place value and possession value***. Out of these four values, logistics creates two values, *i.e.,* time value and place value. Manufacturing creates form value as inputs are converted to finished goods. Possession value is the responsibility of marketing, engineering and finance (through advertising, technical support and pricing and credit availability). Logistics has control over time and place values through transportation, information flows and inventories. But supply chain management includes production and logistics, so it has responsibility for three values namely form value, time value and place value.

6. Customers Want Quick and Customised Response

Advancement in communication technology and transportation has resulted in services such as automatic telling machines, overnight package delivery (courier service), electronic mail (through Internet) and fast food retailing. In addition, improved information system and flexible manufacturing processes have facilitated mass customisation at the market place. Logistics and supply chain management enable the firms to offer products that meet individual customer needs and achieve higher customer satisfaction.

➤ THIRD PARTY/CONTRACT LOGISTICS SERVICES

Asset productivity can be improved by the use of third party-logistics (3 PL) services. A third party-logistics provider (3 PL) is an external service provider who performers all or part of a firm's logistics functions. This approach would reduce the investment in logistics assets such as transportation carriers and handling equipments for loading and unloading the trucks etc., which in-turn increases the firm's asset productivity. Further, the current trend is to involve the fourth-party (4PL) service providers to help manage a number of 3 PLs which may be involved with a firm's logistics operations, A fourth party logistics (4PL) service provider is a firm that assembles and manages the resources, capabilities and technology of its own organisation with those of complementary service provider to deliver a comprehensive supply chain solution. A fourth-party logistics service provider manages a number of 3 PLs and also provides competencies relating to knowledge availability, information technology and skills in forming and sustaining successful supply chain relationships.

➤ REVIEW QUESTIONS

1. Define the terms "supply chain" and "supply chain management."
2. State the needs for supply chain management and its potential benefits.
3. Discuss the relevance of supply chain management to TQM.
4. Explain the elements of supply chain management.
5. Discuss the strategic, tactial and operational issues in supply chain management.
6. State the objectives of the supply chain.
7. State the reasons for outsourcing.
8. What is JIT purchasing?
9. What is vendor analysis? Explain the methods used for vendor evaluation and rating.
10. Explain the following : *(i)* supplier audit, *(ii)* supplier certification, *(iii)* supplier partnerships.
11. Explain "logistics management" as a part of supply chain management.
12. What is "distribution requirement planning"?
13. Describe the various opportunities in supply chain management to enhance value.
14. What is meant by "benchmarking supply chain management"? Elaborate.
15. Describe the various process tools used in supply chain management.
16. Discuss the various considerations for the make-or-buy decision.
17. Discuss the various points about supply chain dynamics.
18. What is meant by coordination in the supply chain? Explain how it is achieved.
19. Explain how supply chain performance is measured.
20. Discuss the nature and scope of supply chain management.
21. Write short notes on

    (a) Purchasing cycle *(b)* Value analysis *(c)* Outsourcing

    (d) JIT purchasing *(e)* Vendor analysis *(f)* Supplier partnerships
22. Discuss the various opportunities available to enhance the value of a supply chain.
23. Discuss the four major process tools used in supply chain management.
24. What is "supply chain dynamics"?
25. What is meant by coordination in the supply chain?
26. How do you measure supply chain performance?
27. "There are two basic ways to improve supply chains, by changing structure and infrastructure"- Discuss.
28. Describe a model of supply chain management with a diagram.
29. Distinguish between logistics management and supply chain management.
30. What are "supply chain drivers"? Explain the role of supply chain drivers in the supply chain decision making network.
31. Briefly outline the evolution of supply chain management.

32. Discuss the importance of logistics/supply chain management.
33. What is "strategic fit"?
34. Discuss the obstacles a firm's supply chain has to face in achieving the strategic fit.
35. What is meant by third party/contract logistics?

❖ ❖ ❖ ❖

DEMAND FORECASTING

Every day managers need to make decisions not only regarding the activities carried out on a daily basis but also for what is going to happen in the future. They order inventory for the production and sales of products for the future period, purchase new machinery and equipments despite uncertainty about demand for products and make investments without knowing what would be the profits. Managers are always trying to make better estimates of what will happen in the future in the face of uncertainty.

Planning is an integral part of a manager's job. If uncertainties exist in the future planning period, it will be difficult for managers to plan effectively. **Forecasts** help managers by reducing some of the uncertainties, thereby enabling them to develop more meaningful plans. *A forecast is an estimate about the future*. Effective approaches to forecasting and preparing the forecasts have become integral part of business planning. Forecasts help managers to determine in the present what courses of action they will take in the future.

Forecasting Defined : Forecasting is the first step in planning. It is defined as ***estimating the future demand for products and services and the resources necessary to produce these outputs***. Estimates of the future demand for products or services are commonly referred to as ***sales forecasts.*** The sales forecasts or demand forecasts are the starting point for the entire planning in production and operations management. *For example,* material planning, capacity planning, manpower planning, financial planning and production scheduling, all depend on sales forecasting.

Forecasting is the art and science of predicting future events. It is not a mere guess or prediction about the future without any rational basis. It may involve taking historical data and projecting them into the future. It may include a manager's good judgement or a subjective or intuitive prediction in the absence of historical data.

Any business organisation can not afford to avoid forecasting and just wait to see what happens and then take its chances. Effective planning in both the short and the long run depends on forecast of demand for the company's products.

Uses of Forecasts : Forecasts help managers **plan the productive system** and also help them **plan the use of the system**. Planning the productive system involves **long-range plans** regarding the type of products and services to offer, what facilities and equipments to have, where to locate and the like. Planning the use of the system refers to **short-range and intermediate range planning** involving tasks such as planning inventory and workforce levels, planning purchasing and production, scheduling and budgeting.

Forecasts are also used to predict profits, revenues, costs, productivity changes, prices and availability of energy, and raw materials, interest rates, movements of key economic indicators (such as Gross National Product, inflation etc.,) and prices of stocks and bonds. But this chapter is limited in scope to the discussion of forecasting demand (*i.e.,* forecasting of sales) eventhough the concepts and techniques apply equally well to other variables.

➤ NEED FOR DEMAND FORECASTING

Some reasons why forecasting is necessary in production and operations management are :

(i) **New Facility Planning :** Designing and building a new facility (factory) or designing and implementing a new production process may take as long as five years or even more. These strategic activities are based on long-range forecasts of demand for existing and new products to allow the needed lead time for production and operation managers for plant location, plant layout, installation of machinery and equipments to produce the products and services to meet the demand.

(ii) **Production Planning :** The rate of producing the products must be matched with the demand which may be fluctuating over the time period in the future. Since it may take several months to change the rate of output of the production processes, production mangers need medium or intermediate range demand forecasts to enable them to arrange for the production capacities to meet the monthly demands which are varying.

(iii) **Workforce Scheduling :** The forecasts of monthly demand may further be broken down to weekly demands and the workforce may have to be adjusted to meet these weekly demands. This may be done through reassignment of jobs to workforce, allowing overtime work, layoffs or hiring in order to match the weekly production rates with the weekly demands. Hence, short-range forecasts are needed to enable managers to have the necessary lead time to fine tune the workforce changes to meet the weekly production demands.

(iv) **Financial Planning :** Sales forecasts are the driving force in budgeting. Sales forecasts provide the timing of cash inflows (sales revenues) and also provide a basis for budgeting the requirements of cash outflow for purchasing materials, payments to employees and to meet other expenses of power and utilities etc. Hence, sales forecasts help finance manager to prepare budgets taking into consideration the cash inflows and cash outflows.

➤ FORECASTING TIME HORIZONS

A forecast is usually classified by the *future time horizon* it covers. Accordingly, the three categories of forecasts are :

(i) *Short-range forecast :* This forecast has a time span of upto one year, but is generally less than three months. It can be even for monthly or weekly forecasts. It is used for planning purchasing, job-scheduling, workforce levels, job assignments and production levels.

(ii) *Medium-range forecast* (or intermediate range) : A medium range or intermediate range forecast generally spans from 3 months to 3 years. It is used in sales planning, production planning and budgeting (quarterly or yearly), cash budgeting and analysing various operating plans.

(iii) *Long-range forecast :* Generally 3 years or more in time span, long range forecasts are used in new product planning and development, capital expenditure planning and planning for facility location or expansion and research and development.

Three features which differentiate short-range forecasts from medium range and long range forecasts are :

(i) Intermediate and long-range forecasts pertain to more comprehensive issues and support management decisions (strategic and tactical decisions) regarding planning for products, plants and processes.

(ii) The forecasting methodologies used in short-term forecasting are different from those used for long-term forecasting.

(iii) Short-range forecasts tend to be more accurate than longer range forecasts because as time horizon lengthens forecast accuracy will diminish because factors influencing forecasts change everyday. *Exhibit 5.1* illustrates characteristics of forecasts based on time horizon.

Exhibit 5.1 : Types and characteristics of forecasts based on time horizon

Forecast Horizon	*Applications*	*Characteristics*	*Forecast Methods*
Long-range (3 to 5 yrs. or more)	Business planning, Product planning, Capital planning, Facility planning Location planning	Broad, general, often only qualitative	Technological, Economic, Demographic Marketing studies, Judgement
Medium or intermediate (3 months to 3 years)	Aggregate planning Capital and cash budgets, Production planning and budgeting, inventory planning and budgeting	Numerical, not necessarily at the item level. Estimate of reliability needed	Collective opinion, Time series/Regression analysis, Judgement
Short-range (1 week to 3 months)	Short run adjustment of production and personnel levels, purchasing, job scheduling, capacity changes by over time, lay offs etc.	May be at item level for planning of activity level, should be at item level for purchasing and inventory control.	Extrapolation of trends, Judgement, Exponential-Smoothing

➢ TYPES OF FORECASTS

1. **Technological forecasts** are concerned with rates of technological progress. Technological changes will provide many companies with new products and materials to offer for sale. Even if the products remain unchanged, a new process for producing the products can be developed with a new or improved technology using new machinery and equipment.

2. **Economic forecasts** are statements of expected future business conditions published by governmental agencies. There forecasts address the business cycle by predicting inflation rates, money supplies, housing starts and other economic indicators such as tax revenues, levels of employment, gross national product etc. These forecasts give ideas about long range and intermediate range business growth to business organisations.

3. **Demand forecasts** are projections of demand for a company's products or services. These forecasts, also called *sales forecasts* give the expected level of demand for a company's goods or services throughout some future period and usually provide the basis for the company's planning and control decisions. These forecasts drive a company's production, capacity and scheduling systems and serve as inputs to financial, marketing and human resource (manpower) planning. Economic and technological forecasting are specialised techniques which fall outside the scope of production and operations managers and hence not discussed in this book.

➤ FEATURES COMMON TO ALL FORECASTS

Eventhough a wide variety of forecasting techniques which are quite different from each other are used to determine the demand forecasts, there are certain features which are common to all forecasting techniques. They are :

(i) Forecasting techniques generally assume that same underlying reasons (causal system) that existed in the past will continue to exist in the future.

(ii) Forecasts are rarely perfect. Actual results (demand) usually differ from forecasted results (demand) Allowances should be made for inaccuracies.

(iii) Forecasts for groups of items tend to be more accurate than forecasts for individual items.

(iv) Forecast accuracy decreases as the time period covered by the forecast (forecasting time horizon) increases.

Elements of a Good Forecast (or Requirements of a Good Forecast)

(i) The forecast should be **timely**. This means that the forecasting horizon must have the time necessary to implement possible changes in production capacity, financial needs etc.

(ii) The forecast should be **accurate** and the degree of accuracy should be known.

(iii) The forecast should be **reliable** (should be consistent in accuracy).

(iv) The forecast should be expressed in **meaningful units** such as rupees, units of products, machines and skills needed.

(v) The forecast should be in the **written form** to permit an objective basis for evaluating the forecast once the actual results are known.

(vi) The forecasting techniques **should be simple** *to understand and use* (comfortable for users).

➤ OBJECTIVES OF DEMAND FORECASTING

The objectives of demand forecasting are divided into : *(i)* Short-range objectives and *(ii)* Medium or Long range objectives.

Short Range Objectives

Short range objectives of demand forecasting are :

(i) **Formulation of production strategy and policy**, to bridge the gap between demand and supply of a product offered by the firm and to ensure :

(a) **Estimating the requirement of materials** to be purchased on a regular basis. The material requirements are based on volume of production in a prescribed time period which in turn is based on the forecasts of demand.

(b) **Optimum utilisation of plant and equipments**, by adjusting the production capacity using overtime, subcontracting, lay offs or hiring casual employees etc.

(c) **Planning the availability of labour on a regular basis to meet the requirement of production schedules.**

(ii) **Formulation of pricing policy** : Demand forecasts enable management to formulate a suitable mechanism for fixing the prices for products to be sold.

(iii) **Planning and control of sales** : Demand forecasts facilitate territory design and determination of sales quotas to be assigned to sales people.

(iv) **Financial planning** : Demand forecasts facilitate estimating cash inflows and cash outflows for the products for which forecasts are made. Accordingly, the funds requirements can be properly planned and cost of funding can be reduced.

Medium or Long-Range Objectives

(i) **Long-range planning for production capacity** : The installed capacity of the plant is usually based on long-term demand forecasts.

(ii) **Labour requirements** *(Employment levels)* : Employment levels are based on reliable medium/long term demand forecasts so as to optimise the cost of production over the long term planning horizon.

(iii) **Restructuring the capital structure** : Long term forecasts facilitate planning for long-term finance requirements at reasonable financial costs and other terms and conditions for obtaining finance from lending institutions as well as planning for internal financial resources to meet the long-term financial needs.

➤ STEPS IN THE FORECASTING PROCESS

The *seven* basic steps involved in forecasting are :

(i) **Determine the purpose (objectives) of the forecast** : What are the objectives of forecasting? When the forecasts are needed? Questions such as the above are required to be answered to determine the level of details required in the forecast, the amount of resources (manpower, computer time, rupees etc.,) that can be justified and the level of accuracy needed.

(ii) **Select the items for which forecasts are needed** : Determine whether the forecast is needed for a single product or for a group of products (product line).

(iii) **Determine the time horizon for the forecast** : Is it short-term, medium-term or long-term? The forecast must indicate the time horizon and whether to develop forecasts weekly, monthly, quarterly or yearly.

(iv) **Select the forecasting model (method or technique)** : Determine whether to use statistical models (quantitative) including moving averages, exponential smoothing and regression analysis or qualitative techniques such as judgemental or market research methods (customers buying plans).

(v) **Gather and analyse the data needed for the forecast** : Before preparing the forecast, data must be gathered and analysed. Identify any assumptions that are made in conjunction with preparing and using the forecasts.

(vi) **Prepare the forecast** : Using the selected method.

(vii) **Monitor the forecast :** Monitor the forecast to determine whether it is performing satisfactorily. If not, review the method, assumptions, validity of data and modify the forecast if needed and prepare a revised forecast.

Forecasting Approaches : The two general approaches to forecasting are : *(i)* Qualitative and *(ii)* Quantitative. Qualitative methods consist mainly of subjective inputs, often of non-numerical description. Quantitative methods involve either projection of historical data or the development of association models which attempt to use *causal variables* to arrive at the forecasts.

➤ OVERVIEW OF QUALITATIVE METHODS

1. **Jury of Executive Opinion :** It is a forecasting technique in which the opinions of a small group of high-level executives (managers) are taken, based on which a group estimate of demand is obtained as the forecast.

   Advantages :

   (i) Uses experience and knowledge of two or more managers to arrive at a single forecast.

   (ii) Can be used for technological forecasting.

   (iii) Can be used for forecasting the demand for new products.

   (iv) Can be used to modify an existing forecast to account for unusual circumstances.

   Disadvantages :

   (i) Executive opinion can be costly because it takes valuable executive time.

   (ii) It sometimes gets out of control or gets delayed.

   (iii) Difficult to obtain consensus opinion of several experts.

2. **Sales Composite Method :** This is also known as **"Pooled salesforce estimate"** method. Each sales person estimates what sales will be in his or her territory. These estimates are then reviewed to ensure that they are realistic. Then they are combined at the district and national level to arrive at the overall forecast.

   Advantages :

   (i) The sales force is the group closest to the customers. The sales persons are most likely to know which products or services, customers will be buying in the near future and in what quantities.

   (ii) Sales territories often are divided into districts or regions and forecasts for districts or regions will be useful in inventory management, distribution and salesforce staffing.

   Disadvantages :

   (i) Individual biases of sales people may affect the sales forecast (some are optimistic and some are pessimistic).

   (ii) Sales people may be unable to distinguish between what customers would like to do and what they actually will do.

   (iii) Sometimes, sales people may be overly influenced by their recent experiences.

   (iv) If the firm uses individual sales person's estimate as a performance measure, sales people may deliberately underestimate their forecasts so that their performance will look good when they exceed their quotas which are fixed based on their estimates.

3. **Market Research Method (or Consumer Survey Method) :** This is a systematic approach to determine consumer interest in a product or service by conducting a consumer survey and sample consumer opinions. This method may be used to forecast demand for the short, medium and long term.

Advantage is that consumers' opinion regarding their future purchasing plans are better than executive opinion or sales force opinion because it is the consumers who ultimately determine demand. Also, information that might not be available elsewhere can be obtained by consumer surveys.

Disadvantages are :

(i) It may not be possible to contact every customer or potential customer and opinions are obtained from sample customers which may lead to forecast error if the sample size is inadequate.

(ii) Surveys require considerable amount of knowledge and skill to handle correctly.

(iii) Surveys can be expensive and time consuming.

(iv) The response rate for mailed questionnaire may be poor.

(v) The survey results may not reflect the opinions of the market.

4. **Other Judgemental Methods : Delphi Method :** In this method opinions are solicited from a number of other managers and staff personnel. The decision makers consist of a group of 5 to 10 experts who will be making the actual forecast. The staff personnel assist decision makers by preparing, distributing, collecting and summarising a series of questionnaires and survey results.

The managers whose judgements are valid are the respondents. This group provides input to the decision makers before forecast is made. Responses of each respondent are kept anonymous which tends to encourage honest responses. Each new questionnaire is developed using the information extracted from the previous one, thus enlarging the scope of information on which participants can base their judgements. The goal is to achieve consensus forecast.

Advantages :

(i) This method can be used to develop long-range forecasts of product demand and sales projections for new products.

(ii) A panel of experts may be used as participants (respondents).

Disadvantages :

(i) The process can take a long time.

(ii) Responses may be less meaningful because respondents are not accountable due to anonymity.

(iii) High accuracy may not be possible.

(iv) Poorly designed questionnaire will result in ambiguous or false conclusions.

➢ OVERVIEW OF QUANTITATIVE METHODS

There are five quantitative forecasting methods, all of which use historical data. They fall into two categories.

1. (a) Naive approach
(b) Moving averages method
(c) Exponential smoothing method
} Time series models

2. (a) Trend projection
(b) Linear regression analysis
} Causal models

Time series models predict on the assumption that the future is a projection of the past. They look at what has happened over a period of time and use a series of past data to make a forecast for the future.

Causal (or association) models such as linear regression, incorporate the variable or factors that might influence the quantity being forecast. The demand or sales forecast is a dependent variable and other factors that affect demand are independent variables (causal variables). In linear regression the dependent variable (*i.e.,* demand or sales) is related to one or more independent variables by a linear equation. The time series models and causal models are discussed in greater detail in the following section.

Time Series Forecasting Methods

A **time series** is a time-ordered sequence of observations taken at regular intervals over a period of time (*e.g.,* hourly, daily, weekly, monthly, quarterly or annually). The data may be measurement of demand, earnings, profits, outputs, productivity, consumer price index etc.

Decomposition of a Time Series

Analysis of time series data requires the analyst to identify the underlying behaviour of the series. This can be done by plotting the data with time on the 'X' axis and data on 'Y' axis and visually examining the plot. One or more patterns might appear. They are **trends, seasonal variations, cycles** and **random** or **irregular variations** (error).

Trend refers to gradual, long term, upward or downward movement in the data over time. Changes in income, population, age distribution or cultural views may account for such movements.

Seasonality refers to short-term, fairly regular variations related to factors such as weather, holidays, vacation etc. Seasonal variations can be daily, weekly or monthly.

Cycles are wavelike variations of more than one year's duration or which occur every several years. They are usually tied with business cycle related to a variety of economic, political or agricultural conditions.

Random variations are residual variations which are blips in the data caused by chance and unusual situations which can not be predicted (*e.g.,* war, earthquake, flood etc.).

Techniques for Averaging

Historical data contain a certain amount of random variation, or **noise** which tends to observe systematic movement in the data. It is desirable to completely remove any randomness from the data and leave only "real" variation such as changes in demand.

Averaging techniques smooth fluctuations in a time series so that the forecast can be based on an average, to exhibit less variability than the original data. Averaging techniques generate forecasts to reflect recent values of a time series. Three techniques for averaging are :

(i) Naive forecasts or Naive approach, *(ii)* Moving averages (Simple and weighted) and *(iii)* Exponential smoothing.

1. **Naive Approach :** The simplest way to forecast is to assume that forecast of demand in the next period is equal to the actual demand in the most recent period (*i.e.,* the current period). *For example,* if the actual sales for a product in January 2003 is 100 units, the forecast demand for February 2003 will also be 100 units.
2. **Moving Averages Method :** A moving average forecast uses a number of most recent historical actual data values to generate a forecast. The moving average for 'n' number of periods in the moving average is calculated as :

$$\text{Moving average} = \frac{\sum \text{demand in previous n periods}}{\text{n}}$$

n may be 3, 4, 5 or 6 periods for 3, 4, 5 or 6 period moving average.

The "simple moving average method" is used to estimate the average of a demand time series and remove the effects of random fluctuation. It is most useful when demand has no pronounced trend or seasonal fluctuations. In this method, if we use 'n' period moving averages, the average demand for the 'n' most recent time periods is calculated and used as forecast for the next time period. For the next period, after the demand is known, the older demand from the previous average is replaced with the most recent demand and the average is recalculated. *For example,* We use a 3 month simple moving average method and the demand data is as below :

Month (period)	*Actual Demand*	*Forecast Based on Simple Moving Average*
1	d_1	
2	d_2	
3	d_3	
4	d_4	$\frac{d_1 + d_2 + d_3}{3}$ (forecast for month 4)
5	d_5	$\frac{d_2 + d_3 + d_4}{3}$ (forecast for month 5)
6	d_6	$\frac{d_3 + d_4 + d_5}{3}$ (forecast for month 6)
7	?	$\frac{d_4 + d_5 + d_6}{3}$ (forecast for month 7)

In the **weighted moving average method** each historical demand in the moving average can have its own weight and the sum of the weight equals one. *For example,* in a 3 period weighted moving average model, the most recent period might be assigned a weight of 0.50, the second most recent period might be assigned a weight of 0.30 and the third most recent period with a weight of 0.20.

Then forecast,

$$F_{t+1} = \frac{0.50\ D_t + 0.30(D_{t-1}) + 0.20\ D_{t-2}}{\text{Sum of the weights } (i.e.,\ 0.5 + 0.3 + 0.2)}$$

(*i.e.*, the average is obtained by multiplying the weight of each period by the value for that period and by adding the products together).

The advantage of a weighted moving average method is that it allows to emphasise recent demand over earlier demand.

3. **Exponential Smoothing Method :** It is a sophisticated weighted moving average method that is still relatively easy to understand and use. It requires only three items of data : this period's forecast, the actual demand for this period and α which is referred to as *smoothing constant* and having a value between 0 and 1. The formula used is

$$\text{Next period's forecast} = \text{This period's forecast} + \alpha \left(\begin{matrix} \text{This period's} \\ \text{actual demand} \end{matrix} - \begin{matrix} \text{This period's} \\ \text{forecast} \end{matrix} \right).$$

or

$$F_t = F_{t-1} + \alpha(A_{t-1} - F_{t-1})$$

Where F_t = Forecast for the this period (t)

F_{t-1} = Forecast for the previous period (t – 1)

A_{t-1} = Actual demand for the previous period (t – 1)

α = Smoothing constant (value varies from 0 to 1)

Selecting a smoothing constant is basically a matter of judgement or trial and error. Commonly used values of α range from 0.05 to 0.5. Detailed discussion of causal models is beyond the scope of this book.

Factors to be considered in the selection of a forecasting method are : *(i)* cost, *(ii)* accuracy, *(iii)* data available, *(iv)* time span, *(v)* nature of products and services and *(vi)* impulse response and noise dampening.

These factors are discussed below :

(i) **Cost and Accuracy :** A trade-off may result between cost and accuracy in choosing a forecasting method. This means high forecast accuracy can be obtained at a high cost. High accuracy approaches use more data, which are more difficult to obtain and the models are costly to design, implement and operate. Examples of high cost models are complex econometric models, Delphi and market research methods. Statistical models based on historical data and jury of executive opinion method are of low or moderate cost.

(ii) **Data Available :** The availability of relevant data for forecasts is an important factor in the choice of forecasting method. *For example,* if the attitudes and intentions of customers are relevant for the forecasts and if the data can be economically obtained from customers about their attitudes and intentions, then a survey of customers (market research method) may be an appropriate method for forecasting the demand.

(iii) **Time Span :** The choice of an appropriate forecasting method is affected by the nature of the production resource to be forecasted. Workforce, cash, inventories and machine schedules are short range in nature and can be forecasted using moving average or exponential smoothing models. Long-range production resources such as plant capacities and capital funds can be forecasted by regression analysis, executive committee consensus (*i.e.*, jury of executive opinion) or market research methods.

(iv) **Nature of Products and Services :** Different forecasting models have to be used for different products. The choice of the forecasting method is affected by factors such as volume of

production, cost of the product, nature of the products (*i.e.*, goods or services), whether product demand has seasonal fluctuations or growth or decline and whether the product is in its life cycle etc.

(v) **Impulse Response and Noise Dampening :** How responsive we want the forecasting model to be to changes in the actual demand data must be balanced against our desire to suppress undesirable chance variation or noise in the data. Each model differs in its impulse response and noise dampening abilities and the model selected must fit the forecasting situation.

Some Reasons for Ineffective Forecasting

1. Not involving a broad cross section of people in forecasting.
2. Not recognising the fact that forecasting is integral to business planning.
3. Not recognising that forecasts will never be correct or accurate.
4. Not forecasting the right things. *For example,* forecasting the demand for raw materials that go into the products is not necessary as it can be computed based on the demand for products.
5. Not selecting an appropriate forecasting method.
6. Not tracing the performance of the forecasting models so that forecast accuracy can be improved and the forecasting model can be modified if needed.

MONITORING AND CONTROLLING FORECASTS

Once a forecast has been completed, it needs to be monitored and corrected periodically by determining why actual demand (or whatever variable is being examined) differed significantly from that projected. This can be done by setting upper and lower limits on how much the performance characteristic of a forecasting model can deteriorate before we change the parameters of the model.

One way to monitor forecasts to ensure that they are performing well is to use a *tracking signal.* A **tracking signal** is a measurement of how well the forecast is predicting actual values.

$$\text{Tracking signal} = \frac{\text{Running sum of the forecast errors}}{\text{Mean Absolute Deviation}}$$

$$= \frac{\text{RSFE}}{\text{MAD}}$$

$$\text{RSFE} = \sum_{i=1}^{n}\left[\begin{pmatrix}\text{Actual demand}\\ \text{in period i}\end{pmatrix} - \begin{pmatrix}\text{Forecast demand}\\ \text{in period i}\end{pmatrix}\right]$$

$$\text{MAD} = \sum_{i=1}^{n}\left[\frac{\begin{bmatrix}\text{Actual demand} & - & \text{Forecast demand}\\ \text{in period i} & & \text{in period i}\end{bmatrix}}{n}\right]$$

or

$$= \sum_{i=1}^{n}\left[\frac{|\text{Forecast errors}|}{n}\right]$$

Implication of Tracking Signal

Positive tracking signals indicate that demand is greater than forecast. Negative tracking signals mean that demand is less than forecast.

A good tracking signal – that is one with a low RSFE – has about as much positive error as it has negative error. In other words, small deviations are okay, but positive and negative errors should balance one another so that the tracking signal centres closely around zero.

Once tracking signals are evaluated, they are compared with predetermined control limits. When a tracking signal exceeds an upper or lower limit, there is some problem with the forecasting method and hence the forecasting method must be reevaluated. *Exhibit 5.2* illustrates a plot of tracking signals.

Exhibit 5.2 : A Plot of Tracking Signal

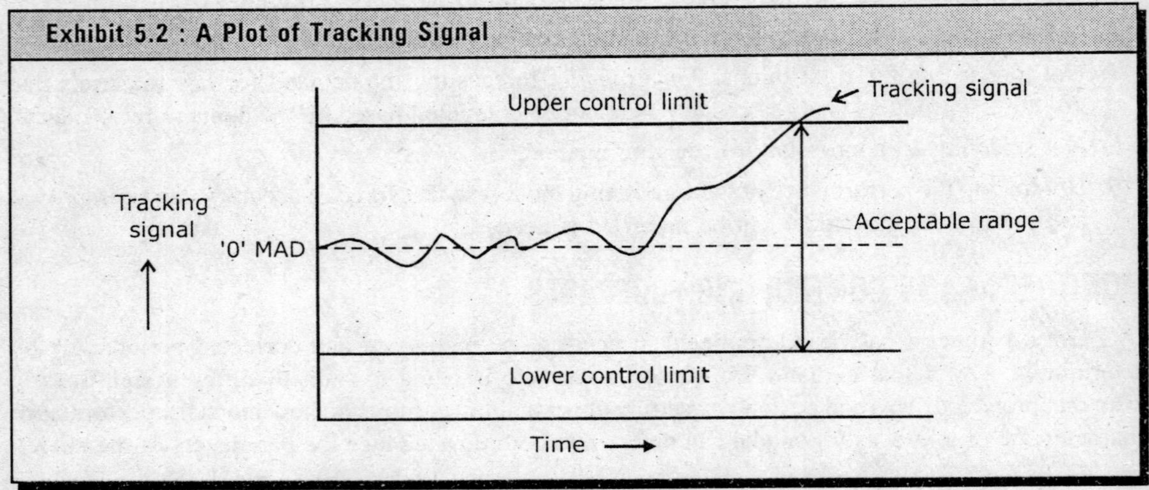

For instance, if the tracking signal for a forecasting model, say exponential smoothing model exceeds the range of acceptable variation, perhaps the smoothing constant needs to be readjusted.

How do firms decide what the upper and lower limits of tracking signal should be?

There is no single answer to this question. But forecasting experts try to find reasonable value, *i.e.,* limits not so low as to be triggered with every small forecast error and not so high as to allow bad forecasts to be regularly overlooked. *For example,* George Plossl and Oliver Wight, two inventory control experts have suggested using maximums of ±4 MADs for high volume stock items and ± 8 MADs for low-volume items.

Since one MAD is approximately equal to 0.8 standard deviation, ±2 MADs = ±1.6 standard deviation, ±3 MADs = ± 2.4 standard deviation and ±4 MADs = ± 3.2 standard deviation. This suggests that for a forecast to be "in control", 89% of the errors are expected to fall within ±2 MADs, 98% within ±3 MADs and 99.9% within ±4 MADs.

Illustration :

K.S. Bakery's quarterly sales (in thousands) as well as forecast demand and error computations for an item are shown below. The objectives is to compute the tracking signal and determine whether forecasts are performing adequately.

Quarter	Forecast Demand (F)	Actual Demand (D)	Error (D – F)	RSFE	[Forecast error]
1	100	90	–10	–10	10
2	100	95	–5	–15	5
3	100	115	+15	0	15
4	110	100	–10	–10	10
5	110	125	+15	+5	15
6	110	140	+30	+35	30

Quarter	Cumulative Forecast Error	Cumulative MAD	Tracing signal
1	10	$\frac{\sum\lvert\text{Forecast error}\rvert}{n} = 10$	$\frac{\text{RSFE}}{\text{MAD}} = (-1)$
2	15	$\frac{15}{2} = 7.5$	–2
3	30	$\frac{30}{3} = 10.0$	0
4	40	$\frac{40}{4} = 10.0$	–1
5	55	$\frac{55}{5} = 11.0$	+0.5
6	85	$\frac{85}{6} = 14.2$	+2.5

Tracking signal for 6th quarter

$$= \frac{\text{RSFE}}{\text{MAD}} = \frac{35}{14.2} = 2.5 \text{ MADs}$$

This tracking signal is within acceptable limits as it drifts from – 2.0 MADs to +2.5 MADs.

➢ SOLVED PROBLEMS

1. *The table below shows the monthly demand over 6 months period for a product.*
   (a) Determine the forecast of demand for the 7th month using 3 month simple moving average method.
   (b) If the weightage given for the demand for 6th, 5th and 4th months are 0.5, 0.3 and 0.2 respectively. Determine the forecast of demand for 7th month using weighted moving average method.

Month	*1*	*2*	*3*	*4*	*5*	*6*
Demand (units)	*120*	*130*	*110*	*140*	*110*	*130*

Solution :

(a) Forecast of demand for 7th month using simple moving average (3 month) is calculated as below :

$$\left.\begin{array}{r}\text{Forecast of demand}\\ \text{for 7th month}\end{array}\right\} = \frac{d_6 + d_5 + d_4}{3}$$

$$= \frac{130 + 110 + 140}{3} = \frac{380}{3} = 126.67 \text{ units}$$

(b) Forecast of demand for 7th month using weighted moving average (3 month) is calculated as follows :

$$\left.\begin{array}{r}\text{Forecast of demand}\\ \text{for 7th month}\end{array}\right\} = \frac{w_1 d_6 + w_2 d_5 + w_3 d_4}{w_1 + w_2 + w_3}$$

$$= \frac{(0.5 \times 130) + (0.3 \times 110) + (0.2 \times 140)}{0.5 + 0.4 + 0.3} = 126 \text{ units}$$

2. *ABC company predicted the sales for a product as 150 units for February 2003. Actual demand for February 2003 was 158 units. Using a smooth constant (α) of 0.3, forecast the demand for March 2003.*

Solution :

$$F_{March} = F_{Feb} + \alpha\,(D_{Feb} - F_{Feb})$$

F_{Feb} = Forecast for Feb. = 150 units

D_{Feb} = Actual demand for Feb. = 158 units

F_{Mar} = Forecast for March

α = Smoothing constant.

$$F_{Mar} = 150 + 0.3\,(158 - 150)$$

$$= 150 + (0.3 \times 8) = 152.4 \approx 152 \text{ units}$$

➤ REVIEW QUESTIONS

1. Define the term "forecasting".
2. Mention the uses of forecasts.
3. State the elements of a good forecast.
4. Define the terms "mean absolute deviation" and "tracking signal".
5. State the reasons for ineffective forecasting.
6. Discuss the need for forecasting.
7. What is "forecasting time horizon"? Discuss the characteristics of the three categories of forecasts based on time horizon for forecasting.
8. Write short notes on *(a)* Technological forecast, *(b)* Economic forecast and *(c)* Demand forecast.
9. Discuss the features which are common to all types of forecasts.
10. Discuss the short range and long range objectives of demand forecasting.
11. Explain the steps involved in the forecasting process.
12. Briefly discuss the qualitative and quantitative methods used for forecasting demand.
13. Discuss the factors to be considered in the selection of a forecasting method.
14. State the reasons for ineffective forecasting.

CHAPTER 6

MATERIALS PLANNING AND CONTROL

In the earlier days, the purchasing activity was thought of merely a supporting function to provide service to the production and operations managers. But as the buying activity became specialised and a professionalised staff function, the purchasing department's function is being viewed today as a **proactive** function rather than a **reactive** function.

Today with the concept of "integrated materials management" and "supply-chain management", materials managers have learnt that a majority of the material needs of their organisations over a period of one year or so can be forecast in advance with acceptable accuracy. Hence, most purchase managers develop an annual buying plan for key materials. Materials planning, materials budgeting and material control have taken prominent roles in the integrated materials management. Planning for materials and working out realistic materials budget not only help motivate people but also serve as a control device.

Materials planning has to be done for non-programmed decisions such as import policy, foreign exchange availability and credit squeeze. Also, planning has to be done for highly programmed decisions such as inventory levels and working out delivery schedules.

The relationship between materials planning and other major functions is shown in *Exhibit 6.1.*

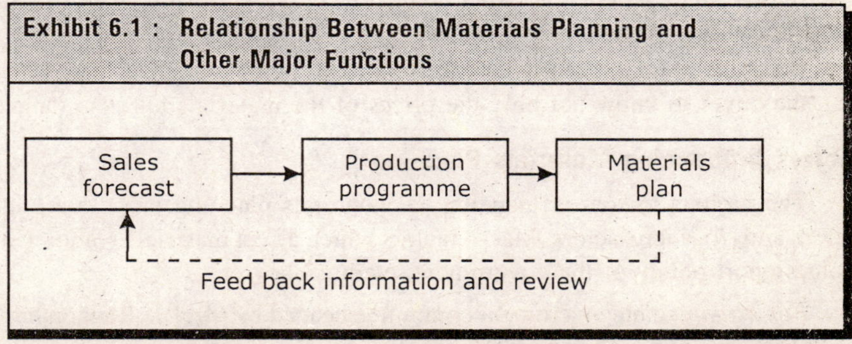
Exhibit 6.1 : Relationship Between Materials Planning and Other Major Functions

➤ WHAT IS MATERIALS PLANNING?

Materials planning is the scientific way of determining the requirements of raw materials, components, spares and other items that go into meeting the production needs within economic investment policies. Materials planning is a sub-set of the overall production planning and control system which has a broad perspective. Materials budgeting is an estimate of expenses to be incurred in the procurement of materials and it helps effective execution and control of materials plans.

Significance of Materials Planning

(i) Lack of proper materials planning and coordination leads to *over-ordering* or *under-ordering* of materials, over-ordering results in over-investment and unproductive use of costly working capital. It creates the need for extra storage facilities to hold unnecessary surplus stocks and may lead to deterioration and obsolescence of materials. Under-ordering results in material shortages that cause unnecessary delays and costly interruption in executing production commitments.

(ii) Poor planning for materials may lead to unwarranted emergency or rush orders, usually processed by costly means of transport.

(iii) Materials planning activity raises the level of the buyer from a mere order placer to a purchase executive or manager. Planning enables the purchase people to spend money in an optimum manner.

(iv) Materials planning aims at motivating people and saves as an effective control device.

(v) Efficiency in materials management function cannot be visulised without a sensible or effective materials planning function.

Benefits of Materials Planning

(i) Materials planning – both quantity and value in terms of rupees – for each item and overall, tries to avoid the practice of *crisis management* of struggling at the last minute to procure materials to meet the production requirements or pressurising unnecessarily the purchase people by sitting on their neck to get the materials at the last moment.

(ii) It helps to get things done efficiently and effectively by better forecasting of future material needs and working pro-actively rather than reacting to the situations.

(iii) A well-designed materials planning system provides steps for effective materials budgeting, follow-up of suppliers to procure materials in-time, thereby avoiding material shortages and its undesirable effects on production.

(iv) Purchase planning which is based on materials planning, if carried out properly, will enable the buyer to know not only the prices of the materials but also their costs.

Factors Influencing Materials Planning

The various factors influencing the materials planning process are classified as : *(a)* Macro factors and *(b)* Microfactors. Macro factors which affect materials planning are price trends, business cycle, import policy of the government, credit policy etc.

For example, the government committee headed by Mr. P.L. Tandon has given certain guidelines for inventory levels of raw materials, stock-in-process or work-in-process and finished goods inventories as well as for receivables and bills purchased and discounted. These guidelines are followed by banks while extending credit to industrial firms. Microfactors affecting materials planning include corporate objectives, working capital, seasonality, delegation of powers and communication systems used by the firm. *Box 6.1* lists A to Z influencing factors which influence materials planning process.

Box 6.1 : A to Z Influencing Factors

(a) State of health of national economy, *(b)* price trends, *(c)* credit policies, *(d)* direct and indirect taxes, *(e)* foreign exchange regulations, *(f)* import policy, *(g)* international market conditions, *(h)* business cycles, *(i)* corporate objectives, *(j)* technology availability, *(k)* demand for the item, *(l)* supply of the item, *(m)* transportation losses, *(n)* total procurement lead time, *(o)* rejection rate, *(p)* working capital, *(q)* storage capacity, *(r)* plant utilisation, *(s)* seasonal factors, *(t)* communication system, *(u)* delegation of power, *(v)* information available, *(w)* location of plant and location of suppliers, *(x)* cost, criticality, reliability and availability of items, *(y)* information on substitute products, *(z)* demand forecasting techniques used.

The Approach to Materials Planning : The basis for materials planning is generally the firmwide **annual production** *or* **operating plan** which in turn is based on the demand or sales forecast for finished goods produced by the firm. The annual sales forecast may be further divided into quarterly or monthly sales forecast for each product line or individual product. The sales forecast is then translated into an *aggregate production plan* and *master production schedule* taking into consideration finished goods inventory levels as well as desired in-process inventory levels for specific items. Obviously short term sales forecasts (monthly, quarterly or yearly) can be converted into a production schedule more accurately than that is possible when intermediate or long term sales forecasts are used to prepare production plans.

All materials planning subsequently flows from the preliminary master production schedule. Requirements of various materials (raw materials, parts, components, subunits etc.,) are worked out by exploding the master production schedule for the planning period through the planning horizon. This technique is referred to as **"Bill of Materials Explosion".** Bill of materials is nothing but a document which shows for a given product or sub-unit, the list of materials required, unit consumption, and location code (for storage). The condition of supply such as "**boughtout**" or "**made in-house**" will also be indicated. Computers can be very effectively used for exploding bill of materials with demand forecasts as basis and the product structure (part lists) as the input data to the computer system. *Exhibit 6.2* illustrates the generation of bill of materials for a product.

Exhibit 6.2 : Bill of Materials Explosion

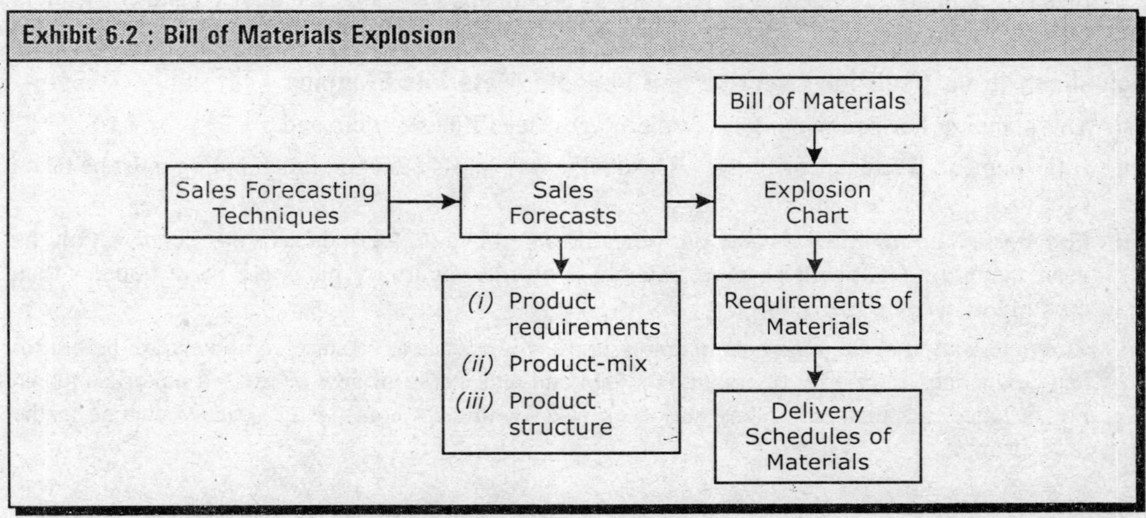

Another approach to materials planning is based on *past consumption analysis*. This method is used for items that are consumed on a continuous basis (*i.e.*, independent demand items) and for which no bill of materials can be prepared. The past consumption data is analysed and a projection for the future is made, taking into account the past and future production programs for end products.

Certain guidelines are worked out for each item based on the "**average**" or **mean** consumption and the **standard deviation** on the *mean* assuming that the consumption follows a "**normal distribution**" (statistical) pattern. The stock levels to be held such as minimum stock levels, maximum stock levels, re-order levels and order quantities are computed using statistical formulae.

Problems Encountered in Materials Planning

(i) Even though materials planning is done based on the short-term sales forecast (usually for quarterly time periods) as the time-horizon (*i.e.*, planning period) extends, sales forecasts become less reliable. Hence, material planners will always have some materials in short-supply or in excess supply and these must be rectified. The ordering is done on suppliers with firm commitments for the whole year and delivery schedules are scheduled on a need basis from time to time.

(ii) There are constraints regarding import policy of the government, foreign exchange components of production requirements, credit availability etc., which affect the efficiency of materials planning.

In order to overcome the above problems, materials planning executives must consider the following:

(i) In working out the materials plan, anticipated lead times for procurement must be taken into account.

(ii) The external environment within which the firm is operating, must be carefully analysed to allow for errors or fluctuations in sales forecasts and/or the effects of seasonal variations in the trend of demand.

(iii) When materials planning extends beyond one year, it becomes more unrealistic because of many uncontrollable factors affecting demand and supply.

(iv) Without a computerised planning and information system, it may become difficult to revise the material estimates, rescheduling deliveries to accommodate changes in demand and consequent changes in production plans.

Guidelines to be Used for Effective and Reliable Materials Planning

(i) The planning horizon should cover the longest lead times anticipated.

(ii) If the demand fluctuates or shows a seasonal variation, its effect on the planning must be taken care of.

(iii) For short planning horizons (say one year) if more planning periods are considered within the year, materials plans will be more reliable. However, quarterly plans are more popular than monthly or weekly plans.

(iv) Computerisation of the materials planning process is advisable because computers are helpful to handle changes caused by fluctuations in demand and work out new or revised materials plans. For instance, the materials plans may be revised within 24 hours of effecting a change in the product mix.

(v) Computerisation of materials planning results in savings in time and effort apart from obtaining accurate forecasts.

Relationship of Materials Planning with Production Programs and Sales Forecasts

For many industries, it is possible to project future sales (*i.e.*, sales forecasts) fairly accurately so that they are closely related to actual sales. In such cases, the production programs are planned to match sales forecasts, which are quite stable. Hence, large quantities of materials and components are ordered prior to the commencement of actual production. When purchases involve longer procurement lead times, for short-run seasonal products, marketable sales volume is controlled by availability of raw materials and components. Thus forecasting of sales and scheduling of deliveries of bought out materials to meet the production needs. When the procurement is planned in such a way that materials are received when they are needed for production, the inventories can be considerably reduced, thereby saving on inventory carrying costs. When the production schedule matches with the sales forecast, the finished goods inventories are at the minimum. The relationship of materials planning with production programs and sales forecasts is shown in *Exhibit 6.3*.

Exhibit 6.3 : Relationship of Materials Planning with Production Programs and Sales Forecasts

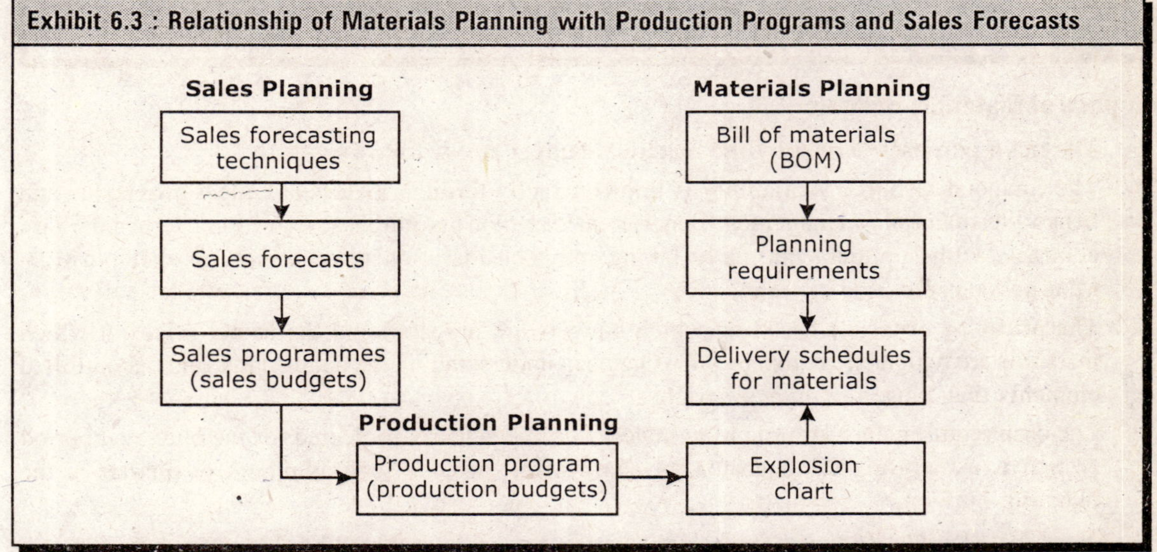

➤ MATERIALS BUDGETING

Once the materials requirements have been established and worked out, the material budget is prepared taking into account inventory on order, and inventory in transit (also known as pipe-line inventory). The process of preparing material budgets is illustrated in *Exhibit 6.4*.

From the *Exhibit 6.4*, it can be seen that the purchase budget (or materials budget) takes into account the inventory on hand and orders on hand. Also, the budget may be formulated to attain certain targeted inventory levels as per the inventory policy of materials management. Usually budgets are formulated both in terms of quantity and money value of materials to be purchased over a period of time (referred to as budgeted period). The financial control aspect is highlighted whenever budgeted expenditure norms are exceeded or actual expenditure falls short of budgeted expenditure. The variances are reported at the end of budgeted period and corrective actions are taken.

Exhibit 6.4 : The Process of Preparing Material Budgets

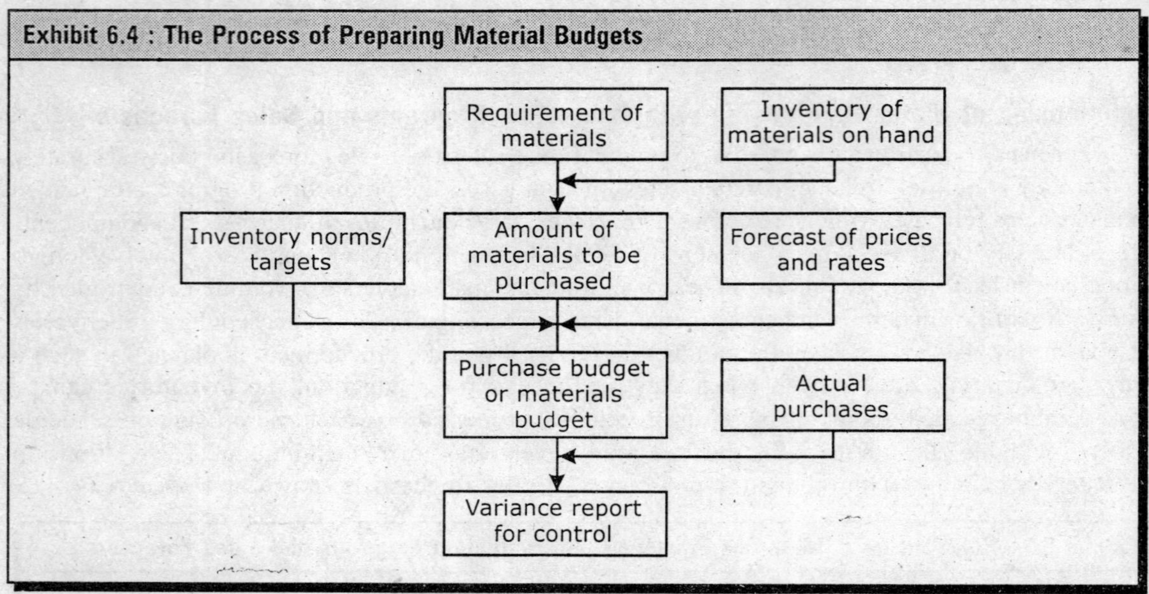

Purpose of Materials Budgets

The main purposes served by the materials budget are as follows :

(i) The financial resource availability is known exactly through materials budget provisions and hence the materials management department can plan its purchases and long term purchase contracts with suppliers optimally taking into consideration price trends, market position, trend in sales etc.

(ii) The prices of materials based on which budgets are prepared and the actual prices at which materials are bought are compared. This helps in understanding the controllable and uncontrolled elements that cause the budget variance.

(iii) The cash requirements for procuring materials can be clearly projected for the budgeted period (which is usually a year) and also for shorter time periods such as month or quarter in the planning horizon.

Need for Flexible Budget : The basic materials budget is prepared based on the sales forecast and the planned production volume for the budgeted period. Since sales forecasts are rarely very accurate and actual production levels deviate from planned levels, the budget becomes erroneous for those items whose costs vary with the level of production (*i.e.,* direct materials). This situation has led to the formulation of flexible budgeting system. The **flexible budget** makes use of supplementary data which adjust variable costs in accordance with the production levels actually experienced.

Also, since materials budget is based on an estimated level of production, preparation of a detailed annual materials budget is practical only for those products whose sales can be forecast reasonably accurately or for materials which are used in a variety of products for which aggregate demand can be forecast accurately. Hence, it becomes difficult for a firm to prepare annual material budgets one full year in advance. Some firms may be able to prepare material budgets only for selected key materials.

Benefits of Materials Budgets

(i) When a material budget is to be expressed in terms of rupees, the purchase manager has to provide the budget department with two types of information. *(i)* estimate of material prices during the coming year and *(ii)* plans for the specific timing of purchases. This information helps the finance department to draw up a realistic schedule of cash requirements for each operating period (a month or a quarter).

(ii) In purchasing, reasonably precise knowledge of materials requirements over an extended period of time facilitates forward buying and permits the advantageous use of contract purchasing and blanket order purchasing techniques.

(iii) Inventory investment and its associated risks can be reduced by advance planning of material requirements.

(iv) Materials budget provide maximum *purchasing lead time.* This facilitates careful selection of qualified suppliers, negotiations without pressure of deadlines and an opportunity to obtain maximum value for each rupee spent.

(v) Additional lead time also produces savings by the use of routine rather than premium (costly) transportation, by a reduction in expediting costs and by smoothing of purchasing work load.

(vi) Supplier relationships can be improved and costs can be reduced because of availability of time to most purchasing requirements with the supplier's production schedule more effectively.

➤ MATERIALS CONTROL

The American Production and Inventory Control Society defines materials control as "The function of maintaining constantly available supply of raw materials, purchased parts and supplies that are required for the manufacture of products". Functional responsibilities include the requisitioning of materials for purchase in economic quantities at the proper time, and their receipts, storage and production, the issuing of materials to production upon authorised request and the maintenance and verification of inventory records.

Importance of Materials Control : Providing raw materials and parts in **proper quantities and when they are needed** is one of the major concerns of any manufacturing organisation. If this is not done properly, workers and machines will be idle and delivery promises will not be met.

In **process industries** the procurement of raw materials and the follow-up to ensure that these materials arrive at the plant when they are needed are the responsibility of vice president of materials or director of purchase. In these industries large quantities of materials must be scheduled into the plant in sufficient quantities to meet the production needs but without excessive accumulation in stock piles.

The **materials control manager** who reports to the materials manager is responsible for ensuring supply of raw materials, parts and supplies to meet the needs of production departments to carry out their production programs. The materials control manager maintains the flow of materials into the plant through production and into finished products storage or into the shipping department. It is a completely centralised and integrated cycle.

To facilitate proper materials control, materials are grouped into classes. Five such classes are: *(i)* **raw materials**, *(ii)* **component parts**, *(iii)* **supplies**, or **indirect items**, *(iv)* **work in-process**, *(v)* **finished products**.

Materials control is usually concerned with the procuring of raw materials and purchased parts and supplying of these to production. Usually in-house manufactured parts, when they are completed, are returned to stores, where they are under the control of materials control department until they are issued to the assembly floor. Also, materials control section sometimes stores and controls supplies and indirect items, (consumables, stationery etc.) recording these when necessary. Work-in-progress is the primary concern of manufacturing department and finished goods may be stored in warehouses under the control of shipping department or sales department. Hence, these two classes of inventory are not a concern of the materials control section.

➤ ORGANISING FOR MATERIALS CONTROL

In most manufacturing operations the provision of materials is a function of the production planning and control manager who normally reports to the Chief Production Manager or Director-Production. The production planning and control manager is responsible for planning the availability of man-power (labour), materials and production facilities so as to achieve the goals/objectives of the production-management function.

The responsibility of production planning and control manager is usually considerably greater than that of the materials control manager. The production planning and control manager is responsible for ensuring that all parts are produced in the plant according to schedule and the finished product is completed and shipped to customer on time. Thus placing materials control under the materials control manager maintains the flow of materials into the plant through production and into finished goods storage and into the shipping department.

A typical organisation of the production planning and control department is shown in *Exhibit 6.5*.

Exhibit 6.5 : Organisation of Typical Production Planning and Control (to include material control)

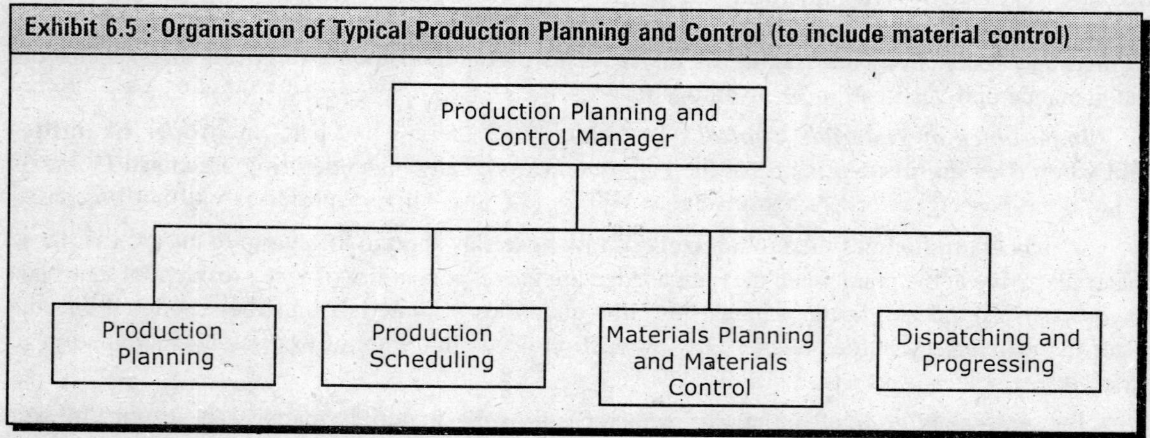

In some cases, inventory planning and control function is combined with materials planning and control function and the materials control manager is made responsible for both these functions.

Establishing the Bases for Materials Control

Some of the important basic decisions which have to be made before properly setting up a materials control system are:

(i) Grouping materials into classes and deciding which department or section is responsible for each class of materials;

(ii) Determining inventory status with reference to the policy of producing finished goods:

(a) To individual customer order only

(b) To a grouping of customer orders.

(c) To a grouping of customer orders plus stock orders for finished items.

(d) To stock by means of a sales forecast or production schedule.

(iii) Modifying control methods and stock status according to the value of the items involved.

The above steps must be taken before setting up a materials control system on a proper basis. The consideration involved in each of the above decisions are discussed in the following paragraphs:

(i) Grouping Materials into Classes :

Materials can be grouped or classified according to their general nature, use or physical condition. Accordingly materials can be classified as:

(i) **Raw materials** which comprise items that must be purchased and processed to convert them into component parts which are then assembled into a finished product.

(ii) **Component parts** which are used in finished assemblies or for maintenance spare parts and are of two kinds:

(a) Parts purchased from vendors in the completed form to be used in the assemblies or as spare parts,

(b) Parts produced in the plant from raw materials and then used in assemblies or as spare parts.

(iii) **Supplies or indirect items** which are used in the production process but do not form a part of the finished product. Such items are usually purchased. They include cutting oils, lubricating oils, coolants, cleaning solutions, cotton waste, janitor's supplies, office supplies, construction materials, spare parts for repair and maintenance of machines and equipments etc.

(iv) **Work-in-process** which includes all materials, parts, sub-assemblies and assemblies that actually undergo production operations or which are in temporary storage between processes or operations in manufacturing departments.

(v) **Finished products** which are units or major assemblies carried in stock in complete form ready for delivery to customers.

The raw materials, component parts, work-in-process and finished products are referred to as **direct materials** because they go into the product or are the product which is delivered to the customer. Supplies do not form a part of the finished product and hence referred to as **indirect materials**.

Materials control is generally concerned with the procurement of **raw materials** and **purchased items** and supplying them to production. Usually, those parts which are produced in-house using the raw materials are stored in holding stores in assembly department and are controlled by materials control department until they are issued to the assembly floor or assembly line.

The materials control department in some organisations stores and controls supplies and indirect items such as spare parts for maintenance department, reordering them when necessary.

Work-in-process is the primary concern of production department since this comprises all materials which are at various stages in the conversion process controlled by the production manager.

Finished products are often shipped directly to customers by the shipping department or they may be stored in warehouses under the control of sales and distribution managers of marketing department.

The work-in-process and finished products are usually not a concern of materials control section or department.

Materials Utilisation: In the flow of materials through the manufacturing process, certain losses occur due to shrinkage, defective workmanship, scrap and the like. In the design process, expected losses, scrap and shrinkage are specified and taken into consideration in estimating the materials requirement and also in materials costing. Materials utilisation provides a measure of the effectiveness of the estimates of required materials.

$$\text{Materials utilisation} = \frac{\text{Output(yield)} + \text{Expected scrap}}{\text{Input}}$$

For example, suppose 10 tons of plastic granules are required to make 8 tons of a plastic moulded part as per design and at the material utilisation rate of 100%. But in actual production, if 12 tons of plastic granules are used to produce the mouldings, then material utilisation would be 10/12 or 83.33%.

Optimum Stock Requirements: The most important determinant of which materials to stock is the lead time between receipt of customer order and the time when the finished product must be shipped. The lead time determines the minimum inventory which the company must carry by classes of materials.

Other reasons for stocking standard parts and raw materials, even though there would be sufficient lead time to purchase them after receipt of customer order are:

(i) **Price advantage** due to purchasing or producing parts in larger quantities than presently needed.

(ii) **Flexibility advantage** for producing on short notice additional quantities of finished goods over and above those forecast or scheduled.

(iii) **Protection against market change:** Some additional stock of raw materials and purchased parts are held to avoid production stoppage when supplies are delayed (*i.e.*, lead time for procurement gets extended beyond the normal lead time).

Materials Control Cycle : The materials control cycle comprises all of those procedures which are necessary for the provision of materials for the manufacturing process with a minimum investment and at lowest cost possible. A knowledge of this cycle is fundamental to an understanding of the principles and practice of materials control. The various steps in the **materials control cycle** are as follows.

(i) Determining materials needs.

(ii) Preparing requisitions for purchased items and requests for work orders for parts made in the shops.

(iii) Receiving purchased materials and finished parts into the plant.

(iv) Inspecting purchased materials and parts and inspection of finished shop made parts. Delivering all parts and materials to the stores for storage.

(v) Entering receipts in stores records, apportioning materials in the records to current orders, authorising requisitions of materials from stores for production of shop parts and requisitions of parts from stores for assembly into finished products.

(vi) Issuing of parts and materials to the shop for production and assembly.

(vii) Recording the issue in store records.

(viii) Entry of receiving and issuing transactions to cost and accouning records.

(ix) Determination of necessity for replacement of stores which leads to step number one and the cycle repeats.

Other activities of materials control section are :

(i) Determining the proper quantity to requisition for each item of materials for each purchased and manufactured part.

(ii) Physical stock checking in stores to check quantity on hand of each part and materials in order to verify the balances shown in stock on store records.

(iii) Standardising materials and parts for lowest cost manufacturing or purchasing.

Records and Procedures for Materials Control

Bill of Materials: Most fabrication and assembly manufacturing organisations are required to keep records that describe the structure of the products to be manufactured. These records are needed for planning and implementing the manufacturing process. Product structure records are referred to as *bills of materials*, *parts lists* or *where-used lists*.

A centralised bill of materials file (computerised) should be maintained to serve the requirements of engineering, finance, purchase and manufacturing departments.

Normally, the product structure records would be kept in two sequences:

(a) Assembly or bill-of-materials sequence

(b) Where used.

Product structure data originate in the engineering department (or Research and Development department) from the design process. The data are usually released as a series of lists of materials or assemblies showing a detailed break-down of the following:

(i) Top level assemblies into sub-assemblies

(ii) Sub-assemblies into fabricated detailed parts and purchased part numbers

(iii) Fabricated parts into raw materials used.

The bill of materials lists the components of the assembly along with the quantity used per assembly. The next any-where used list shows the higher level assemblies on which a particular assembly is used and the quantity required and end item use, showing the end items or end products on which this assembly is used and the total quantity used.

(i) **Multilevel Bills of Materials:** The product structure can be displayed as a "tree" or a series of levels or tiers as shown in *Exhibit 6.6* below.

Exhibit 6.6 : Product Structure Tree

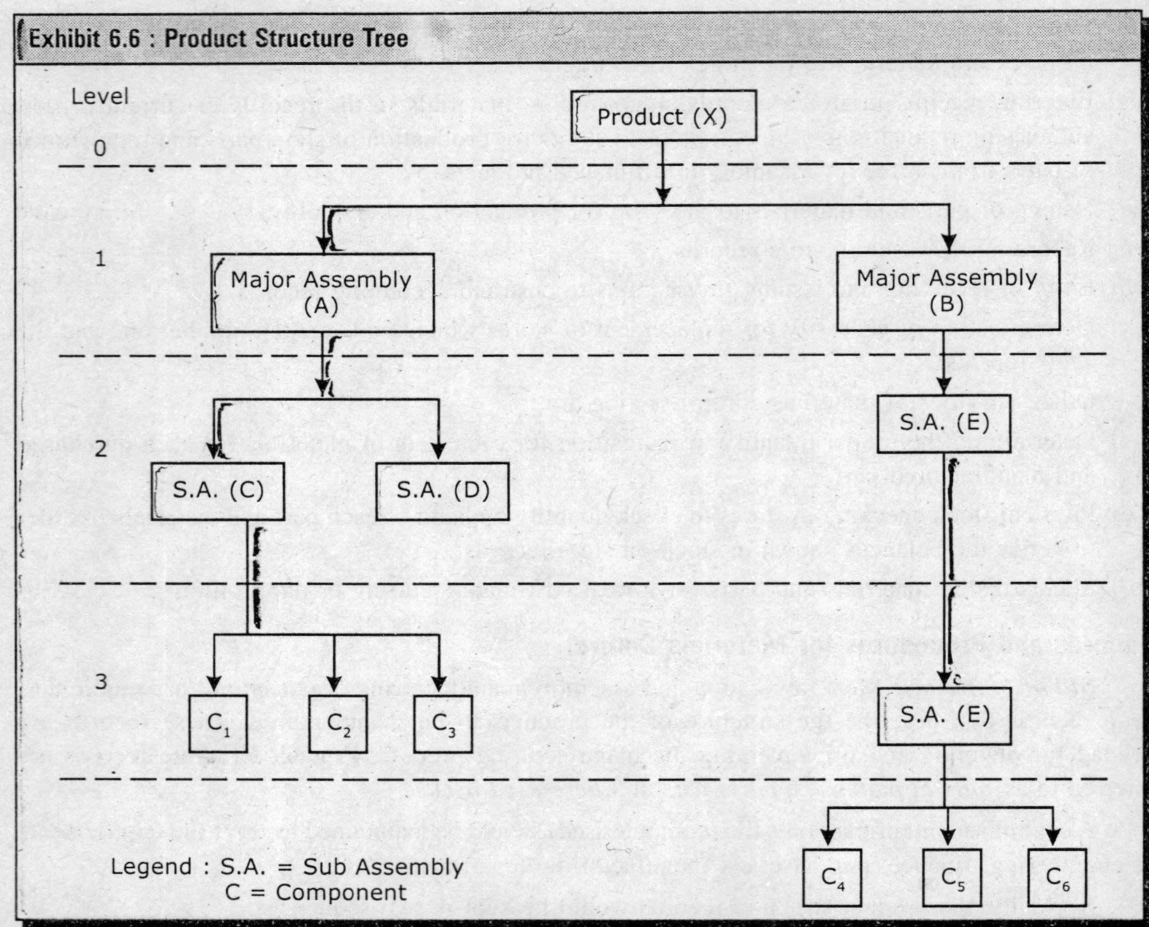

This product structure tree shows that Product (X) is broken down into major assemblies (A) and (B). These major assemblies, in-turn, are broken down into multiple levels of sub-assemblies down to the level of individual components making up the subassemblies.

(ii) **Bill of Materials Explosion:** This refers to a retrieval process which divides a product or an assembly into its immediate components or lower level components through their sub-assemblies. The outcome of the explosion results in an assembly order depicting the quantity per assembly of the various components required.

(iii) **Bill of Materials Implosion:** This retrieval technique traces the direct or indirect uses of a part on higher level assemblies. This is the explosion process which is in the backward direction. The implosion process shows where the part is used throughout the assembly. It is also useful to show which assemblies will be affected and when, by late delivery of a basic component.

(ii) Determining Materials Needs

Material control department uses order systems for standard items, parts, components, supplies and spare parts determined by a feasibility study. Two different methods for ordering standard stock items are *(i)* **fixed order system** and *(ii)* **periodic reordering system**. These systems will be discussed in detail later in the chapter titled "Inventory Management".

Fixed Order System: In this system materials are re-ordered whenever the stock on hand reaches a certain predetermined level (referred to as re-order level) established by usage and ordering policy. Orders are placed whenever the balance declines to this re-order level. At that point, a new order is placed for a quantity equal to or greater than an economical-order quantity (referred to as EOQ). This order point is also called the "review point".

Stores Record Method: The simplest form of a stores record or **perpetual inventory card** shows the receipts, issues and balance on hand at any point of time. Receipts are posted on bin cards from receiving reports. Issues are posted from stores requisition (or material requisition) for materials or parts from the user departments. The difference between the quantity received and the quantity issued is the balance in stock. The posting of receipts and issues and the balance in stock may be done manually or by using a personal computer.

Allocation Method: Allocating or appropriating of materials is carried out when the production programmes are originated. When the kinds and quantities of products to be made in the forthcoming period are scheduled, materials are ordered in kinds and quantities to carry on such production and to deliver finished products at the time specified. The stores records are set up so that by including "**allocation**" and "**available**" columns in the record, materials may be allotted (or reserved) to current orders in advance of production. This plan avoids stock outs which may happen when the stores record shows only the balance on hand of the needed items and not how much of each will be withdrawn for work still to go into manufacturing.

The stores record indicates the following: *(a)* Quantity on order (total) *(b)* Quantity on hand (balance) *(c)* Quantity allocated (total) and *(d)* Quantity available.

The correctness of the record can be checked against the equation:

[Quantity on order (total) + Quantity on hand (balance)]

= [Quantity allocated (total) + Quantity available]

Demand and Supply Methods : Demand and supply methods of materials control utilise principles of planning the demand for and supply of each item at the lowest cost possible and the lowest possible inventory consistent with operating requirements.

Economic purchasing and manufacturing lot sizes are also developed to minimise the total cost of procuring, storing and utilising each specific item of materials and parts. In order to use this method of materials control, the following information must be known or estimated for each part and raw material item controlled:

(i) **Average usage:** The expected usage of the particular part or raw material in the future.

(ii) **Lead time:** The average elapsed time between the initiation of the order paper work and the receipt of the materials from the vendor or the in-house manufacturing shop.

(iii) **Reorder point:** The quantity expected to be consumed during the replenishment lead time plus a reserve quantity.

Reorder point or reorder level = Normal lead time in time period (say weeks)
× Average usage in time period (say weeks)
plus a reserve quantity.

(iv) **Reserve stock:** An extra quantity which is kept on hand to take care of greater than normal usage during the replenishment lead time or an average usage during the extension of normal lead time or both.

(v) **Economic order quantity:** The quantity which is most economical to order and stock, considering all factors bearing on the situation.

All the above terminologies used will be explained in detail in the later chapter on "Inventory Management".

Requisitions for New Orders : Requisitions for the purchase of production material or for making a part in the manufacturing shop are usually initiated by the materials control section. The various ways to initiate **requisition for procuring materials**, depending on the method of control are:

(i) On the fixed-order basis, purchase orders and shop requisitions (for manufacturing parts in-house) are initiated whenever the reorder point (or reorder level) is reached for the stock items. Special items are purchased or produced as needed.

(ii) On the periodic order basis, requisitions for purchased raw materials and parts are initiated whenever manufacturing schedules are reviewed and the need to place orders determined.

Purchase Requisitions : The sources of purchase requisitions for specific purchases are mainly: *(i)* the materials control section, for items carried regularly in stores and controlled through store records *(ii)* the production planning or scheduling section, for production items which are not regularly stored or which are controlled by a production schedule and *(iii)* individuals authorised to issue purchase requisitions as needs arise.

Receiving and Inspection of Inwards Goods : In many companies, receiving is a function of materials control although sometimes materials control takes over after the materials are received, inspected and accepted at the inwards goods or transit stores. The basic receiving functions are unloading and unpacking materials received, checking materials against purchase order and invoice, having any necessary inspection carried out, preparing receiving and inspection reports, putting materials into standard containers and delivering the materials to the store room.

➤ REVIEW QUESTIONS

1. What is materials planning?
2. Discuss the significance of materials planning.
3. State the benefits of materials planning.
4. Discuss the factors affecting materials planning.
5. Describe the approach to materials planning.
6. What is "Bill of Materials"? What is its relevance in materials planning?
7. Discuss the problems encountered in materials planning.
8. Mention the guidelines to be used for effective and reliable materials planning.
9. Discuss the relationships among materials planning, production program and sales forecasts.
10. What is materials budgeting?
11. State the main purposes served by the materials budgets.
12. Discuss the need for flexible budgets in materials budgeting.
13. State the benefits of materials budgets.
14. What is "material control"?
15. Bring out the importance of materials control.

16. What is a "materials control cycle"? What are the various steps involved in it? Explain.
17. What is meant by organising for material control?
18. Explain how various bases are established for material control.
19. What is meant by "materials utilisation"?
20. Explain some of the records and procedures used in materials control.
21. Write short notes on: *(i)* Bill of materials, *(ii)* Product structure tree, *(iii)* Bill of materials explosion, *(iv)* Bill of materials implosion, *(v)* Multi-level bill of materials.
22. Discuss the following functions of materials control section:
    (i) Determining materials needs.
    (ii) Stores recording and allocating.
    (iii) Determining the supply quantities to meet demand.
    (iv) Initiating purchase requisitions for new orders.
    (v) Receiving and inspecting inwards goods.

❖ ❖ ❖ ❖

INVENTORY MANAGEMENT

CHAPTER 7

Inventory analysis is one of the most popular topics in Production and Materials Management. One reason is that almost all types of business organisations have inventory. For many firms inventory is the largest current asset. Inventory is usually thought in terms of stock of materials or idle goods that are held by an organisation for use some time in the future. Inventory also includes partially finished products at different stages of a manufacturing process, raw materials and components, resources, finished products, labour or cash. The purpose of inventory is to meet customer demand, to avoid stock-out of materials which may cause stoppage of production or even to hedge against strikes and lock-outs and to meet uncertainties in supply from vendors. Whatever form inventory takes or whatever its purpose, it often represents a significant cost to a business firm. If a firm carries excessive inventories, it is estimated that the average annual cost of carrying inventory would be approximately 30% of the total value of inventory held by the firm. Conversely, if the firm is a manufacturer, the stock-out could, in extreme cases, bring production to a halt and cause huge losses due to idling of machinery, equipments and labour. Hence, if the amount of inventory could be reduced to an optimal level, both stock-out cost and inventory carrying cost can be reduced to the minimum possible level. Skillful inventory management can make a significant contribution to a firm's profit.

➤ NATURE AND IMPORTANCE OF INVENTORY

The term inventory refers to any resource that has a certain value, which can be used at a future occasion when the demand arises. Alternatively inventory may be defined as **"stock of items kept on hand by an organisation to be used to meet customer demand"**.

Virtually every type of organisation maintains some form of inventory. A department stores or retail store carries inventories of all the retail items it sells, a family household maintains inventories of food, clothing, medical supplies, an automobile dealer maintains inventory of automobiles, a manufacturing firm maintains inventory of raw materials, bought-out components, semifinished goods or work-in-progress items, finished goods, spare parts for maintenance of equipments and machinery, inventory of skilled labour, liquid funds such as cash and also inventory of plant and equipment.

In an organisation, the importance of inventory can be recognised for the following reasons.

(a) Inventories represent resources acquired at a cost, thereby locking up substantial working capital.

(b) Inventories allow for smooth flow of production process by ensuring that adequate supply of raw materials, components and manufactured items are available to the production lines.

(c) Inventories serve as buffers against uncertain and fluctuating usage and reduce stock-out situations, thereby avoiding production hold-ups and loss of customer good will.

The inventory problem is common to all organisations and poses a challenge to management. The specific questions for which satisfactory answers have to be found by the managers are :

(i) What are the inventories that have to be acquired and maintained?

(ii) From what sources should they be acquired?

(iii) How much of the inventories should be acquired when inventory replenishment is needed?

(iv) When should the inventories be replenished?

➤ CLASSIFICATION OF INVENTORIES

Inventories are usually classified as :

(a) **Raw materials**, *(b)* **Bought-out components** or **sub-assemblies**, *(c)* **Semi-finished goods** or **work-in-progress** or **work-in-process**, *(d)* **Consumable stores**, *(e)* **Maintenance spare parts**, *(f)* **Finished goods stored** or **in transit to warehouses or customers**.

Box 7.1 lists the various types of inventory

Box 7.1 : Types of Inventory

***(A)* Based on nature of materials**

(i) **Production Inventories :** Raw materials, parts and component which become part of the firm's finished product in the production process.

(ii) **MRO Inventories :** Maintenance, repair and operating supplies which are consumed in the production process, but which do not become part of the finished product (*e.g.*, lubricants, grease cotton waste, spare parts for machine repairs).

(iii) **In-process Inventories :** Also known as "work-in-process" or work-in-progress or semi-finished goods inventories – these are parts or sub assemblies found at various stages in the production process.

(iv) **Finished Goods Inventories :** Completed products kept in stores ready for shipment.

***(B)* Classified by how it is created**

(i) **Cycle Inventory :** The position of total inventory which varies directly with lot size (*i.e.*, quantity ordered). *For example,* if Q is the order quantity or the lot size and the supply is received exactly when the stock is nil, then the minimum inventory is nil, maximum inventory is Q and the average cycle inventory is half of quantity ordered.

(ii) **Safety Stock Inventory :** Safety stock inventories are held to avoid stock out conditions which cause production stoppages and to project against uncertainties in demand, lead time, supply and consumption rates.

(iii) **Anticipation Inventory :** Inventory of materials purchased in bulk quantities in anticipation of price rise and products having seasonal demand produced in quantities more than the demand during off-seasons and held in inventory to meet higher demand rate (more than production rate) during seasons of high demand.

(iv) **Pipe-line Inventory :** Inventory moving from point to point in the materials flow system. Materials move from supplier to a plant, from one operation to the next in the plant and from the plant to the warehouse or distribution centre or to the customer. Pipe line inventories also include materials that have been ordered but not received.

(v) **Fluctuation Inventory :** Inventory held as reserve stock to meet the unexpected fluctuating demand over a period which cannot be predicted accurately.

➤ FUNCTIONS OF INVENTORY

One reason organisations maintain inventory is that it is rarely possible to predict sales levels, production levels, demand and usage patterns exactly. In such situations, inventory serves as a buffer against uncertain and fluctuating demand and keeps a supply of items available in case items are needed by the organisation or its customers.

The many functions that inventories perform can be summarised as follows :

(a) **Smoothing out irregularities in supply :** Inventories provide a buffer to overcome the problems of uncertainties in supplies such as delayed deliveries and supply of short quantities by vendors as against the promised delivery schedules and quantities. Also, the customer demand for the goods may increase suddenly which affects the ability of the manufacturer to meet the customer demand. In such cases also, an inventory of finished goods held in the warehouses will act as a buffer against the uncertainties in demand. Thus, inventories fill the gap between supply and demand.

(b) **Buying or producing in lots or batches :** When the demand for an item does not justify its continued production throughout the year, it is produced in batches or lots on an intermittent basis. During the time when the item is not being produced, demands are met from the inventory which is accumulated by batch production.

(c) **To meet seasonal or cyclical demand :** Companies will produce items at a constant production rate more than the demand rate in order to meet the seasonal demand occurring at a later period for which the production capacity is insufficient.

(d) **To take advantage of price discounts while buying items :** A company will often purchase large amounts of inventory to take advantage of price discounts, as a hedge against anticipated price increases in the future. In some cases large quantities are ordered because the cost of an order may be very high and it is more cost-effective to have higher inventories than to order small quantities several number of times in an year.

(e) **To maintain continuity to operations in production processes :** Many companies find it necessary to maintain in-process inventories at different stages in a manufacturing process to provide independence between operations and to avoid work stoppages or delays and to continue production smoothly if there are temporary machine breakdowns or other work stoppages.

Box 7.2 summarises the functions of inventory.

Box 7.2 : Functions of Inventory

The most important functions of inventory are :

(i) To meet anticipated demand.

(ii) To smooth production requirements.

(iii) To decouple components of the production - distribution system.

(iv) To protect against stockouts.

(v) To take advantage of order cycles.

(vi) To take advantage of quantity discounts.

(vii) To hedge against price increases.

INVENTORY COSTS

There are two types of costs associated with inventory namely :

(a) Costs associated with the purchase of inventory items *i.e.,* cost of materials purchased.

(b) Costs on materials consisting of three basic costs namely,

(i) **Ordering costs or acquisition costs** which are costs associated with the placement of an order for the acquisition or replenishment of the stock of inventory. Ordering costs are expressed as rupees per order and are independent of the order size. Ordering costs per year vary with the number of orders placed in an year. Costs incurred each time an order is made can include requisition costs, purchase orders, transportation and shipping, receiving, inspection, handling and placing in storage, accounting, bills payment and auditing costs.

(ii) **Carrying or holding costs** are the costs of holding items in storage. These vary with the level of inventory and with the length of time an item is held *i.e.,* the greater the level of inventory over time, the higher the carrying cost. Carrying costs include the direct storage costs such as rent, lighting, security, refrigeration, record keeping, interest on capital tied up in holding the inventory (*i.e.,* cost of capital), depreciation of equipments used for materials handling, costs due to pilferage, spoilage, obsolescence, and taxes and also the cost of opportunity lost due to loss of funds tied up in inventory.

Carrying costs are expressed as rupees per unit of item held in inventory per time period such as a month or year. Alternately, carrying costs are sometimes expressed as a percentage of the value of an item or as a percentage of average inventory value per year.

(iii) **Shortage costs,** also referred as stock-out costs, occur when customer demand can not be met because of insufficient inventory on hand. Shortages may result in permanent loss of sales of items demanded but not provided, resulting in loss of profits. Shortages can also cause customer dissatisfaction and a loss of goodwill which may result in permanent loss of customers and future sales. In some instances delayed deliveries to customers due to shortages may result in specified penalties in the form of price discounts or rebates. When demand is internal, a shortage can cause work stoppages in the production process and create delays resulting in downtime costs and cost of lost production.

The three costs are related to each other in some way or the other. The ordering costs per year decreases as the order size (*i.e.,* the quantity ordered in each order) increases, thereby decreasing the number of orders per year. However, an attempt to place few orders per year results in bigger order size which in turn increases the average inventory held and the carrying cost or holding cost. Shortage occurs because it is too costly to carry inventory in stock. As a result shortage costs are inversely related to carrying costs. As the amount of inventory on hand increases, the carrying cost increases while shortage costs decrease. The objective of inventory management is to employ an inventory control system that will indicate **how much should be ordered** and **when orders should be placed** in order to minimise the sum of the three costs *i.e.,* ordering costs, carrying costs and shortage costs.

➢ INVENTORY DECISIONS

There are two basic inventory decisions managers must take in order to effectively manage inventories. They are :

1. **How much of an item should be ordered when the inventory is replenished?**
2. **When should the inventory be replenished?**

Inventory Models

We will first consider *deterministic* inventory models in which we assume that the rate of demand for the item is constant or nearly constant. Later we will consider *probabilistic* inventory models in which the demand for the item fluctuates and can be described only in probabilistic terms.

Deterministic Inventory Models

1. Economic Order Quantity (EOQ) Model

The EOQ model is applicable when the demand for an item has a constant or nearly constant rate and when the entire quantity ordered arrives in inventory at one point of time (instantaneously).

The EOQ model system is also known as **fixed-order quantity system (Q system)** or **a continuous** or **perpetual review system.** In this system order is placed for the same constant or fixed amount (known as economic order quantity) whenever the inventory on hand reaches a certain predetermined level known as **re-order level** or **re-order point.** Continual record of inventory level for every item is maintained. The order that is placed to replenish the stock of inventory is for a fixed quantity which minimises the total inventory carrying, ordering and shortage costs.

A positive feature of a continuous review system is that inventory level is closely and continuously monitored so that management always knows the inventory status. This is advantageous for critical items such as replacement parts of raw materials or supplies.

The function of the EOQ model, also referred to as the economic lot size model is to determine the *optimal order size* that minimises total inventory costs.

There are several variations of the EOQ model, depending on the assumptions made about the inventory system. Three such variations are : *(a)* the basic EOQ model, *(b)* the EOQ model with non-instantaneous receipt or gradual arrival of supplies and *(c)* the EOQ model with shortages.

1. The Basic EOQ Model

The formula for EOQ and Re-order level are derived under a set of simplifying and restrictive assumptions, as follows :

- Demand is known with certainty and is relatively constant over time.
- No shortages are allowed.

– Lead time for the receipt of orders is constant.

– The order quantity is received all at once *i.e.,* instantaneously.

The *Exhibit 7.1* illustrates these basic model assumptions.

Exhibit 7.1 : Basic Inventory Model (Instantaneous Supply)

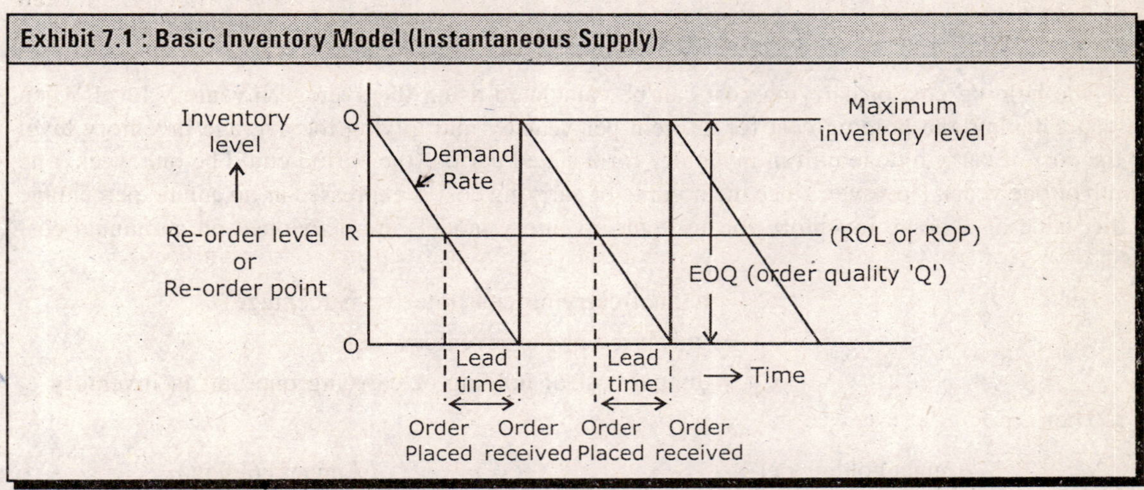

The diagram above describes the continuous inventory order cycle system inherent in the EOQ model. An order quantity 'Q' is received and is used up over time at a constant rate. When the inventory level decreases to the re-order point 'R', a new order is placed and a period of time referred to as the lead time, is required for delivery. The order is received all at once just at the moment when demand has used up the entire stock of inventory (*i.e.,* the inventory level reaches zero), thus allowing no shortages. This cycle is continuously repeated for the same order quantity, re-order point and lead time. *Box 7.3* lists the assumptions used in the basic EOQ model.

Box 7.3 : Assumptions Used in the Basic EOQ Model

(i) Only one product is involved.
(ii) Annual demand requirements are known.
(iii) Demand is spread evenly throughout the year.
(iv) Demand rate for the item is constant and known with certainty.
(v) No constraints (*e.g.,* truck capacity or materials handling limitations) on the size of each lot.
(vi) Only two relevant costs are the inventory carrying cost and the ordering cost.
(vii) No uncertainty in lead time or supply. The lead time is constant and known with certainty.
(viii) Each order is received in a single delivery.
(ix) Quantity received is exactly what was ordered and it arrives at once (*i.e.,* instantaneous supply).
(x) There are no quantity discounts.

Derivation of EOQ Formula

(a) The How-Much-To Order Decision

Let 'D' be the annual demand for an item in units. If 'Q' is the order size (*i.e.,* EOQ) to be determined then, the number of orders/year $= \frac{D}{Q}$.

Let C_o be the cost per order or ordering cost.

Then, annual ordering cost $= \left(\begin{matrix}\text{Number of orders}\\ \text{per year}\end{matrix}\right) \times (\text{Cost per order})$

$$= \frac{D}{Q} C_o$$

The holding cost or carrying cost can be calculated using the average inventory level. Then we can calculate the holding cost for an item per year by multiplying the average inventory level by the cost of carrying one unit in inventory for a stated period (the period could be one week, one month or one year). However, since the holding or carrying cost is expressed as an annual percentage of the value of average inventory for an item, inventory models are developed on an annual cost basis.

Let C_i = annual carrying cost rate (as percentage)

p = unit price of the inventory item

C_e = annual cost of holding or carrying one unit in inventory

Then $C_e = pC_i$

$$\left.\begin{matrix}\text{Annual holding or}\\ \text{carrying cost}\end{matrix}\right\} = (\text{Average Inventory Level}) \times \left(\begin{matrix}\text{Annual holding}\\ \text{cost per unit}\end{matrix}\right)$$

$$\text{Average inventory} = \frac{\text{Initial Inventory} + \text{Final Inventory}}{2}$$

$$= \frac{Q+0}{2} = \frac{Q}{2}$$

Exhibit 7.2 illustrates calculation of average inventory

Exhibit 7.2 : Calculation of Average Inventory

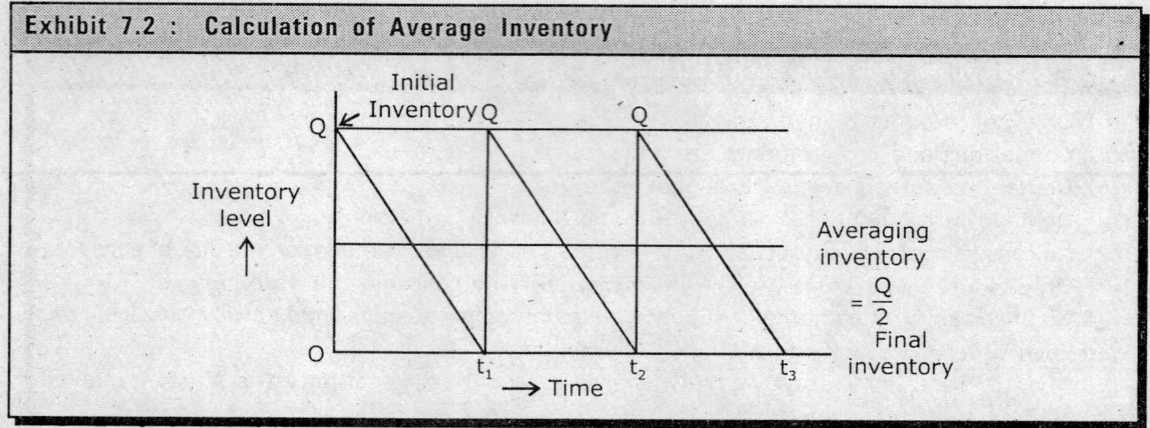

$$\left.\begin{matrix}\text{Annual holding}\\ \text{or carrying cost}\end{matrix}\right\} = \left(\frac{Q}{2}\right) \times C_c$$

Total annual inventory cost = Annual ordering cost + Annual holding cost

$$TC = \frac{D}{Q} C_o + \left(\frac{Q}{2}\right) \times C_c$$

The cost functions are illustrated in *Exhibit 7.3*.

Exhibit 7.3 : Cost Functions

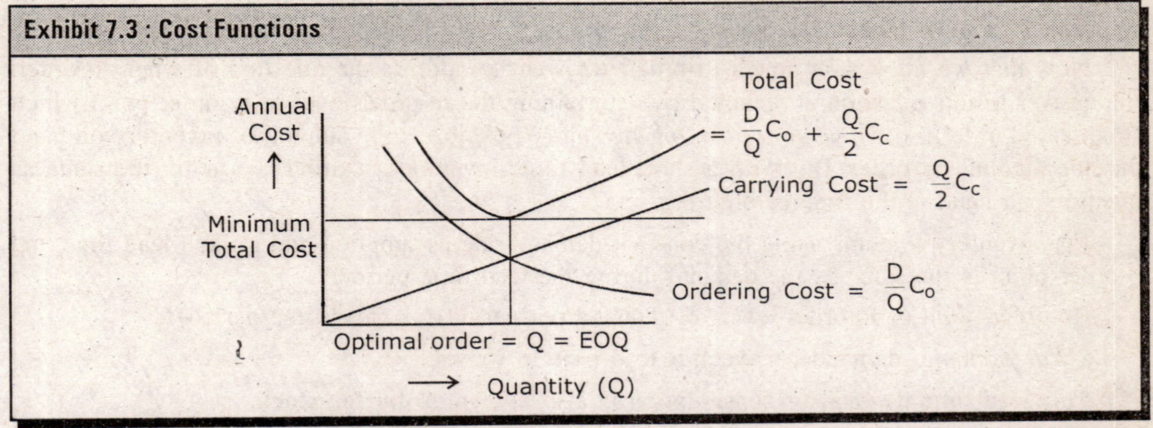

The optimal order quantity occurs at the point where the total cost curve is at the minimum, which also coincides exactly with the point where the ordering cost curve intersects with the carrying cost curve. This enables us to determine the optimal values of the order quantity (Q) or EOQ by equating the two cost functions and solving for Q as follows :

$$\frac{D}{Q}C_o = \frac{Q}{2} \times C_c$$

or $$Q^2 = \frac{2\,DC_o}{C_c}$$

or $$Q = \sqrt{\frac{2\,DC_o}{C_c}}, \text{ where } C_c = p\,C_i$$

Alternately, the optimal value of Q can be determined by differentiating the total cost equation with respect to Q and equating the resulting function to zero and then solving for Q as follows :

$$TC = \frac{D}{Q}C_o + \left(\frac{Q}{2}\right) \times C_c$$

$$\frac{dTC}{dQ} = -\frac{DC_o}{Q^2} + \frac{C_c}{2}$$

$$0 = -\frac{DC_o}{Q^2} + \frac{C_c}{2}$$

or $$\frac{DC_o}{Q^2} = \frac{C_c}{2}$$

or $$Q^2 = \frac{2\,DC_o}{C_c}$$

or $$Q_{(EOQ)} = \sqrt{\frac{2\,DC_o}{C_c}} = Q_{opt}$$

$$\text{Minimum Total Cost, } TC_{minimum} = \frac{D}{Q_{opt}}C_o + \frac{Q_{opt}}{2} \times C_c$$

(b) **The When-To-Order Decision**

Now that we know how much to order, we want to address the question of when to order. The answer to this question is obtained by determining the re-order level or re-order point which is expressed in terms of *inventory position*. Inventory position is the amount of inventory on hand plus the amount on order. But with a short lead time, inventory position is usually the same as inventory on hand at the time of ordering.

For inventory systems using the constant demand rate assumption and a fixed lead time, the re-order point is the same as the demand during the lead time period.

Re-order point or Reorder level = (demand per period)* × (lead time period)*

* *For example,* demand per week × lead time in weeks.

This lead time demand or consumption is also known as **buffer stock**.

(c) **Calculation of Cycle Time**

The question of how frequently the order will be placed (or the time interval between two successive orders) can now be answered. The period between orders is referred to as the cycle time which is determined as follows:

$$\left.\begin{array}{r}\text{Optimal number of}\\ \text{orders per year}\end{array}\right\} = N$$

$$= \frac{D}{Q_{opt}} = \frac{D}{\sqrt{\dfrac{2DC_o}{C_c}}} = \sqrt{\frac{DC_c}{2C_o}}$$

$$\text{The cycle time T} = \frac{\text{No. of days per year}}{N} \text{ days} \quad \textit{i.e.,} \quad \frac{365}{N} \text{ days}$$

$$= \frac{\text{No. of weeks per year}}{N} \text{ weeks} \quad \textit{i.e.,} \quad \frac{52}{N} \text{ weeks}$$

$$= \frac{\text{No. of months per year}}{N} \text{ months} \quad \textit{i.e.,} \quad \frac{12}{N} \text{ months}$$

The Manager's Use of the EOQ Model

The EOQ model results in a recommended order quantity (say, Q units). But this quantity need not be the final decision of the manager. He may have to exercise his judgement into establishing the final inventory policy regarding how much to order (*i.e.,* EOQ or otherwise) and when to order (*i.e.,* the order level or re-order point). The decision maker may have to modify the final order quantity and re-order level recommendation to meet the unique circumstances of the inventory situation. Several alternatives may arise such as :

(a) Ordering a quantity more than EOQ if the vendor offers a lesser unit price for higher order quantities.

(b) Ordering a quantity which will result in whole number of orders per year, even though their order quantity is slightly more or less than EOQ.

(c) Ordering a quantity other than EOQ which may be stipulated by the vendor as the minimum order quantity (*i.e.,* MOQ) which he may accept to supply.

(d) Ordering a quantity deviating from EOQ to facilitate cheaper transportation cost.

Also, the inventory control manager may have to recognise the fact that EOQ model is based on the constant demand rate assumption whereas in reality the demand rate may fluctuate from time to time. Also, the reorder level is so fixed that the EOQ order when arrives, the inventory level reaches zero level. This assumes that the lead time assumed will be exactly met by the supplier which may not be the case in reality. The estimation of lead time exactly becomes critical to protect against shortages. Hence, to protect against shortages due to higher than expected demand or slightly delayed incoming orders, the inventory control manager may have to increase the re-order level by some amount. This quantity by which the reorder level exceeds the expected lead-time demand is referred to as **safety stock.**

Quantity Discounts for the EOQ Model

It is often possible for a customer to receive a price discount on an item if a predetermined number of units is ordered. The basic EOQ model can be used to determine the optimal order size with quantity discounts, however, the application of the model is slightly altered. The total inventory cost function must now include the purchase order price (*i.e.,* cost of materials ordered) as follows:

$$TC = \frac{D}{Q}C_o + \frac{Q}{2}C_c + Dp$$

Where, p = per unit price of the item

D = Annual demand in units

The optimal order size will not change with the purchase price. However, when a discount price is available associated with a specific order size that may be different from the optimal order size, the customer must evaluate the trade-off between possibly high carrying costs with the discount quantity versus EOQ cost.

Quantity discounts can be evaluated using the basic EOQ model under two different options – with constant carrying costs and with carrying cost as a percentage of the purchase price. In this case of quantity discount, carrying cost will vary with the change in price if it is computed as a percentage of purchase price. Assume that we have a product in which the basic EOQ model is applicable. Then the optimal order quantity $Q_{opt} = \sqrt{\frac{2\,DC_o}{pC_i}}$ where 'p' is the unit price and C_i is the carrying cost as a percentage.

If the supplier quotes the following discount schedule,

Order size 0 to Q_1 – Discount x_1% Unit price p_1

Order size > Q_1, < Q_2 – Discount x_2% Unit price p_2

Order size > Q_2, < Q_3 – Discount x_3% Unit price p_3

Then, we should prepare a thorough cost analysis before making a final ordering and inventory policy recommendation.

The EOQ model provides EOQ = $Q_{opt} = \sqrt{\frac{2DC_o}{pC_i}}$

With three discount categories providing three different unit prices, we obtain

$$Q_{opt1} = \sqrt{\frac{2DC_o}{p_1C_i}} \quad ; \quad Q_{opt2} = \sqrt{\frac{2DC_o}{p_2C_i}} \quad ; \quad Q_{opt3} = \sqrt{\frac{2DC_o}{p_3C_i}}$$

Since the only difference in the EOQs calculated as above are slight difference in the carrying cost due to differences in unit price, the EOQ resulting from the above formulae will be approximately same. However, these optimal order quantities will usually not all be of the size necessary to qualify for the discount price offered.

Hence, we have to examine the feasibility of the optimal order quantities calculated as above by comparing them with the order size (range of quantities) for which the various discount prices are applicable and find out the **feasible optimal quantity** which while calculated for a particular discounted price, also fall between the minimum and maximum quantity limits applicable to that discounted price offered by the vendor.

After determining the feasible optimal order size, we have to evaluate the total cost for this optimal order size [say Q_{Disc}] and compare the same with the total cost for EOQ option without discount. This is done as shown as follows :

(a) EOQ option

$$\text{Optimal order quantity} = Q_{opt}$$

$$\text{Unit price} = p$$

$$(TC)_{EOQ} = \frac{D}{Q_{opt}} C_o + \frac{Q_{opt}}{2} pC_i + Dp \qquad \text{(Equation 1)}$$

(b) Discount option

$$(TC)_{Disc} = \frac{D}{Q_{Disc}} + \frac{Q_{Disc}}{2} p_{Disc} C_i + Dp_{Disc} \qquad \text{(Equation 2)}$$

Decision Criteria

If $(T.C)_{EOQ} \leq (T.C)_{Disc}$ do not accept the discount offer.

If $(T.C)_{Disc} \leq (T.C)_{EOQ}$ then accept the discount offer.

➤ IMPORTANCE OF INVENTORY MANAGEMENT

Inadequate control of inventories can result in both understocking and overstocking of items. Understocking results in production holdups, lost sales, dissatisfied customers, delayed delivery of finished goods to customers and so on. Overstocking unnecessarily ties up working capital funds that might be used more productively elsewhere and also causes inventory carrying costs, obsolescence, wastage due to loss of shelf-life, damage in storage, pilferage and so on.

Two main concerns of inventory management are :

(i) **Level of customer service** *i.e.,* to have the right goods, in sufficient quantities, in the right place at the night time.

(ii) **Costs of ordering and carrying inventories** and **the shortage costs** or **stock out costs**. The overall objective of inventory management is to achieve satisfactory levels of customer service while keeping inventory costs within reasonable limits.

Two basic decisions to be made are the **timing** and **size** of orders (*i.e.,* when to order and how much to order).

The inventory performance is measured by **customer satisfaction** (measured by the number and quantity of back orders and for customer complaints) and by **inventory turnover ratio** which is the ratio of annual cost of goods sold to average inventory investment. The higher this ratio the better will be the inventory performance, which implies more efficient use of inventories.

To be effective inventory management must have the following :

(i) A system to keep track of the inventory on hand and on order.

(ii) A reliable forecast of demand that includes an indication of possible forecast error.

(iii) Knowledge of lead time and variation in lead time (probability of variation and extent of variation *i.e.,* extension of lead time).

(iv) Reasonable estimates of inventory carrying costs, ordering costs and shortage costs.

(v) A classification system for inventory items (*e.g.,* ABC or XYZ classification).

➤ INVENTORY CONTROL SYSTEMS

Two fundamental issues which underlie all inventory planning and control systems are :

(i) **How much to order** of each material when orders are placed with either outside suppliers or production departments in-house.

(ii) **When to place the orders** (*i.e.,* at what stock or inventory level).

Order quantities (called lot sizes which may be EOQ or otherwise) and when to place these orders, called **order points** or **re-order levels**, determine the amount of materials held inventory at any given time.

Dependent Demand and Independent Demand Inventories : Inventories may contain materials which have either **dependent demand** or **independent demand.** In independent-demand inventories, the demand for an item carried in inventory is independent of the demand for any other item carried in inventory. *For example,* inventories of finished products, tools, spare parts, stationery items etc., are examples of independent-demand inventories. Dependent -demand inventories consist of items whose demand depends on the demand for other items held in inventory. *For example,* the raw materials, components, parts, sub-assemblies etc., which will become part of the finished product and the packing materials required to pack and ship the finished goods-all have dependent demand. This means the demand for all these items (called bill-of-materials items) depend on the demand for the end product made from these items. Order quantity and order point decisions for dependent-demand inventories are, therefore, distinctly different from those of independent-demand inventories.

➤ INVENTORY CONTROL SYSTEMS FOR INDEPENDENT-DEMAND ITEMS

Two inventory control systems used for independent-demand items are:

(i) Perpetual review system or continuous review system or re-order point system or fixed order quantity variable order cycle system (also popularly referred to as 'Q' system).

(ii) Periodic review system or fixed order interval–variable order quantity system (also popularly known as 'P' system).

Continuous Review System ("Q" System)

In this system a fixed quantity of the material or item is ordered every time whenever the inventory on hand reaches a certain level referred to as **re-order level** (ROL) or **order point**. The advantages of this system are :

(i) Control is provided by continuous monitoring of inventory withdrawals and inventory levels.

(ii) Since the order quantity is fixed, the economic order quantity (EOQ) is justified.

However, the disadvantages are the added cost of : *(i)* record keeping and *(ii)* physical count of inventories must be performed periodically to verify records because of errors, pilferage, spoilage etc., *(iii)* orders are raised at irregular intervals which may not be convenient to the suppliers. The inventory control decisions are : *(i)* how much to order (*i.e.,* EOQ) and *(ii)* when to order (*i.e.,* when the inventory level falls to reorder level.

The order quantity is EOQ which is calculated as $Q = \sqrt{\dfrac{2\,DC_o}{p\,C_i}}$ where D is the annual demand in units, C_o is ordering cost per order, p = unit price in rupees and C_i is the inventory carrying changes as a percentage of the value of average inventory.

The other decision is regarding the reorder level. When the demand rate and lead time are known for certain, the re-order level is calculated as the inventory which meets the demand during lead time (also referred as **buffer stock**).

$$\text{Re-order level (ROL)} = \begin{pmatrix}\text{Normal or average}\\ \text{demand rate}\end{pmatrix} \times \begin{pmatrix}\text{Normal or average}\\ \text{lead time}\end{pmatrix}$$

$$= dL$$

where d is the demand rate per time period (say per day or per week and L is the lead time in the same units of time period (per day or per week).

When the demand rate and lead time are not certainly known, which means either the demand rate varies with a certain mean and a standard deviation about the mean (under normal distribution pattern) or the variation following Poisson distribution pattern or the lead time gets extended by some time period with the probabilities of extension by certain time period (say days or weeks) and the cumulative probability of maximum extension of lead time is known or variations in both lead time and demand rate may occur.

When the lead time gets extended by say 'x' weeks (maximum extension) and the probability of this maximum extension is 'P_x' then, the extra stock or cushion to be provided to take care of the consumption need in the extended lead time period (referred to as **safety stock**) is computed as:

$$\text{Safety stock} \begin{pmatrix}\text{For extension}\\ \text{of lead time}\end{pmatrix} = \begin{pmatrix}\text{Normal or average}\\ \text{consumption rate}\end{pmatrix} \times \begin{pmatrix}\text{Maximum extension}\\ \text{of lead time}\end{pmatrix} \times \begin{pmatrix}\text{Cumulative probability}\\ \text{of that extension}\end{pmatrix}$$

$$= dx\,P_x$$

On the other hand, when the consumption rate or demand rate is varying, we need to keep certain stock as cushion to meet the extra quantity demanded in normal lead time (referred to as reserve stock), and a particular desired service level has to be maintained. **Service level** refers to the probability that a stockout will not occur during lead time, usually a service level of 85 to 95 per cent is desired which means the probability that all customer orders can be immediately filled out of inventory is between 85 to 95 perc ent. The reserve stock is calculated as below :

(i) $\left.\begin{array}{l}\text{Reserve stock (when the}\\ \text{variation follows a normal}\\ \text{distribution pattern)}\end{array}\right\} = K\sigma_L$

Where K is the **service level constant** whose value depends on the service level desired (values of K can be obtained from Annexure C; area under the normal probability distribution), σ_L

is the standard deviation for the lead time period *i.e.,* $\sigma_L = \sigma\sqrt{L}$ where σ is the standard deviation per unit time period and L is the average or normal lead time in the same units of measurement of time period.

(ii) When the variation in demand during lead time follows Poisson distribution, the reserve stock $= K\sqrt{D_L}$. Where K is the service level constant and D_L = demand during average or normal lead time (which is also known as buffer stock)

Once the safety stock, reserve stock and buffer stocks are calculated, the reorder level is calculated as:

ROL = Safety stock + Reserve stock + Buffer stock.

Exhibit 7.4 illustrates the continuous review model.

Exhibit 7.4 : Continuous Review Inventory Model

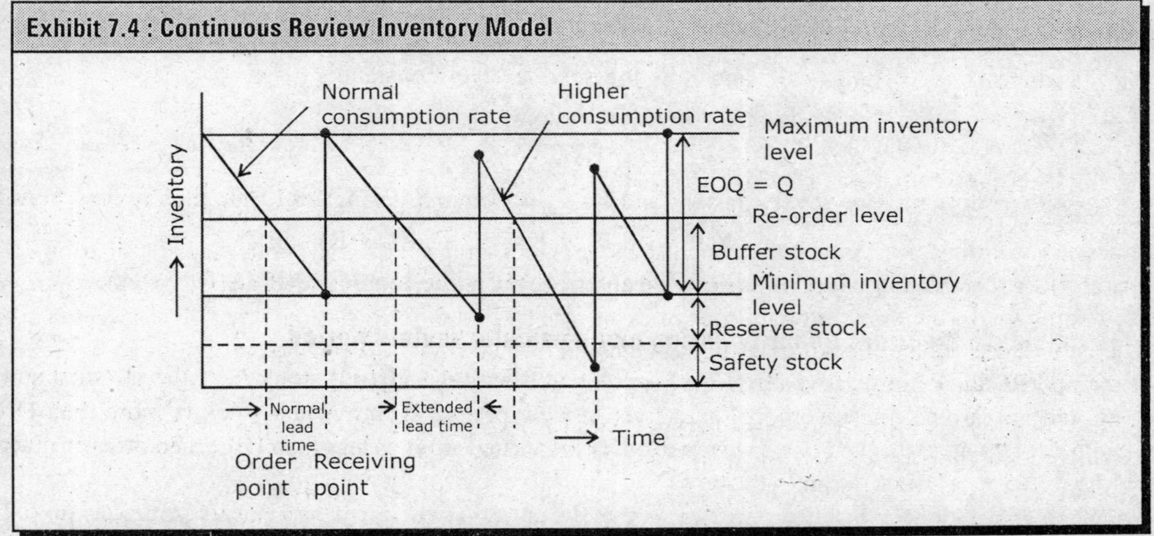

Periodic Review System ("P" System)

Under this system, inventory levels are reviewed at fixed time intervals (known as review periods) and orders are placed for enough quantity of material to bring the inventory level back to some predetermined level referred to as **desired inventory level (DIL)** or **target inventory level.** The **review period** is calculated as below :

$$\text{Number of orders per year (N)} = \frac{\text{Annual demand (units)}}{\text{EOQ}}$$

i.e.,

$$N = \frac{D}{Q}$$

$$\text{Review period R} = \frac{12}{N} \text{ months} \quad \text{or} \quad \frac{52}{N} \text{ weeks} \quad \text{or} \quad \frac{365}{N} \text{ days}$$

Review period is expressed in the same unit of measurement used for lead time (*i.e.,* if the lead time is in weeks, review period is also calculated in weeks).

Then the reorder level is calculated as equal to the consumption during a time period which is the sum of the average lead time and review period *i.e.,*

Reorder level (or Buffer stock) $= d\ (L + R)$

Where d is the demand rate, L is the average lead time and R is the review period.

When the lead time and demand rate vary, Re-order level is calculated as:

Re-order level = Safety stock + Reserve stock + Buffer stock.

Safety stock for extension of lead time

$$= d\chi\ P_{\chi}$$

Where d is the demand rate, χ is the maximum extension of lead time and P_{χ} is the cumulative probability of maximum extension of lead time.

Reserve stocks $= K\sigma_{L+R}$

(for normal distribution pattern)

where $\sigma_{L+R} = \sigma\sqrt{L + R}$ and K is the service level constant

Reserve stock (for Poisson distribution pattern)

$$= K\sqrt{D_{L+R}}$$

Where K = Service level constant and D_{L+R} = Demand during lead time plus review period.

i.e., $\text{ROL} = d_{\chi}P_{\chi} + K\sigma_{L+R} + d(L + R)$

Target inventory level or desired inventory level is the reorder level in 'P' system.

To calculate the order quantity during any particular review period

The DIL or Target inventory level is compared with the **virtual stock** (*i.e.,* the physical stock on hand plus pipe line inventory) at a given review period. If the virtual stock is more than DIL no order is placed till the next review period. If the virtual stock is less than DIL, then order is placed for quantity = DIL – virtual stock.

Exhibit 7.5 illustrates the periodic review system or 'P' system of inventory control.

Exhibit 7.5: Periodic Review System (or 'P' System) of Inventory Control

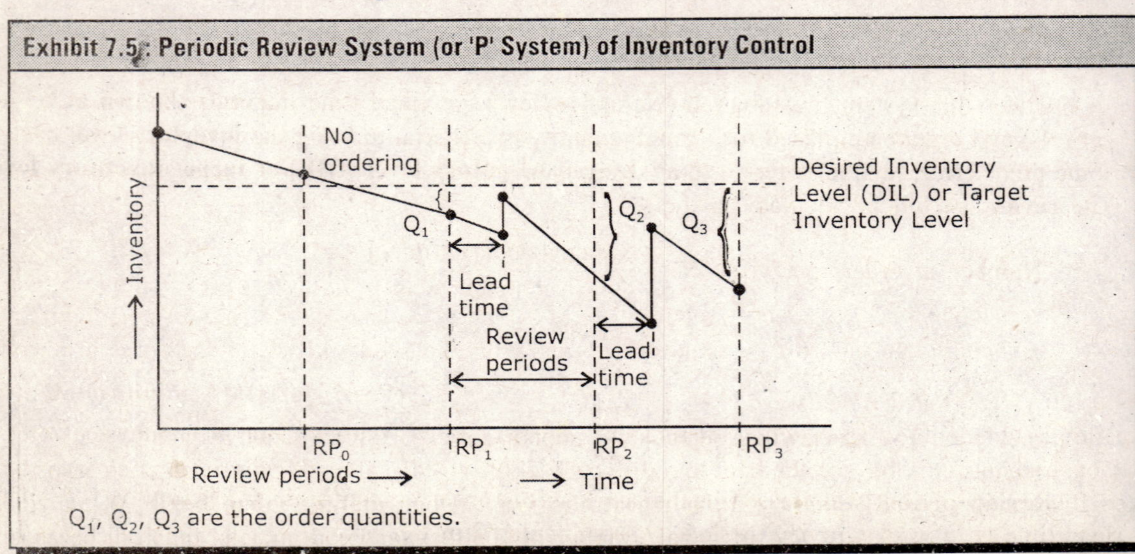

Q_1, Q_2, Q_3 are the order quantities.

Selective Inventory Control

Because of the large number of materials used in production at many manufacturing plants, it is desirable to classify materials according to the amount of analysis that can be justified. Selective inventory control means that the method of inventory control varies from item to item and the differentiation should be on a selective basis.

The philosophy behind selective inventory control technique is **"to put the efforts where results are worth putting the efforts"**. The importance of materials can be due its costs, its consumption value, its criticality, its availability and consumption. A number of selective inventory control technique are used. *Exhibit 7.6* lists the selective inventory control techniques, the criteria on which they are based and their main use or application.

Exhibit 7.6 : Selective Inventory Control Techniques

Sl.No.	*Type of Control*	*Criteria*	*Application*
1	A-B-C analysis (Always Better Control)	Annual consumption value of the item.	To control inventory of raw materials and W.I.P. inventory.
2	X-Y-Z analysis	Inventory value of items in stores.	To review the actual inventories, their uses etc., at scheduled intervals of stock-checking.
3	V-E-D analysis	Criticality of the item. Consumption pattern of the item.	To determine the stocking level of spare parts for machines and equipments.
4	F-S-N analysis	Unit price of the item.	To control obsolescence.
5	H-M-L analysis	Purchasing problems in regard to availability.	To control purchases and to develop vendors.
6	S-D-E analysis (scarce, difficult to procure and easy to procure)	Nature of supplies and seasonality.	Lead time analysis and purchasing strategies.
7	S-O-S analysis (Seasonal-Off-Seasonal)	Source of supply of materials.	Procurement and holding strategies for seasonal items (agricultural products).
8	G-O-L-F analysis (Government, Open market, Local and Foreign source).		Procurement strategies.

The selective inventory techniques listed above are briefly discussed in the following paragraphs.

1. A-B-C Analysis (or Classification)

This is also referred to as **"always better control"** or **Pareto Analysis** A-B-C analysis is a basic inventory control technique which is often the starting point. It can be applied to almost all aspects of materials management such as purchasing, receiving, inspection, storekeeping and issue of materials from stores, verification of bills, inventory control, value analysis etc.

Pareto's Law : Pareto, a German economist who worked out the distribution of income in East Prussia, found that 20% of the people owned 80% of the country's economy. Based on this finding, his law referred to as **Pareto's law** states *"In any series of elements to be controlled, only a small* *fraction in terms of elements will usually account for a large fraction in terms of results"*. It is also usually called **80/20 rule**. The underlying principle of Pareto's law is the saying **"the vital few and trivial many"** which applies to many areas of selective inventory control. In inventory management, it may be noticed that usually nearly 20% of the items contribute to 80% of the **annual consumption value** or **value of materials held in stores** at any given time. Since the primary objective of inventory control is to reduce costs, 80/20 rule is useful in the sense that we need to focus on only 20% of the total items used or inventoried in order to effect reduction in 80% of the total **annual consumption value or value of inventory held in stores** (These 20% of the items are the vital few and the balance 80% are trivial many).

ABC classification further refines 80/20 rule into a classification system using the **annual consumption value** (*i.e.*, annual consumption quantity of an item multiplied by its unit price) have three classes of items namely A, B and C item. 'A' items generally consist of 10 to 15 per cent of the **total number** of items and contribute for 65 to 70% of the **total annual consumption** value, 'B' items consist of about 20 percent of the total number and account for about 20 to 25 per cent of total consumption value and the balance items categorised as 'C' items consist of the remaining 60 to 70 per cent of the total number of items account for 5 to 15% of the total annual consumption value. The more common basis used for A-B-C classification is shown in *Box 7.4* below :

Box 7.4 : Basis for A-B-C Classification

Class of item	*Percentage of total number of items*	*Percentage of total annual consumption value*
A (Vital few)	10%	70%
B (Moderate importance)	20%	20%
C (Trivial many)	70%	10%
	Total 100%	100%

Mechanics of A-B-C Analysis

The steps involved in A-B-C Analysis are as follows :

Step 1. Calculate the **annual consumption value (ACV)** (rupees) for each item proposed to be used for manufacturing a product by **multiplying** the **number of units** used by the **unit price** of the item.

Step 2. Arrange all the items in the order of **descending sequence** of annual consumption value.

Step 3. Calculate the **cumulative** annual consumption value for each item, item-by-item.

Step 4. Compute the cumulative percentage of annual consumption value for each item.

Step 5. Locate the item in the list for which the cumulative annual consumption value is 70% of near 70% of the total annual consumption value. Categories all the previously listed items upto this item as 'A' category items.

Step 6. Locate the item in the list for which the cumulative annual consumption (ACV) is 90% of the total ACV. Categorise the items listed after 'A' category items and upto this item as 'B' category items.

Step 7. Categorise the remaining items as 'C' category items.

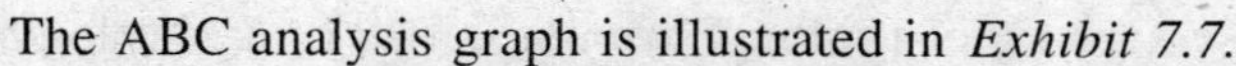

The ABC analysis graph is illustrated in *Exhibit 7.7*.

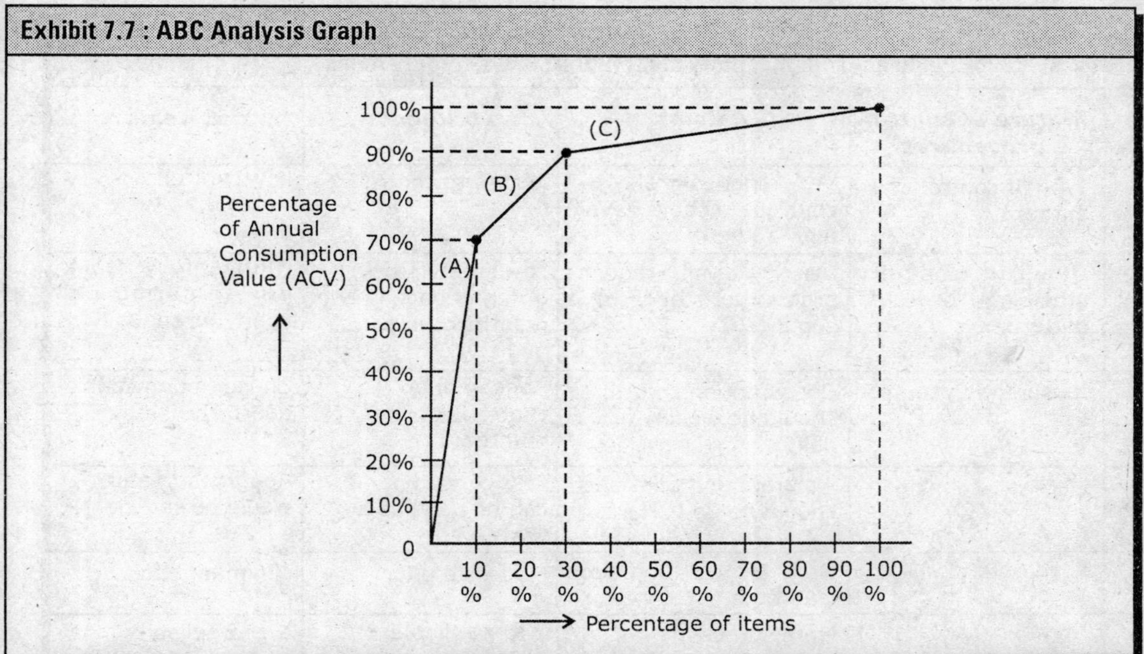

Exhibit 7.7 : ABC Analysis Graph

Advantages of ABC Analysis

This approach helps the materials manager to exercise selective control and focus attention on 'A' category items. By controlling the inventory of 'A' category items, the total inventory costs can be considerably reduced. Usually, fixed order quantity system or **'Q' system** of inventory control is used for 'A' category items advising the supplier to follow staggered supplies (*i.e.,* EOQ is ordered and the supplier is asked to supply fractions of EOQ on weekly basis to match the consumption rate). For 'B' category items the fixed-order cycle system or **'P' system** is used without appreciably increasing the average inventory value. For 'C' category items **"two-bin system"** is used wherein the annual requirement of the item is ordered in one or two lots and the quantity received is distributed into two bins - bin number one keeping the re-order level inventory and bin number two keeping the balance quantity. The item is consumed from bin number two and once it becomes empty, the repeat order is placed for the annual or six month's requirement. Item is issued from the first bin till the supply is received.

Limitations of ABC Analysis

(i) To be fully effective, it should be carried out with standardisation and codification.

(ii) Importance is given to an item based only on its annual consumption value and not on its criticality for the production

(iii) It should be reviewed periodically so that changes in prices and consumption are taken into account.

(iv) It does not apply to dependent demand inventory which is controlled by Material Requirement Planning (MRP) system.

Exhibit 7.8 illustrates broad policy guide lines for controlling inventory of A, B, & C category items.

Exhibit 7.8 : Policy guide lines for inventory control of A, B, C category items

Sl. No.	***Nature of control procedures***	***A items***	***B items***	***C items***
1.	Type of control and authority.	Very strict control, controller should have high authority.	Moderate control.	Low control.
2.	Quantity of safety stock and ordering pattern.	Very low or nil, Frequent ordering or staggered supply.	Low safety stock, ordering once in two months or in a quarter	High safety stock, Bulk ordering half yearly or annually.
3.	Consumption control.	Consumption control should be weekly or daily.	Consumption control fortnightly or monthly.	Consumption control quarterly.
4.	Material planning.	Accurate and data base should be up to date.	Past consumption can be used as a basis.	Rough estimates would be sufficient.
5.	Lead time.	Max. efforts to reduce lead time.	Moderate effort.	Minimum effort.
6.	Number of sources of supply.	More sources, centralised purchasing and storage.	2 to 4 reliable sources, combined purchasing.	1 or 2 reliable sources, Decentralised purchasing.
7.	Follow up	Regular expediting and maximum follow-up.	Periodic follow up.	Normally no follow up is necessary.
8.	Value analysis and wastage reduction.	Rigorous value analysis.	Moderate value analysis.	Minimum value-analysis.
9.	Forecasts in material planning.	Accurate forecasts.	Estimates based on past data on present plans.	Rough estimates for planning.
10.	Review of obsolete and surplus.	Review once in 15 days.	Quarterly review.	Annual review.

2. X-Y-Z Analysis (or Classification)

This classification is based on the value of inventory of materials actually held in stores at a given time (usually during stock checking annually or half-yearly). X-Y-Z analysis helps to control average inventory value by focussing efforts to reduce the inventory of 'X' items which are usually 10% of the number of items stored, but accounting for 70% of the total inventory value. Similarly 'Y' items are 20% of the number of items stored and account for 20% of the total inventory value. The remaining 70% of the items accounting for 10% of the total inventory value are 'Z' items. The X-Y-Z classification is done in the same way as ABC analysis, the difference being the actual inventory value of items in stores instead of their estimated annual consumption value.

3. V-E-D Analysis (or Classification)

'V' stands for vital, 'E' for essential and 'D' for desirable. This classification is usually applied for spare parts to be stocked for maintenance of machines and equipments based on the **criticality**

of the spare parts. The stocking policy is based on the criticality of the items. The vital spare parts are those which can cause stoppage of the plant, if not available. Usually such spare parts are known as **capital or insurance spares**. The inventory policy is to keep at least one number of the vital spare irrespective of its value. Also, spare parts to be supplied by foreign manufacturers are treated as 'Vital spares because of the long lead time required for procurement. Essential spare parts are those whose non-availability may not adversely affect production. Such spare parts may be available from many sources within the country and the procurement lead time may not be long. Hence, a low inventory of essential spare parts is held. The desirable spare parts are those which, if not available, can be manufactured by the maintenance department or may be procured from local suppliers and hence no stock is held usually.

4. F-S-N Analysis (or Classification)

It stands for Fast-moving, Slow-moving and Non-moving items. The classification is based on **past consumption pattern**. Items which are usually drawn from stores frequently are classified as fast moving items, items which are drawn only once or twice a year are classified as slow-moving and items not at all drawn for the past two years are classified as non-moving items. F-S-N analysis is useful to control obsolescence of raw materials, components, tools and spare parts.

5. H-M-L Analysis (or Classification)

This stands for High value, medium value and Low value items based on unit price of the item. For instance, a firm may decide to categorise items having unit price more than Rs. 5000 as 'H' items. From Rs. 1000 to 5000 as 'M' items and below Rs. 1000 as 'L' items. On this basis, materials management may delegate authority to various levels of purchase officers/managers to authorise and sign purchase orders. Also, for high value items, alternative sources of suppliers are developed.

6. S-D-E Analysis (or Classification)

This stands for Scarce items, Difficult to procure items and Easy to procure items. A scarce item is one which is not easily available in the market and reliable source may have to be developed. *For example,* imported items may have to be stocked because it is difficult to procure and takes a long lead time.

7. S-O-S Analysis (or Classification)

'S' stands for Seasonal items and 'OS' stands for Off-Seasonal items. It may be advantageous to buy seasonal items at low prices and keep inventory or buy at high price during off seasons. Based on the fluctuation in prices and availability, suitable decision has to be taken regarding how much to purchase and at what prices.

8. G-O-L-F Analysis (or Classification)

This stands for Government, Open market, Local or Foreign source of supply. For many items, imports are canalised through government agencies such as State Trading Corporations, Mineral and Metals Trading Corporation, Indian Drugs and Pharmaceutical etc.

For such items the buying firms can not apply any inventory control techniques and have to accept the quota allotted by the Government. 'Open market' category are those who form bulk of suppliers and procurement is rather easy. 'L' category includes those local suppliers from whom items can be purchased off-the-shelf on cash purchase basis. 'F' category indicates foreign suppliers. Since an elaborate import procedure is involved, it is better to buy imported items in bigger lots usually covering the annual requirements.

Measurement of the Effectiveness of Inventory Management

Like purchasing and stores, the performance of inventory management should be measured to ensure that the functions of inventory management are effectively carried on. Traditional indicators, like the *number of months' holdings in stores as compared to budgeted consumption, or number of months' finished goods inventory vis-a-vis budgeted sales*, serve as broad, over-all signals for bankers or top management, but are not adequate for functional managers, who are most concerned with sorting out day-to-day problems of co-ordination in respect of materials, and matching production or despatch schedules with commitments. So, in addition to the traditional methods, there is the felt need for developing a further set of indicators, which relate organisational goals to departmental goals. The following are some of the performance indicators of inventory management :

1. $$\left.\begin{array}{r}\text{Overall inventory}\\ \text{turnover ratio}\end{array}\right\} = \frac{\text{Cost of goods sold}}{\text{Average inventory at cost}}$$

2. $$\left.\begin{array}{r}\text{Raw materials inventory}\\ \text{turnover ratio}\end{array}\right\} = \frac{\text{Annual consumption of raw materials}}{\text{Average raw materials inventory}}$$

3. $$\left.\begin{array}{r}\text{Work - in - process inventory}\\ \text{turnover ratio}\end{array}\right\} = \frac{\text{Cost of manufacture}}{\text{Average w - i - p inventory at cost}}$$

4. $$\left.\begin{array}{r}\text{Finished goods inventory}\\ \text{turnover ratio}\end{array}\right\} = \frac{\text{Cost of goods sold}}{\text{Average finished goods inventory at cost}}$$

5. $$\left.\begin{array}{r}\text{Week's inventory of}\\ \text{raw materials on hand}\end{array}\right\} = \frac{\text{Raw materials inventory on hand}}{\text{Weekly consumption of raw materials}}$$

6. $$\left.\begin{array}{r}\text{Week's raw material}\\ \text{on order}\end{array}\right\} = \frac{\text{Raw materials on order}}{\text{Weekly consumption of raw materials}}$$

7. $$\left.\begin{array}{r}\text{Week's inventory of}\\ \text{finished goods on hand}\end{array}\right\} = \frac{\text{Finished goods inventory}}{\text{Weekly sale of finished goods}}$$

8. $$\left.\begin{array}{r}\text{Average age of raw}\\ \text{materials in inventory}\end{array}\right\} = \frac{\text{Average raw materials inventory at cost}}{\text{Aveage daily purchase of raw materials}}$$

9. $$\left.\begin{array}{r}\text{Average age of}\\ \text{finished goods inventory}\end{array}\right\} = \frac{\text{Average finished goods inventory at cost}}{\text{Aveage cost of goods manufactured per day}}$$

5. $$\text{Out of stock index} = \frac{\text{Number of times out of stock}}{\text{Number of times requisitioned}}$$

11. $$\text{Spare parts index} = \frac{\text{Value of spare parts inventory}}{\text{Value of capital equipment}}$$

➢ INVENTORY CONTROL OF DEPENDENT DEMAND ITEMS

A major distinction in the way inventories are managed results from the nature of demand for those items. When demand for items is derived from production plans for certain and products, for instance, demand for raw materials, components, parts and sub-assemblies used in producing the finished product, these items are referred to as those having **dependent demand.** The required quantities of such items are computed by multiplying the quantities indicated in the bill of materials for the product by the quantity of end product demand (as indicated in master production schedule) *i.e.,*

$$\begin{pmatrix}\text{Gross requirement}\\ \text{of an item}\end{pmatrix} = \begin{pmatrix}\text{Bill of materials}\\ \text{quantity for the item}\end{pmatrix} \times \begin{pmatrix}\text{Master production}\\ \text{schedule quantity}\\ \text{for the end product}\end{pmatrix}$$

Independent demand items have a fairly stable demand, once allowances are made for seasonal variations in the forecast but dependent demand items have sporadic or lumpy demands depending on the demands for the end products in which these items are used. Independent demand items are stocked on a continual basis while dependent demand items need only to be stocked or made available just prior to the time of their need in the production process. Moreover, when the forecast of demand for the end product is fairly accurate and the production programme is stable, there is little or no need to have safety stock to take care of variations in demand for the dependent demand items.

Inventory control techniques for dependent demand items are :

(i) **Materials Requirements Planning (MRP-I).**

(ii) **Just-In-Time systems (JIT).**

Materials Requirements Planning (MRP-I)

Materials Requirements Planning is a computer based information system designed to handle ordering and scheduling of dependent-demand inventories (raw materials, sub-assemblies, parts, components). A production plan for a specified number of finished products (usually over a quarterly or monthly time period) in the form of a **"master production schedule"** is translated into requirements of component parts and raw materials working backward from the due date (need date in the production process) using lead times and other information (regarding how the product is built) to determine **when to order** and **how much to order**. Hence, requirements of end items generate the requirements for lower-level components which are broken down by planning periods (*e.g.,* weeks) so that ordering, fabrication and assembly can be scheduled for timely completion of end items while inventory levels are kept reasonably low.

Materials requirement planning is a philosophy as well as technique and also an approach to production scheduling, procurement scheduling and inventory control.

Objectives of MRP

The objectives of materials requirements planning in operations management are :

1. To improve customer service by meeting delivery schedules promised and shortening delivery lead times.
2. To reduce inventory costs by reducing inventory levels.
3. To improve plant operating efficiency by better use of productive resources.

Three facets of MRP technique are :

1. The MRP technique as a requirements calculator.
2. The MRP – A manufacturing, planning and control system.
3. The MRP – A manufacturing resource planning system.

The MRP technique as a requirements calculator was originally used as an inventory control tool providing reports that specify how many components should be ordered, when they should be ordered and when they should be procured or produced in-house. Since MRP is a computer based system, it was possible to expand the system into a manufacturing, planning and control system by providing information for planning and controlling both the material and the capacity required to manufacture the products. Hence, MRP serves as a key component in an information system for planning and controlling production operations and procurement of materials. It is the basic foundation for production activity control or shop floor control, for vendor follow up systems and for detailed capacity requirements planning. When both the MRP and CRP are integrated within one system, the system is known as "Materials Requirements Planning" abbreviated as 'MRP' or MRP-I. When MRP is extended to include feedback from and control of vendor orders and production operations, it is called "closed-loop MRP" which helps managers achieve effective manufacturing control.

Manufacturing Resource Planning or MRP-II

When the capabilities of closed-loop MRP are extended to integrate financial, accounting, personnel, engineering and marketing information along with the production planning and control activities of basic MRP system, the resulting broad-based resource-coordination system is known as manufacturing resource planning or MRP-II. MRP-II is the heart of corporate management information system for many companies, as it provides information about inventory investment levels, plant expansion needs and work-force requirements, that is useful for co-ordinating marketing, financial, engineering and manufacturing efforts to achieve the company's overall business plans.

The projections of what materials and components will be purchased and when, can be used to develop purchase commitments and a projected purchasing budget. The labour hours projected in capacity requirement plan for each work centre can be aggregated to develop personnel needs and labour budgets. The projected on hand inventory of material can be used to develop inventory budgets.

General Overview of MRP (Materials Requirements Planning)

Basically, MRP consists of a set of computer programs that are run periodically (once a week or once a month) to incorporate the latest schedule of production requirements. MRP performs three important functions, *viz.,*

1. Order planning and control, *i.e.,* when to release orders and for what quantity?
2. Priority planning and control, *i.e.,* comparison of expected date of availability with the need date of each item.
3. Provision of a basis for planning capacity requirements and development of broad business plans.

MRP is applicable primarily to companies that carry out fabrication of parts and assembly of standard products in batch quantities.

Exhibit 7.9 shows a flow chart that provides a general overview of MRP as a means of co-ordinating purchasing activities to support manufacturing as well as materials requirements and capacity requirements.

Exhibit 7.9 : Information Flow for Planning and Controlling with MRP

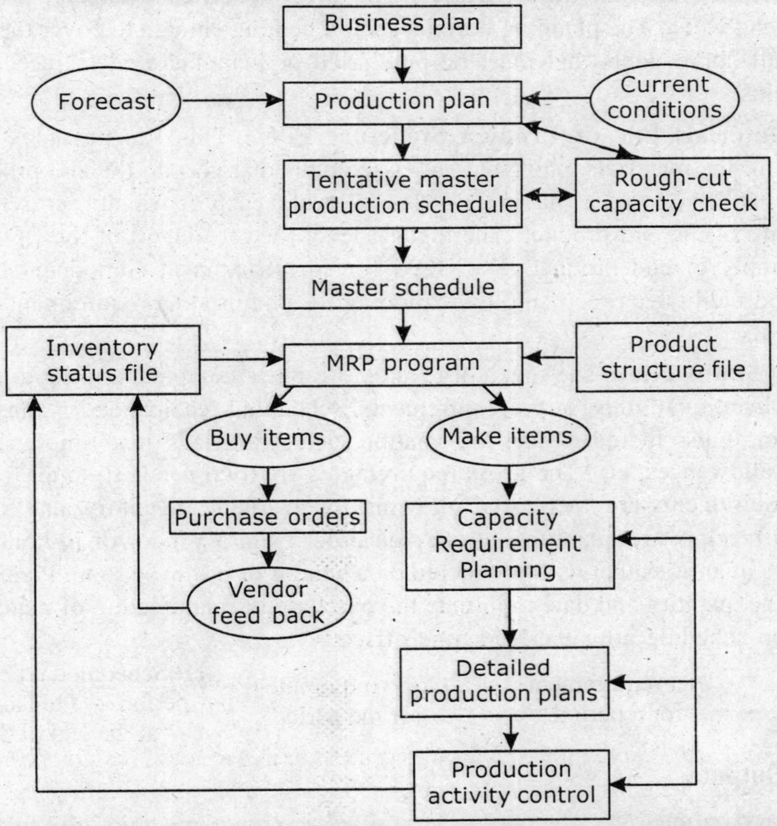

Business plan
Forecast
Production plan
Current conditions
Tentative master production schedule
Rough-cut capacity check
Master schedule
Inventory status file
MRP program
Product structure file
Buy items
Make items
Purchase orders
Capacity Requirement Planning
Vendor feed back
Detailed production plans
Production activity control

Operation of the MRP System

Exhibit 7.10 illustrates the operation of MRP system.

Exhibit 7.10 : Operation of MRP System

Inputs
Processing
Outputs
Inventory status file
MPS file
BOM file
MRP Systems
Inventory transaction data
Planned order schedule
Exception reports

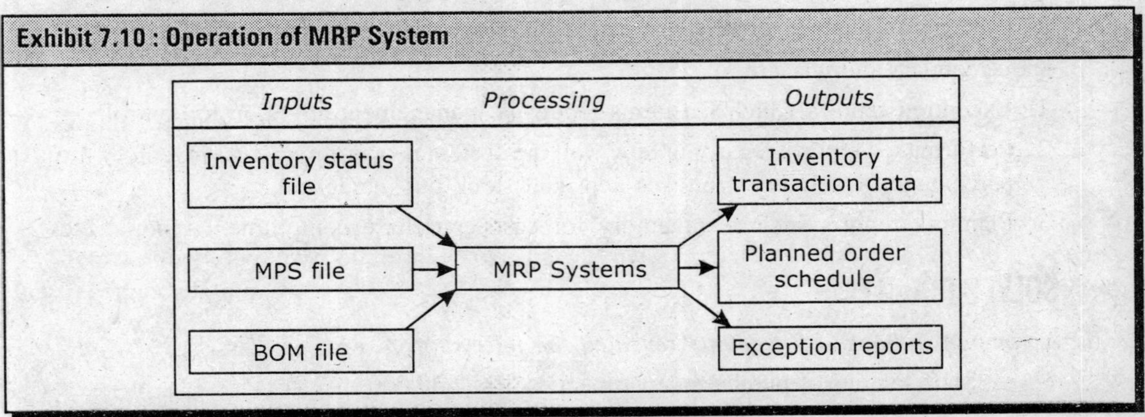

The entire MRP system is driven by the MPS. The bill of materials file and inventory status file are fed to the MRP computer program to generate the outputs.

MRP System Inputs

1. **Master Production Schedule (MPS) :** The MPS specifies what end products are to be produced and when. The planning horizon should be long enough to cover the cumulative lead times of all components that must be purchased or manufactured to meet the end product requirements.
2. **Bill of Materials File or Product Structure File :** This file provides the information regarding all the materials, parts and sub-assemblies that go into the end product. The Bill of Materials can be viewed as having a series of levels, each of which represents a stage in the manufacture of the end product. The highest level (or zero level) of the BOM represents the final assembly or end product. The BOM file identifies each component by a unique part number and facilitates processing by exploding the end product requirements into component requirements.
3. **Inventory Status File :** The inventory status file gives complete and up-to-date information on the on-hand quantities, gross requirements, scheduled receipts and planned order releases for the item. It also includes other information such as lot sizes, lead times, safety stock levels and scrap allowances, etc. The gross requirements are total needs from all resources whereas the net requirements are "net" after allowing for available inventory and scheduled receipt. Scheduled receipts are quantities already on order from a vendor or in-house shop. Planned receipts are quantities that will be ordered on a vendor or in-house shop. Planned order release indicates the quantity and date to initiate the purchase or manufacture of materials that will be received on schedule after the lead time offset.

$$\begin{pmatrix}\text{Net requirement}\\ \text{for a period}\end{pmatrix} = \begin{pmatrix}\text{Gross requirement}\\ \text{for the period}\end{pmatrix} - \begin{pmatrix}\text{Scheduled receipt for the}\\ \text{period + On hand inventory}\\ \text{at the end of the period}\end{pmatrix}$$

MRP System Outputs

Two primary outputs are :

1. Planned order schedule which is a plan of the quantity of each material to be ordered in each time period. The order may be a purchase order on the suppliers or production orders for parts and sub-assemblies on production departments.
2. Changes in planned orders - *i.e.,* modification of previous planned orders.

The secondary outputs are :

1. Exception reports which list items requiring management attention to control.
2. Performance reports regarding how well the system is operating - *e.g.,* inventory turnovers, percentage of delivery promises kept and stock out incidences.
3. Planning reports such as inventory forecasts, purchase commitment reports, etc.

➤ SOLVED PROBLEMS

1. A company's books of accounts revealed the following.

Staff salaries of purchase department = Rs. 2,50,000

Expenses incurred in ware - house personnel salaries = Rs. 2,75,000

Cost of security for ware house = Rs. 80,000

Travelling and purchase follow up expenses = Rs. 80,000

Taxes and insurance = 1.0% p.a.

Interest rate on inventory value = 20% p.a.

Cost of bills payment = Rs. 30,000

Cost of materials handling in store = Rs. 1,50,000

Obsolescence and pilferage = Rs. 20,000

Cost of inwards inspection = Rs. 48,000

The company has an average inventory of Rs. 60 lakhs and has placed 3400 orders in the year of review. Calculate the cost per order and inventory carrying the cost as percentage based on the above costs. What would be the EOQ if the annual demand of an item is 12,000 numbers and unit price is Rs. 60 per unit.

Solution :

In order to calculate the ordering cost/acquisition cost per order and the inventory carrying cost, as a percentage of the value of average inventory, it is necessary to bifurcate the various items of cost data under two heads, *viz.,* ordering cost and inventory carrying cost as below :

Ordering cost (Rupees)		*Inventory carrying cost (Rupees)*	
(a) Staff salaries of purchase department =	2,50,000	(a) Expenses incurred in warehouse personnel salaries	= 2,75,000
(b) Travelling & purchase follow up expenses =	80,000	(b) Cost of security for warehouse	= 80,000
(c) Cost of bills of payment =	30,000	(c) Taxes and insurance @ 1%	$= \frac{1}{100} \times 60{,}00{,}000$ = 60,000
(d) Cost of inward inspection =	48,000	(d) Interest @20% of the value of average inventory	$= \frac{20}{100} \times 60{,}00{,}000$ = 12,00,000
Total	4,08,000	(e) Cost of materials handling in store	= 1,50,000
Ordering cost per order (C_o) $= \frac{\text{Total ordering cost}}{\text{No. of orders per year}}$ $= \frac{4{,}08{,}000}{3400}$ = Rs. 120		(f) Obsolescence and pilferage cost	= 20,000
		Total inventory carrying cost	= 17,85,000
		Inventory carrying charges (C_i)	$= \frac{17{,}85{,}000}{60{,}00{,}000} \times 100$ = 29.75%

Calculation of E.O.Q. : Annual demand (D) = 12,000 units

Unit price (P) = Rs. 60/-

$$\text{E.O.Q.} = \frac{2\times\begin{pmatrix}\text{Annual demand}\\ \text{(units)}\end{pmatrix}\times\begin{pmatrix}\text{Ordering cost}\\ \text{per order}\end{pmatrix}}{\text{Unit price}\times\begin{pmatrix}\text{Inventory carrying}\\ \text{charges (as \%)}\end{pmatrix}}$$

$$= \sqrt{\frac{2DC_o}{PC_i}} = \sqrt{\frac{2\times 12{,}000\times 120}{60\times 0.2975}}$$

$$= 401.67 \approx \text{Rs. } 402$$

2. *An auto industry purchases spark plugs at the rate of Rs. 25 per piece. The annual consumption of spark plug is 18,000 nos. If the ordering cost is Rs. 250 per order and carrying cost is 25% p.a., what would be the EOQ? If the supplier of spark plugs offers a discount of 5% for order quantity of 3,000 nos. per order, do you accept the discount offer?*

Solution :

(a) Calculation of EOQ :

Annual demand (D) = 18,000 nos.

Unit price (P) = Rs. 25/-

Ordering cost per order (C_o) = Rs. 250/-

Carrying charges (as %) (C_i) = 25%

$$EOQ = \sqrt{\frac{2DC_o}{PC_i}} = \sqrt{\frac{2\times 18{,}000\times 250}{25\times 0.25}}$$

$$= \sqrt{\frac{20\times 18{,}000}{0.25}}$$

$$= \sqrt{80\times 18{,}000} = \sqrt{10^4\times 8\times 18}$$

$$= 10^2 \times \sqrt{144}$$

$$= 100 \times 12 = 1200 \text{ nos.}$$

(b) Decision regarding discount offer for Q = 3000.

(i) EOQ option :

$$\left.\begin{matrix}\text{Total cost of materials plus}\\ \text{cost on materials per annum}\end{matrix}\right\} = DP + \frac{D}{Q}C_o + \frac{Q}{2}PC_i$$

$$= 18{,}000 \times 25 + \frac{18{,}000}{1200}\times 250 + \frac{1200}{2}\times 25\times\frac{25}{100}$$

$$= 4{,}50{,}000 + 3750 + 3750$$

Total cost $TC_{(EOQ)}$ = Rs. 4,57,500

(ii) Discount option :

Discount offered for order qty. (Q_1) of 3,000 nos. = 5% of unit price

New price after discount, P_1 = 0.95 × 25 = 23.75

$$\left.\begin{array}{r}\text{Total cost of materials plus}\\ \text{cost on materials } TC_{(Discount)}\end{array}\right\} = DP_1 + \frac{D}{Q_1}C_o + \frac{Q_1}{2}P_1C_i$$

$$= 18{,}000 \times 23.75 + \frac{18{,}000}{3000} \times 250 + \frac{3000}{2} \times 23.75 \times 0.25$$

$$= 4{,}27{,}500 + 1500 + 8906.25$$

$$TC_{(Discount)} = \text{Rs. } 4{,}37{,}906.25$$

(iii) Decision rule :

If TC (Discount) $\leq$ TC (EOQ) $\rightarrow$ Accept discount

If TC(Discount) > TC(EOQ) $\rightarrow$ reject discount offer

In this case, since $TC_{Discount}$ (*i.e,* 4,37,906.25) is less than TC_{EOQ} (*i.e.,* 4,57,500), discount offer of 5% on unit price for ordering 3000 nos. per order is acceptable.

3. *The ABC Fun novelty company buys 80,000 shipping containers per year. Price of each container is Rs. 0.40. Cost of purchase Rs. 80 per order, cost of holding one container per year = Re. 0.10. Bank rate of interest 15% including a charge for taxes and insurance. Find*
   (i) the economic order quality and time between orders based on 220 working days per year.
   (ii) the minimum variable cost per year.
   (iii) if the company had been following a policy of quarterly ordering, what would have been the increase in the variable cost?

Solution :

Annual demand (D) = 80,000 units

Unit price (P) = Re. 0.40

Ordering cost per order (C_o) = Rs. 80/-

Holding cost per item per year = Re. 0.10/-

Bank rate of interest including charge for taxes and insurance = 15% of unit price

$$= \frac{15}{100} \times 0.40 = \text{Re. } 0.06$$

Inventory carrying cost per item per year C_c = 0.10 + 0.06 = Re. 0.16

Calculation of EOQ :

$$(i)\ \text{EOQ} = \sqrt{\frac{2DC_o}{C_c}} = \sqrt{\frac{2 \times 80{,}000 \times 80}{0.16}} = 8944.27 \approx 9000 \text{ nos.}$$

Calculation of time between orders based on 220 working days per year:

$$\left.\begin{array}{r}\text{Time between orders}\\ \text{(in days)}\end{array}\right\} = \frac{\text{No. of working days per year}}{\text{No. of orders per year (N)}}$$

$$\left.\begin{array}{r}\text{No. of orders}\\ \text{per year (N)}\end{array}\right\} = \frac{\text{Annual demand (D)}}{\text{EOQ}}$$

$$N = \frac{D}{Q} = \frac{80,000}{9000} = 8.88 \approx 9$$

$$\text{Time between orders} = \frac{220}{9} = 24.44 \text{ days} \approx 24 \text{ days}$$

(ii) Calculation of minimum variable cost per year :

Variable cost comprises ordering cost per year and inventory carrying cost per year and this would be minimum when the order qty. equals economic order qty. (*i.e.*, EOQ).

$$\left.\begin{matrix}\text{Minimum variable}\\ \text{cost per year}\end{matrix}\right\} = \begin{pmatrix}\text{Ordering cost}\\ \text{per year}\end{pmatrix} + \begin{pmatrix}\text{Inventory carrying}\\ \text{cost per year}\end{pmatrix}$$

$$= \begin{pmatrix}\text{No. of} \\ \text{orders}\end{pmatrix} \times \begin{pmatrix}\text{Ordering}\\ \text{cost per order}\end{pmatrix}$$

$$+ \begin{pmatrix}\text{Average inventory}\\ \text{units}\end{pmatrix} \times \begin{pmatrix}\text{Inventory carrying}\\ \text{cost / unit / year}\end{pmatrix}$$

$$= (9 \times 80) + \left(\frac{9000}{2}\right) \times 0.16$$

$$= 720 + 720 = \text{Rs. } 1440$$

(iii) Policy of quarterly ordering (ordering once in 3 months)

$$\text{No. of orders per year} = \frac{12}{3} = 4$$

$$\text{Order Qty. per order} = \frac{80,000}{4} = 20,000 \text{ units}$$

$$\text{Ordering cost per year} = 4 \times 80 = \text{Rs. } 320$$

$$\text{Inventory carrying cost per year} = \frac{20,000}{2} \times 0.16 = \text{Rs. } 1600$$

$$\text{Total variable cost per year} = 320 + 1600 = \text{Rs. } 1920/-$$

$$\left.\begin{matrix}\text{Increase in the variable}\\ \text{cost as compared with}\\ \text{that of EOQ ordering}\end{matrix}\right\} = 1920 - 1440 = \text{Rs. } 480/-$$

4\. *Determine safety stock, reserve stock and buffer stock for the data given below :*

Normal usage = *100 per week*

Lead time = *4 to 6 weeks*

Minimum usage = *50 per week*

Maximum usage = *150 per week*

Re-order quantity = *600 nos.*

Also, calculate the Re-order level, minimum and maximum levels of inventory and also average inventory level.

Solution :

$$\text{Buffer stock} = \begin{pmatrix}\text{Average}\\ \text{lead time}\end{pmatrix} \times \begin{pmatrix}\text{Average}\\ \text{usage rate}\end{pmatrix}$$

$$= 5 \times 100 = 500 \text{ nos.}$$

Safety stock is for usage at normal rate during the extension of lead time.

Max. extension of lead time = 6 – 5 = 1 week

Normal usage rate = 100 per week

Safety stock = (6 – 5) × 100 = 100 nos.

Reserve stock is to meet the excess usage requirement during normal lead time.

Excess usage requirement = 150 – 100 = 50 per week

Reserve stock = 5 × 50 = 250 nos.

Re-order level = Safety Stock + Reserve Stock + Buffer Stock

= 100 + 250 + 500 = 850 nos.

Minimum inventory level = S.S.+ R.S. = 100 + 250 = 350 nos.

Max. inventory level = Minimum level + Order quantity

= 350 + 600 = 950 nos.

$$\text{Average inventory level} = \frac{\text{Min. level} + \text{Max. level}}{2}$$

$$= \frac{350+950}{2} = 650 \text{ nos.}$$

5. *A company uses 1200 units per month of an electronic component each costing Rs. 2/-. Placing each order costs Rs. 50/- and the carrying cost is 6% per year of the average inventory.*

(i) Find EOQ.

(ii) If the company gets 5% discount if it places single order, should they accept the discount offer?

(iii) Find break even discount percentage which matches EOQ ordering.

Solution :

Annual demand for the component (D) = 1200 × 12 = 14,400 nos.

Unit price of the component (P) = Rs. 2/-

Ordering cost per order (C_o) = Rs. 50/-

Inventory carrying charges per year (C_i) = Rs. 6%

(i) Determination of EOQ :

$$\text{EOQ} = \sqrt{\frac{2DC_o}{PC_i}} = \sqrt{\frac{2 \times 14{,}400 \times 50}{2 \times 0.06}} = 3464$$

$$\text{No. of orders per year} = \frac{14{,}400}{3464} = 4.15 \approx 4$$

$$\text{Modified EOQ} = \frac{14{,}400}{4} = 3600$$

$$\begin{pmatrix}\text{Total cost for}\\ \text{EOQ ordering}\end{pmatrix} = \begin{pmatrix}\text{Cost of}\\ \text{materials / year}\end{pmatrix} + \begin{pmatrix}\text{Ordering cost}\\ \text{per year}\end{pmatrix} + \begin{pmatrix}\text{Inventory carrying}\\ \text{cost per year}\end{pmatrix}$$

$$TC_{(EOQ)} = DP + \frac{D}{Q} C_o + \frac{Q}{2} P C_i$$

$$= 14{,}400 \times 2 + \frac{14{,}400}{3600} \times 50 + \frac{3600}{2} \times 2 \times 0.06$$

$$= 28{,}000 + 200 + 216 = \text{Rs. } 29{,}216/-$$

(ii) Decision regarding discount offer of 5%

$$\left.\begin{array}{r}\text{Discounted}\\ \text{unit price}(P_1)\end{array}\right\} = 0.95 \times 2 = \text{Rs. } 1.90$$

$$\left.\begin{array}{r}\text{Order qty. to}\\ \text{avail discount}(Q_1)\end{array}\right\} = 14{,}400 \text{ nos. (i.e., single order per year)}$$

$$\left.\begin{array}{r}\text{Total cost under}\\ \text{discount offer}\end{array}\right\} = T.C._{(Disc)}$$

$$T.C._{(Disc)} = DP_1 + \frac{D}{Q_1} C_o + \frac{Q_1}{2} P_1 C_i$$

$$= 14{,}400 \times 1.90 + \frac{14{,}400}{14{,}400} \times 50 + \frac{14{,}400}{2} \times 1.90 \times 0.06$$

$$= 27{,}360 + 50 + 820.80 = \text{Rs. } 28{,}230.80$$

Since, $T.C._{(Disc)} < T.C._{(EOQ)}$, the decision is to accept the discount offer of 5% on unit price.

(iii) Determination of break even discount percentage which matches EOQ ordering.

Let x be the new discounted price to match EOQ ordering.

$$\text{Then, total cost } T.C._{(BE/Disc)} = D(x) + \frac{D}{Q_1} C_o + \frac{Q_1}{2} (x) C_i$$

$$T.C._{(BE/Disc)} = 14{,}400\,(x) + \frac{14{,}400}{14{,}400} \times 50 + \frac{14{,}400}{2} \times (x) \times 0.06$$

$$= 14400x + 50 + 432x = 14832x + 50$$

$$T.C._{(BE/Disc)} = T.C._{(EOQ)}$$

$$\text{i.e., } 14832x + 50 = 29216$$

$$14832x = 29216 - 50 = 29166$$

$$\therefore x = \frac{29166}{14832} = 1.966$$

$$\text{Break even \% discount} = \left(\frac{P - x}{P}\right) \times 100 = \left(\frac{2 - 1.966}{2}\right) \times 100 = 1.7\%$$

6. *A factory uses annually 24,000 units of a raw material which costs Rs. 1.25 per unit. Placing each order costs Rs. 25/- and carrying cost is 6% per year of the average inventory.*

   (a) Find the economic order quantity and the total inventory cost including the cost of material.

   (b) The factory works for 320 days a year. If the procurement time is 10 days and safety stock is 450 units, find the re-order point, the minimum, maximum and average inventories.

Solution :

Annual demand (D) = 24,000 nos.

Unit price (P) = Rs. 1.25

Ordering cost per order (C_o) = Rs. 25/-

Inventory carrying charges per year (C_i) = 6%

(a)

$$EOQ = \sqrt{\frac{2DC_o}{PC_i}} = \sqrt{\frac{2 \times 24{,}000 \times 25}{1.25 \times 0.06}}$$

$$EOQ = 4000 \text{ units}$$

$$\text{Total cost} = \text{Cost of materials} + \text{Cost on materials}$$

$$= \left(\begin{matrix}\text{Cost of materials}\\ \text{per year}\end{matrix}\right) + \left(\begin{matrix}\text{Ordering cost}\\ \text{per year}\end{matrix}\right) + \left(\begin{matrix}\text{Inventory carrying}\\ \text{cost per year}\end{matrix}\right)$$

$$= DP + \frac{D}{Q} C_o + \frac{Q}{2} PC_i$$

$$= 24{,}000 \times 1.25 + \frac{24{,}000}{4000} \times 25 + \frac{4{,}000}{2} \times 1.25 \times 0.06$$

$$= 30{,}000 + 150 + 150$$

$$\text{Total cost} = \text{Rs. } 30{,}300/-$$

(b) If the factory workers for 320 days a year,

$$\text{Consumption rate per day} = \frac{\text{Annual demand}}{\text{No. of working days per year}}$$

$$= \frac{24{,}400}{320} = 75 \text{ units}$$

$$\text{Safety stock} = 450 \text{ units}$$

$$\text{Procurement lead time} = 10 \text{ days}$$

$$\left.\begin{matrix}\text{Buffer stock } i.e., \text{ lead}\\ \text{time consumption}\end{matrix}\right\} = \text{Lead time} \times \text{Consumption rate}$$

$$= 10 \times 75 = 750$$

$$\left.\begin{matrix}\text{Re-order point}\\ \text{(or re-order level)}\end{matrix}\right\} = \text{Safety stock} + \text{Buffer stock}$$

$$= 450 + 750 = 1200 \text{ units}$$

$$\text{Minimum inventory level} = \text{Safety stock} = 450 \text{ units}$$

$$\text{Maximum inventory level} = \left(\begin{matrix}\text{Minimum}\\ \text{inventory level}\end{matrix}\right) + \left(\begin{matrix}\text{Order qty.}\\ (i.e., \text{ EOQ})\end{matrix}\right)$$

$$= 450 + 4000 = 4450 \text{ units}$$

$$\text{Average inventory level} = \frac{\left(\begin{matrix}\text{Minimum}\\ \text{inventory level}\end{matrix}\right) + \left(\begin{matrix}\text{Maximum}\\ \text{inventory level}\end{matrix}\right)}{2}$$

$$= \frac{450 + 4450}{2} = \frac{4900}{2} = 2450 \text{ units.}$$

7. *Veena industries, manufacturers of computer peripherals require certain item costing Rs. 3.75 each. The annual demand is 24,000 nos. Average lead time is 6 weeks and the demand per week is 460 with a standard deviation of 50 nos. per week. The company stipulates the policy of maintaining a service level of 95% (K = 1.64). Though normal lead time is 6 weeks, it is fluctuating and maximum lead time that occurred is 10 weeks. The cumulative probability of its occurrence, i.e., 7,8,9,10 weeks is 0.25. The ordering cost is Rs. 180 per order and the inventory carrying cost is 30% p.a. Based on the above information, design fixed order quantity inventory system and explain how it operates.*

Solution :

Annual demand (D) = 24,000 units

Ordering cost per order (C_o) = Rs. 180/-

Inventory carrying charges/year (C_i) = 30%

Unit Price of the item (P) = Rs. 3.75

$$\text{Economic Order Quantity (EOQ)} = \sqrt{\frac{2DC_o}{PC_i}}$$

$$\text{EOQ} = \sqrt{\frac{2 \times 24{,}000 \times 180}{3.75 \times 0.30}} = 2771.28$$

$$\text{No. of orders per year} = \frac{24{,}000}{2771.28} = 8.66 \approx 9 \text{ orders}$$

$$\text{Modified EOQ} = \frac{24{,}000}{9} = 2667 \text{ nos.}$$

Design of fixed order qty. system or Q system involves determination of how much to order *i.e.*, EOQ and when to order *i.e.*, Re-order level (ROL).

Re-order level = (Safety stock + Reserve stock + Buffer stock)

Normal or average consumption = 460 nos. per week

Safety stock (for variation in lead time) = (Normal consumption rate × Max. extension lead time × Cumulative probability of max. extension of lead time)

$= 460 \times (10 - 6) \times 0.25$

$= 460 \times 4 \times 0.25 = 460$ nos

Reserve stock = $K.\sigma_L = k\sigma \times \sqrt{L}$

For variation in consumption rate = $1.64 \times 50 \times \sqrt{6}$

= 200.85 say 201.

Buffer stock (*i e.*, normal consumption during normal lead time) = Normal consumption rate × Normal lead time

Buffer Stock = 460 × 6 = 2760 nos.

Re-order level = 460 + 201 + 2760 = 3421 nos.

Operation of 'Q' model of inventory control :

Whenever stock on hand falls to re-order level of 3421 nos., a fresh order is placed for EOQ *i.e.*, 2667 nos.

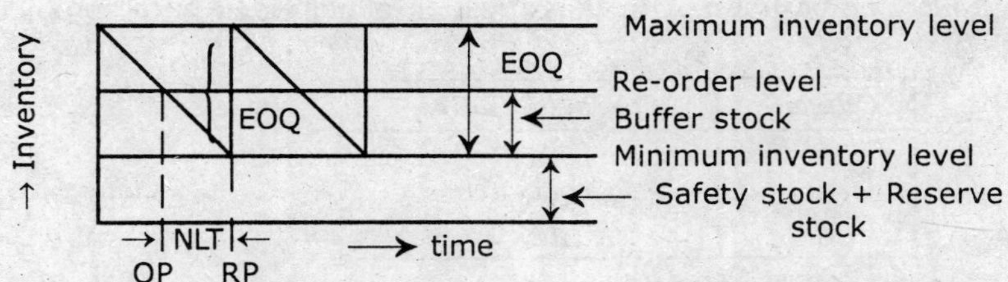

NLT – Normal Lead Time ; OP – Order Point ; RP – Receiving Point

8. *From the following data draw an ABC analysis graph after classifying A, B & C class items.*

Item	*Unit price (Rs.)*	*Annual consumption (units)*
1	*200.0*	*3,000*
2	*2.0*	*60,000*
3	*5000.0*	*20*
4	*12.5*	*200*
5	*9.0*	*350*
6	*25.0*	*6,000*
7	*1000.0*	*40*
8	*70.0*	*300*

Solution :

Step No. 1 : Determination of annual consumption value:

Item	***[Annual consumption (units) × Unit price (Rs.)]***	***Annual consumption value (Rs.) (ACV)***
1	3000 × 200	6,00,000
2	60,000 × 2	1,20,000
3	20 × 5000	1,00,000
4	200 × 12.5	2,500
5	350 × 9	3,150
6	6000 × 25	1,50,000
7	40 × 1000	40,000
8	300 × 70	21,000

Step No. 2 : Re-arrange the item in the descending order of annual consumption value and calculate cumulative ACV.

Item	***Annual Consumption Value (ACV) in descending order***	***Cumulative ACV***
1	6,00,000	6,00,000
6	1,50,000	7,50,000
2	1,20,000	8,70,000
3	1,00,000	9,70,000
7	40,000	10,10,000
8	21,000	10,31,000
5	3150	10,34,150
4	2500	10,36,650
	10,36,650	

Step No. 3 : Since the basis for ABC classification is not given in the problem, assume the following basis.

Category	*% ge of total ACV*
A	70%
B	20%
C	10%

70% of Total ACV = 0.70 × 10,36,650 = 7,25,655

Since this value is near to cumulative ACV of Rs. 7,50,000, categorize items 1 and 6 under 'A' category.

(A + B) together account for 90% of ACV

$$90\%\ \text{ACV} = 0.9 \times 10{,}36{,}650 = \text{Rs. } 9{,}32{,}985$$

Since this value is nearer to cumulative ACV of Rs. 9,70,000 categorize items 2 and 3 under 'B' category. The remaining items, 7, 8, 5 and 4 are categorized under 'C' category.

Step No. 4 : Construction of ABC analysis graph

$$\left.\begin{array}{r}\text{Exact \%ge of ACV of}\\ \text{'A' category items}\end{array}\right\} = \frac{7{,}50{,}000}{10{,}36{,}650} \times 100 = 72.34\%$$

$$\text{Exact \%ge of (A + B) items} = \frac{9{,}70{,}000}{10{,}36{,}650} \times 100 = 93.57\%$$

$$\text{\%ge of ACV of 'B' item} = 93.57 - 72.34 = 21.23\%$$

$$\text{\%ge of ACV of 'C' item} = 100 - 93.57 = 6.43\%$$

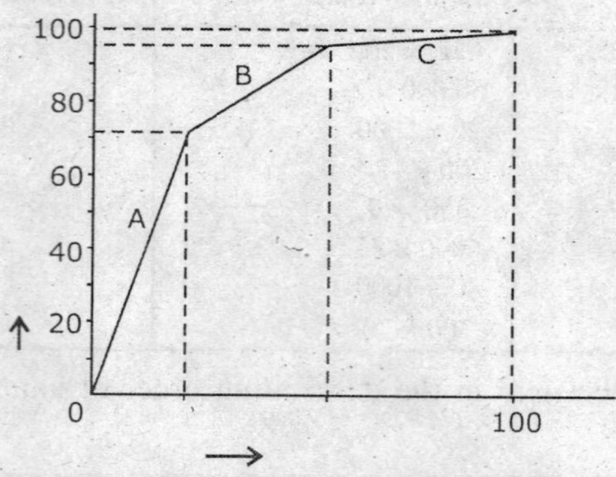

11. The following data is available on consumption pattern of certain materials in an organisation.

Group	*No. of items*	*Monthly consumption (units)*	*Price item (Rs.)*
I	*40*	*300*	*90*
II	*20*	*270*	*100*
III	*100*	*1700*	*5*
IV	*200*	*1500*	*4*
V	*60*	*340*	*50*
VI	*300*	*2500*	*1*
VII	*250*	*2000*	*2*
VIII	*30*	*170*	*500*

Find out A, B ,C items when,
'A' item account for 85% of consumption value.
'B' item account for 10% of consumption value.
'C' item account for 5% of consumption value.

Solution :

Step No. 1 : Calculation of Monthly consumption value (MCV)

Group	*No. of items per group*	*Monthly consumption (units)*	*Unit price (Rs.)*	*Monthly consumption value (MCV)*
I	40	300	90	10,80,000
II	20	270	100	5,40,000
III	100	1700	5	8,50,000
IV	200	1500	4	12,00,000
V	60	340	50	10,20,000
VI	300	2500	1	7,50,000
VII	250	2000	2	10,00,000
VIII	30	170	500	25,50,000
			Total	89,90,000

Step No. 2 : Rearrange the groups in the decreasing order of MCV and calculate cumulative MCV for each group.

Group	*MCV in descending order (Rs.)*	*Cumulative MCV (Rs.)*
VIII	25,50,000	25,50,000
IV	12,00,000	37,50,000
I	10,80,000	48,30,000
V	10,20,000	58,50,000
VII	10,00,000	68,50,000
III	8,50,000	77,00,000
VI	7,50,000	84,50,000
II	5,40,000	89,90,000

Step No. 3 : Classifying the group as A, B & C based on MCV

$$85\% \text{ of total MCV} = 0.85 \times 89{,}90{,}000$$
$$= 76{,}41{,}500$$

Since this value is nearer to cumulative MCV of 77,00,000, the groups VIII, IV, I, V, VIII and III are categorized under group 'A'.

(A + B) Comprise 95% of MCV.

$$95\% \text{ of MCV} = 0.95 \times 89{,}90{,}000$$
$$= \text{Rs. } 85{,}40{,}500/-$$

Since this value is nearer to 84,50,000, groups VI is under category 'B' and group II is under category 'C'.

➤ REVIEW QUESTIONS

1. Define the term "inventory".
2. Discuss the nature and importance of inventory for a manufacturing organisation.
3. How are inventories classified?
4. Briefly explain the various functions of inventory.
5. Discuss the various costs associated with inventory.
6. What are inventory decisions? Discuss basic EOQ model and the quantity discounts for EOQ model.
7. What is inventory management? What are its concerns?
8. Distinguish between dependent demand and independent demand inventories.
9. Explain the 'Q' system and 'P' system of inventory control for independent demand inventories.
10. Define the terms safety stock, reserve stock and buffer stock.
11. What do you understand by *(i)* Minimum level, *(ii)* Maximum level, *(iii)* Reorder level and *(iv)* Average level with respect to inventory.
12. What is selective inventory control? What are the various types of selective inventory control technique? Briefly discuss the same.
13. What is Pareto's law? What is its relevance in selective inventory control techniques?
14. What is material requirements planning? What are its objectives?
15. What is manufacturing resource planning?
16. Briefly discuss the operation of the MRP system.

❖ ❖ ❖ ❖

CHAPTER 8

MATERIALS REQUIREMENT PLANNING

Aggregate capacity plans develop plans for employment levels (manpower) machinery and utility, subcontract and purchase and facility modification. The planning horizon for aggregate capacity plans usually vary from six to eighteen months and short range master production schedule (MPS) are developed within the capacity constraints stipulated by aggregate plans. The time horizon for short range master production schedules vary from few weeks to several months and indicate the finished products or end items to be manufactured. The entire resource requirements planning system is based on the master production schedules.

➤ RESOURCE REQUIREMENTS PLANNING

Resource requirements planning is directed at determination of the amount and timing of production resources such as personnel, materials, cash and production capacity needed to produce the finished products or end items as per the master production schedule.

Resource requirements planning is also known as rough-cut capacity planning. It can be used to evaluate the feasibility of a trial master production schedule. It is an aggregate planning tool that is used to sum up and evaluate the work load that a production plan (MPS) imposes either on all work centres or on only selected key work centres where resources are limited, expensive or difficult to obtain from outside sources (subcontractors). This step ensures that a proposed MPS does not overload any key work centres or departments or machines making the MPS unworkable. Rough-cut capacity planning is usually applied to the critical work centres which are most likely to be bottlenecks.

Steps involved in rough-cut capacity planning are:

1. Developing a trial production plan (or trial master production schedule) that indicates the company's products that are planned for production during each week or month of the planning horizon.
2. Computing the work load this production plan will impose on each key work centre and key sub contractors for each period (week or month) of the planning horizon.

3. The load profile *i.e.,* the load on each work centre over time, is evaluated for feasibility by comparing the load with the available capacity in each of the key work centres or key subcontractors.
4. If the trial production plan does not appear to be feasible or does not make optimal use of the resources in the key work centres, the plan may be revised.
5. The capacity requirements of the revised production plan (revised MPS) can then be evaluated to determine the feasibility of the plan.
6. Step 4 and 5 are repeated until a plan considered to be satisfactory is developed.

Resource Requirements Planning System

Exhibit 8.1 illustrates the working of a resource requirements planning system.

Exhibit 8.1 : Resource Requirements Planning System

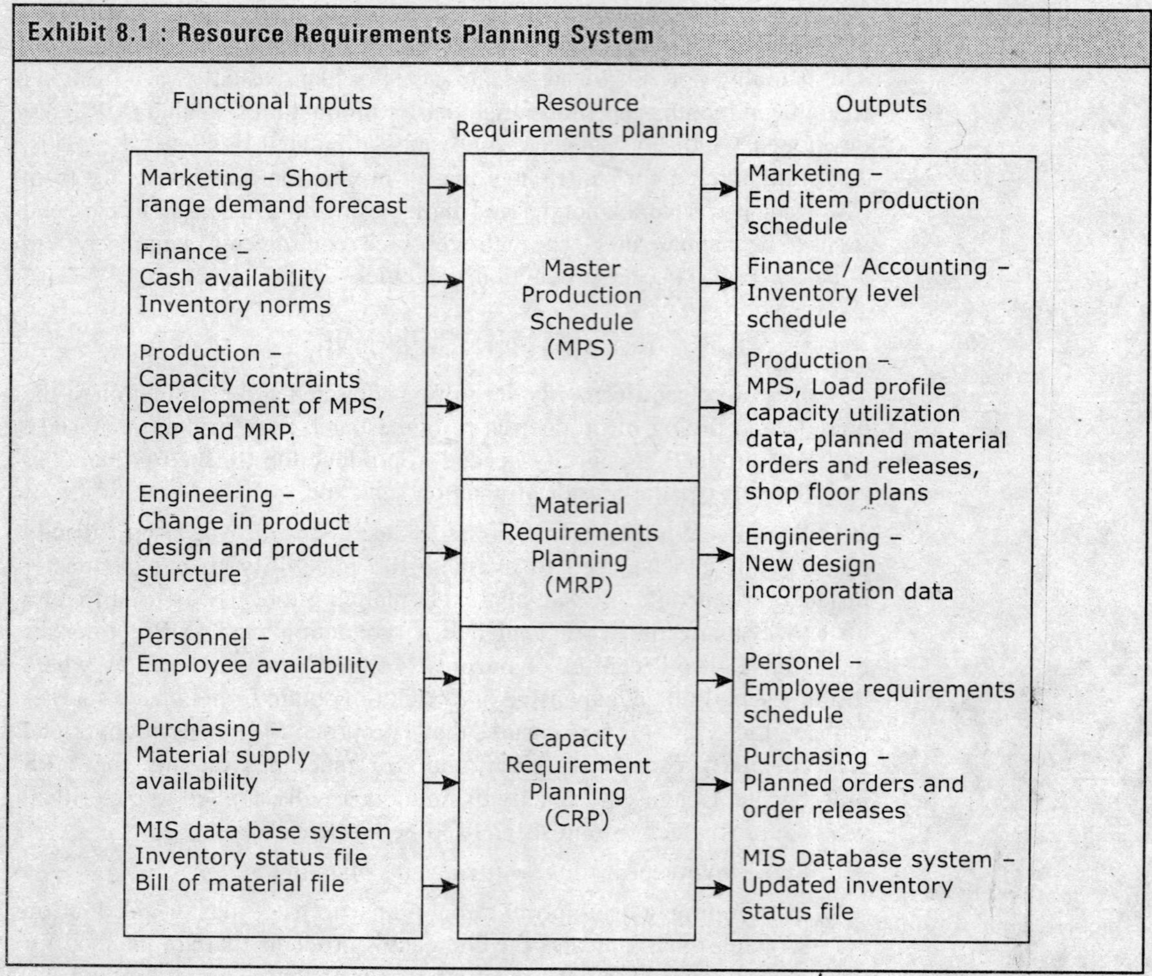

Exhibit 8.2 illustrates the major elements of resource requirements planning system.

It is seen from the above flow chart that there are two main elements of resource requirements planning systems namely (*a*) Material requirements planning (MRP) and

(*b*) Capacity requirements planning (CRP)

Exhibit 8.2 : Flow Chart of Resource Requirements Planning System or Rough-cut Capacity Planning Process

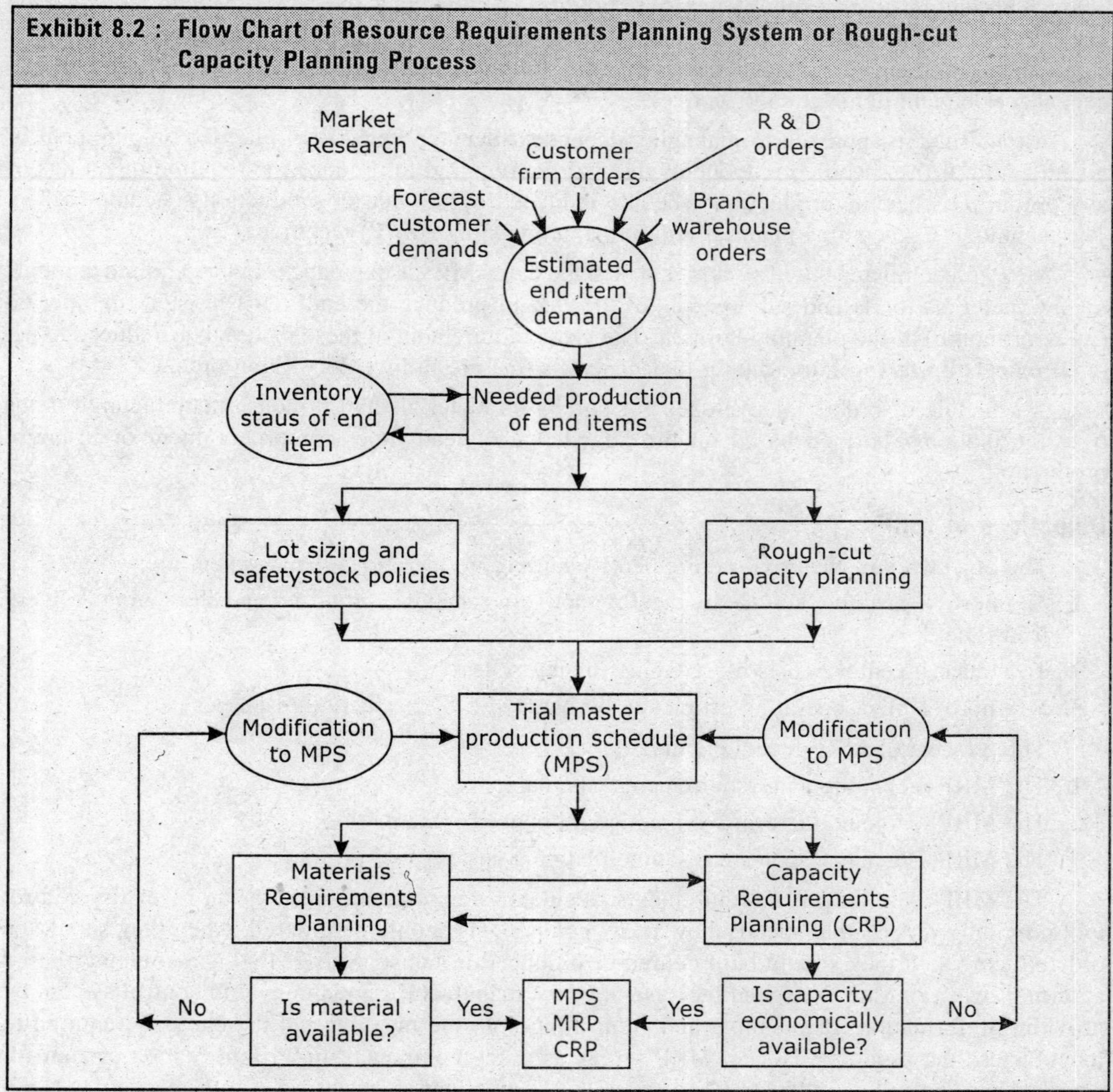

➤ MATERIAL REQUIREMENTS PLANNING (MRP OR MRP-I OR mrp)

For a manufacturing company to produce end items to meet demand, the availability of sufficient production capacity must be co-ordinated with the availability of all raw materials and purchased items from which the end items are to be produced. In other words, there is a need to manage the availability of dependent demand items from which the products are made. Dependent-demand items are the components *i.e.*, materials or purchased items, fabricated parts or subassemblies that make up the end product.

One approach to manage the availability of dependent-demand items is to keep a high stock of all the items that might be needed to produce the end items and when the on-hand stock dropped below a present re-order level, the items are produced or bought as the case may be to replenish the stock to the maximum level. However this approach is costly due to the excessive inventory of components, fabricated parts and sub assemblies to ensure high service level (*i.e.,* availability of dependent demand items at short notice).

An alternative approach to managing dependent-demand items is to plan for procurement or manufacture of the specific components that will be required to produce the required quantities of end products as per the production schedule indicated by the master production schedule (MPS). The technique is known as material requirements planning (MRP) technique.

MRP is a computer-based system in which the given MPS is exploded into the required amounts of raw materials, parts and sub assemblies, needed to produce the end items in each time period (week or month) of the planning horizon. The gross requirement of these materials is reduced to net requirements by taking into account that materials that are in inventory or on order.

A schedule of orders is developed for purchased materials and in-house manufactured items over the planning horizon based on the knowledge of lead times for procurement or in-house production.

Objectives of MRP

The objectives of material requirements planning in operations management are:

1. To improve customer service by meeting delivery schedules promised and shortening delivery lead times.
2. To reduce inventory costs by reducing inventory levels.
3. To improve plant operating efficiency by better use of productive resources.

Three facets of MRP technique are:

1. The MRP technique as a requirements calculator
2. The MRP - A manufacturing, planning and control system
3. The MRP - A manufacturing resource planning system

The MRP technique as a requirements calculator was originally used as an inventory control tool providing reports that specify how many components should be ordered, when they should be ordered and when they should be procured or produced in-house. Since MRP is a computer based system, it was possible to expand the system into a manufacturing planning and control system by providing information for planning and controlling both the material and the capacity required to manufacture the products. Hence, MRP serves as a key component in an information system for planning and controlling production operations and procurement of materials. It is the basic foundation for production activity control or shop floor control, for vendor follow up systems and for detailed capacity requirements planning. When both the MRP and CRP are integrated within one system, the system is known as "Material Requirements Planning" abbreviated as 'mrp' or MRP-I. When MRP is extended to include feed back from and control of vendor orders and production operations, it is called "closed-loop MRP" which helps managers achieve effective manufacturing control.

Purpose of MRP

The main purposes of a basic MRP system are to control inventory levels, assign operating priorities for items and plan capacity to load the production system. These are briefly discussed under three areas viz., *(i)* ***Inventory :*** Order the right item, order in the right quantity and order at the right time in order to receive the supplies at the right time.

(ii) ***Priorities :*** Order with the right due date and keep the due date valid.

(iii) ***Capacity :*** Plan for a complete load, plan an accurate load and plan for an adequate time to view future load.

The *theme* of MRP is "getting the right materials (whether bought-out or in-house manufactured) to the right place at the right time in the right quantities".

Advantages and Disadvantages of MRP

Advantages : *(i)* Reduced inventory, *(ii)* Reduced idle time, *(iii)* Reduced set up time, *(iv)* Ability to change the master production schedule, *(v)* Ability to price more competitively, *(vi)* Better customer service, *(vii)* Better response to market demands, *(viii)* Reduced sales price. In addition the MRP system enables the following:

(i) Aids capacity planning, *(ii)* Helps managers to use the planned schedule before actual release orders, *(iii)* Tells when to expedite or deexpedite, *(iv)* Delays or cancels orders, *(v)* Changes order quantities, *(vi)* Advances or delays order due dates.

Disadvantages : Even though MRP system has many advantages, there are some problems with MRP systems which make them fail in many firms. Three major causes for failures of an MRP system are:

(i) Lack of top management commitment. MRP must be accepted by top management as a planning tool with specific reference to profit results. All executives concerned with the implementation of the MRP system must be educated emphasizing the importance of MRP as a closed-loop, integrated strategic planning tool.

(ii) MRP was presented and perceived as a complete and stand-alone system to run a firm, rather than as part of the total system.

(iii) The issue of how MRP can be made to function with just-in-time production system.

MRP also needs a high degree of accuracy for operation, which often requires *(i)* changing how the firm operates and *(ii)* updating files.

The major complaint by users of MRP is that MRP is too rigid because when MRP develops a schedule, it is quite difficult to deviate from the schedule if need arises.

➤ MANUFACTURING RESOURCE PLANNING OR MRP-II

When the capabilities of closed-loop MRP are extended to integrate financial, accounting, personnel, engineering and marketing information along with the production planning and control activities of basic MRP system, the resulting broad-based resource-coordination system is known as manufacturing resource planning or MRP-II. MRP-II is the heart of corporate management information system for many companies as it provides information about inventory investment levels, plant expansion needs, and work-force requirements that is useful for co-ordinating marketing, financial, engineering and manufacturing efforts to achieve the company's overall business plans.

The projections of what materials and components will be purchased and when, can be used to develop purchase commitments and a projected purchasing budget. The labour hours projected in capacity requirement plan for each work centre can be aggregated to develop personnel needs and labour budgets. The projected on hand inventory of material can be used to develop inventory budgets.

➤ GENERAL OVERVIEW OF MRP (MATERIAL REQUIREMENTS PLANNING)

Basically, MRP consists of a set of computer programs that are run periodically (once a week or once a month) to incorporate the latest schedule of production requirements. MRP performs three important functions, *viz.*,

1. Order planning and control, *i.e.,* when to release orders and for what quantity?
2. Priority planning and control *i.e.,* comparison of expected date of availability with the need date of each item.
3. Provision of a basis for planning capacity requirements and development of broad business plans.

MRP is applicable primarily to companies that carry out fabrication of parts and assembly of standard products in batch quantities.

Exhibit 8.3 shows a flow chart that provides a general overview of MRP as a means of co-ordinating purchasing activities to support manufacturing as well as material requirements and capacity requirements.

Exhibit 8.3 : Information Flow for Planning and Controlling with MRP

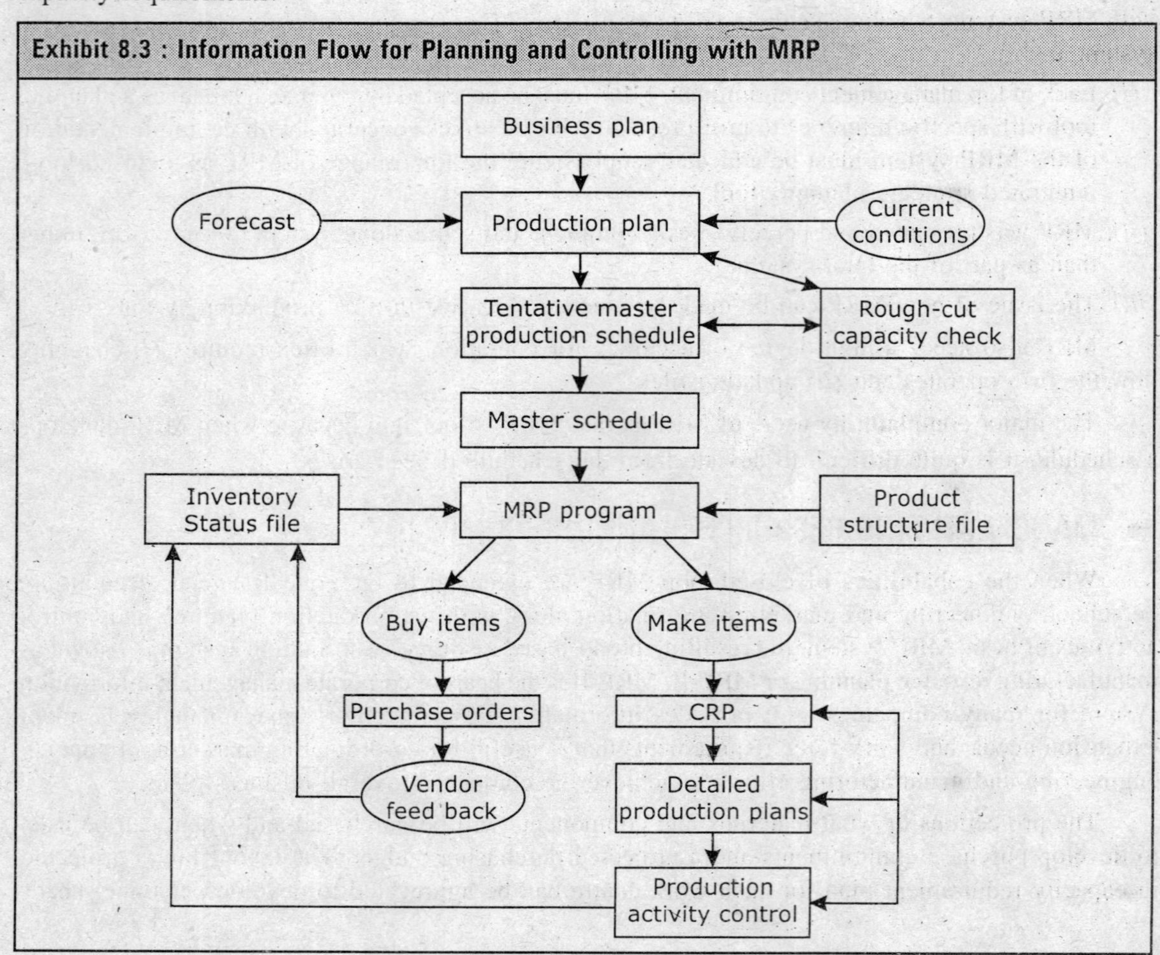

➤ OPERATION OF THE MRP SYSTEM

Exhibit 8.4 illustrates the operation of MRP system.

Exhibit 8.4 : Operation of MRP System

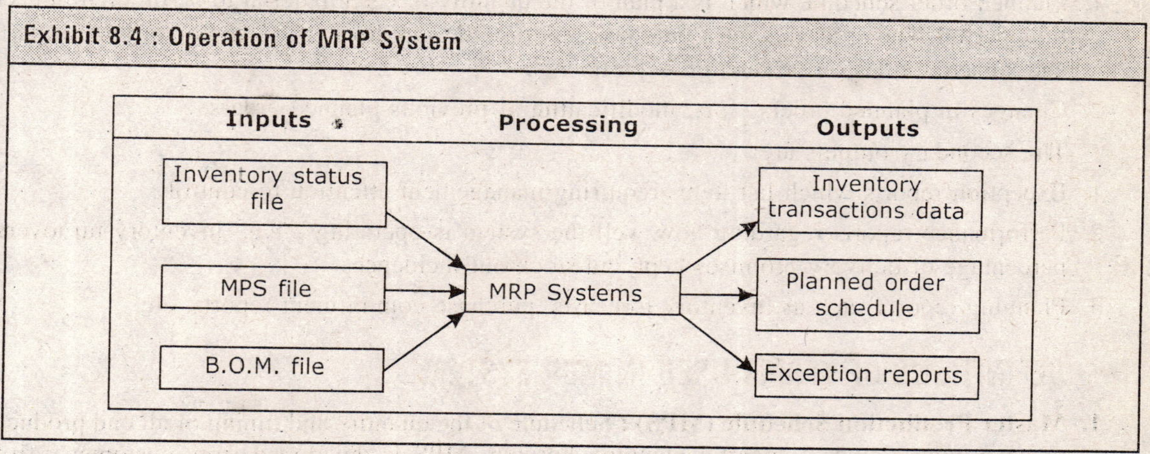

The entire MRP system is driven by the MPS. The bill of materials file and inventory status file are fed to the MRP computer program to generate the outputs.

MRP System Inputs

1. **Master Production Schedule (MPS) :** The MPS specifies what end products are to be produced and when. The planning horizon should be long enough to cover the cumulative lead times of all components that must be purchased or manufactured to meet the end product requirements.
2. **Bill of Material file or Product Structure file :** This file provides the information regarding all the materials, parts and sub assemblies that go into the end product. The Bill of Materials can be viewed as having a series of levels, each of which represents a stage in the manufacture of the end product. The highest level (or zero level) of the BOM represents the final assembly or end product. The BOM file identifies each component by a unique part number and facilitates processing by exploding the end product requirements into component requirements.
3. **Inventory Status file :** The inventory status file gives complete and up-to-date information on the on-hand quantities, gross requirements, scheduled receipts and planned order releases for the item. It also includes other information such as lot sizes, lead times, safety stock levels and scrap allowances, etc. The gross requirements are total needs from all resources whereas the net requirements are "net" after allowing for available inventory and scheduled receipt. Scheduled receipts are quantities already on order from a vendor or in-house shop. Planned receipts are quantities that will be ordered on a vendor or in-house shop. Planned order release indicates the quantity and date to initiate the purchase or manufacture of materials that will be received on schedule after the lead time offset.

$$\begin{pmatrix}\text{Net requirement}\\ \text{for a period}\end{pmatrix} = \begin{pmatrix}\text{Gross requirement}\\ \text{for the period}\end{pmatrix} - \begin{pmatrix}\text{Scheduled receipt for the period}\\ \text{+ on hand inventory at the end}\\ \text{of the period}\end{pmatrix}$$

MRP System Outputs

Two primary outputs are:

1. Planned order schedule which is a plan of the quantity of each material to be ordered in each time period. The order may be a purchase order on the suppliers or production orders for parts and subassemblies on production departments.
2. Changes in planned orders - *i.e.,* modification of previous planned orders.

The secondary outputs are:

1. Exception reports which list items requiring management attention to control
2. Performance reports regarding how well the system is operating - *e.g.,* inventory turnovers, percentage of delivery promises kept and stock out incidences.
3. Planning reports such as inventory forecasts, purchase commitment reports, etc.

➤ DEFINITIONS OF TERMS USED IN MRP SYSTEM

1. **Master Production Schedule (MPS) :** Schedule of the quantity and timing of all end products to be produced over a specific planning horizon. MPS is developed from customer's firm orders or from forecasts of demand or both. It is an input to the MRP system.
2. **Product structure :** Indicates the level of components required to produce an end product.
3. **Bills of Material (BOM) :** A list indicating the quantities of all raw materials, parts, components, sub assemblies and major assemblies that go into an end product. It gives details of the build-up of a product. It may also be called as indented parts list.
4. **Bills of Material file :** A bills of material file, also known as product-structure file is a computerized file listing all finished products, the quantity of raw materials, parts, sub assemblies and assemblies in each product. The bills of material file must be kept up-to- date as and when the products are redesigned or modified with addition/deletion of some parts, components and subassemblies.
5. **Inventory status file :** It is a computerized file with a comprehensive record of each and every material held in inventory. The information included in this file are materials on hand or on order, planned orders, planned order releases, allocated materials, lot sizes, lead times, safety stock levels, costs and suppliers for each material. The inventory file must be kept up-to-date taking into consideration the daily inventory transactions such as receipts, issues, scrapped materials, planned orders and order releases.
6. **MRP computer program :** It is a computer program which processes the MRP information. Its inputs are the MPS, inventory status file and bills of material file. The primary outputs are : planned order schedule, planned order releases and changes to planned orders.
7. **Available inventory :** Materials that are held in inventory or which are on order but are not either safety stock or allocated to other uses.

$$\left.\begin{array}{r}\text{Available inventory}\\ \text{of an item at the end}\\ \text{of a time period}\end{array}\right\} = \left\{\begin{array}{l}\text{[Scheduled receipts + planned}\\ \text{order receipts − gross requirements}\\ \text{for that period] + Quantity available}\\ \text{from the previous period}\end{array}\right.$$

8. **Allocated inventory :** Materials that are held in inventory or on order but which have been

allocated to specific production orders (committed for use) in the future. These materials are not available to meet future requirements for use on other orders.

9. **On-hand inventory :** The quantity of a material physically held in inventory at a point of time. It may include safety stock and allocated inventory except materials on order.
10. **Planning horizon :** The number of time periods (days, weeks or months) included in the MPS, CRP, MRP and departmental schedules.
11. **Action Bucket :** The unit of time measurement in MRP systems. It is a particular period of time in the planning horizon. *For example*,, Bucket # 10 means the tenth period (usually a week in duration) of the planning horizon.
12. **Gross requirements :** The total quantity of an item needed at the end of a period to meet the planned output levels, not considering any availability of the item in inventory or scheduled receipts.
13. **Scheduled receipts :** The quantity of an item that will be received at the beginning of a time period from a supplier as result of orders already placed (open orders).
14. **Planned order receipts :** The quantity of an item that is planned to be ordered so that it will be received at the beginning of the time period to meet the net requirements for that time period. The order is yet to be placed.
15. **Planned order releases :** The quantity of an item that is planned to be ordered and the planned time period for releasing this order so that the item will be received when needed. This time schedule is determined by offsetting the planned order receipts schedule to allow for lead times, *i.e.*,

$$\begin{pmatrix}\text{Planned order release}\\ \text{(time schedule)}\end{pmatrix} = \begin{pmatrix}\text{Planned order receipt}\\ \text{(time schedule)}\end{pmatrix} - \text{(Lead time)}$$

When this order is released, it becomes a scheduled receipt.

16. **Net requirements :** The quantity of an item that must be procured to meet the scheduled output for the period.

$$\begin{pmatrix}\text{Net requirements}\\ \text{for the period}\end{pmatrix} = \left[\begin{pmatrix}\text{Gross}\\ \text{requirements for}\\ \text{the period}\end{pmatrix} - \begin{pmatrix}\text{Scheduled}\\ \text{requirements for}\\ \text{the period}\end{pmatrix}\right] - \begin{pmatrix}\text{Qty. available}\\ \text{from the}\\ \text{previous period}\end{pmatrix}$$

$$\begin{pmatrix}\text{Net requirements}\\ \text{for the period}\end{pmatrix} = \begin{pmatrix}\text{Gross requirements}\\ \text{for the period}\end{pmatrix} - \begin{pmatrix}\text{Material available}\\ \text{for the period}\end{pmatrix}$$

17. **Low-level coding :** The coding of each material at the lowest level in any product structure that it appears. A component can appear at more than one level in the product structure. Because MRP computer programs process net requirements calculations for all products level by level from end items down to the raw materials, low level coding avoids redundant net requirements calculations.
18. **Lot-sizing decisions :** Whenever there is a need for the net requirement of a material, a decision must be taken regarding the quantity of material to be ordered (either purchase order or production order). Lot sizing decisions include both the batch or lot size (quantity) as well as the timing of these lots.

19. **Dependent Demand :** Demand for a raw material, part or a component, that is dependent on the demand for the end product in which these materials are used.

20. **Independent demand :** Demand for a material that is independent of the demands for other materials. *For example,* demand for end products are independent of demand for parts, raw materials or components as their demands are determined by customers outside the organization.

21. **Lumpy demand :** If the demand for the materials varies greatly from time period to time period (say week to week), the demand is said to be "lumpy demand".

22. **Capacity requirement planning :** The process of reconciling the Master Production Schedule to the available capacities of production departments (viz., machine and labour capacities) over the planning horizon.

23. **Load Schedules :** A load schedule is a device for comparing the actual labour-hours and machine-hours required to produce the MPS against the available labour-hours and machine-hours in each week.

24. **Net change MRP :** MRP systems that generate outputs emphasizing only the changes to last MRP outputs. Planned order schedules in these systems would indicate only the changes to the previous report and not a completely new schedule.

25. **Regenerative MRP :** MRP systems that periodically generate one complete set of MRP outputs. In these systems, a planned order schedule would be a complete report not be comprised solely of changes to an earlier report.

26. **Product Explosion :** The process of determining from the product structure and planned order releases and the gross requirements for components.

27. **Pegging :** The process of tracing through the MRP records and all levels in the product structure to identify how changes in the records of one component will affect the records of other components. Pegging shows the level-by-level linkages among components and their time-phased status in the MRP records.

28. **Cycle counting :** Counting on-hand inventories at regular intervals to verify inventory quantities shown in the MRP.

29. **Time fence :** A designated length of time that must pass without changing the MPS, to stabilize the MRP system.

30. **Lot-for-lot ordering :** A lot sizing policy in which order quantity equals net requirement for the period.

31. **Period-order quantity (POQ) method :** Also known as part-period method, it is a lot-sizing policy in which order quantity varies according to a comparison of holding versus ordering costs.

$$\text{P.O.Q.} = \frac{\text{No. of weeks per year}}{\text{No. of orders per year (N)}} = \frac{52}{\text{N}} \text{ weeks}$$

$$\text{No. of orders per year (N)} = \frac{\text{Annual Demand (units)}}{\text{Economic Order Quantity}}$$

$$\text{Order quantity} = \text{Net requirements of periods equal to POQ}$$

32. **Frozen MPS :** The early time periods of the MPS that can be assumed to not to be subject to change. Frozen periods of MPS enables managers to commit funds, order materials as such plans will not need to be subsequently changed.

Questions Answered in MRP Processing

Questions	*Answers*
1. What end products do we want to produce and when?	Input to MRP program through the MPS.
2. What components/parts are required to make the end products and how many are required?	Provided by Bills of materials.
3. How many components/parts are already scheduled to be available in each future period?	Obtained from inventory status file.
4. How many more components/parts do we need to obtain for each future period?	Gross requirements minus scheduled receipts.
5. When do we need to order these quantities in order to make them available when needed (not too early or not too late)	Need date for the item minus procurement lead time or production lead time as the case may be (*i.e.*, whether the item is bought out or manufactured in-house)

➢ THE MRP COMPUTATIONAL PROCEDURE

The MRP system is shown below in *Exhibit 8.5*.

Exhibit 8.5 : MRP System

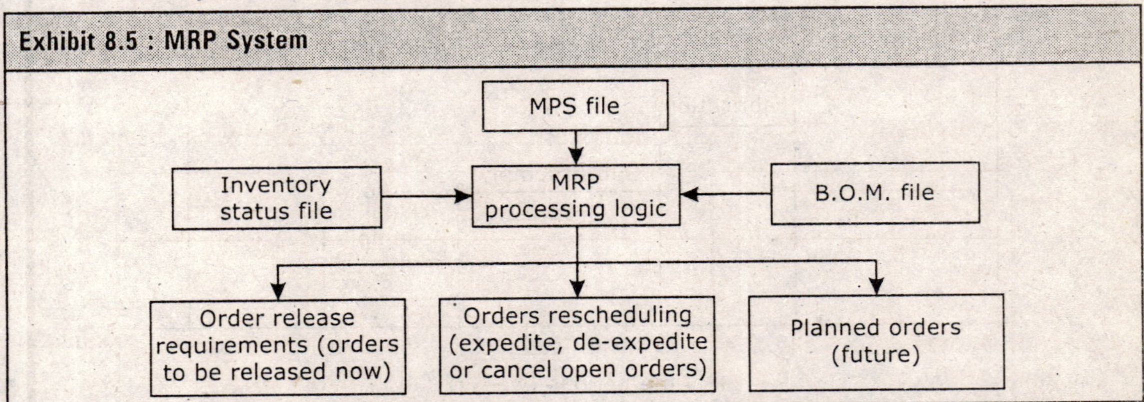

Inputs : M.P.S. file, B.O.M. file and Inventory status file

Outputs : Planned order release, order reschedules, order release requirements.

MRP Inputs

1. The master production schedule is the key input which drives the MRP program. The MPS tells the program what the company intends to produce. As an illustration, let us consider a portion of the MPS for XYZ company which is given below in *Table 8.1*.

Table 8.1

End item	*Week Number*											
	1	*2*	*3*	*4*	*5*	*6*	*7*	*8*	*9*	*10*	*11*	*12*
001-3 drawer filing cabinet							200			200		200
002-4 drawer filing cabinet				120			120	240		120		
003-Desk						300			300		180	

The above figure shows the Master Production Schedule of XYZ company manufacturing office equipments and furnitures. The MPS is prepared for one quarter (12 weeks period). The time bucket in the planning horizon is one week. The quantities indicated in the MPS may include both plans to produce end items that have been ordered by customers (customer's firm orders) and plans to produce end items for forecast sales.

The minimum planning horizon for each product must usually be greater than the cumulative time required for procurement of raw materials and components and for performance of all other production operations such as fabrication, subassembly and final assembly as illustrated in *Exhibit 8.6*.

This minimum planning horizon (*i.e.,* time period) may be considered as a 'time fence' within which changes to the MPS are not permitted except in extreme situations (*e.g.,* a customer's order is cancelled)

The maximum length of time that is planned in a MPS will depend on the company's ability to forecast demand and its requirements, but a one-year span is usually common.

Exhibit 8.6 :

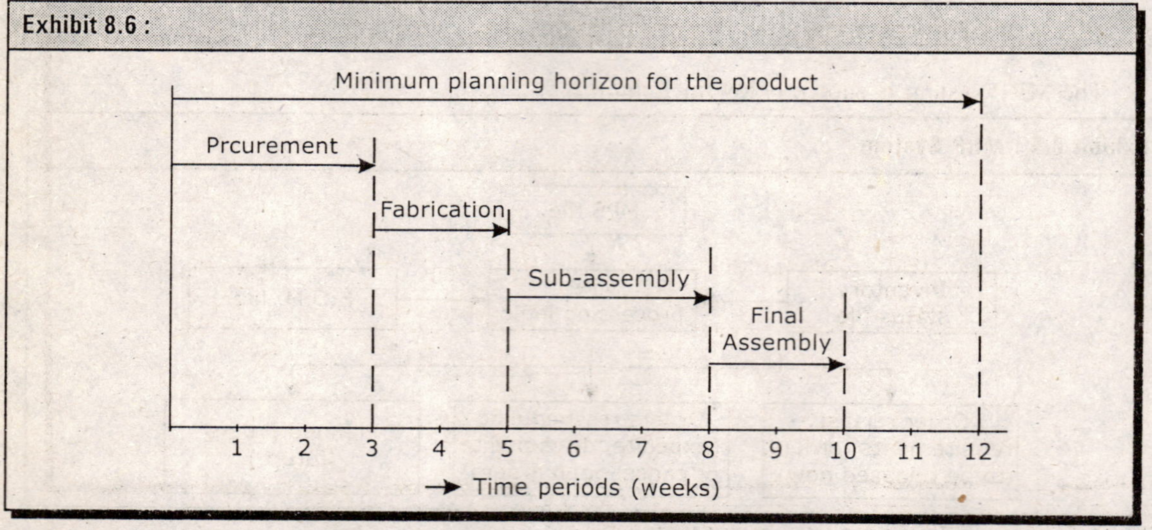

Source : James B. Dilworth, *Production and Operations Management*, 4th Edition, McGraw Hill Co., p.295

2. Bill of Materials file : The MRP program obtains information about the components needed to make an end product from the bill-of-materials file, which is also known as product-structure file. A bill of material not only lists all the required parts but also is structured to reflect the sequence of steps required to produce the end product. The B.O.M. has a series of levels, each of which represents a stage in the manufacture of the end product.

The highest level or zero-level of the B.O.M. represents the final assembly or end product. The next lower level might represent the sub assemblies that are combined to make the final assembly. The next lower level might represent the parts needed to make the sub assemblies and the bottom most level might represent the raw materials from which the parts are made.

Each component at any level of the B.O.M. is identified by a unique part number. Determining all the lower-level components needed to make a parent item is called 'exploding' the requirements of the bill-of-materials. A 'where-used list' indicates the next assembly in which a component or part is used and can be used to determine what products cannot be made if some components are not available on time.

Exhibit 8.7 (see p.285) shows the product-structure tree for 3 drawer filing cabinet manufactured by XYZ company :

The bill-of-material for the three-drawer cabinet would contain the following items are listed in *Table 8.2.*

Exhibit 8.7 : Product Structure Tree for 3 Drawer Filing Cabinet

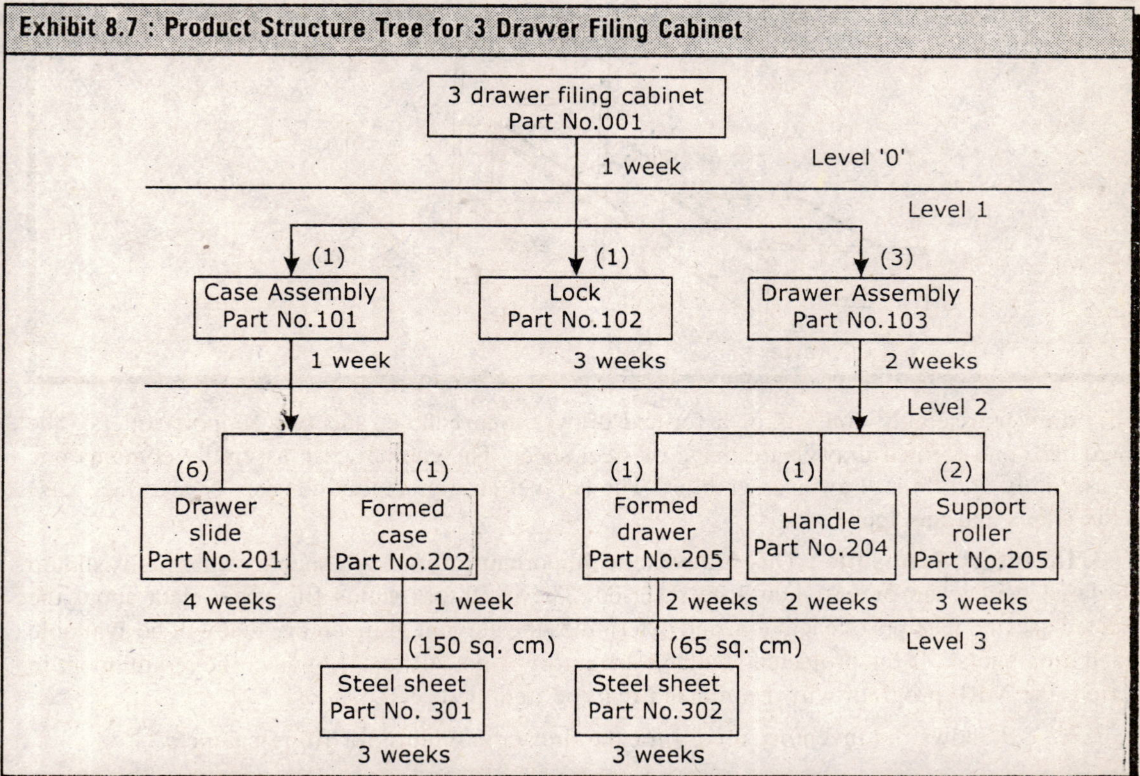

Table 8.2 : Bill of Materials for three-drawer cabinet

Part No.	Quantity	Description
001	1 no.	3 drawer filing cabinet
101	1 no.	Case assembly
102	1 no.	Lock
103	3 nos.	Drawer assembly
101	1	Case assembly
201	6	Drawer slides
202	1	Formed case
103	1	Drawer assembly
203	1	Formed drawer
204	1	Handle
205	2	Support rollers
202	1	Formed case
301	150 sq.cm.	Steel sheet
203	1	Formed drawer
302	65 sq.cm.	Steel sheet

Exhibit 8.8 shows the 3 drawer filing cabinet

Exhibit 8.8 : Three Drawer Filing Cabinet

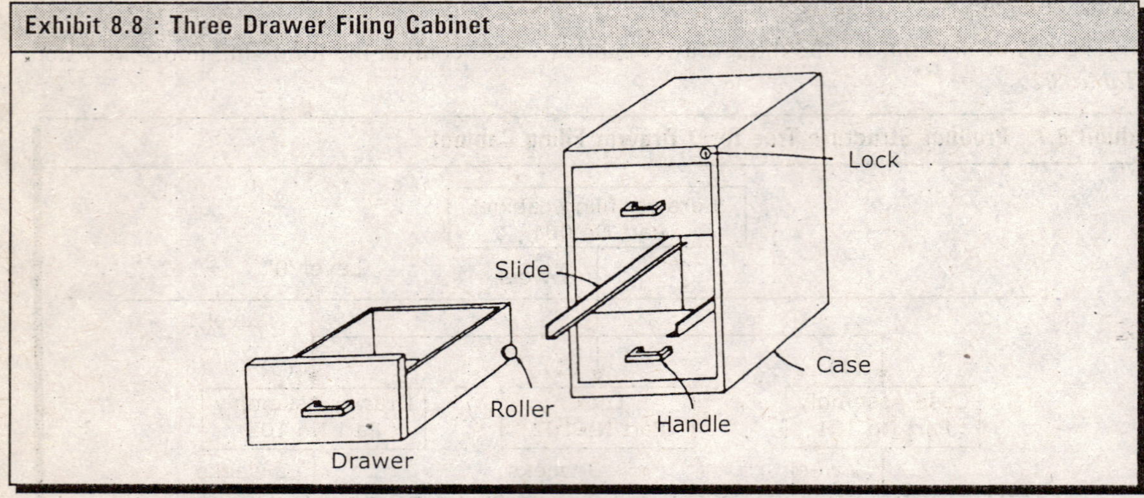

A drawer assembly consists of a formed drawer, one handle, and two support rollers. The formed case and formed drawer are made of steel sheet. The cabinet case assembly contains one case assembly and three drawer assemblies. The cabinet case assembly consists of a formed case and six slides and one lock.

3. Inventory Status file ; This file contains important information such as what items should be ordered, and when orders should be released. The inventory status file keeps data about the projected use and receipts of each item and determines the amount of inventory that will be available in each time bucket. If the projected available inventory is not sufficient to meet the requirement in a period, the MRP program will recommend that the item be ordered.

Table 8.3 shows the inventory record for the drawer assembly for filing cabinets.

Table 8.3 : Inventory Record for the Drawer Assembly for Filing Cabinets

Item 103 Lead time = 2 weeks. Drawer Assembly	Week											
	1	2	3	4	5	6	7	8	9	10	11	12
Gross reqmnts.						600			600		600	
Scheduled receipts		800										
On hand	40	40	840	840	840	840	240	240	240	-360	-360	-960
Net reqmts.									360		600	
Planned order release							360		600			

4. Gross Requirements : The gross requirements shown in *Table 8.3* project the use of the item viz., drawer assembly (part no.103) in the end product viz., 3-drawer filing cabinet (part no.001). In this example, the company needs 600 drawers in week No. 6 to make the 200 nos of 3 drawer filing cabinets that are to be started in week no.6 so that they will be completed by week no.7 as specified in MPS (Ref. *Table 8.1*). An additional 600 drawers are to be started into assembly in week no.9 to meet the requirement of 200 nos of 3 drawer filing cabinet in the week no.10 (Ref. *Table 8.1*).

5. Scheduled Receipts : The numbers in the scheduled receipts row indicate when the previously released orders (*i.e.*, open orders) if any are scheduled to be received and available for use. In the example, an order for 800 nos of drawers is scheduled to be completed in week no.2.

6.On Hand inventory : The numbers in the 'on hand' row indicate the number of units projected to be available at the end of each time period (*i.e.*, week). The quantity of 40 nos indicates the beginning inventory in the beginning of week no.1. The numbers in other blocks of the 'on hand' row represent the quantity scheduled to be on hand at the end of each period (*i.e.*, week).

$$\begin{pmatrix}\text{'On hand' inventory}\\ \text{for period 'n'}\end{pmatrix} = \begin{pmatrix}\text{'On hand' for}\\ \text{the period 'n – 1'}\end{pmatrix} + \begin{pmatrix}\text{Scheduled receipts}\\ \text{for the period 'n'}\end{pmatrix} - \begin{pmatrix}\text{Gross requirements}\\ \text{for the period n}\end{pmatrix}$$

7. Net requirements : The amount of net requirements in any period can be calculated by subtracting from the gross requirements for that period, any scheduled receipts for that period and any positive quantity 'on-hand' for the previous period.

$$\begin{pmatrix}\text{Net requirement}\\ \text{for the period 'n'}\end{pmatrix} = \begin{pmatrix}\text{Gross}\\ \text{requirements}\\ \text{for period 'n'}\end{pmatrix} - \begin{pmatrix}\text{Scheduled}\\ \text{receipts}\\ \text{for period 'n'}\end{pmatrix} - \begin{pmatrix}\text{On hand inventory}\\ \text{at the end of}\\ \text{period 'n – 1'}\end{pmatrix}$$

For *e.g.*, $\begin{pmatrix}\text{Net requirement}\\ \text{for } 9^{th} \text{ week}\end{pmatrix} = (600 - \text{NIL} - 240) = 360$ numbers

8. Planned order releases : Numbers in 'planned order releases' row indicate when orders should be placed to meet the requirement for the item. The time period at which the order should be released is found by subtracting the lead time from the 'net requirement' period (this procedure is called 'offsetting' by lead time)

9. Lot-for-lot ordering : In this method, one order is planned for each period in which there is a net requirement. The planned order release will be for the quantity which is indicated in the 'net requirement' row for that period. In this example, the lead time to produce a drawer assembly is 2 weeks. Hence the net requirement of 360 drawers for the week no. 9 should be planned for order release in week no.7 and the net requirement of 600 drawer assemblies in week no. 11 should be planned for order release in week no. 9.

Issues in MRP

Some of the issues which deserve consideration in any comprehensive treatment of MRP are:

1. Lot-sizing : The MRP system generates planned order releases, which trigger purchase orders for outside suppliers or production orders (or work orders) for in-house production departments. As certain costs such as the set up cost (or ordering cost) and holding cost (or inventory carrying cost) are associated with each order, it is necessary to consider the trade-off between these two types of costs and take decision regarding how much to order (ie., batch size/lot size) A question that should be examined is whether there is some economic lot size (EOQ or EBQ) that should be purchased or produced as the case may be. In production a minimum lot size is sometimes established to reduce the set up cost per unit produced. Such minimum lot sizes may cause excessive inventory if it exceeds very much the net requirement of a period and followed by periods with no requirements, which is counter to the benefit of MRP system.

Various methods of lot sizing are:

(a) *Lot-for-lot ordering (LFL)* in which order quantity equals the net requirements for a given period. Separate orders are released for each period's net requirement.

(b) *EOQ technique* in which the order quantity is larger than a single period's net requirement so that ordering cost and holding costs balance out.

(c) Requirements may be batched until they reach some arbitrary minimum order size. If the requirement exceedes this exceeds this minimum, the requirement will determine the order size.

(d) The lot size may be determined by the *period order quantity (POQ)* technique.

$$\text{Period order qty. (POQ)} = \frac{\text{No. of weeks per year}}{\text{No. of orders per year}} = \frac{N}{D/Q} \text{ weeks}$$

where D = Annual demand (units)

Q = Economic order Qty (EOQ)

N = Number of weeks per year.

The ordering policy is to order the net requirements of the number of periods equal to POQ.

(e) The lot size can be chosen to approximately balance ordering and holding costs. One method of doing this is known as *part-period method or part-period algorithm (PPA)*. This is a simple approach to lot-size selection when a series of requirements which are not necessarily uniform are to be batched into orders so that the total cost will be near the minimum. This method does not provide an optimal lot size (ie EOQ) but it approaches optimality by attempting to make holding cost for a lot nearly equal to the ordering cost for the lot.

Unlike the EOQ model, the part period algorithm method may select a different quantity to be ordered each time the order is to be placed. The PPA assumes that an order will be scheduled in the first period in which there is a net requirement. The requirement for the next period is added into this order if the cost of holding these units until they are used is less than the cost of receiving them as a separate order. Requirements for future periods continue to be added to the lot until the total holding cost for the lot comes as close as possible to the order cost without dividing a period's requirement.

2. Safety stock : There are divergent views by MRP users regarding whether safety stock should be used in MRP systems or not. One side of argument supporting the use of safety stock is that it performs the function of avoiding excessive stockouts caused by uncertain lead times and daily demands. On the other hand those who oppose the use of safety stock in MRP argue that safety stock is not required because MRP systems adopt to changing conditions that affect demand and lead times.

The use of safety stock can be justified only by the sources of uncertainty present during lead times. Safety stock is normally maintained for end items which have independent demand. For lower-level items such as raw material and parts, the uncertainty of demand is adequately controlled because the demand is a dependent demand which is set by the M.P.S. However uncertainties may be present during lead times because of uncertainity of lead time and the uncertainty of demand that occurs because of changes in the MPS. Keeping some safety stock can be justified for raw materials. parts and other low-level items although at significantly reduced levels.

3. Scrap allowances : The bill of materials explosion could include multiplication by a factor (more than one) to make an allowance for the usual scrap loss in manufacturing an item.

4. Pegging : Pegging is a technique which enables the planner to trace from a work load in a work centre back through its higher-level assemblies to determine what end item in the MPS caused the load. Single level pegging is used often which simply tells the immediately higher-level parent of a component. When material plans are disrupted, pegging helps to identify which components are affected by such disruptions. Pegging shows the level-by-level linkages among components and their time-phased status in MRP records. *Table 8.4* gives an example of pegging showing the current records for an end item 'X' and for its sub components Y and Z at two lower levels in the product structure.

Table 8.4 : Pegging the MRP Records

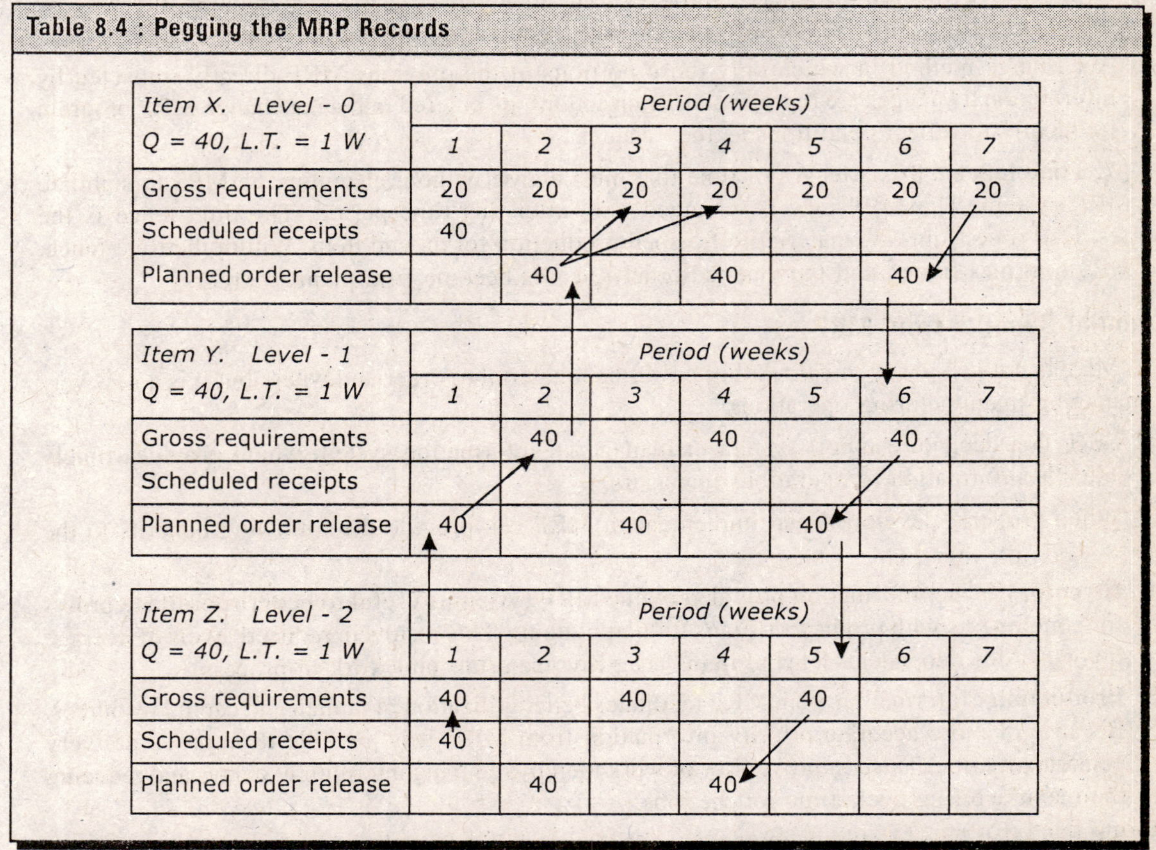

Item X. Level - 0	*Period (weeks)*						
Q = 40, L.T. = 1 W	*1*	*2*	*3*	*4*	*5*	*6*	*7*
Gross requirements	20	20	20	20	20	20	20
Scheduled receipts	40						
Planned order release		40		40		40	

Item Y. Level - 1	*Period (weeks)*						
Q = 40, L.T. = 1 W	*1*	*2*	*3*	*4*	*5*	*6*	*7*
Gross requirements		40		40		40	
Scheduled receipts							
Planned order release	40		40		40		

Item Z. Level - 2	*Period (weeks)*						
Q = 40, L.T. = 1 W	*1*	*2*	*3*	*4*	*5*	*6*	*7*
Gross requirements	40		40		40		
Scheduled receipts	40						
Planned order release		40		40			

If it is found out that 40 units of Z (scheduled receipts) for period 1 can not be completed, then plan for Y & X are affected. The planned order release for Y (40 units in period 1) should be cancelled because its supporting material (Z) will not be available. Consequently the planned order release for 40 units of X in period 2 also should be cancelled.

Similarly, if the master production schedule were to increase week 7's gross requirements for X from 20 to 60 to meet a special customer order, the pegging procedure traces down through the

MRP records to identify associated changes at lower levels. The planned order release for X in week 6 has to be raised from 40 to 60 and the associated requirements for Y and Z has to be changed accordingly.

5. Cycle counting : Cycle counting is the process of counting on-hand inventories at regular intervals to verify inventory of components including defective items at each stage of production and in storage areas. This ensures that on-hand inventories tally with the quantities shown in MRP records. Based on cycle counting, the MRP records are updated daily or weekly to show the actual inventory status. This knowledge of actual inventory is helpful in adjusting the production schedules at various work centres.

6. Updating : Whenever changes occur in MPS, in inventory status file, (*e.g.*, revised lead times) or in product structure file, or changes in product design occurs, the MRP system must be updated. Two approaches to update MRP system are:

(a) Regenerative method which is a process used to update the MRP at regular intervals by reprocessing the entire set of information and regenerating the entire MRP.

(b) Net change method in which only those portions of the previous MRP directly impacted by informational changes are reprocessed. Transactions are entered into a net change MRP program frequently to reflect conditions as they change.

7. Time fence : It is a length of time that must elapse without changing the MPS to stabilize the MRP system. The MPS may be changed only after this time period. The time fence is the shortest lead time from raw material to finished production for an end item. Within the time fence, the MPS becomes frozen and the planned order releases become firm planned orders.

Potential Benefits from MRP

MRP is not just a way of calculating how much material to order and when; but it is a new way of managing manufacturing operations.

MRP is a decision support system or managerial information system which provides timely and valuable information to operations managers.

When properly developed and implemented, MRP can provide the following benefits to the firm :

1. **Inventory :** The information provided by the MRP system is useful to better coordinate orders for components with production plans for parent items. This results in reduced levels of average inventory for dependent-demand items (*i.e.*, raw materials and work-in-process).
2. **Production :** Information from MRP facilitates better utilization of human and capital resources. Because of more accurate priority information from MRP, it is possible to improve delivery performance. It can also improve flow of work thereby reducing intermittent delays and reducing the manufacturing cycle time for the jobs.
3. **Sales :** MRP helps to check in advance whether the desired delivery dates are achievable. It improves the company's ability to react to changes in customer orders, improves customer service by helping production meet assembly dates and helps cut delivery lead times.
4. **Engineering :** MRP helps in planning the time of design releases and design changes.
5. **Planning :** MRP can simulate changes in the MPS for purpose of evaluation of alternative MPS. It facilitates projection of equipment and facility requirements, workforce planning and procurement expenses for a proposed MPS.

6. **Purchasing :** MRP helps purchase department by making known the real priorities and recommending changes in due dates for orders so that the purchase staff may expedite or delay the orders placed on vendors. Because of this the vendor relations can be improved.
7. **Scheduling :** Better scheduling can result from MRP through better knowledge of priorities.
8. **Finance :** MRP can help better planning of cash flow requirements. It can identify time capacity constraints or bottleneck work centres thereby helping operations managers to make better capital investment decisions.

Implementation of MRP

Successful implementation of MRP depends on the following factors:

1. **Management commitment :** Top level managers and other managers in all parts of the organization that will be affected by MRP must be aware of the efforts needed to achieve the new way of managing other activities.
2. **User involvement :** A team consisting of people from all those parts of the company that will use the MRP system, will be responsible for the development and implementation of MRP. This will ensure that the participation of users of the system in its development will make them more familiar with the system and its use.
3. **Education and training :** All of the people who work with the MRP system must understand it and must know how to use it. They must know what information to provide and how to provide it, what information to ask and how to obtain it. Hence, it is necessary that all people connected with MRP system must be trained in its application and use.
4. **Selection of packages :** The potential user must be able to decide about the use of net change or regenerative MRP package knowing their advantages and disadvantages. Also the user must decide whether to develop his own programs for MRP system or to purchase and adapt the available packages.
5. **Data accuracy :** After a MRP system is installed, careful attention and discipline must always be exercised to ensure that all data used by the system are accurate. Managers must exert effort to see that accurate and timely data are supplied to the system.
6. **Realistic MPS :** The MPS developed should be realistic and achievable. The MPS should not overload the plant capacity. The company must develop MPS that effectively uses its capacity without causing bottlenecks or overloads.

Problems in Using MRP

1. **Preparation of MPS** which is realistic in the midst of uncertainties in market environment and non-availability of adequate lead time from customers for delivery of end products. Frequent changes in MPS aggravate the problem.
2. **Maintaining accurate BOM files** *:* Changes incorporated in BOM by design department should be communicated to all users of BOM.
3. **Incorrect stock (inventory) status** *:* A major problem is to know the correct status of all materials at all stages. Incorrect stock status results in erroneous net requirement of materials.
4. **Unrealistic lead times** *:* Most crucial step in MRP system which minimizes inventory is the time-phasing of requirements and release of orders; by advancing by the lead time required so that materials arrive just when required.

Problems in Designing the MRP System

1. Inadequacies of software chosen.
2. Deficient systems design.
3. Improper and untimely information flow among various related departments.

Solution to overcome the above problems in the design of MRP system are:

1. Careful choice of software package to suit organization's specific needs.
2. Careful planning of activities and scheduling.
3. Assigning work to competent manpower.
4. Continuous monitoring of progress against schedule.
5. Substantial education and training at all levels.
6. Involvement of users at the systems design stage itself.
7. Maximum attention at the stage of creating the data base.

Problems in Managing the MRP System

1. Need for formal systems and role of systems.
2. Need for proper organization of functions *viz.*, production planning and control, materials, production, quality, engineering, etc.
3. Importance of proper appreciation of planning and control systems.
4. Timeliness of generating information required in managing the plant.
5. Effective communication system.
6. Proper motivation of people concerned with the implementation of the system.
7. Right leadership.

Evaluation of MRP

The advantages of MRP system over conventional inventory-planning approaches viz., fixed order quantity system (Q system) and fixed order-point system (P system) are:

(a) improved customer service,

(b) reduced inventory levels and

(c) improved operating efficiencies of production departments.

However, MRP systems cannot be used in all production systems. Conventionally, MRP is applied only to manufacturing systems which process discrete products for which BOM can be generated. MRP is seldom used in service systems viz., petroleum refineries, retailing systems, transportation firms and other non-manufacturing systems.

The production systems suitable for MRP should have the following desirable characteristics:

1. An effective computer system,
2. Computerized BOM files and inventory status file for all end products and materials with highest possible accuracy.
3. A production system that manufactures discrete products made up of raw materials, parts, sub assemblies and major assemblies which are processed through several production steps or operations.

4. Production processes or operations requiring long processing times.
5. Short and reliable lead times for procurement of raw materials and components from vendors.
6. The time fence for the frozen MPS should be sufficient to procure materials without undue expediting effort.
7. Support and commitment of top management.

MRP is more useful in process-focussed systems that have long processing times and complex multi-stage production steps. It simplifies production and inventory planning in process-focussed systems by its ability to offset planned order receipts to planned order releases to account for long lead times for in-house processed items or raw materials and components purchased from suppliers.

For MRP to be effective, supplier lead times must be short and reliable and the MPS must be frozen before the start of actual production to the MPS. What is to be produced (*i.e.*, the MPS) must be known with certainty and quantity and timing of receipts of raw materials and components must be dependable. MRP offers advantages in inventory planning when lot sizes are small and demand is highly variable.

However it should be remembered that MRP is not a panacea to solve all our inventory planning problems. Basically MRP is a computerized information system for production and operations managers. MRP will not be of much help when computer systems are ineffective, inventory status and BOM files are inaccurate and MPS are unrealistic. MRP is best applied when production systems are well managed and when a comprehensive production and inventory planning system is needed.

➢ MANUFACTURING RESOURCE PLANNING (MRP II)

Manufacturing Resource Planning (MRP II) has been developed by manufacturing managers to address the planning and controlling of a manufacturing process and all of its related support functions. It encompasses logically correct planning and control activities related to materials, capacity, finance, engineering, sales and marketing. MRP II is universally applicable to any manufacturing organization regardless of its size, location, product or process.

MRP II is a management process for taking the business plan and breaking it down into specific, detailed tasks that people evaluate, agree upon and are held accountable for. It involves all departments *viz.*, materials department, engineering department that must maintain bill of materials, sales/marketing department that must keep sales plan upto date, purchasing and manufacturing departments that must meet due dates for bought out items and in-house manufactured items respectively.

From MRP I to MRP II : Manufacturing resource planning (MRP II) is a natural outgrowth of Materials Requirement Planning (MRP I) Whereas MRP I focuses upon priorities of materials, CRP is concerned with time. Both material and time requirement are integrated within the MRP system (*i.e.*, MRP I). Beyond this, MRP II has been coined to 'close the loop' by integrating financial, accounting, personnel, engineering and marketing information along with the production planning and control activities of basic MRP systems. MRP II is the heart of corporate management information system for many manufacturing firms.

Evolution of MRP II

The earlier resource requirement planning systems were quite simple and unsophisticated. The MRP technique was used for its most limited capability to determine what materials and components are needed, how many are needed and when they are needed and when they should be ordered so that they are likely to be available when needed. In other words, MRP simply exploded the MPS into the required materials and was conceived as an inventory control tool or a requirements calculator. Later the logic of MRP technique was extended to serve as the key component in an information system for planning and controlling production operation and purchasing. It was helpful to production and operations managers to determine the relative priorities of shop orders and purchase orders. As a manufacturing planning and control system, MRP laid the basic foundation for production activity control or shop-floor control.

Closed-loop MRP : Later during 1970s, closing the loop in MRP systems was thought of by experts in manufacturing management. The term "closed-loop" MRP means: "A system built around material requirement planning (MRP I) and also including additional planning functions such as master production scheduling and capacity requirement planning. Once the planning phase is complete and plans have been accepted as realistic and attainable, execution functions such as shop-floor control function (viz., input-output measurement, detailed scheduling, dispatching, anticipated delay reports from both shop and vendors, purchase follow-up and control etc.) came into the picture. The closed-loop MRP system implies that not only the above elements included in the system but also that there is feed back from the execution functions so that planning can be kept valid at all times". Further to the closed-loop MRP systems, the MRP I was improved to manufacturing resource planning (MRP II).

Exhibit 8.9 : MRP II – An Integrated System of Planning and Control

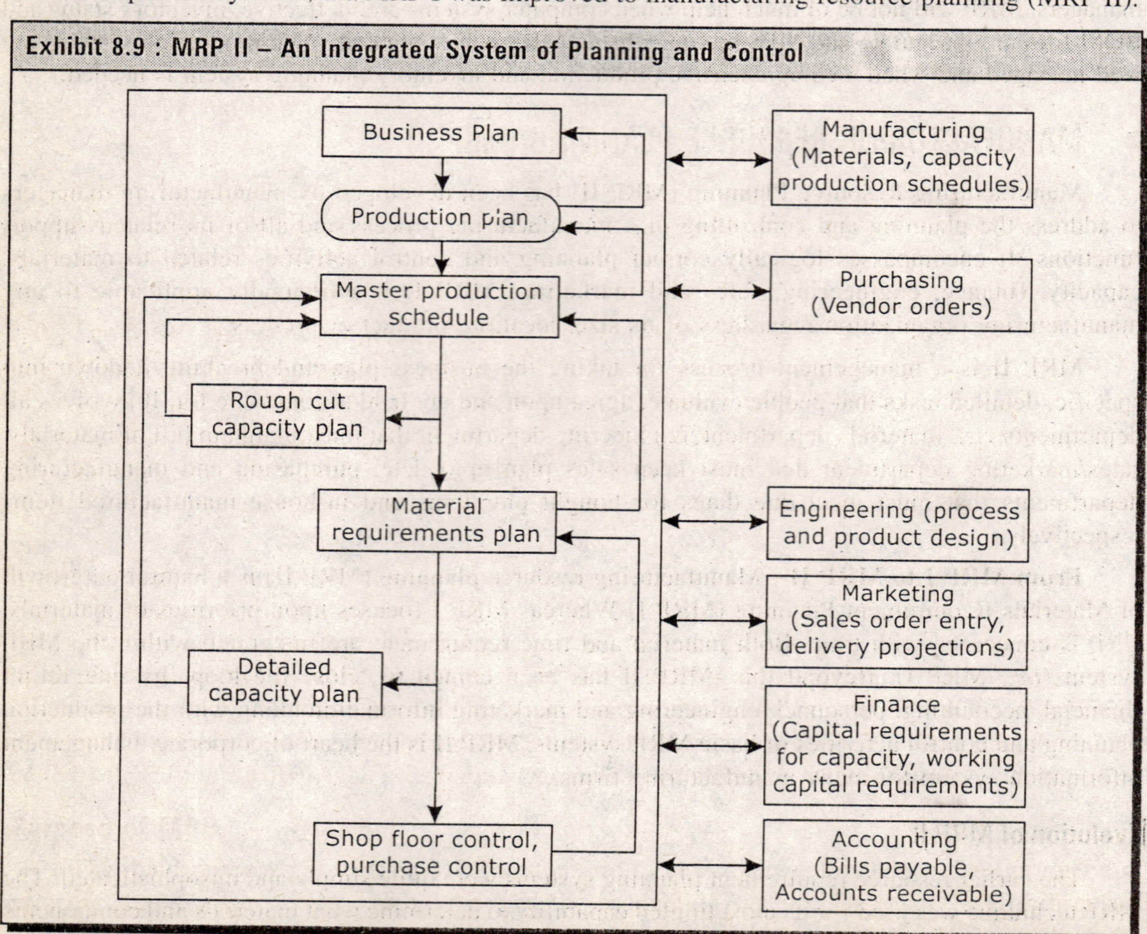

Manufacturing resource planning is a broader resource co-ordination system. In this the capabilities of closed-Loop MRP are extended to provide information on financial resources, personnel needs and labour budgets. It provides a means of simulating to provide information on the use of various assured plans. Information about inventory investment levels, plant expansion needs and work force requirements is useful for co-ordinating marketing, finance, engineering and manufacturing efforts to achieve the overall business plan of the firm. MRP II is a direct outgrowth and extension of closed-loop MRP.

Exhibit 8.9 shows MRP II as an integrated system for planning and control. In this process a production plan is developed from a business plan to specify production levels for each month for each product line for the next one to five years. Once the production plan is accepted by all the functional departments, it becomes a commitment for all concerned. *i.e.,* the production department is expected to produce at the committed levels, the sales department to sell at these levels and the finance department to ensure adequate financial resources for these levels of production. Based on the production plan the MPS specifies the quantities of specific products to be produced every week. Rough-Cut capacity planning is done to determine whether the capacity available is roughly adequate to sustain the proposed MPS. The MPS is then used to generate material requirements and priority schedules for production. Then detailed capacity planning is done to determine whether the capacity is sufficient for producing specific components at each work centre during the scheduled time periods. After a realistic capacity-feasible schedule is developed, the plan is executed. Purchase schedule and shop floor schedules are generated, based on which work centre loadings, shop floor control and vendor follow-up activities can be determined to ensure that the MPS is met.

➢ ENTERPRISE RESOURCE PLANNING

Enterprise resource planning, popularly known as ERP, is today's buzz-word in the corporate world. Companies world-wide use ERP to integrate business processes and thereby reduce costs and increase productivity. It has established its base as a global phenomena.

Traditionally, companies developed isolated computer applications to suit and satisfy each of their functional segments such as sales, purchase, production, inventory, personnel and accounts. Materials Requirement Planning (MRP I) and Manufacturing Resource Planning (MRP II) were developed basically to address the requirements of the manufacturing set-up. But the information available in various functional segments was so scattered that it was almost impossible to consolidate the information and provide the same to the people in the top management to enable them to take vital business decisions. Hence, the companies, whether in the manufacturing or the service sector have been searching for the 'total solution' on an integrated system which could provide for the information needs of the entire enterprise. ERP software was developed to provide such a *'total solution'* to the business enterprise.

To be highly successful in today's global competitive market, it is necessary that business enterprises continuously strive for developing a high level of interaction and co-ordination along the supply chain and improve in the area of quality, time to reach the market, customer satisfaction, performance and profitability. The ERP software fulfils this need.

What is ERP?

ERP is a software package developed for optimum use of resources of an enterprise in a planned manner. ERP integrates the entire enterprise starting from the supplier to the customer, covering logistics, financial and human resources. This will enable the enterprise to increase productivity by reducing costs. ERP is a package for cost saving. Once the ERP is implemented, a single solution addresses the information needs of the whole organisation. *Exhibit 8.10* shows the general model of ERP.

Functioning of ERP

The following example gives a simple understanding of how ERP functions.

Suppose, an order is placed by the dealer, then the ERP checks for the stock, reserves the inventory for despatch, opens the dealer account to verify the credit limit of the dealer and processes the order. If the credit limit exceeds, then it places hold on the order. All these functions are carried out instantaneously, as ERP integrates production, logistics, distribution, marketing, Human Resource Development and Finance.

Features of ERP

The general ERP model shown in *Exhibit 8.10* has a central data base shared by all functions of the enterprise, represented by four quadrants in the figure. The figure represents the concept of enterprise resources planning and execution; symbolizing integrated functionality and the global nature of today's enterprises.

Some of the salient features of ERP are:

1. **Accommodating variety :** The ERP software solution provides both multi-lingual and multi currency capabilities. Also, multi mode manufacturing and multi-facility provide the capability required to compete and succeed globally.
2. **Integrated Management Information :** Today's business managers use ERP for
   (*a*) Flexible reporting tools to extract the information as and when needed without depending on an information system department (MIS department).
   (*b*) Electronic data interchange (EDI) to electronically accept customer information like purchase orders, schedule amendments or cash payments and electronically send order acknowledgment and invoices to customers.
   (*c*) Imaging to provide the ability to display drawings or specifications, ability to store original sale orders, purchase orders, quotations and contracts.
   (*d*) Data base creation : Starting with time and attendance reporting, monitoring and control of machines and post-sales statistics.
3. **Seamless integration :** Integration of new product introductions or changes to existing product fully into the enterprise system, also known as 'engineering change management', is crucial to the enterprise. The reengineering change management should include electronic approval routing, change-order process routing, revision-level control and automatic generation of product structures.
4. **Supply chain management :** End-to-end supply chain management is crucial for enterprise having multiple manufacturing units and distribution networks. Intelligent Resource Planning (IRP) is used to optimise the overall flow of demand and supply data and to build relationship between various activities to optimally identify the demand supply chain.

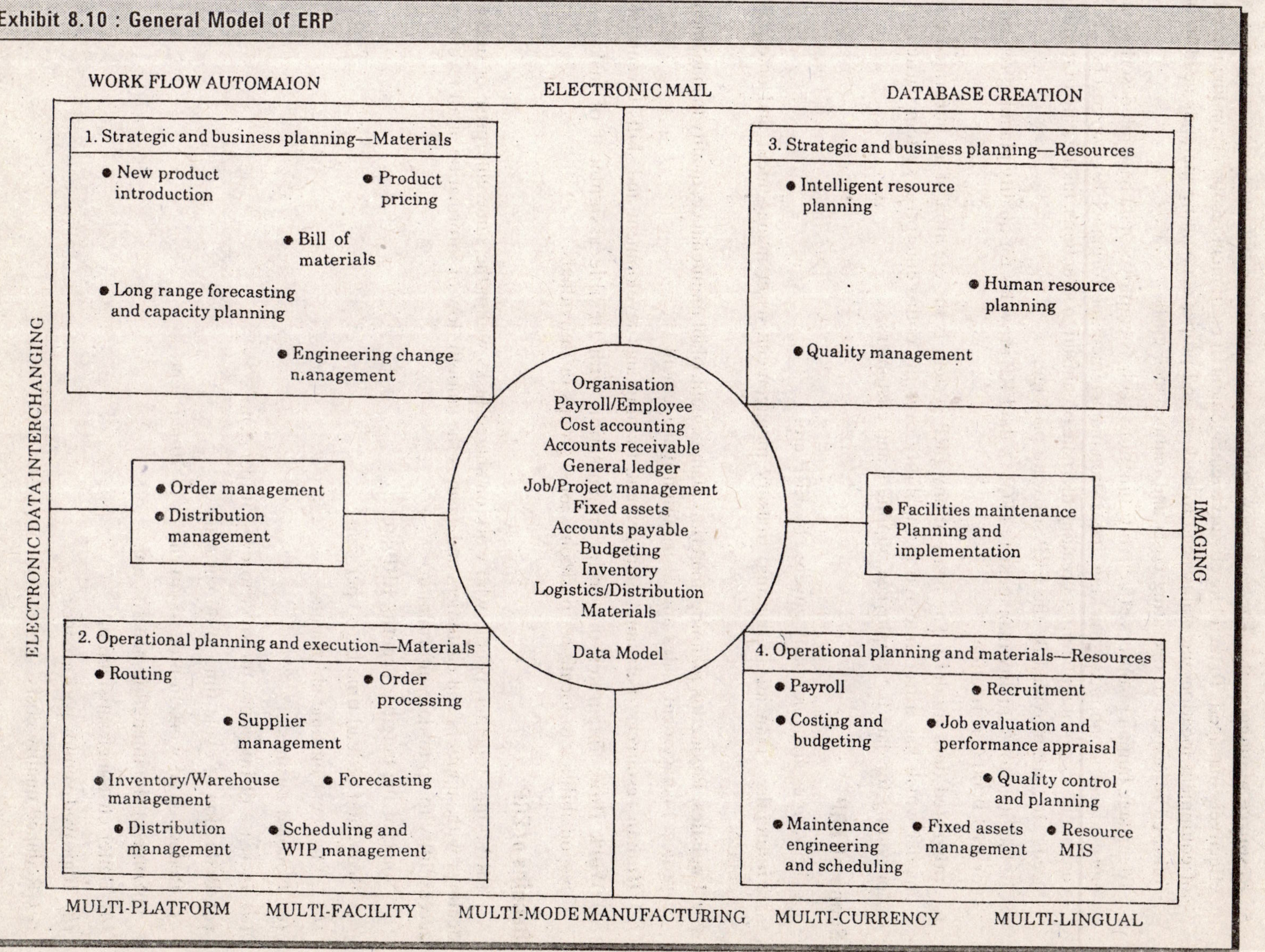
Exhibit 8.10 : General Model of ERP
WORK FLOW AUTOMAION
ELECTRONIC MAIL
DATABASE CREATION
1. Strategic and business planning—Materials
New product introduction
Product pricing
Bill of materials
Long range forecasting and capacity planning
Engineering change n.anagement
3. Strategic and business planning—Resources
Intelligent resource planning
Human resource planning
Quality management
ELECTRONIC DATA INTERCHANGING
Order management
Distribution management
Organisation
Payroll/Employee
Cost accounting
Accounts receivable
General ledger
Job/Project management
Fixed assets
Accounts payable
Budgeting
Inventory
Logistics/Distribution
Materials
Data Model
Facilities maintenance Planning and implementation
IMAGING
2. Operational planning and execution—Materials
Routing
Order processing
Supplier management
Inventory/Warehouse management
Forecasting
Distribution management
Scheduling and WIP management
4. Operational planning and materials—Resources
Payroll
Recruitment
Costing and budgeting
Job evaluation and performance appraisal
Quality control and planning
Maintenance engineering and scheduling
Fixed assets management
Resource MIS
MULTI-PLATFORM
MULTI-FACILITY
MULTI-MODE MANUFACTURING
MULTI-CURRENCY
MULTI-LINGUAL

5. **Resource management :** The resources such as equipment and human resources should be effectively managed. To facilitate effective management of equipment resources, on line records of equipment location and status need to be kept and proper accounting methods need to be followed in respect of operating costs and maintenance costs.

   To manage human resources effectively, functions such as employee data base job descriptions and evaluations, applicant tracking, requisition management, performance review, cost benefits, career and succession planning, creating alternate organisation structures, taking care of training needs etc., are provided by the ERP software package.

   To facilitate total quality management (TQM), the ERP provides for quality planning required for ISO 9000 certification.

6. **Integrated data model :** The heart of any ERP system is the creation of an integrated data model which has a true integration capability over the entire enterprise system particularly providing for data for employees, suppliers and customers.

Scope of ERP

The various areas normally covered by ERP are:

(a) **Financials***:* Financial accounting, treasury management, asset management and enterprise control.

(b) **Logistics***:* Production planning, materials management, plant maintenance, quality management, project management, sales and distribution management.

(c) **Human resources***:* Personnel management, training and development and skills inventory.

(d) **Work flow***:* Integrates the entire organisation with flexible assignment of tasks and responsibilities to locations, positions, jobs, groups or individuals.

Benefits of ERP

ERP brings together, people who work on shared tasks within the same enterprise or in their dealings with suppliers and customers and ensures the smooth flow of information at all levels and accessibility to up-to-date information.

Some of the tangible benefits ERP are:

(a) Reduction of lead time by 60 per cent.

(b) 99 per cent on-time shipments.

(c) Doubled business.

(d) Increase of inventory turnover to over 30 per cent.

(e) Reduction of cycle time to 80 per cent.

(f) Reduction of work-in-process inventory to 70 per cent.

Some of the intangible benefits are:

(a) Better customer satisfaction.

(b) Improved vendor performance.

(c) Reduced quality costs.

(d) Improved resource utilisation.

(e) Improved information accuracy.

(f) Improved decision-making capability.

Application of ERP

ERP is gaining popularity in India at a rapid pace. This is mainly due to the need for reducing costs especially when the sales are sluggish in the sub-merging markets.

With the entry of MNCs into the Indian markets, need for quality service to the customer is gaining momentum. Hence, many Indian enterprises, both large, medium and small scale have implemented ERP. *For example,* Reliance, Tata Group of Industries and Hindustan Lever Limited (HLL) have already implemented ERP and more than 300 Indian companies are in the process of implementing ERP according to the recent reports. In the global market, ERP Group of Industries sales have increased from $ 13 billion in 1997 and is expected to increase considerably in the future.

Selection of ERP Package

As the money involved ranges from a few lakhs to a few crores, careful selection of ERP package assumes greater importance.

Before deciding to go in for the ERP implementation, a through introspection of the company's activities is necessary to understand one's exact requirements, Lack of proper planning and preparation may result in the selection of the wrong vendor which in turn may not ensure the expected returns on the resources employed. Implementation period may take 12 to 24 months, depending on the scale and scope of operation.

Once the platform is built, then the company should decide to go in for the right vendor for the software and the right consultant for implementation. It is necessary to evaluate the services offered by different ERPs before selecting the appropriate one.

The giants in the ERP field are SAP, Oracle applications and Baan. Other vendors are JD Edwards, People Soft, Scala, Ramco Marshal, QAD etc. While ERP can be tailor made to suit needs of specific customers, packaged product is gaining more popularity compared to customised software. If ERP can't be tailor made to fit into company's requirement, then the company's requirement can be tailor made to fit the ERP. However, it is important to remember that no ERP implementation will be successful, unless there is a very high commitment from the management.

➢ JUST-IN-TIME SYSTEMS (JIT)

Just-in-time (or JIT) is defined as "a philosophy of manufacturing based on planned elimination of all wastes and continuous improvement of productivity".

JIT is an approach that seeks to eliminate all sources of waste in production activities by providing the **right part** at the **right place** at the **right time.**

JIT encompasses the successful execution of all manufacturing activities required to produce a final product, from design to delivery and including all stages of conversion from raw materials onward. The primary elements of JIT are to have only the required inventory when needed, to improve quality to zero defects, to reduce lead times by reducing set-up times, que-lengths and lot sizes, to incrementally revise the operations themselves and to accomplish these things at minimum cost.

In short, JIT means :

(i) Producing the *quantity* of units *that is needed,* no more or no less.

(ii) Producing them *on the date* and at the *time required,* not before, not after.

Objectives of JIT Manufacturing

The ultimate goal or objective of JIT system is a balanced system, that is one that achieves a smooth, rapid flow of materials through the system. The idea is to reduce the process time to as low as possible by making best of the resources. The specific goal or objective is to provide the *right quality level* at the *right place.* JIT tries to build only what internal (employees) and external customers want and when they want it. The supporting goals or objectives of JIT are :

(i) Produce only the products that customers want.

(ii) Produce products only as quickly as customers want to use them.

(iii) Produce products with perfect quality.

(iv) Produce products with features that customers want.

(v) Produce with no waste of labour, materials or equipment and with zero inventory.

The major focus in JIT is on reduction of wastes. Wastes includes : *(i)* Overproduction, *(b)* waiting time or delays, *(c)* unnecessary handling or transportation, *(d)* unnecessary inventory, *(e)* processing waste (scrap), *(f)* inefficient work methods (waste of labour effort), *(g)* defective products.

Building Blocks of JIT

The design and operation of a JIT system provide the foundation to achieve the goals or objectives of JIT system. The four building blocks of this foundation are : *(i)* Product design, *(ii)* Process design, *(iii)* Personnel and organisational elements and *(iv)* Manufacturing planning and control.

Three elements of product design that are key to JIT systems are : *(i)* standard parts, *(ii)* modular design and *(iii)* quality.

Seven aspects of process design that are particularly important for JIT systems are : *(i)* small lot sizes, *(ii)* set-up time reduction, *(iii)* cellular manufacturing, *(iv)* limited work-in-process inventory, *(v)* quality improvement, *(vi)* production flexibility and *(vii)* minimum inventory.

The five elements of personnel and organisation are : *(i)* workers as assets, *(ii)* cross-trained (multi-skilled) workers, *(iii)* continuous improvement, *(iv)* cost accounting and *(v)* leadership.

Five elements of manufacturing planning and control are : *(i)* level loading, *(ii)* pull systems, *(iii)* visual systems (kanban), *(iv)* close vendor relationships, *(v)* reduced transaction processing.

Characteristics of JIT System

The salient characteristics are :

(i) pull method of material flow, *(ii)* constantly high quality, *(iii)* small lot sizes, *(iv)* uniform workstation loads, *(v)* standardised components and work methods, *(vi)* close supplier ties,

(vii) flexible workforce, *(viii)* line flow strategy, *(ix)* automated production and *(x)* total preventive maintenance.

JIT Purchasing : JIT purchasing has the same pull type approach used in JIT manufacturing, applied to purchasing shipments of parts from suppliers. The essentials of JIT purchasing are :

(i) Supplier–development and supplier relationship.

(ii) Long-term relationships with few supplier (referred to as JIT suppliers).

(iii) Suppliers are rated not based on price, but on product quality, delivery schedules, reliability of supply and flexibility.

(iv) Suppliers are located near the buying firm.

(v) Shipments are delivered directly to the customer's production line.

(vi) Parts are delivered in small size containers.

(vii) Delivered material is of near-perfect quality.

Benefits of JIT System

(i) Inventory levels are drastically reduced and high inventory turnovers (50 to 100 times per year) have been achieved.

(ii) Reduced production cycle time or product throughput time.

(iii) Improved product quality and minimum scrap.

(iv) Root-cause elimination approach to solve production problems.

(v) Multiskilled and flexible work-force reduces worker idle time, overheads, fewer lay-offs etc.

(vi) Elimination of unpleasant suppliers.

(vii) Reduced customer-related problems.

(viii) Near zero defects.

(ix) Improved communications.

(x) Lesser work-in-process and finished goods inventory.

(xi) Shorter procurement lead times.

(xii) Improved employee morale due to high employee involvement and employee empowerment.

(xiii) Reduced amount of inspection.

SOLVED PROBLEMS

1. *For the product structure tree shown below determine (a) Quantities of items B, C, D, E and F needed to assemble one unit of end product X. (b) Determine the quantities of these items that will be required to assemble 100 nos of product X, taking into account the inventory on-hand of these components given below:*

Product structure tree

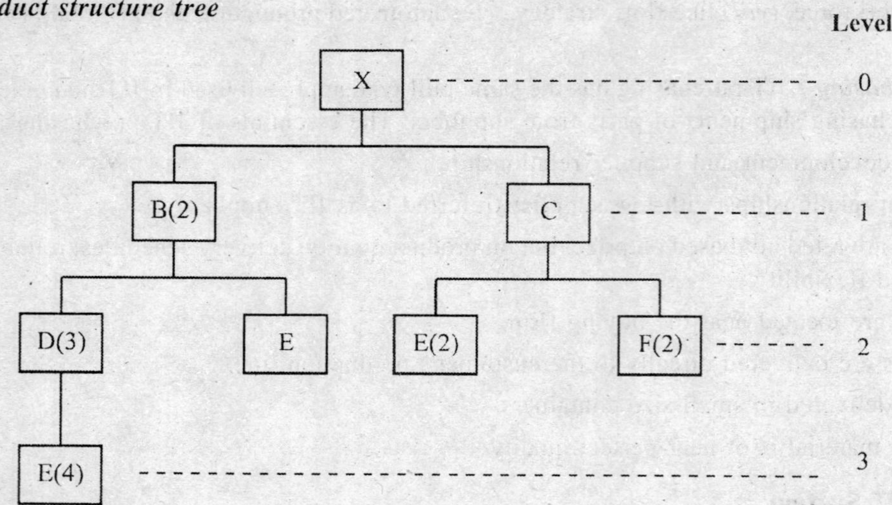

Inventory on-hand

Item	*On-hand*
B	*40*
C	*50*
D	*180*
E	*800*

(*a*) *Determination of quantities of items B, C, D, E and F required to assemble one unit of end product (X).*

Solution :

Level 1 : B = 2 nos. C = 1 no.

Level 2 : D = 3 × 2 = 6 nos. E = 1 × 2 = 2 nos.

E = 2 × 1 = 2 nos. F = 2 × 1 = 2 nos.

Level 3 : E = 4 × 3 × 2 = 24 nos.

Bill of materials to produce 1 unit of (X) =
B = 2 nos.
C = 1 no.
D = 6 nos.
E = 2 + 2 + 24 = 28 nos.
F = 2 nos.

Item	*Quantity*
B	2
C	1
D	6
E	28
F	2

(b) *Determination of quantities of items B, C, D, E and F required to produce 100 nos. of assembly (X) taking into consideration the inventories on hand.*

Solution :

Quantities of items required to produce 100 nos. of assembly (X) are obtained by multiplying the bill-of-materials quantities by the quantity of end item 'X' to be produced.

Items	*Quantity (Gross requirements)*
B	2 × 100 = 200
C	1 × 100 = 100
D	6 × 100 = 600
E	28 × 100 = 2800
F	2 × 100 = 200

Quantities required (Net requirement) are computed by subtracting the inventories on hand from gross requirements of the items B, C, D, E and F.

Item	*Gross requirement*	*Inventory on-hand*	*Net requirement*
B	200	40	200 – 40 = 160
C	100	50	100 – 50 = 50
D	600	180	600 – 180 = 420
E	2800	800	2800 – 800 = 2000
F	200	NIL	200 – NIL = 200

2. *End item A has a product structure tree shown below. There are 25 units of B and 900 units of H in stock. (a) Prepare the bill of materials (b) What net requirements of H are needed to supply 300 units of A?*

Product structure tree

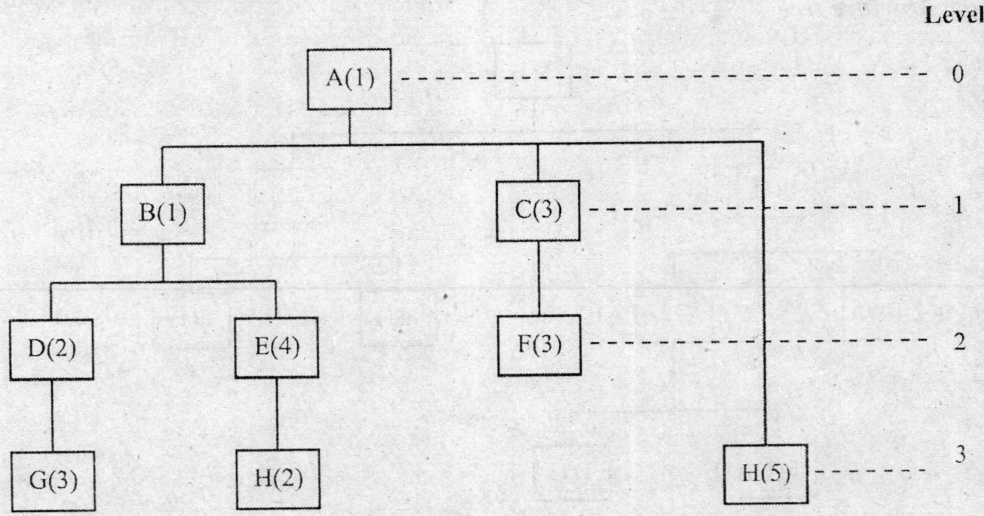

Solution :

Bill of materials

Level 1: B = 1 no. C = 3 nos.

Level 2: D = 2 × 1 = 2 nos. E = 4 × 1 = 4 nos. F = 3 × 3 = 9 nos.

Level 3: G = 3 × 2 x 1 = 6 nos. H = 2 × 4 × 1 = 8 nos. H = 5 × 1 = 5 nos.

Bill of material

Item	*Quantity*
B	1
C	3
D	2
E	4
F	9
G	6
H	13

(b) ***Determination of the net requirements of H to supply 300 nos of A, given that 25 units of B and 900 units of H are in stock:***

Since there are 25 units of 'B' in stock, the nos. of item B to be built for 300 units of A would be 275 units, (*i.e.,* 300 – 25) To build one unit of B, we need 8 units of H. Therefore to build 275 units of B, we require 275 × 8 = 2200 nos. of item H. On the right hand branch we require 5 x 300 = 1500 nos. of H, to build assembly A. Therefore we need a total of (2200 + 1500) =3700 units of H. The stock on hand of H is 900 nos. therefore quantity of H required = 3700 – 900 = 2700 nos.

3. *For the product structure tree shown below for product "A" determine (a) Bill of materials and (b) Gross requirements of items to produce 10 nos. of product A. (c) Determine the net requirement of items if inventory on hand is taken into consideration.*

Product structure tree

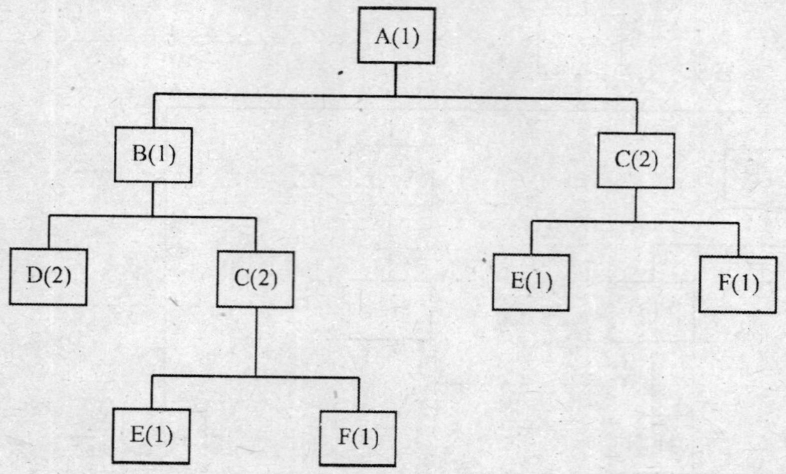

Inventory on-hand

Item	*Quantity*
B	2 nos.
C	10 nos.
D	6 nos.
E	12 nos.
F	8 nos.

Solution :

(a) To compute the bill of materials

Level	*Item*	*Quantity required*
0	A	1 no.
1	B	1 no.
	C	2 nos.
2	D	2 nos.
	C	2 nos.
	E	1 × 2 = 2 nos.
	F	1 × 2 = 2 nos.
3	E	1 × 2 = 2 nos.
	F	1 × 2 = 2 nos.

Bill of material

Item	*Quantity*
B	1 no.
C	2 + 2 = 4 nos.
D	2 nos.
E	2 + + = 4 nos.
F	2 + 2 = 4 nos.

(b) To determine the gross requirement of items to produce 10 nos. of product A.

Item	*Bill of material quantity*	*Gross requirement*
B	1	1 × 10 = 10 nos.
C	4	4 × 10 = 40 nos.
D	2	2 × 10 = 20 nos.
E	4	4 × 10 = 40 nos.
F	4	4 × 10 = 40 nos.

(c) To determine net requirement of items considering inventory on-hand.

Item	*Gross requirement*	*Inventory on-hand*	*Net requirement*
B	10 nos.	2 nos.	10 – 2 = 8 nos.
C	40 nos.	10 nos.	40 – 10 = 30 nos.
D	20 nos.	6 nos.	20 – 6 = 14 nos.
E	40 nos.	12 nos.	40 – 12 = 28 nos.
F	40 nos.	8 nos.	40 – 8 = 32 nos.

4. *Determine the net requirement of the two items A and B using the data given below.*

Data	*Item A*	*Item B*
Projected (Gross) requirements	*30*	*45*
On-hand inventory	*12*	*22*
Scheduled receipts (Inventory on-order)	*10*	*NIL*

Solution :

Net requirement = Gross requirement – [Inventory on-hand + Scheduled receipts]

Net requirement for item A = 30 – (12 +10) = 8 nos.

Net requirement for item B = 45 – (22 + 0) = 23 nos.

5. *Compute the MRP table for item 'X' for which details are given below:*

Order quantity = 70 *Lead time = 4 weeks* *Safety stock = 40*	*Week*											
	1	*2*	*3*	*4*	*5*	*6*	*7*	*8*	*9*	*10*	*11*	*12*
Gross requirements	*20*	*20*	*25*	*20*	*20*	*25*	*20*	*20*	*30*	*25*	*25*	*25*
Scheduled receipts		*70*										
On-hand at the end of period = 65												

Solution :

MRP table will be as shown below.

Order quantity = 70 Lead time = 4 weeks Safety stock = 40	Week											
	1	2	3	4	5	6	7	8	9	10	11	12
Gross requirements	20	20	25	20	20	25	20	20	30	25	25	25
Scheduled receipts		70			70			70			70	
On-hand at the end of period = 65	65 – 20 = 45	(70+45) –20 = 95	(95-25) = 70	70–20 = 50	(70+50) – 20 = 100	100–25 = 75	75–20 = 55	(55+70) –20 = 105	105–30 = 75	75–25 = 50	(70+50) – 25 =	95–25 = 70
Planned order release	70			70			70					

6. *Compute the MRP table shown below and find the amount of inventory on-hand at the end of week no. 8.*

Order Qty = 500	*Week*							
Lead time = 4 Weeks	*1*	*2*	*3*	*4*	*5*	*6*	*7*	*8*
Projected(Gross)requirements	*150*	*150*	*150*	*150*	*200*	*200*	*180*	*320*
Planned receipts		*500*						
On-hand inventory At the end of period = 300								

Solution :

The MRP table will be as shown below.

Order Qty = 500	Week							
Lead time = 4 Weeks	1	2	3	4	5	6	7	8
Projected (Gross) requirements	150	150	150	150	200	200	180	320
Planned receipts			500			500		500
On-hand inventory At the end of period = 300	300 – 150 = 150	150 – 150 = Nil	500 – 150 = 350	350 – 150 = 200	200 – 200 = Nil	500 – 200 = 300	300 – 180 = 120	(500 + 120) – 320 = 300
Planned order release		500		500				

➤ REVIEW QUESTIONS

1. Define the term "Resource requirement planning"?
2. What is "Material requirement planning"?
3. What is "Manufacturing resource planning"?
4. What is "Enterprise resource planning"?
5. What is closed loop MRP?
6. Discuss the role of master production schedule, manufacturing resource planning and capacity requirement planning in "Resource requirement planning".
7. State the objectives of material requirement planning. Explain how these objectives are achieved.
8. Distinguish between MRP-I and MRP-II.
9. Briefly describe the operation of the MRP system.
10. Discuss the various inputs and outputs of MRP system.
11. Discuss the potential benefits from implementation MRP system in managing manufacturing operations.
12. Explain the factors on which successful implementation of MRP depends.

13. Explain the features of "Enterprise Resource Planning".
14. Discuss the problems faced in using the MRP system.
15. Explain how you would evaluate the MRP system.

CHAPTER 9

PURCHASING MANAGEMENT

Purchasing is the most important function of materials management. The material planning function determines the requirements of raw materials, parts, components, spare parts etc., needed for production and takes decision regarding: *(i)* What to buy? *(ii)* How much to buy? and *(iii)* When to buy? All these decisions result in the preparation of material requisitions which are then passed on to purchase department for further action towards procurement of the materials listed in materials requisitions.

"Purchasing" refers to the function of procuring of materials, supplies, machines, equipments, tools, spare parts and services required for meeting the needs of production department and maintenance department.

Purchasing implies the act of exchange of goods and services for money whereas procurement is a genuine term with a wider connotation for the total responsibility of acquiring goods and services. In its narrow sense, 'purchasing' refers to merely to the act of buying an item at a price. In a broader sense, purchasing is a managerial activity involving planning and policy formulation, research and development strategies required for the proper selection of materials and sources of supply, negotiating with supplies for best price terms, placing purchase orders, follow-up to ensure timely delivery, co-ordinating with other departments *viz.*, receiving, inwards inspection, stores and accounting (bills payable section).

The term 'procurement' is broader in its meaning and covers the duties performed by the purchasing department as well as such additional functions of materials supervision and management as **inventory control**, **incoming material inspection** and **salvage operations**.

➢ FUNCTIONS OF PURCHASING DEPARTMENT

It is entrusted basically with the procurement duty. The functions of the purchasing department is to procure the needed materials, supplies, machines, tools and services at an ultimate cost consistent with economic conditions surrounding the item being purchased, while safeguarding the standards of quality, continuity of service, competitive position and the company's reputation for fairness and integrity. The purchasing department must also ensure that it does not violate the laws governing commercial transactions. The major functions of purchasing management are listed in *Box 9.1*.

Box 9.1 : Major Functions of Purchasing Management

(i) Materials requirements review
(ii) Specifications development for materials
(iii) Make-or-buy analysis
(iv) Materials standardisation
(v) Determination of inventory levels
(vi) Determination of quality requirements
(vii) Negotiation of price and terms of supply
(viii) Supplier selection
(ix) Joint problem solving with supplies
(x) Supplier monitoring (follow up) and analysis
(xi) Communication of specification changes
(xii) Productivity/cost improvements
(xiii) Development of sourcing strategy
(xiv) Vendor analysis and vendor rating
(xv) Vendor development
(xvi) Market analysis
(xvii) Price forecasting
(xviii) Long-range purchasing planning
(xix) Determination of purchasing policy
(xx) Value analysis.

Importance of Purchasing

(i) Purchasing is a basic function of any industrial enterprise. Since any industrial enterprise manufacturing products (tangible goods) need raw materials and components for converting them into finished goods, purchasing function is of major importance. Purchasing department is responsible for purchasing materials of **right type**, in **right quantities**, at the **right price**, made available at the **right time** and procured from the **right supplier**.

(ii) In any manufacturing industry the materials cost ranges from 50 to 80 per cent of the product cost, depending on the nature of the product. Procurement of goods through purchase accounts for about 50 percent of the money spent by the average industrial enterprise and ranges from 20 to 90 per cent among different industries. Hence, the financial aspect of purchasing is of great importance. A one percent of savings in the material cost is equivalent to nearly 10 per cent increase in sales turnover. Savings in cost of materials is achieved mainly through efficient buying.

(iii) A large amount of working capital is usually tied up in the inventories of raw materials, components and supplies held by an industrial firm. Since high financial stakes are involved in buying, the purchase manager who is the custodian of a firm's working capital is obliged to have utmost integrity in spending the company's valuable money.

(iv) Purchasing can effectively contribute to import substitution and thereby saving the nation's precious foreign-exchange resources. Purchase managers are continuously aware of external industrial activities and are able to gather vast information regarding new products, materials, equipments, machinery, tools and processes for the benefit of their firms.

(v) Purchasing function has a crucial role in the completion of major projects undertaken by a firm. Any delay in procurement of materials for the project will eventually cause delay in completion of the project.

(vi) Purchasing is a key function in materials management. Other functions of materials management are built around the purchasing function.

(vii) Four specific factors which have contributed to the rising importance of purchasing are :

(a) Post-war shortages and increasing requirements of defence and government departments.

(b) The cyclical swings of surpluses and shortages of materials and fast rising materials costs.

(c) Stiff domestic and international competition in the manufacturing industries.

(d) growing world-wide markets, foreign purchasing to assume international scope.

Box 9.2 summarises the importance of purchasing department.

Box 9.2 : Importance of Purchasing Department

(i) It is a primary function, directly influencing the major cost of operating a business.

(ii) Efficient operation of any industry depends upon proper turnover of investment. The purchasing department must ensure receipt of proper materials when needed, in sufficient quantities to maintain production, at the same time it must not increase investment beyond that required to meet current needs and maintain a reasonable factor of safety against stock out conditions.

(iii) Discovering new materials which may be used to advantage as substitutes for materials in use.

(iv) Identifying possible new line of products to be added.

(v) Building up goodwill in the business world with which it deals.

(vi) See changes in trends, either in price or other factors, that will affect the sales of the company.

(vii) Its knowledge of vendors, and the manufacturing and marketing policies of other industries make it possible for the purchasing department to contribute invaluable help in framing plans for initiation of new products, scheduling of production and determination of marketing policies.

Objectives of Purchasing

The overall objective of purchasing is understood as buying materials of the **right quality**, in the **right quantity**, at the **right time**, at the **right price** and from the **right source**. This objective indicates broadly the scope of purchasing function which also involves policy decisions and analysis of various alternative possibilities (such as make-or-buy or evaluating alternative vendors) before the act of purchase.

The **specific objectives** of purchasing are :

(i) To obtain the necessary materials and supplies of proper quality.

(ii) To procure the materials, and supplies in time for plant requirements and have them delivered to the proper place.

(iii) To procure them at the lowest possible ultimate cost.

(iv) To keep inventories as low as possible without affecting the smooth flow of production.

(v) To develop satisfactory source of supply and maintain good vendor relationships.

(vi) To ensure good vendor performance including prompt deliveries and acceptable quality.

(vii) To implement activities such as make-or-buy analysis, cost analysis and value analysis to reduce cost of purchases.

(viii) To employ high calibre personnel and train and develop them to their maximum abilities.

(ix) To achieve a high degree of co-operation and co-ordination with other departments in the organisation.

(x) To keep top management informed of the latest developments taking place in the field of materials which would affect company's performance and profits.

(xi) To keep the expenses incurred by the purchase department (as a cost centre) as low as possible.

(xii) To ensure continuity of supply of raw materials, sub-contracted items and spare parts and at the same time reduce the ultimate cost of the finished goods.

Exhibit 9.1 Illustrates objectives of purchasing in terms of purchase parameters.

EXHIBIT 9.1 : Purchase Parameters

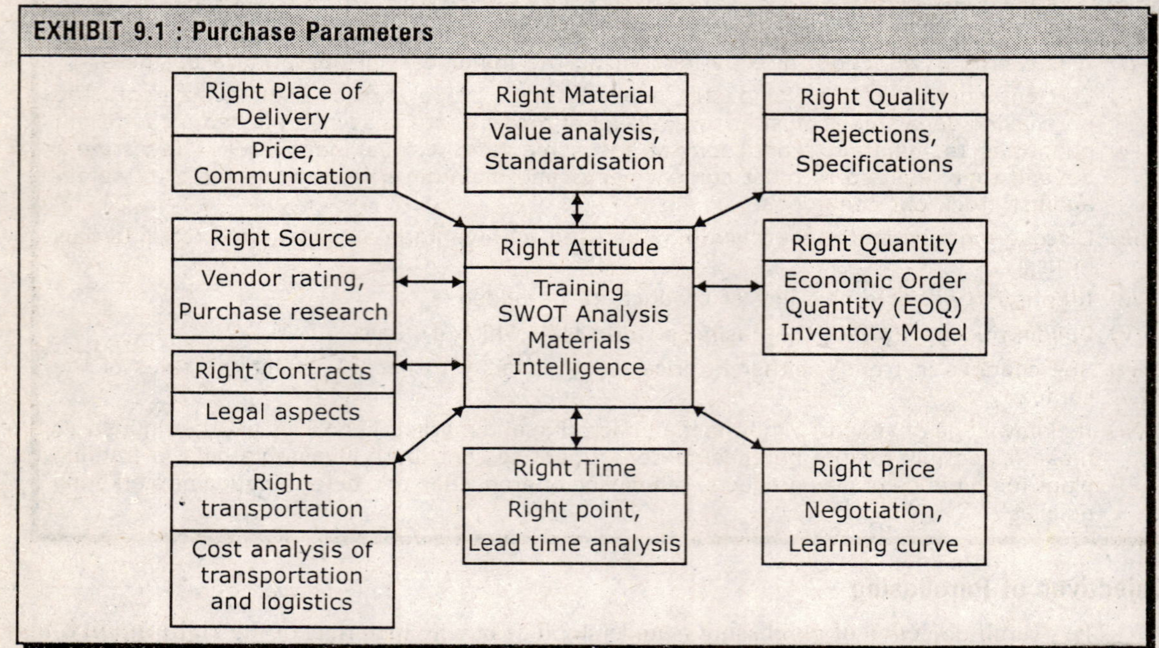

➤ PURCHASE PARAMETERS

(i) **Right Price :** Purchasing an item at the right price is the primary concern of purchase department. But right price need not be the lowest price. While it is difficult to determine the right price, the cost structure of the product can be used as a guide to arrive at the right price. In the "tender system" of buying used in public sector organisations, the objective should be to identify the lowest responsible bidder and not the lowest bidder, for purchase decision. If

the labour content of the purchased item is high, then the concept of "learning curve" helps the buyer to determine the price of the item. Price negotiation also helps to determine the right price on the basis of evaluation of prices offered by alternative suppliers. In addition, prices can be kept low by proper planning and not by "rush" buying or "crisis" buying.

(ii) **Right Quality :** Quality of product depends on the quality of its inputs *i.e.,* raw materials, parts and components that build the product as well as the quality of manufacturing processes used to convert the inputs into outputs. Quality of the outputs depends on *quality of design* and *quality of conformance*. The design specifies the quality characteristics or specifications of raw materials and components and purchase department ensures that these quality specifications are met by the materials purchased by it. (*i.e.,* the quality of conformance or the extent to which the purchased materials and components conform with their specifications).

Also, since the quality of the product depends on *quality at source, i.e.,* the quality has to be ensured right at the input materials stage. This means the purchase department has to ensure the input quality while buying the materials from the suppliers because the product quality very much depends on quality of inputs (*i.e.,* material which is one of the inputs)

(iii) **Right Quantity :** This is the most important parameter in buying because both over ordering or under ordering increase costs of inputs. Over ordering increases inventory carrying costs whereas under ordering results in idling of machines and labour and stoppage of production due to storage of materials. Concepts of economic order quantity (EOQ), economic purchase quantity, inventory control techniques such as fixed order quantity system (Q system) andfixed order period system (P system) etc., serve as guidelines for processing the right quantity of materials. But the buyer has to use his knowledge, experience and common sense to determine the quantity to be bought after taking into consideration factors such as price structures, discounts, availability of the item etc. The purchase manager has to take two important decisions while buying : *(i)* How much to buy? and *(ii)* When to buy?

(iv) **Right Source :** The source of supply of material should be dependable and capable of supplying materials of uniform quality. The buyer should decide which materials should be directly purchased from which supplier/manufacturer. Aspects such as source development and vendor rating help buyer to choose the right source. Right source also requires the analysis of transportation costs along with basic price to choose between a local supplier and a distant supplier.

(v) **Right Time :** For determining the right time to purchase, the buyer should have information regarding lead time for all items to be purchased. Lead time is the total time elapsed between the recognition of the need for an item till it arrives and is made available for use. The buyer should negotiate with suppliers to reduce the lead time for supply of materials. The buyer should have contingency plans when the suppliers are not able to supply materials within the promised lead time due to uncontrollable factors such as strike, lockout, floods, earth quakes etc.

(vi) **Right Transportation :** The buyer should decide about right mode of transportation, trading off between *time* needed for transportation from supplier's premises to the buyer's premises and the transportation *costs*. The buyer should have knowledge of alternative transportation modes and their costs, schedules, merits and demerits and should seek constant improvements in transportation, achieving greater speeds and better quality of service and at the same time with reduction in transportation costs.

(vii) **Right Place of Delivery :** The supplier should try to arrange supply of materials directly to the consuming units or departments so that rehandling of materials is reduced to the minimum.

(viii) **Right Procedure :** The buyer should develop the right procedure to be used at the pre-purchase, ordering and post-purchase stages of the purchasing activity. In the pre-purchase stage, purchase is initiated through requirements of indents, planning the source, selecting the supplier, obtaining quotations, making comparative study of the quotations for evaluating the suppliers and selecting the best among them. In the ordering stage, the purchase order is sent to the supplier along with an order acknowledgment copy which should be duly signed by the supplier and sent back to the buyer as a token of acceptance of the purchase order. This also indicates acceptance of the supplier to abide by the terms and conditions mentioned in the purchase order. In the post-purchase stage, the buyer will send a copy of the inspection cum receiving report to the supplier for the purpose of submitting his/her bills for payment for the materials supplied.

(ix) **Right Contract :** Since purchase order is a legal document which binds the supplier and the buyer firms, the buyer should clearly indicate various terms and conditions regarding insurance, sales tax, octroi, excise duties, custom duties, breach of contract, settlement of disputes etc., in the purchase order or in the purchase contract executed between the buyer and supplier.

➤ PURCHASING MANAGEMENT

Purchasing management refers to all activities required to manage relationship with suppliers. It focuses on structuring and continuously improving purchase processes within the organisation and between the organisation and its suppliers. Purchasing management is also referred as **business resource management**.

➤ THE TRANSITION TO SUPPLY MANAGEMENT

The impact of purchasing and materials managers on company assets became very significant and very visible. The manufacturing industries started implementing techniques such as *Kanban, quality circles, just-in-time* and *Kaizen* (continuous improvement) and these changes coupled with electronic purchasing systems provided stimulus for more changes. Purchasing and materials managers identified the need for two types of resources in their organisations:

(i) a team of people who manages the operational and tactical activities of purchasing and materials management. These people are referred to as **materials coordinators** and

(ii) **supply managers** who are involved in the development of broader policy aspects of the function.

Supply managers participate in new product development and are responsible for **selecting sources, managing costs, developing and nurturing supplier partnerships** and issuing long-term agreements with carefully selected suppliers.

Materials co-ordinators are responsible for placing orders against these purchase agreements, keeping the production lines running and also minimising inventories.

Supply managers also actively participate in the organisation's strategic planning process. An organisation's supply strategy is becoming equally important as the firm's marketing, production and finance strategies as a strategic weapon. These four strategies when integrated become the organisation's strategic plan.

Paradigm Shifts in Focus

Two major paradigm shifts in the progression from **purchasing to supply management** are:

(i) from a focus on **internal processes to value-adding benefits** and

(ii) from **tactical** to **strategic** focus.

Value-Adding Benefits

Historically, the performance of purchasing managers was measured and evaluated on the following parameters:

(a) changes in the purchase price of materials,

(b) ability to keep the production line running,

(c) the cost of operating the purchase department.

But today, purchasing and supply management function in many world-class organisations focus on the following value-adding outputs of supply management which involves proactive procurement:

(i) **Quality :** The quality of purchased materials and services (virtually defect free).

(ii) **Cost :** The supply management function must focus on strategic **cost management** which is the process of reducing the total cost of processing, moving, holding, converting and supporting products containing purchased materials and services throughout the supply chain.

(iii) **Time :** The supply management and its outside suppliers must play active roles in reducing the time period required to bring new products to market.

(iv) **Technology :** The supply management must ensure that the firm's supply base provides appropriate technology in a timely manner and also it must ensure that technology which affects the firm's core competencies is carefully controlled when dealing with outside suppliers.

(v) **Continuity of Supply :** The supply management function must monitor supply trends, develop appropriate supplier alliances and take action to reduce the risk of supply disruptions

Strategic Focus

Historic focus of purchasing has been on **purchase price** and **continuity of supply**. The following strategic activities are added by supply management:

(i) **Integration :** The firm's supply strategy must be integrated with the organisation's marketing, conversion and finance strategies and also that of the corporation or strategic business unit (SBU).

(ii) **Business Environment :** Supply management must address the identification of threats and opportunities in the firm's supply environment.

(iii) **Technology :** Supply management must address issues of technology access and control.

(iv) **Component and Commodity Strategies :** Supply management must develop-formalised market-driven supply plans for critical purchased materials and services.

(v) **Management Information System (MIS) :** Supply management must ensure that a timely, cost-effective and comprehensive information system is in place to provide data required to make optimal supply decisions.

(vi) **Centralisation of Development and Management :** The development and management of the firm's supply strategy will be centralised while low value-adding supply activities will be decentralised.

(vii) **Use of Professional Personnel :** There will be fewer but far more *professional* personnel assigned to purchasing/procurement/supply-chain management functions.

(viii) **Use of Senior Procurement Professionals :** The senior procurement professionals are assigned the responsibility of managing five to ten key supply relationships or supplier partnerships.

➢ MAJOR DEVELOPMENTS IN SUPPLY MANAGEMENT

In traditional manufacturing organisations, the production department and purchase department functioned independent of each other and there was no proper co-ordination among these two departments. Neither purchase department personnel involved in the product design process nor the production department person involved in source selection process. Such functional biases did not reduce cycle time nor did they reduce costs.

In modern manufacturing processes this myopic approach is being replaced by a focus on what is in the best interest of the customer. This effective approach uses **cross-functional teams** which tend to be adhoc organisations brought together to meet specific stated objectives such as the development of a new product or negotiating a purchase contract with a supplier.

The current and future approach (individual or team) of the purchasing personnel to the following activities were studied:

(i) Materials requirement review, *(ii)* Specification development, *(iii)* Make-or-buy analysis, *(iv)* Materials standardisation, *(v)* Determination of inventory levels, *(vi)* Determination of quality requirements, *(vii)* Selection of suppliers, *(viii)* Supplier partnerships, *(ix)* Problem-solving jointly with suppliers, *(x)* Communication of specification changes to supplier, *(xi)* Monitoring of suppliers, *(xii)* Analysis of supplier performance, *(xiii)* Productivity improvements (cost reductions), *(xiv)* Developing sourcing strategy, *(xv)* Market analysis, *(xvi)* Forecasting price, *(xvii)* Long range purchase planning, *(xviii)* Determining purchasing policy, *(xix)* Value analysis.

The study revealed that, for all the above purchasing activities, transformation was taking place from individual to team responsibility. *For example, a new product development team* may be headed by a design manager or a marketing manager (product manager) and other members may come from departments such as supply management, manufacturing engineering, production/operations, quality and one or more customer and supplier organisations.

Usually, membership on a cross-functional team is a part-time assignment or full-time for a specified time period. The functional experts retain their identification with their functional areas and they function part-time as members of cross-functional teams.

➢ SUPPLY CHAINS

Supply management has led to the development and management of the firm's *supply chain.* The supply chain which is a part of the firm's *value chain* is responsible to ensure that the right materials, services and technology are purchased from the right source, at the right time, in the right quantity and for right price.

Supplier Partnerships

Parallel with the development of supply chains, supplier partnerships and strategic alliances with suppliers are in progress. These partnerships and alliances are mutually beneficial relationships and are not legal entities. They are needed for both parties (supplier and buyer) to achieve satisfaction and benefit mutually.

The key characteristics of supplier partnerships and strategic alliances are:

(i) a compatibility of interests, *(ii)* mutual need, *(iii)* a willingness to be open, sharing information as well as benefits which result from the relationship and *(iv)* trust between them.

Exhibit 9.2 illustrates a continuum of supply relationships

Exhibit 9.2 : Continuum of Supply Relationships

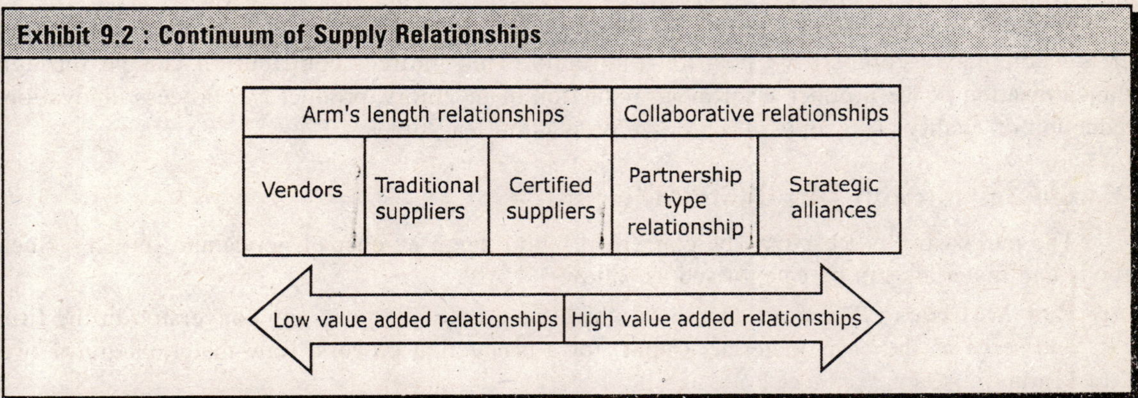

The role of purchasing and supply management personnel requires a combination of technical expertise and leadership communication and team skills.

The Future : The purchasing or supply function is growing in importance in all kinds of organisations – manufacturing and/or service industries, institutions and government organisations. Many of the manual tasks performed by purchasing personnel will be automated or reassigned. The personnel in supply management will be responsible for value addition and not mere paper work. They will become more technically proficient so that they can work with technical customers (internal customers such as R & D, production, quality etc.) and external suppliers. People functioning as supply management personnel need to possess sound knowledge of all the commercial aspects of purchasing and materials management. They start their career as purchasing personnel or buyers and will progress to become supply managers.

Importance of Supply Management in Business

In manufacturing firms, it has been observed that the largest part of the cost of goods sold is due to purchased materials and services. Hence saving on purchasing related expenditures for a firm may lead to an improvement of the return on net asset. On the other hand, a lack of a well defined purchase policy and a lack of a structure in the purchasing process may result in a lack of control over purchasing costs which may lead to unforeseen financial loss.

Purchasing contributes to improvement of a firm's return on net assets in two ways:

(i) By reducing all direct material costs which will result in increase in the firm's sales margin which in turn will increase the return on net assets.

(ii) By reducing the net capital employed in the firm. This will increase the firm's capital turn over ratio. Capital employed can be reduced by reduction of inventories of base materials through just-in-time (JIT) agreements with suppliers, improving quality at the source (*i.e.,* suppliers), leasing instead of buying and resorting to longer payment terms. Nowadays firms aim at improving logistics, improving quality of incoming materials and cycle time or lead time reduction, thereby reducing materials costs. Also, purchasing policies contribute to business success in several ways:

(a) Significantly improve sales margins through realising substantial cost savings.

(b) Improving quality and having logistics arrangements with suppliers.

(c) By properly addressing suppliers to contribute to the firm's innovation processes.

In addition to the above benefits, purchasing function can also contribute to the improvement of the company's competitive position indirectly. This indirect contribution can be through standardisation of the product assortment, reduction of inventory, product and process innovation, reduction of quality costs and cutting down production lead times.

➢ CLASSIFICATION OF PURCHASING GOODS

The purchasing process may be concerned with a large number of goods and services. Such goods and materials can be categorised as follows:

(i) **Raw Materials :** These are materials which have not undergone any conversion in the firm and serve as the basis materials (input) for a production process. Raw materials are of two kinds :

(a) **physical raw materials** such as iron ore, coal and the like and *(b)* **natural raw materials** such as food grains, coffee, tea, fruits etc.

(ii) **Supplementary Materials :** These are materials which are not absorbed physically in the end product, but are used or consumed during the production process. *For example*, lubricants, coolants, polishing materials, welding electrodes and the like.

(iii) **Semi-finished Products :** These are parts or products which have been processed partially and will be processed further at a later stage of production. They will be physically present in the end product. *For example*, steel plants, rolled wires, plastic foils etc.

(iv) **Components :** These are manufactured goods which will not undergo further physical changes but may be assembled with other parts to produce sub assemblies or finished products. *For example*, batteries, electrical motors, fans, switches, head light units, transformers, gears, bearings etc. Components can be classified as: *(a)* **standard components** and *(b)* **specific components**. Standard components are produced according to some standard specifications of the supplier whereas specific components are produced according to the design specification of the customer.

(v) **Finished Products :** These are products which are purchased and sold after negligible value addition along with other finished products and/or manufactured products: *Examples* are accessories such as car radios, security systems etc. The firm manufacturing a particular product of its own design for its customers buy these finished items from other specialised suppliers.

(vi) **Capital Equipment :** These are products which are not consumed immediately but replaced after their purchase value is depreciated over a period of time of use. For example, machine tools computers, furnaces, photo copiers, fax machines and the like.

(vii) **Maintenance, Repair and Operating Materials (MRO Items) :** These are items referred to as indirect materials or consumable items which are necessary for keeping the machinery and equipments in good working conditions and also for use in offices. *For example*, cleaning materials, office supplies, maintenance spare parts, stationery items etc.

(viii) **Services :** These are activities which are executed by suppliers and contractors on a contract basis. Examples are services such as cleaning services, maintenance services, transportation services, construction work and the like.

➤ PURCHASING CYCLE

A purchasing department buys many different types of materials and services, and the procedures used in completing a total transaction normally vary among the different types of purchases.

However, a **general cycle of activities** in purchasing most operating materials and supplies is fairly standardised. The following steps constitute the typical **purchasing cycle**.

(i) Recognition of the need.

(ii) Definition and description of the need.

(iii) Investigation, qualification and selection of a suitable source for the supply (often a source may have to be developed).

(iv) Determination of price and availability of materials.

(v) Preparation and issue of purchase order.

(vi) Supplier's acceptance of the purchase order (*i.e.*, order acknowledgment).

(vii) Follow-up of the purchase order to ensure timely delivery of the material (includes expediting and de-expediting).

(viii) Receiving and inspecting the material supplied.

(ix) Checking the invoice and approving payment of bills.

(x) Closing the orders.

The above activities involved in the purchasing cycle are illustrated in *Exhibit 9.3*.

The activities involved in the purchasing cycle are briefly discussed in the following paragraphs.

(i) **Recognition of the need :** The need for a purchase typically originates in one of a firm's operating departments (*i.e.*, user department or indenting department) or in its inventory control section. The purchasing department is usually notified of the need by means of *(i)* a standard **purchase requisition** issued by the user department or *(ii)* a **material requirement planning** *(MRP)* **schedule** issued by the inventory control section or stores department or materials planning and control section. If the need is one-time purchase, then an engineering **bill of materials** is sometimes used.

(ii) **Description of the need :** Regardless of how the need is transmitted to the purchase department by the industry or user department, material requirements must be defined clearly and described in detail with part name, part number, coding, specifications, quantities required etc. The purchase requisition must include all necessary information about the material to be purchased, in a form that can be readily checked and verified.

Exhibit 9.3 : The Purchasing Cycle

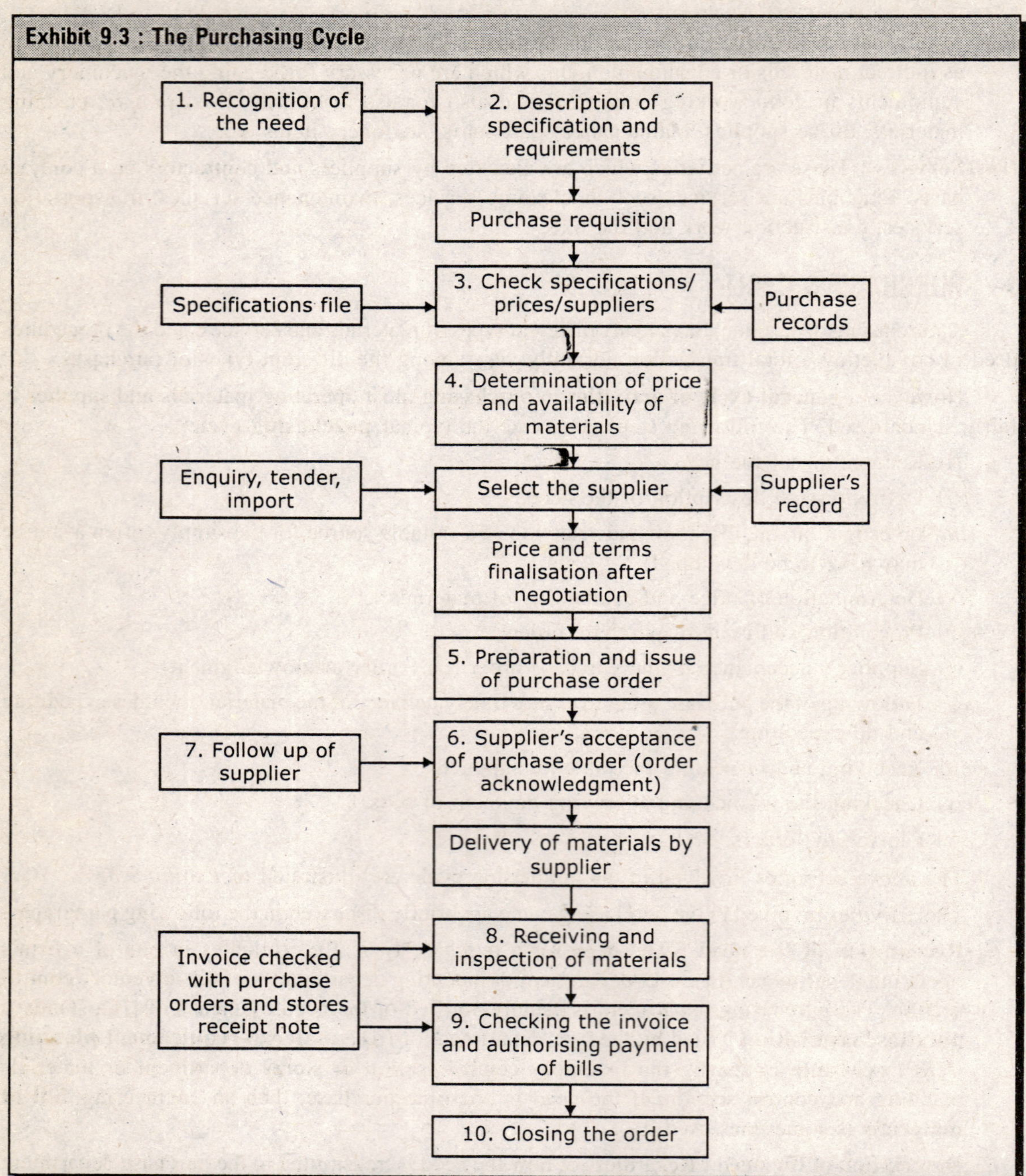

(iii) **Supplier selection :** As soon as a need has been established and precisely described, the buyer begins an investigation of the market to identify potential sources of supply. In case of routine items (repetitively bought) for which supplier relationships have already been developed, little additional investigation may be required to select a good source of supply. But for the purchase of a new or a high-value item a thorough investigation of potential suppliers may be necessary.

The buyer may refer to the approved supplier's list or register maintained in the purchase department to select a few suppliers to whom enquiries are to be sent for getting the quotations. Sometimes it becomes necessary to advertise in the newspapers inviting tenders from suppliers.

After qualifying a preliminary group of potential sources, the buyer may employ the techniques of competitive bidding or negotiation or both. When competitive bidding is used, the buyer initiates the procedure by requesting quotations from a reasonable number of firms with whom the buying group is willing to do business.

Whatever is the method, it is essential that a right source must be selected. A right supplier is one who delivers materials of the correct specifications on the stipulated delivery dates. The qualifications of a right supplier are : *(a)* ethical in behaviour, *(b)* stands by the promises, *(c)* regards for cordial buyer-seller relationships, *(d)* progressive in business, *(e)* seeks technological advancements in improving quality of his products, *(f)* charges reasonable prices, *(g)* can be relied upon, *(h)* honest and fair in his dealings all the times, *(i)* has adequate plant facilities and know-how.

Before selecting a right source, the buyer has to decide which to have: a single source or multiple sources, both having their own advantages and disadvantages.

The factors in source selection are : *(a)* reliability, *(b)* technical abilities, *(c)* after sales service availability, *(d)* buying convenience, *(e)* past experience, *(f)* location, *(g)* financial position, *(h)* labour relations, *(i)* reciprocal relations.

(iv) **Determination of price and availability :** After selecting the potential sources of supply, the next step is to secure the price for the items to be purchased. This can be done in three ways : *(a)* For standard items, vendor's catalogues and price lists are available. For such items, the buyers need only check current listings to obtain the price, *(b)* Negotiating with potential suppliers for establishing the price and *(c)* Inviting tenders or quotations from the potential suppliers.

(v) **Preparation and issue of purchase order :** Once a supplier has been selected, the purchasing department prepares and issues a serially numbered purchase order. In most cases the purchase order becomes a *legal contract document*. Hence, the buyer should take great care in preparing and wording the purchase order. Quality specifications must be described precisely. Quantity requirements, price and delivery and shipping requirements must be specified accurately. The purchase order may also include terms and conditions designed to give legal protection to the buyer on such matters as contract acceptance, delivery performance and contract termination, shipment rejections, assignment and subcontracting of the order, patent rights and infringements, warranties, compliance with legal regulations, and invoicing and payment procedures etc. Usually these terms and conditions are printed on the back of the firm's purchase order form.

(vi) **Order acknowledgment by the supplier :** In most cases, the original copy of the purchase order which is sent to the supplier constitutes a legal "offer" to buy. No purchase "contract" exists, however, until the supplier accepts the buyer's offer. Hence, it is necessary for the buyer to obtain the order acknowledgment from the supplier in a copy of the purchase order sent to the supplier.

The purpose of order acknowledgment is twofold : *(a)* The supplier can complete the order acknowledgment and return the same to the buyer, acknowledging acceptance of the order, *(b)* The supplier can indicate whether or not he or she is able to meet the desired delivery date. If the supplier ships the ordered item immediately, it is not necessary to send the order acknowledgment.

(vii) **Follow up and expediting :** The purchasing department's responsibility for an order does not terminate with making of a satisfactory contract with seller by placing a purchase order. Purchasing bears full responsibility for an order until the material is received and accepted. Even though a supplier intends to meet a required delivery date, many problems may arise to prevent the supplier from making his/her delivery commitments. When there is a possibility that the supplier may not stay on schedule, important orders with critical delivery dates should be actively followed-up by the buyer. At times such orders are placed, the buyer may have to determine specific dates for follow-up checks to be made.

Follow up is usually done through a fax or a telephone cell for critical orders. Routine follow-up for the less critical orders is usually accomplished by mailing a preprinted enquiry to the supplier.

(viii) **Receipt and inspection**: When a supplier ships materials, a *packing slip* which itemises and describes the contents of the shipment is kept along with the items shipped. The receiving clerk or stores person uses this packing slip along with his/her copy of purchase order to verify that the correct material has been received.

After the consignment of materials received has been inspected for *quantity* and general condition of the material, the receiving clerk issues a *receiving report.*

Before shipments can be accepted, technical inspection may be necessary for some materials. A copy of the receiving report may be sent to the inwards goods inspection section. The inspectors carry out the necessary technical inspection and record their remarks and quantity of materials which are accepted as well as those which are rejected. Copies of this report known as **inspection cum receiving report** (ICRR) will be sent to purchase department, stores department, supplier and "bills payable" section of accounts department for necessary action.

(ix) **Checking the invoice and approval for payment :** Once the inspection is completed and if all the quantities ordered are supplied and accepted, then the purchase executive checks the inspection cum receiving report received by him/her with the copy of the purchase order and verifies the bill sent by the supplier for payment. If the bill is priced correctly and if no rejections occur in the quantity supplied, the bills are passed by the purchase executive and sent to "bills payable" section of the accounts department for payment to the supplier.

(x) **Closing the purchase order :** If the supplier supplies materials in quantities as specified in the purchase order and if no rejection occurs, then the order can be closed. Closing the order entails a consolidation of all documents and correspondence relevant to the order, the completed order is then filed in the closed order file as a part of historical record. In cases where the supplier supplies partial quantities or some of the items supplied are rejected, the supplier is asked to expedite supply of balance quantities or rejection replacements and after the order quantities are completely received and accepted, the purchase order is treated as closed. The supplier may be paid for the partial supplies or for the accepted quantities which are less than the ordered quantities as per the terms of the purchase order. In cases where the supplier refuses to supply the balance quantities or rejection replacements, the purchase order may be short closed to the extent of accepted quantities and payments made accordingly and the purchase order is amended to this effect.

Purchasing Methods and Techniques

Before discussing the various purchasing methods and techniques, it is necessary to have the knowledge of purchasing policies and how the purchasing department is organised to achieve the objectives of purchasing within the guidelines set by purchasing policies.

Purchasing Policies : Every organisation needs purchasing guidelines within which purchasing decisions are made and the day-to-day activities of the buyers are carried out. Well-established purchasing policies reduce the number and complexity of the purchasing decisions that must be made by the buyers and ensure a reasonable uniformity of action.

Purchasing Policies define the basic decisions of top management as they relate to buying actions, whether first time or repetitive. In most companies, the following areas are covered by policy statements:

(i) A definition of authority and responsibility for purchasing.

(ii) Relationship with vendors/suppliers.

(iii) Treatment of sales representatives of vendor/supplier firms.

(iv) Proper handling of competitive bidding.

(v) Proper handling of vendor technical service and design work.

(vi) Reciprocity.

(vii) Employee purchases.

(viii) Ethical practices in purchasing.

Further the purchasing function is influenced by certain policies. These policies refer to : *(a)* make or buy decision, *(b)* ancillarisation, *(c)* speculative buying, *(d)* vendor rating, *(e)* purchasing ethics, *(f)* reciprocity, *(g)* purchasing for employees, *(h)* gifts and *(i)* value analysis.

These are briefly discussed in the following paragraphs.

(a) **Ancillary Development :** Ancillary industries are undertakings having investments in fixed assets in plant and machinery not exceeding Rs. 75 lakhs and engaged in manufacturing of parts, components, sub assemblies, toolings etc., for large industries (parent units) and rendering of services, and supplying or rendering 30% of their production of the total services as the case may be to other units. After make-or-buy decision taken by a firm, some of the buy items for which there are no proprietory supplies, can be subcontracted to ancillary units or other small or medium scale industries located in industrial estates or industrial areas.

(b) **Make-or-Buy** decisions are policy decisions based on the company's investment policy *i.e.*, whether to invest in a huge infrastructure having equipments and machinery to manufacture a wide range of parts or to outsource parts extensively by subcontracting or buying from established suppliers. The make-or-buy consideration is mainly based on economic analysis *i.e.*, if it is costing less to buy an item, it is better to buy the same, otherwise manufacture in-house, utilising the existing production capacity and labour skills.

(c) **Speculative Buying :** This is done with the hope of making profit out of price changes. In one approach, purchasing department buys certain items at low prices in quantities exceeding their requirements and selling excess quantities to others when prices go up. This practice is known as hedging. Another practice is to purchase in excess of forceable requirements in anticipation that the need will rise for the material and the firm will gain profit by purchasing at the current price.

(d) **Vendor Rating :** Vendor appraisal or rating is necessary to objectively compare the performance of vendors and improve the relationship with reliable vendors. The success of purchasing department in its purchasing action depends on its ability to identify and select reliable vendors from whom materials are purchased on repetitive basis for a long term.

(e) **Purchasing Ethics :** Probably more than any employee of a company, the buyer is in a position of ethical temptations. He is prone to ethical errors covering a wide range of situations from outsight dishonest personal gain to a completely unconcious failure to properly consider the company's interests.

The most common ethical problem facing the buyer is the avoidance of any action that places him in a position of obligation to a vendor. Gifts or entertainment or a close personal friendship of a sales representative may lead to favouritism. Not only must the buyer avoid being improperly influenced, he must avoid the appearance of such influence.

Another ethical problem is that of maintaining an atmosphere of complete *competitive fairness* among vendors. The buyer may give a vendor misleading information either about competitive offers or about the conditions of the contract in order to force him to improve his proposal. To exert undue pressure on a supplier is also an unethical practice which the buyer may be tempted to use. Completely ethical conduct in a purchase department can be maintained by having strict, positive policy statements covering the area of ethics.

(f) **Reciprocity :** Reciprocal buying means purchasing from one's customers in preference to others. It is a practice of giving preference in buying to those vendors who are customers of the buying firm as opposed to vendors who do not buy from the company. Reciprocity is not viewed as unethical and hence can be practised. But it is often found that less efficient manufacturers and distributors gain by reciprocity what they are unable to gain by price and quality. Since this tends to discourage competition and might lead to higher prices and fewer suppliers, reciprocity should be practised on a selective basis.

(g) **Purchasing for Employees :** This refers to the practice of using the company's facilities for obtaining merchandise for employees of the company at better terms than they could individually obtain through their own efforts.

(h) **Gifts :** Since the practice of vendors giving gifts to the buyers has become an established practice over a period of years, it is difficult for the buyer to draw line between the unethical and ethical aspects of accepting gifts from vendors.

(i) **Value Analysis :** It refers to the examination of the function of purchased parts and materials in an effort to reduce cost and/or improve performance. It is a joint effort of purchasing department and methods engineering department. Purchasing people contribute to value analysis by aiming at modifying the specifications of materials, parts and components to reduce their costs without affecting the performance of the end product in which these materials, parts and components are used.

Purchasing Manuals : Purchasing manuals are designed to avoid conflicts between departments, to clarify responsibility, and to provide consistent instructions covering the regular activities of the purchasing department. Two types of purchasing manuals are : *(i)* The policy manual and *(ii)* the procedures manual. These manuals may be issued separately or together.

Policy manual is a written statement of the company's general purchasing policies for use by all concerned, both inside and outside the company. Copies of the purchasing policy manuals may be made available to the vendors.

Procedures manual is a detailed precise statement of the intra-company procedural responsibilities. This helps to ensure that all repetitive actions carried out in the purchasing department will be performed in a consistently efficient manner.

➢ PURCHASING SYSTEMS

Almost all buying situations involve a complex set of conditions under which the purchase must be made. Many approaches to the buying decisions have been developed and used by the skillful buyer. The buyer is required to have through knowledge of all the methods and techniques of purchasing and ability to apply the most appropriate one to a given situation. The key factors are timing, quantity and duration of the commitments whatever may be the approach to purchasing. The various purchasing systems and methods are discussed in the following paragraphs.

(i) The purchasing systems are classified as :

(a) Pre-purchase system,

(b) Ordering system and

(c) Post purchase system.

The salient features in each of these systems are :

(a) **Pre-Purchase System :** This involves initiating the purchase through purchase requisitions, requirements programs, selection of suppliers, obtaining quotations and evaluating them. The department which is in need of a material usually presents a completed purchase requisition form indicating the description of material, quantity required, suggested supplier and the approximate date when material is required. The requisition prepared by the purchasing clerk or purchasing assistant has to be countersigned by a purchase executive or purchase manager depending on the value of the materials to be purchased. It may be noted that capital equipments can not be requisitioned in their manner as they require the sanction of the top management.

Many organisations often invite suppliers to quote rates for supply of materials. A standard format similar to a purchase order with words such as "*this is only a request for quotation*" is used for obtaining quotation for enquires sent by the purchasing department.

(b) **Ordering System :** After selecting the supplier and rates are agreed upon by both buyer and supplier, the buyer places the purchase order on the supplier indicating the terms and conditions of purchase. The purchase order once accepted becomes a legal contract which is binding on both supplier and buyer.

The following details are normally furnished in a purchase order :

(i) Purchase order reference number, *(ii)* Date of the purchase order, *(iii)* Name and address of the supplier, *(iv)* Consignee's (buyer's) name and address, *(v)* Description of the materials and detailed specifications, *(vi)* Quantity to be supplied, *(vii)* Required delivery schedule, *(viii)* Supplier's quotation reference and date, *(ix)* Price terms and discounts if any, *(x)* Shipping instructions, *(xi)* Location where the materials are to be shipped and delivered, *(xii)* Billing instructions, *(xiii)* Mode of payment, *(xiv)* Packing instructions, *(xv)* Transport instructions, *(xvi)* Freight payment terms, *(xvii)* Inspection procedure, *(xviii)* Insurance requirements, *(xix)* Warranty, *(xx)* Cancellation provisions, *(xxi)* Signature of the purchase executive or manager who can authorise the purchase, *(xxii)* Acknowledgment from supplier, *(xxiii)* Detailed terms and conditions (usually printed at the back of the purchase order), *(xxiv)* Removal of rejections and rejection replacement terms, *(xxv)* Penalty clauses for late delivery.

Normally five to six copies of the purchase order are prepared. The original purchase order with an acknowledgment copy is sent to the supplier. The supplier is expected to sign the order acknowledgment copy and send the same back to the purchaser. One copy of the purchase order is sent to the inwards goods stores or receiving department to facilitate identification. When the consignment is delivered by the supplier - one copy is sent to the indenting department for information. One copy is sent to the finance department (bills payable section) for subsequent matching of purchase order with the invoice of the supplier along with goods received notes (inspection cum receiving report) for payment of bills to the supplier.

(c) **Post-Purchase System :** This includes follow-up procedure, receipt and checking invoices with purchase orders.

(i) **Follow-up :** Follow up is necessary to ensure that the supplier meets the supply commitment. Since follow up involves expenditure of money and time, only *critical* items are selected for follow up. Purchase order status reports (pending supplies) are generally prepared so that selective follow up is ensured.

(ii) **Receipt :** A systematic record of the consignments received, carrier details and descriptions are to be maintained in chrological sequence to facilitate quick identification of materials so that inspection can be arranged prior to acceptance. A receiving section in the inwards goods stores or transit stores does the function of receiving materials and arranging for inspection.

(iii) **Invoice Checking :** The supplier usually sends an invoice for the materials supplied, for the purpose of claiming payment. The invoice is compared with the receipt details (inspection cum receiving report) to check the quantity accepted, against the quantity ordered and quantity received, so that payments can be made accordingly. The invoice checking is done by bills payable section before authorising payment to the supplier.

➤ PURCHASING METHODS

(i) **Purchasing by Requirements :** This means that no purchase is made until a need arises and then the quantity bought covers only the current need. This method applies to emergency requirements or to infrequently used goods which would not be stocked. This kind of purchasing requires good relationships with vendors who are dependable and fill such orders promptly. Manufacturers of specialty products produced on contract to customer specifications may use this type of routine purchasing.

(ii) **Purchasing for a Specified Future Period :** This is a standard practice for goods regularly used, but not in large quantities and for which price variations are negligible. Most supplies are bought by this method. The period for which the purchase is made may be fixed by a production schedule or by the record of past use or by a combination of both.

(iii) **Purchasing According to Market :** This method is designed to take advantage of price fluctuations. The quantities purchased conform to the production schedule and its possible changes or to the demands of the plant or business. In cases where the firms have definite manufacturing or construction programs, the purchase department studies the market statistics and factors that affect prices and forecast the trend of market prices and buy to best advantage. When the prices are close to the peak and that the trend will be downward, a *hand-to-mouth* purchasing programme is followed until prices have become stabilised at a lower level. On the other hand, when the price range is at a reasonably low point and that the future trend will be toward higher levels, the purchasing department will cover its requirements for a considerable period ahead.

(iv) **Speculative Purchasing :** This refers to buying when the market is low (low price), more than can possibly be used in manufacturing, with the idea of reselling much of the material at a higher price to users who may come to the market when the price is high. Speculative purchasing is not properly a function of the purchasing department and it should be authorised only by direct action of finance department.

(v) **Forward Buying :** It is nothing but committing an organisation into the future (usually one year). The buyer commits to buy at a future date a **contracted quantity** at **contracted price**, whatever may be the ruling market price in the contracted period. The future commitment is decided depending upon the availability of the item, the financial policies, the economic order quantities, the quantity discounts and staggered delivery. It is different from **speculative buying** where the motive is to make profit out of the price changes, by selling the purchased items at a higher price.

The factors to be considered in forward buying are : *(a)* the availability of the item, *(b)* financial constraints, *(c)* economic order quantity, *(d)* minimum order quantity for obtaining discounts, *(e)* shelf-life of items, *(f)* cash availability.

(vi) **Hedging :** It is different from forward buying. In this, the buyer tries to protect himself in the future by entering into two transactions : A purchase contract and a sales contract in two different markets, whose prices move up and down together. The profit or loss sustained in the buying transaction is compensated by the loss or profit in the selling transaction. The ideal condition one can reach is *zero loss* by a perfect hedge. But such ideal conditions do not occur in practice and hence there will be marginal adjustments of profit or loss. The usual practice is to trade in the spot markets as well as in the future market. Thus hedging is basically a tool for protecting against future loss due to vagaries of prices in the commodities market.

(vii) **Contract Purchasing :** Contract purchasing offers advantages comparable to those of speculative purchasing. By a contract calling for deferred delivery over a period, advantages can be had of low prices in effect on materials at the time of placing the contract, while spreading delivery of materials over a schedule consistent with estimated future requirements. Thus, **the price advantage is obtained without adding unduly to inventory**.

Contract purchasing may be a means of assuring continuous supply as well as a method of getting price advantages. It can be used for the purchase of parts, tools etc. It is particularly useful for those items where the production programs is known, but its timing is not entirely certain. It is some kind of *scheduled purchasing* which is in the form of a contract for better protection of both vendor and buyer.

(viii) **Group Purchasing :** A number of small items can be purchased as group which offers the possibility of large savings. When the items are small and of trivial value, the cost of placing an order often exceeds the value of items purchased. Hence, such items are better bought under the method of "**group purchasing**". In this practice, arrangements may be mode to send orders for all group items to a **single supplier** who agrees to handle and bill them at a fixed percentage of profit above cost, his cost records being open to inspection by the buyer on demand.

When group purchasing is combined with contract buying, the method is sometimes called **systems contracting**. In this, the supplier virtually takes over the complete inventory responsibility for a given category of materials for an agreed renewable contract period.

(ix) **Scheduled Purchasing :** If purchasing of materials on a regular basis and in large quantities can be scheduled properly, then there would be large savings. This method reduces investments in inventory. The suppliers are given approximate estimate of purchase requirements over a period of time. This helps suppliers to be in a position to anticipate orders and be prepared to fill them when received.

The objectives of scheduled purchasing are : *(i)* minimum inventory, *(ii)* good quality, *(iii)* timely deliveries and *(iv)* low cost.

The problems arise in this method due to changes in the requirements or specifications, and goods produced or allocated but not now required may become a matter of dispute between vendor and buyer. Hence, scheduled purchases should be restricted to items for which requirement is definitely known within a closely limited period and for which specifications should be established.

(x) **Blanket Order :** These are purchase orders placed and accepted for large quantities of materials to be delivered as later specified. By the agreement, the vendor agrees to supply and the buyer agrees to accept a stated number units, normally within a given period.

The vendor manufactures or processes the full quantity as per the blanket order based on the assurance that the buyer will authorise shipment in due time. Blanket order is simpler than contract method and has the features of scheduled purchasing but with a greater certainity as to the legal rights involved. Blanket orders are often placed for small fabricated parts or tools and contain a *binding price* based on the vendor's best estimate of his costs and the desirability of having a certain outlet for the vendor's product.

(xi) **Tender Buying :** This method (also known as tender system) is adopted to procure materials at the most competitive rates and to eliminate chances of undue favour to any supplier. The prime objective is to avoid negotiation and give equal opportunity for all vendors. It is usually adopted by the government departments and public sector undertaking to choose the best supplier without any bias. Usually very high value items are bought by tendering method by private sector organisations.

Three kinds of tenders used are: *(a)* **Open tender**, *(b)* **Limited tender** *and (c)* **Single tender**.

In Open tender system, tenders are invited by advertising in at least three or four English newspapers and in Indian trade journal. The suppliers will usually have to quote in the **tender forms** along with **earnest money deposit**. Once the quotations are received, the tenders are opened publicly and a **comparative statement** is made and the tender is awarded to the lowest tender meeting the technical specifications.

Sometimes, to avoid the quotation of an **irresponsible bidder** (who quotes a very low price in order to get the order, but will not be able to execute the orders) **limited tender** system is used. In this, quotations are solicited by sending tender forms to get quotations from a few selected suppliers who are competent to execute the order. For proprietary items or single source items, **single tender system** is adopted.

(xii) **Cash Purchasing :** Some items are bought off-the shelf from the market place (retailer) under the cash purchase system by paying cash on the spot, across the counter. Items which are required urgently and are of low value are purchased by cash purchasing method. Some purchasers ask for at least three oral quotations or get to know the quotations of minimum of three persons over telephone, before going for cash purchase to reduce the purchasing costs.

Some use *imprest purchase* method, where each departmental head is given some *imprest amount* to be spent on urgent purchases of items subject to a ceiling on value per item and overall limit for the imprest amount per year.

(xiii) **Seasonal Purchasing :** Seasonal purchasing refers to "buying the annual requirement of an item during its season". The availability of some items such as agricultural products follow a seasonality pattern and it would be convenient to buy these items at the peak seasons when prices will be the lowest. But this requires enough storage space to store the entire annual requirement. What is important is to compare the ordering cost and inventory carrying cost including the cost of material for the two alternatives :

(i) Buying the annual requirement once during the peak season at the lowest price or

(ii) Buying at regular intervals to meet the requirement, sometimes at a high or sometimes at a low price.

(xiv) **Reciprocal Purchasing :** Reciprocity is defined as a state of exchange, a co-operation for return in kind. The buyer purchases some items needed for his organisation from the customers of the organisation without affecting the interests of the buying organisation in terms of quality, price and delivery schedule. The guiding principle is the overall benefit of the purchasing organisation taking into consideration long term relationships with customers who are also the suppliers.

(xv) **Subcontracting :** This method is used to procure manufactured parts, components and sub-assemblies from properly chosen sub-contractors. The decision to sub-contract is based on factors such as capacity utilisation, cost of manufacture, availability of technology for the sub-contractor etc. Sub-contracting is done for buying items which are unique to the buyer and not available as a standard item of any proprietary manufacturer. Sometimes the whole item or sub unit is sub-contracted and sometimes a few operations are sub-contracted and the raw materials and tools are made available to the subcontractor by the purchasing organisation.

(xvi) **"Just-In-Time" Purchasing** (Also known as stock less purchasing or "zero stock" purchasing) In this system, a blanket order is placed on the supplier for the annual requirement of an item at a firm price. Whenever the item is needed the buyer informs the supplier over phone about the quantity to be delivered at a particular date of need of the item. The buyer may provide some storage area in his organisation to the supplier to keep the stocks under his (supplier's) ownership and supply the items as and when the need arises.

The supplier submits a single invoice for all the items supplied on a monthly basis and receives a single payment for all the items supplied every month.

➤ PURCHASING ORGANISATIONS

A firm's organisational structure reflects the basic attitude of management toward the major activities involved in its operation. The importance attached to purchasing function may be reflected by knowing the position of purchase department in the overall organisational structure of the firm. The most commonly found alternatives are shown in *Exhibit 9.4*.

Exhibit 9.4 : Purchasing Organisation

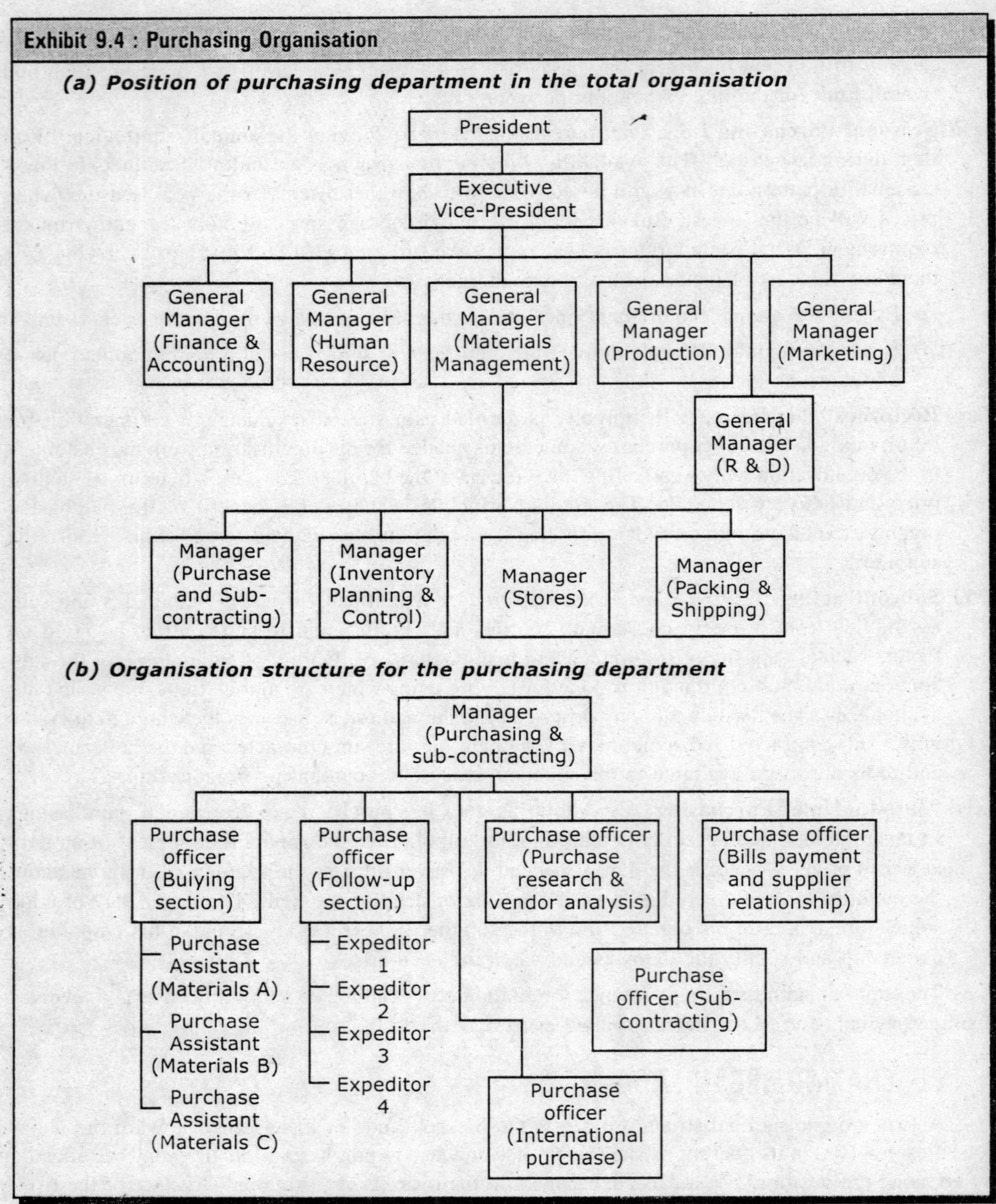

➤ FORMS OF PURCHASING ORGANISATION

There are three ways in which responsibility for purchasing is organised: *(a)* **Centralised purchasing** *(b)* **De-centralised purchasing**, and *(c)* **Centralised-Decentralised purchasing**.

(a) **Centralised Purchasing :** Responsibility for purchasing function should be centralised whenever it can be done without sacrificing the efficiency due to restriction of local initiative. The advantages of centralisation are : *(i)* Undivided responsibility, *(ii)* Consistent purchasing policies and *(iii)* High degree of purchasing power.

With Centralised Purchasing, all purchase records are kept in one place and under one supervision and control, which facilitates easier compiling and consulting the records.

Centralised purchasing is thus more effective for taking action to meet changing market conditions.

Centralisation aids in the standardisation of specifications and tends toward lower inventory investments. The order quantities on vendors will be high resulting in lower purchase prices. Usually any organisation having a single location must adopt centralising purchasing as a rule.

In case of organisation's having multiple plants, centralisation must consider factors such as geogrpahical location of plants, similarity of products produced, type of materials forming the bulk of purchases, special market situations relating to large volume materials, location of suppliers etc.

(b) **Decentralised Purchasing :** When manufacturing plants are widely dispersed geographically and manufacture different products having different material requirements, decentralised purchasing is better than centralised purchasing. In such cases each manufacturing plant will have its own purchasing department. The purchasing manager directly reports to the chief executive of the plant or to the general manager (materials management). But the individual purchase departments of various plants will have functional relationship with director (materials management) at the corporate management level. The corporate director for materials management will establish and enforce general purchasing policies and procedures for all the purchase departments of different plants of the organisation.

Centralised-Decentralised Purchasing

Many firms operating several plants whose geographical locations may not be too widely scattered and whose product and material requirements may cover a large number of similar parts and materials used in common and in large quantities, may adopt centralised-decentralised purchasing approach.

A general purchasing department may be setup to establish general purchasing policies and to do actual buying of common parts and materials and also to supervise and direct the work of local purchasing departments which are set up at each plant.

Responsibilities of the Purchasing Manager : The major responsibilities of the purchasing manager, some of which assigned to their assistants are :

(i) Keeping up the company's standard of quality production by proper choice of materials used.

(ii) Organising and directing the purchase department.

(iii) Spending wisely a large amount of company's finance.

(iv) Supporting the operations of the company's production schedules without interruption.

(v) Maintaining the company's integrity and fair dealing by his/her method of negotiating with suppliers.

(vi) Participating in the preparation of purchase budget.

(vii) Facilitating the progress and competitiveness of the company by conducting purchase research, vendor development and having open mind on new materials, tools, machinery and equipments available in the market.

(viii) Acting as final check, in the interest of economy, on all goods requisitioned, questioning need, quantity and quality specifications.

Personal Duties of Purchasing Manager

(i) Interviewing sales representatives of supplier firms to obtain up-to-date information, securing and comparing quotations, and placing orders for such main commodities as he or she shall receive to himself or herself to purchase.

(ii) Establishing purchasing policies for the purchase department to execute.

(iii) Overseeing the preparation of all general reports on purchasing to be presented to top management.

(iv) Conducting all major adjustment negotiations which are vital to the company's goodwill.

(v) Taking part in interdepartmental meetings representing purchasing department.

(vi) Approving material specifications on major commodities.

(vii) Supervising the functions of purchase officer, in charge of buying, follow up, purchase research, vendor development, sub-contracting, bills payment etc.

➤ PURCHASING POLICY AND PROCEDURES

Tasks and responsibilities assigned to the purchasing department vary widely among companies. In some organisations, purchasing department may be viewed as an ordering agency whose main activity is processing purchase orders, whereas in some other organisations, purchasing may be considered as a strategic activity which is integrated into all other major business processes. The differences in responsibilities and the degree of authority assigned to the purchasing departments arise due to the differences in purchasing portfolio, the characteristics of the supplier markets, the production technology adopted by the buyer firms and their organisational structures. Hence, most organisations share a set of **policies** outlining or detailing the directives of the top management across a range of issues or topics. These **directives** provide guidance while at the same time putting operating constraints on the personal behaviour of purchasing personnel.

What is a policy? The term **policy** includes "all the directives, both explicit and implied, that designate the aims and ends of an organisation and the appropriate means used in their accomplishment".

Policy refers to a set of purposes, principles and rules of action that guide the decisions taken by managers in an organisation. Policies are usually documented in writing but could be written or informal also.

➤ PURCHASING POLICIES

These are policies developed by purchasing department to provide guidance and support to the purchasing personnel and supporting staff. Purchasing policies can be categorised as :

(i) Policies defining the role of purchasing.

(ii) Policies defining the conduct of purchasing personnel (*i.e.,* ethics in purchasing).

(iii) Policies defining social objectives of the business.

(iv) Policies defining buyer-seller relationships.

(v) Policies defining operational issues.

These policies are briefly outlined in the following paragraphs :

(i) Policies defining the role of purchasing include a set of policies defining the purchasing's authority. It usually addresses the objectives of the purchasing function and defines the responsibilities of purchasing personnel at various levels in the purchasing department.

(ii) Policies defining the conduct of purchasing personnel outline management's commitment to ethical and honest behaviour while guiding purchasing personnel who are confronted with difficult situations while discharging their duties and responsibilities.

(iii) Policies defining social objectives include objectives of supporting and developing local sources of supply or awarding supply contracts to qualified minority suppliers. It also includes a set of policies outlining a position related to environmental issues.

(iv) Policies defining buyer-seller relationships cover a wide range of topics related to supplier relations, qualification and supplier selection, principles and guidelines for awarding purchase contracts, managements position concerning labour or other problems at supplier firms etc.

(v) Policies defining operational issues involve policies that provide guidance for operational issues confronting buyers during their normal performance of duties. These include hazardous materials, supplier's responsibility for defective materials supplied by them, management's position concerning continued evaluation of purchased items etc.

Basis for Purchasing Policies

The major principles on which purchasing policies should be based are :

(i) a sound business orientation

(ii) an integrated, cross functional approach and

(iii) a bottom-line orientation.

These principles of purchasing policies are briefly discussed in the following paragraphs :

(i) **Business Orientation :** A thorough understanding of the company's overall business policy is essential to develop purchasing and supply strategies and policies. To understand how purchasing and supply strategies will need to support the company to meet its overall business goals and objectives, the following questions must be answered.

(a) What end-user markets is the company targeting?

(b) What are the major developments going on those markets?

(c) What competition is the company facing?

(d) What advantages does the company have in setting its own pricing policies?

(e) To what extent can increase in price of materials be passed on to the final customer or is this impossible?

(f) What changes are taking place in the company's products, production and information technologies?

(g) What investments will be made by the company in terms of new products and technology?

(h) What products will be withdrawn from the market for the years to come?

(ii) **Integrated, Cross-functional Approach :** Purchasing decisions should not be made aiming only at optimisation of purchasing performance. They should be made taking into consideration their effects on other primary activities such as production planning, inventory control, storage and transportation. Purchasing decisions need to be based on balancing the total cost of owning the materials. Careful decision making in purchasing requires a cross-functional and team-based approach among all the business disciplines affected by it.

(iii) **Bottom-line Orientation:** Purchasing should not be viewed as only a service function which should work on behalf of and comply with its customers requirements. Purchasing personnel should make the internal customers (*i.e.*, employees) more cost aware. They should consistently look for improving the price/value ratio of the goods and services bought by the company. To accomplish this, purchasing should suggest alternatives to existing product designs, materials or components to be used and alternative suppliers. In companies where purchasing is recognised as a bottom-line-driven activity, it is observed that this function contributes to a permanent reduction of the cost price of the end product and stimulating innovation from suppliers at the same time.

➤ PURCHASING PROCEDURES

Procedures are operating instructions detailing the functional duties or tasks to be performed by purchasing personnel. Every organisation develops a unique set of operating instructions to meet its own specific requirements. Since no uniform set of principles exist to guide the development of purchasing procedures, a brief overview of purchasing procedure is given in this section:

Procedure Manual : A procedure manual serves a number of purposes. They are :

(i) As a reference guide for purchasing personnel and especially valuable for new employees of purchase department.

(ii) For experienced personnel, the manual provides clarification or reinforces knowledge about different issues related to their functions.

(iii) The manual provides consistency and order by documenting the steps and activities required to perform a purchasing task. The purchase procedure manual is more detailed than purchase policy manual.

(iv) The procedure manual may also specify the best practices to follow in the industry that are identified through bench making leading firms.

Procedures include information considered essential for successfully deploying purchasing strategies.

Areas of Purchasing Procedure : Most purchasing procedures correspond to one of the following areas :

(i) **The Purchasing Cycle :** The existing purchasing procedures document the steps to be followed during the purchasing cycle or purchasing process. Five steps involved in the purchasing procedure for routinely purchased items are :

(a) Identify or anticipate material and service needs

(b) Evaluate suppliers

(c) Select suppliers based on evaluation

(d) Release and receive purchase requirements and

(e) Continually measure and monitor supplier performance.

(ii) **Proper Use of Purchasing Forms :** The procedure manual describes the proper use of the forms and documents commonly used, the detailed meaning of each information field on the form and also describes the proper handling and storage of each form. Storage can be manual or electronic.

(iii) **The Development of Legal Contracts :** Many organisations have specific procedures for contracting with outside suppliers for goods and services. The purchasing personnel are responsible for becoming familiar and following the procedure covering legal contracts.

(iv) **Operational Procedures :** Operational procedure provides detailed instructions across a broad range of issues or topics. Some of the topics of operational procedures are :

(a) Control of material furnished to suppliers.

(b) Storage of purchasing documents.

(c) Supplier qualification process.

(d) Analysis of competitive quotations.

(e) Use of single source selection.

(f) Order placing and analysis requirements.

(g) Use of computerised systems for purchasing.

(h) Cost analysis procedures.

(i) Intra company transactions.

(j) Processing and handling of overshipments.

(k) Supplier acknowledgment of purchase orders.

(l) Disposal of rejected purchased material.

(m) Withdrawal of tools supplied by the buying firm to the supplier.

➤ PURCHASING MANAGEMENT PROCESS

Purchasing policies and strategies should be based on the overall (financial) objectives and product/market strategies of the company. A company operating in a highly competitive end-user market will have a strong focus on cost reduction and innovation. Hence its purchasing and supply strategies should reflect those aspects and the purchasing activities will be directed through material budgets and cost reduction projects. The purchasing management should be constantly looking for new and more competitive sources of supply (global sourcing). But in a high-tech company having a niche marketing strategy, the purchasing and supply strategy is concerned with early supplier involvement, securing proprietary knowledge, reducing development lead time etc. In addition, the purchasing and supply function need to secure reliable delivery of components and materials required. Innovation and supply assume a higher priority than price and cost aspects.

The purchasing management process is viewed as having the following successive elements :

(i) Purchasing and supply (market) research.

(ii) Determining purchasing and supply objectives.

(iii) Determining purchasing and supply strategies.

(iv) Action planning.

(v) Implementation of purchasing policy and

(vi) Control and evaluation.

Exhibit 9.5 illustrates the purchasing management process schematically.

Exhibit 9.5 : Purchasing Management Process

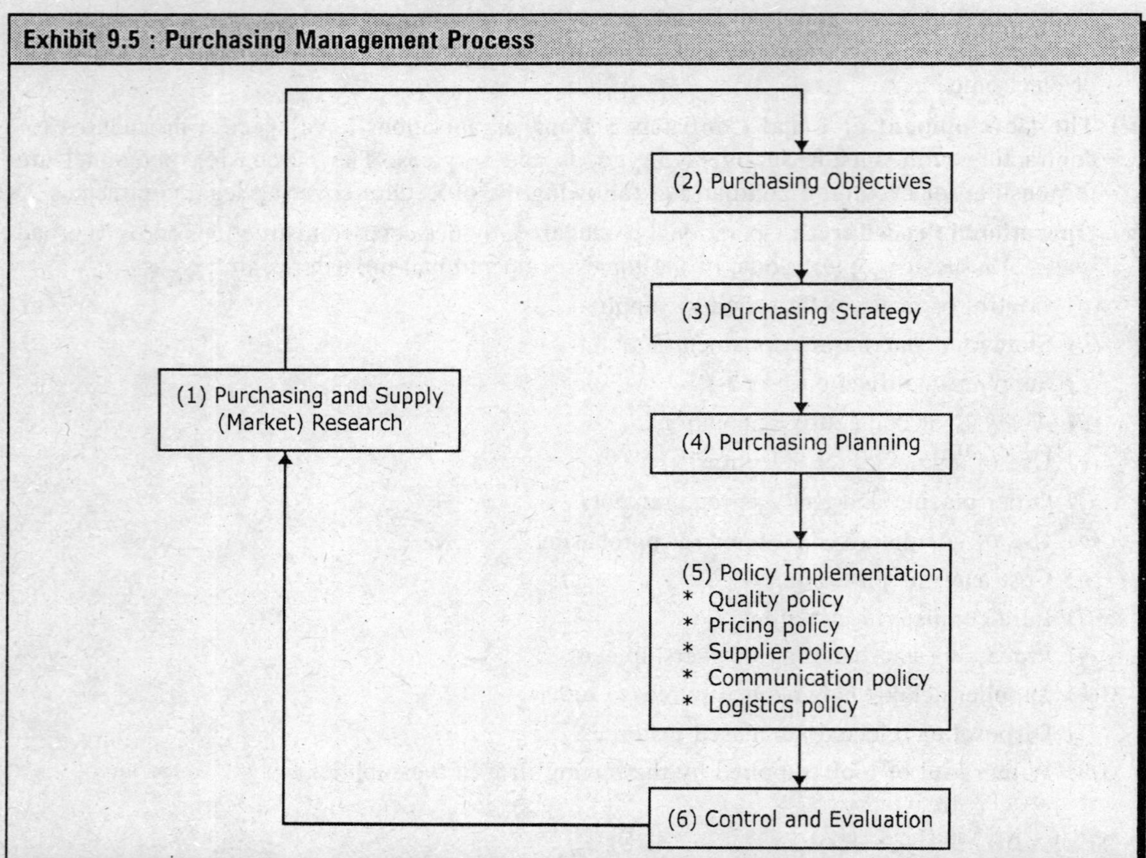

These elements are briefly discussed in the following section :

1. **Purchasing and Supply (Market) Research :** This refers to the systematic study of all relevant factors which may affect supply and demand of goods and services for the current and future requirements of the company. The purchasing and supply research must generate data and alternatives on which the purchasing department can base its purchasing decisions. Purchasing research supports purchasing policies and purchasing decision making.
2. **Purchasing and Supply Obligations :** Purchasing objectives which are based on the company's overall objectives relate to cost reduction, reduction of supplier base, improvement in product quality, reduction of lead time and the like. These objectives help the company to direct, manage and control its purchasing activities and relationships with suppliers.
3. **Purchasing and Supply Strategies :** Some important decisions which need to be made in terms of supplier strategies are:
   (i) How many suppliers are needed per product category?
   (ii) For what product categories the firm is going to increase or reduce the number of suppliers?
   (iii) Is the company going to pursue a relationship with suppliers based upon partnership or based upon competitive bidding?

(iv) For what products does the company need to source globally and for what products to find local suppliers?

4. **Action Planning :** The purchasing management can plan to focus on different areas for action in line with the purchasing and supply objectives. Some of these areas of action in purchasing are:
   (a) **Sourcing policy**: Determining dependency on suppliers & planning to reduce this dependency.
   (b) **Direct versus indirect buying** : Determining the cost benefits of buying directly from the manufacturers or through middle men (importers and distributors).
   (c) **Make-or-buy analysis** : Analysing savings opportunities by eliminating some production activities and buying or leasing them.
   (d) **Integration between purchasing and other activities** : Planning to remove interface problems between purchasing and materials management, purchasing and product design and between purchasing and finance.
   (e) **Setting up a purchasing information and control system** : Analysing the need for purchasing's information and designing an automation plan.
   (f) **Centralised or decentralised purchasing** : Balancing between cost benefits and strategic considerations related to a centralised or decentralised purchasing.
   (g) **Standardisation** : Determining the possibilities of achieving standardisation to reduce product and supplier variety, balancing savings and risks.

5. **Implementation of Purchasing Policy :** The important areas to be considered while implementing purchasing and supply policy are :
   (a) **Supply policy** : Purchasing order processing, and materials and supply planning are the aspects involved. Purchasing order processing entails, handling of purchase requisitions and expediting and development of computer supported order routines. Materials and supply planning is related to issue of materials delivery schedules to suppliers, reducing supplier lead times, reducing pipeline inventories and monitoring delivery performance of suppliers.
   (b) **Product and supplier quality policy** : Aspects involved are early involvement of suppliers in product design and development and improving product and supplier quality performance. Activities that may contribute to this area are :
      (i) standardisation of materials.
      (ii) a purchasing policy focused on the life cycle of the end products.
      (iii) specific quality improvements.
      (iv) extending warranty conditions that are to be provided by the supplier and
      (v) initiating cost reduction programs in the field of value analysis to simplify product design and/or reduce product costs.
   (c) **Materials cost policy** : This involves control of materials costs and prices and reduction of materials costs and prices.
   (d) **Supplier policy** : Aspects involved are : *(i)* sourcing policy and *(ii)* improvement of supplier performance.
   (e) **Communication policy** : This is related with the need to communicate the company's purchasing policy both internally and to external suppliers. Companies use their Intranet for internal communications. Also many companies use their own Purchasing Website to

communicate their future material requirements and ways of working to their suppliers.

6. **Control and Evaluation :** Purchasing management must ensure that both results and activities which have been planned are achieved within the available financial resources. For this, the actual performance must be periodically compared with the purchasing plans (objectives). Reports about the savings and cost reductions realised through purchasing activities are needed for control and evaluation purposes. Further, the performance of suppliers should be checked periodically through vendor performance reports.

➤ MAKE OR BUY DECISIONS

Purchasing often analyses whether a new or existing purchase requirements should be provided internally or sourced from external suppliers (*i.e.,* Insourcing or Outsourcing). For certain standardised items manufactured by proprietary manufacturers, make-or-buy evaluations are not necessary because it is economical to buy always because of cost considerations. For other items, however, make-or-buy analysis assumes strategic importance involving more than simple cost comparisons. Make-or-buy decisions indicate where management is willing to commit the resources required to maintain production ability and also indicate the amount of **vertical integration** a firm is willing to pursue.

Purchasing has an important role in make-or-buy analysis. Regarding outsourcing, purchasing must identify qualified suppliers in the market place. In addition, purchasing has to carry out activities such as visiting potential supplies, negotiating outsourcing contracts and monitoring supplier performance.

When a firm considers which components or subsystems it shall make and which it should buy, it should analyse the issue at two levels : *(i)* **Strategic level** and *(ii)* **Tactical or Operational level**.

Strategic Decisions : The starting point of strategic analysis is to identify the major strengths of the firm and then build on them. The firm's existing *core competencies* must be identified in terms of design skills, unique production skills and equipment, different types of people skills etc. The next step in strategic analysis is to look at the current and expected future environment in which the firm operates — the competition, the government reputation, the changing characteristics of sales and supply markets and the like.

In considering what to make and what to buy, the decisions should cultivate and exploit the firm's core competencies. The items that should be made in-house are those that require capabilities that are closely linked with the core competencies and are mutually reinforcing as opposed to those that can be separated. Firms which follow the concept of "*lean manufacturing* increasingly buy more and make less." Some firms outsource sub-systems and component parts unless they fall into one of the following three categories:

(i) An item that is critical to the success of the product.

(ii) An item that requires specialised design and manufacturing skills or equipment.

(iii) An item that fits well within the firm's core competencies or within those the firm must develop to fulfil future plans.

Components or subsystems that fit into one of these categories are considered strategic and are produced in-house, if possible.

Tactical Decisions: Some of the operating factors that necessitate make-or-buy analysis at the tactical level are : *(i)* unsatisfactory supplier performance in the case of some outsourced items, *(ii)* changing sales demands, *(iii)* restricted manufacturing capacity and *(iv)* modification of an existing product.

From a "make" perspective, these make-or-buy situations involve items for which the firm already possesses most of the necessary production resources. The decisions to make or buy are driven by operating considerations such as efficiency, control of quality and reliability, cost, capacity utilisation and so on.

Factors Influencing Make-or-Buy Decisions

At the tactical level, two factors which stand out above all other factors when considering make-or-buy are : *(i) cost* and *(ii) availability of production capacity.* The following considerations influence firms to make or buy items used in their finished products or their operations.

Considerations which favour making :

(i) Cost (less expensive to make the item).

(ii) Desire to integrate plant operations.

(iii) Productive use of excessive plant capacity.

(iv) Need to exert direct control over production and/or quality.

(v) Design secrecy required.

(vi) Unreliable suppliers.

(vii) Desire to maintain a stable work force in periods of declining sales.

Considerations which favour buying :

(i) Supplier's research and specialised know-how.

(ii) Cost considerations (less expensive to buy).

(iii) Small-volume requirements.

(iv) Limited production facilities.

(v) Desire to maintain a stable work force in periods of rising sales.

(vi) Desire to maintain a multiple-source policy.

(vii) Indirect managerial control considerations.

(viii) Procurement and inventory considerations.

The Volatile Nature of the Make-or-Buy Situations

Although make-or-buy analyses begin with a cost analysis, there are various qualitative factors that frequently portend more far-reaching consequences than does cost analysis. Hence, a make-or-buy decision correctly approached considers the probable composite effect of all factors on the firm's total operations.

A thorough analysis is complicated because of the dynamics and uncertainties of business activity. Certain factors can hold quite different implications for a make-or-buy decision at different points in time and under different operating conditions. Changing costs can turn a good decision into a bad decision in a very short period of time. Also, future costs are influenced substantially by such variable factors as technological innovation and customer demand. The availability of capital for expansion also influences make-or-buy decisions.

The tendency toward "make" decisions in order to stabilise production and work force fluctuation is usually greater in small firms than in large ones.

Finally, labour-relations climate within a firm can influence its make-or-buy decisions. If the union has a hostile attitude towards the management, then it would be difficult for management to buy an item previously made in-house. An amicable labour-management climate may evoke a favourable union reaction towards "buy" decisions for previously "make" decisions. To summarise, it may be stated that there are no rigid formulae or rules of thumb that claim to produce easy "make-or-buy" decisions. This decision is influenced by a multitude of diverse factors that are in a constant state of change. Also the relevant factors vary immensely from one firm to another. For these reasons, every company should periodically evaluate the effectiveness of its past decisions to generate information helpful in guiding future courses of make-buy action.

➤ GLOBAL SOURCING

During the last decade of the 20th century, international business has experienced a major metamorphosis which is irreversible. Today, international business does not mean one way expansion of the developed countries such as the US, Japan and European countries. Today these developed countries face a new reality of global competitors. Eventhough US, Western Europe and Japan still dominate global competition, an increasing number of countries, especially the developing countries are competing head-on for global-leadership. Global competition has resulted in drastically shortened life cycle for most products.

As technology diffused quickly, international business firms should establish **sourcing plans**, distribution and service networks in order to exploit both emerging technology and potential markets around the world simultaneously. A firm can not reach the status of a global firm without having the ability to procure crucial components internally or on a global basis. As a result, the increased pace of new product introduction and reduction in lead time for innovation calls for a more pro-active management of locational and corporate resources on a global basis.

Purchasing component parts, products and services of foreign origin can be quite challenging. Eventhough all the practices and procedures applicable for domestic sourcing are applicable for foreign or international sourcing, many new issues must be addressed if a sourcing team has to ensure that its firm receives the ***right quality***, in the ***right quantity***, ***on time*** with the ***right services*** at the ***right price***.

In recent years the term **"foreign sourcing"** is replaced with **"international sourcing"** which is the process of purchasing from suppliers outside of the firm's country of manufacture. Of late the term, international sourcing is being replaced with a broader international approach called **"global sourcing"** or **"worldwide sourcing"**.

Global sourcing is defined as *"the integration and coordination of requirements across world wide business units, looking at common items, processes, technologies and suppliers"*.

Reasons for Global Sourcing : To start with, the oil embargo of 1970s coupled with shortages of some basic materials forced purchasing to search overseas for suppliers. Also many world wide producers were becoming quality and cost leaders within many industries. While global sourcing requires more efforts when compared to domestic sourcing, it can yield large benefits.

While every firm will have its own reasons to go for global sourcing, the **four major reasons** are:

(i) To achieve cost/price benefits

(ii) To ensure better quality of products and services

(iii) To gain access to advanced technology and

(iv) To access the only source available

The **other reasons** for global sourcing are:

(a) Better timeliness

(b) Broader supply base

(c) Expanded customer base

(d) Introducing competition to domestic supply base

(e) Satisfying counter trade requirements

(f) Reacting to the sourcing patterns of competitors

(g) Establishing a presence in a foreign market and

(h) Increased supplier responsiveness.

The above reasons are briefly discussed in the following section:

Major Reasons

1. **Cost/Price Benefits :** It may be possible to have savings of 20 to 30 percent after considering all the costs associated with international purchasing. Cost differentials between countries arise because of the following reasons: *(a)* lower labour rates, *(b)* different productivity levels, *(c)* a possible willingness to accept a lower profit margin, *(d)* exchange rate differences, *(e)* lower-cost inputs for materials and *(f)* government subsidies if any. Eventhough the major consideration in purchasing is the quality of the product or service, quite often price differentials become the primary criterion behind a foreign sourcing decision.

   It is important to note that in assessing the cost-benefits of international sourcing, purchasing personnel should consider all the relevant costs associated with sourcing (total cost) the item instead of comparing the unit price alone. The costs to be considered while sourcing globally are *(i)* Freight, *(ii)* Import duties, *(iii)* Warehouse charges, *(iv)* Quality costs, *(v)* Damage during transportation, *(vi)* Obsolescence, *(vii)* Freight forwarding charges and *(viii)* Other administrative expenses.

2. **Quality :** A key reason for global sourcing is to obtain products/services of the required level of quality. For instance, producers in some countries such as Japan and Germany are able to achieve superior quality levels compared to other countries and are able to capture increasing share of world markets across a range of industries. The combination of consistently high quality and low-overall price has been a major consideration of foreign buying.

3. **Access to Advanced Technology :** No country holds a monopoly on new technology. Global sources in some industries are more advanced technologically than their domestic counter parts. Not taking advantage of such product or process technologies can result in a manufacturer's losing its competitive position vis-a-vis other firms that incorporate new technologies. Gaining access to the most current technologies leaves many firms with little choice except to pursue worldwide purchasing. *For example,* in the electronic components area, Asian suppliers have developed leading edge technologies and have emerged as technology leaders.

4. **Access to Only Source Available :** In many countries, the economic recession in the early 1980s has resulted in permanent closure of many firms across a wide range of industries. Hence in many industrial sectors, no domestic supplier can adequately meet the requirements

of purchasers, leaving domestic buyers with no viable alternative except foreign sources.

The other reasons are:

(a) **Better Timeliness :** Another reason for global sourcing is to improve certainty of a supplier in meeting schedule requirements of the buyer firm. Foreign suppliers may be able to supply in a shorter lead time compared to domestic suppliers eventhough transportation time is more. As with quality, the timeliness capability of suppliers around the globe has steadily improved.

(b) **Broader Supply Base :** Global sourcing increases the number of possible suppliers from which the buying firm can select. Broadening the supply base does not mean increasing the number of suppliers. It actually increases the opportunity to find better suppliers; thereby enabling the buying firm to decrease the number of contracted suppliers and pursue collaborative partnership or alliance relationships when appropriate.

(c) **Expanded Customer Base :** Sourcing globally can create opportunities to sell in countries where the buying firm's suppliers are based. Where trade restrictions are minimal, the interaction may yield some of the sales opportunities. In some countries where trade restrictions are imposed, non-domestic suppliers of products may have to purchase materials in the buying country as a part of the sales transaction.

(d) **Introducing Competition to Domestic Suppliers :** Firms that rely on competitive forces to maintain price and service levels within their industry may use worldwide sourcing to introduce competition to the domestic supply base.

(e) **Satisfying Counter Trade Requirements :** Counter trade agreements between firms specify that a firm must source a specific quantity of goods from a foreign country if it sells to a firm in that country. Hence, in such cases, purchasing personnel of the buying firm are required to evaluate and select suppliers in the foreign country with which the buyer firm's country has a counter trade agreement.

(f) **Reacting to the Sourcing Pattern of Competitors :** This may not be a widely accepted reason for global sourcing. Most firms may not like to admit that they are reacting to the practice of competitors in their sourcing strategies. A buyer firm may try to duplicate the factors that provide an advantage to a competitor, which may mean sourcing from the same suppliers or regions of the world used by the competitors.

(g) **Establishing a Presence in a Foreign Market :** If a firm's marketing has plans to sell to a foreign market where it currently does not have any business, then, as a way of developing good will with a foreign country, purchasing may first choose to source certain items from that country. The business relationship established with a foreign country may later support an expanded marketing presence.

(h) **Increased Supplier Responsiveness :** Foreign suppliers may respond better than domestic suppliers in term of quality standards, order lead-times, delivery schedules, mode of transport, price discounts etc. Also they may offer better associated services such as spare parts supply, customer training, installation etc.

Problems Associated with Global/International Sourcing

(i) **Cultural Issues :** The cultural differences between the buyer and the seller may be perhaps the biggest obstacle to developing mutually profitable business relations with international sources. The nature, customs and ethics of individuals and business organisations from two different cultures can affect the successful business relations. What is considered ethical in one culture

may not be ethical in another culture. Cultural issues can be a problem in global sourcing because of the wide variety of approaches to conducting business in different regions of the world.

(ii) **Communications :** Language frequently poses a significant barrier to successful international business relations. Communication problems may arise due to differences in culture, language, dialects which may result in miscommunications.

(iii) **Payment Terms and Conditions :** Buyer's prefer to pay after receipt and inspection of the goods. But the seller may prefer advance payment from the buyer. Such a payment term may tie up the purchaser's capital. Letter of credit is the common method of payment in international business. In this method also the buyer's funds may be committed to a longer period of time as compared to a domestic source.

(iv) **Long Lead Times :** The reasons for long lead times associated with global sourcing are: *(a)* variable shipping schedules, *(b)* unpredictable time requirement for customs activities, *(c)* the need for greater coordination in international purchasing, *(d)* strikes by aircraft and shipping company employees, *(e)* storms or cyclones at sea, *(f)* bad weather affecting airfreight etc.

(v) **Additional Inventories :** Eventhough it is difficult to determine the exact quantity of additional inventory needed when purchasing from foreign sources, the inventory carrying costs must be added to the purchase price, the freight costs and administrative costs to determine the true total cost of buying from global sources.

(vi) **Lower Quality :** When a firm which follows metric system of measurement buys from a firm following non-metric system, problem may arise due to variations in manufacturing tolerances. Further, nondomestic suppliers tend to be less responsive to design changes than the domestic suppliers.

(vii) **Social and Labour Issues :** US and some European countries are pressing for retaliatory measures against exporting countries where workers lack clout and labour laws are either week or flouted (for *e.g.*, use of child labour flouting the law).

(viii) **Higher Costs of Doing Business :** The need for translators, communications problems, the distance involved in making site visits etc., all add to the cost of doing business with global suppliers.

(ix) **High Opacity :** Risk of conducting business in different countries varies. A risk factor called **"opacity index"** has been developed to address the risk costs associated with conducting business in a specific country. The areas addressed by the global opacity index are: *(a)* corruption in government bureaucracy, *(b)* laws governing contracts on property rights, *(c)* economic policies, *(d)* accounting standards and *(e)* business regulations.

Barriers to Worldwide Sourcing

Firms with little or no international experience often face obstacles or barriers when beginning worldwide sourcing. The major barrier is the lack of understanding of international purchasing procedures. This includes *(a)* lack of knowledge about potential sources of supply and *(b)* lack of familiarity about the additional documentation required with international purchasing.

Another major barrier is the resistance to change from an established, routine procedure or shifting from a long-standing supplier. Domestic market nationalism is another barrier. Buyers are sometimes reluctant to shift from domestic sources to unknown foreign sources.

Another barrier involves the changes required to accommodate longer lead times. With long lead times, accurate material forecasts over extended time periods become critical. International sourcing may have certain degree of logistical, political and financial risk. Also, lack of knowledge about foreign business practices, language and cultural differences may be barriers which make negotiations with foreign suppliers more difficult.

Approaches Used to Overcome World Wide Sourcing Barriers

Some of the approaches for overcoming world wide sourcing barriers are:

(i) Education and training to generate support for the global sourcing process and to overcome the anxiety associated with change.

(ii) Publicising success stories of buyer firms to let other firms know about the benefits that world wide purchasing provides.

(iii) Use of computer aided systems for overcoming communication problems in engineering design.

(iv) Some firms have created a measurement and reward system that encourages sourcing from the world-class suppliers.

(v) Use of third party or external agents can be valuable particularly when a firm goes for world wide sourcing for the first time. After a period of time, firms may insource this function as the volume of overseas purchase increases.

Regardless of the approaches used to overcome the barriers for worldwide sourcing, it is most important that the top management of the firm extends its support for global sourcing. The objective of top management should be that global sourcing is used as a means to remain competitive by using only world-class suppliers and not to force domestic suppliers out of business.

➢ COSTS ASSOCIATED WITH GLOBAL SOURCING

It is important in global sourcing that purchasing examine closely the additional costs associated with global sourcing. This is one area that requires a ***total cost perspective***.

Certain common costs exists whether the purchase transaction is with a domestic or foreign supplier when compared to domestic purchasing, foreign purchasing includes the additional costs associated with conducting overseas transactions. If price is a major competitive factor, then a buyer must compare the total cost of foreign purchase to the total cost of the domestic purchase.

Common Costs : The costs which are common between domestic and foreign purchasing include the unit purchase price quoted by a supplier, tooling charges and transportation from the foreign supplier. If the purchased item requires tooling, purchasing must compare the benefit of owning the tool versus not owning the tool. The various considerations involved in the evaluation of unit price are: *(a)* effect of quantity breaks, *(b)* minimum purchase quantity necessary for shipping efficiency *(c)* the effect on price due to rush shipments and *(d)* any supplier - specific surcharges or extras. It is also necessary to critically evaluate transportation costs. *For example,* the effect on transportation costs if the purchaser controls a shipment directly from the supplier instead of the supplier arranging shipment or the effect on transportation costs due to longer transportation distances. International transportation is usually a major part of the total cost of international purchasing.

International Transaction Costs : International purchasing involves some costs that are not part of domestic purchasing. These costs must be included in the total cost analysis. Packaging requirements and costs are usually higher with foreign purchases than domestic purchasing. This is due to the longer distances involved in transportation and increased handling of shipments. The costs of packaging can be minimised by efficient packaging design by packaging engineers. Also the items entering a country are subject to customs duty or tariff. Duty rates vary widely over seemingly small differences between items. Total cost analysis must include any duty and broken fees incurred during the international transaction.

International shipments usually have insurance protection because ocean going carrier liability is generally limited. Other costs include port terminal and handling fees. A purchaser has to incur charges for unloading of cargo, administrative services of port authority personnel, and general use of the port.

Box 9.3 provides a generalised list of costs that can increase the total cost of international purchasing.

Box 9.3 : Elements of Total Cost of International Sourcing

(i) **Base Price :** *(a)* Ascertain quantity breaks, minimum purchasing quantity for shipping efficiency and surcharges if any.

(b) Determine price for rush shipments of quantities smaller than planned quantities.

(ii) **Tooling :** *(a)* Ideally, the purchaser should own the tooling and pay for it only once

(b) Consider shipping tooling from a domestic source if transferable.

(iii) **Packaging :** *(a)* It is a hidden cost (may be expensive for long distance and multiple handlings)

(b) A packaging supplier or an internal engineer may be consulted for methods to minimise costs on international shipments.

(c) Disposal of packaging materials can be expensive in some countries.

(iv) **Escalation :** *(a)* Determine how long the quoted price is firm or stable.

(b) Determine components of price escalation.

(v) **Transportation :** *(a)* Obtain assistance from logistics personnel who are experts in international transportation.

(b) Consider consolidation of shipments with other firms from the same geographical area.

(c) Use multinational carriers of freight agents to manage shipments and costs where required.

(d) consult the foreign supplier as a source of information regarding freight sources.

(vi) **Customs Duty :** *(a)* customs duty can vary widely over range of goods and countries.

(b) Items may fall into more than one classification for assessing the duty.

(vii) **Insurance Premiums :** *(a)* Not included in an ocean shipment price (Marine insurance is needed)

(b) Don't pay for extra coverage than needed.

(viii) **Payment Terms :** *(a)* Foreign suppliers may agree for longer payment terms.

(b) While dealing with intermediaries, the payment may be requested upon shipment.

(ix) Additional fees and commissions may have to be paid in some situations.

(x) **Port Terminal and Handling Fees :**

(a) Port handling charges include charges for unloading cargo, administrative services of port personnel and use of port.

(xi) **Customs Broker Fees :** Flat charges per transaction.

(xii) **Taxes :** Consider any additional taxes that may be paid.

(xiii) **Communication Costs :** *(a)* Charges for phone, travel, mailing, telex, fax and e-mail.

(xiv) **Payment and Currency Fees :** Bank transfers, bills of exchange, hedging and forward contracts.

(xv) **Inventory Carrying Costs :** *(a)* Higher levels of inventory due to longer lead times.

(b) Costs include the interest rate forgone by investing funds in inventory, insurance, taxes, storage and obsolescence.

(c) Internal carrying costs (usually 15% to 25% of the value of average inventory)

➤ REVIEW QUESTIONS

1. Enumerate the major functions of purchasing department.
2. Discuss the importance of purchasing.
3. State the objectives of purchasing.
4. Explain briefly the various parameters used in purchasing.
5. Define the term "purchasing management".
6. Discuss the transition of purchasing management to supply management.
7. Distinguish between purchasing management and supply management.
8. Discuss the various value-adding benefits of supply management.
9. Discuss the major developments in supply management.
10. Discuss the importance of supply management in business.
11. How are purchasing goods classified? Elaborate.
12. What is a "Purchase Cycle"? What are the activities constituting a typical purchase cycle?
13. What are "Purchase policies"? Mention the areas covered by policy statements.
14. Briefly discuss the various purchasing functions which are influenced by certain policies.
15. What is a "Purchase manual"? What are its two types?
16. How are purchasing systems classified? Briefly explain them.
17. Mention the various details which are normally furnished in a purchase order.
18. Briefly discuss the various methods of purchasing practised by various types of organisations.
19. Briefly explain the purchasing organisation with an organisational chart.
20. Describe the various ways in which responsibilities for purchasing is organised.
21. List the duties and responsibilities of a purchase manager.
22. What is meant by purchasing policies?
23. Discuss the various purchasing policies.
24. Discuss the basis for purchasing policies.
25. What are purchasing procedures?
26. What is a procedure manual? What are the purposes served by it?
27. Discuss the areas of purchasing procedures.
28. Explain the purchasing management process with a diagram.

29. Discuss the various types of supply policies.
30. What do you mean by "make-or-buy analysis"?
31. Discuss the strategic and tactical or operational decisions involved in make-or-buy analysis.
32. Discuss the factors influencing make-or-buy decisions.
33. Enumerate the various considerations which favour : *(a)* Making in-house and *(b)* Outsourcing, (or buying).
34. Discuss the volatile nature of the make-or-buy situations.
35. What is "global sourcing"?
36. Discuss the major reasons for global sourcing.
37. Discuss the problems associated with global sourcing.
38. What are the barriers for world-wide sourcing? What approaches are used to overcome these barriers?
39. Discuss the costs associated with global sourcing.
40. Discuss the elements of total cost of international sourcing.

❖ ❖ ❖ ❖

CHAPTER 10

VENDOR DEVELOPMENT

Traditionally competitive bidding was the primary method for awarding purchase contracts. In this approach, it was sufficient to obtain three bids (or quotations) and award the purchase contract to the supplier offering the lowest price. But it is not sufficient that the supplier is able to meet the material and service requirements of today. The buyer also wants to determine whether a supplier is capable to meet the company's long-term requirements and needs. This requires the knowledge of supplier's **strengths and weaknesses** and of the strong and weak points in their performance. Also, it is necessary to know whether the supplier can guarantee sustained continuity of supply. Hence, today purchasing managers systematically gather data about supplier performance and capability across many different areas. These data enable purchasing managers to negotiate agreements about improving reject rates, reducing total lead time and cost reduction. Because of all these, evaluation, selection and continuous measurement of supplier performance have become very important in materials management.

➤ NEED FOR VENDOR DEVELOPMENT

Make-or-Buy decisions and outsourcing are major decisions in any manufacturing organisation. The first step in **process planning** is to consider whether to make or buy some or all of a product or to subcontract some or all of a service.

A manufacturer might decide to purchase certain parts rather than make them. Sometimes all parts are purchased and the manufacturer simply performs assembly operations to produce the finished goods. In some cases, a firm might choose to perform part of the work itself and **sub-contract** part of the operations to outside suppliers or vendors. Whatever may be the extent of purchasing some parts or components or sub-units from outside suppliers (out sourcing) or sub-contracting some operations to vendors, good supply management is crucial for the survival and growth of any organisation. The vendors are considered as the best intangible assets of any organisation. Good suppliers are a vital link in the supply chain.

Supplier inefficiencies such as delayed deliveries of parts or materials or missing or defective materials can affect the production schedules, increase inventory carrying costs, and also cause late deliveries of end products to customers. Hence, both new and established vendors are subjected to critical evaluation periodically to review their plant capacities, financial conditions, performance etc. The materials manager must formulate a selective policy for vendor selection and choose only those suppliers who are suitable to the firm's needs. One of the objectives of purchasing is to develop at least two suppliers for each item being purchased.

Since the purchasing activity is a continuous process, it is not only enough if vendors are selected for meeting the immediate outsourcing requirements of a firm, but also for the future requirements. Hence, it is necessary to develop and cultivate the sources of supply which can be used effectively for the future needs.

➢ LEVELS OF VENDOR ASSESSMENT

Vendor assessment may take place at four different levels of abstraction. They are : *(i)* Product level, *(ii)* Process level, *(iii)* Quality assurance system level and *(iv)* Company level.

(i) **Product Level :** At this level, the focus is on establishing and improving the vendor's product quality. Incoming inspections and quality inspections are carried out to establish the degree of quality conformance of incoming materials.

(ii) **Process Level :** At this level, the production process is closely investigated rather than focusing on product inspection. This is because, the quality of the product depends on the quality of the vendor's manufacturing process. If the process is under control through consistent application of quality control procedures (*for example,* statistical process control using control charts), it will result in a product which conforms to the stated quality standards and specifications.

(iii) **Quality Assurance System Level :** Quality assurance means checking the way in which quality inspection procedures are developed, maintained and improved. The entire quality organisation of the vendor is the subject of investigation of the buyer firm.

(iv) **Company Level :** In this approach, not only quality aspects are focused, but also financial aspects are taken into consideration. The quality of the management of the vendor firm is assessed. In this way the buyer tries to establish how competitive that a particular supplier will be in the future.

➢ VENDOR EVALUATION AND SELECTION PROCESS

The overall objective of the vendor evaluation process is to reduce purchase risk and to maximise overall value to the buyer. An organisation must select vendors with whom it can do business over an extended period of time. The degree of effort associated with the vendor selection is related to the importance of the commodity to be purchased. *Exhibit 10.1* illustrates the critical activities and decisions involved in the vendor evaluation and selection process.

These activities and decisions involved in vendor evaluation and selection are briefly discussed in the following section.

Step 1 : Recognise the Need for Vendor Selection

Recognising that a requirement exists to evaluate and select a supplier for an item or service is the first step of the evaluation and selection process. Purchasing may participate in a product development team to get an early insight into new product development plans and thereby obtain some preliminary specifications on the type of materials, services or process required. This preliminary information may trigger initial evaluation of potential sources of supply in anticipation of future material need. The recognition of a purchase requirement occurs when a standard purchase requisition is received by purchase department. Also, a supplier selection decision may arise when existing suppliers fail to perform satisfactorily. Changing suppliers for existing items is termed as **supplier switching.**

Exhibit 10.1 : Vendor Evaluation and Selection Process

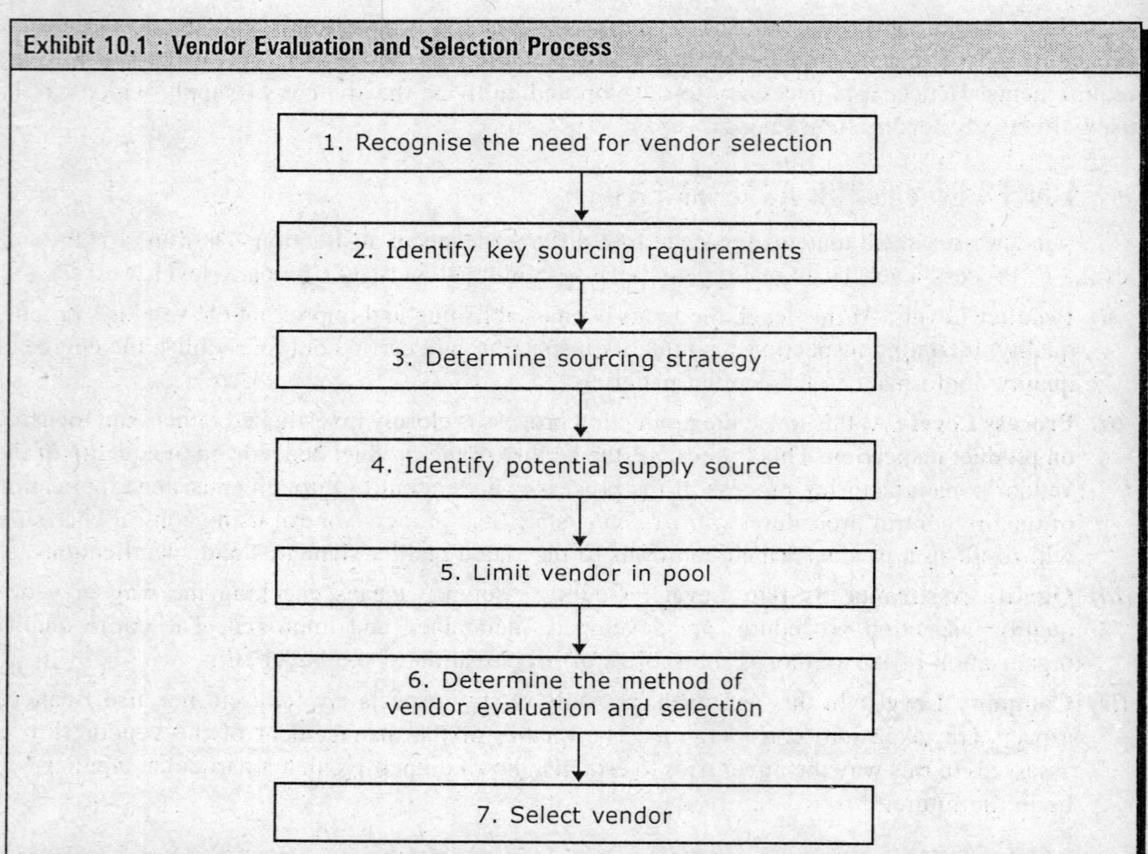

Step 2 : Identify Key Sourcing Requirements

The requirements that are crucial for a purchase often differ widely from item to item, organisation to organisation or industry to industry – while different requirements exist for each evaluation area, the minimum evaluation criteria include ***supplier quality, cost, delivery – performance*** and ***technological capacity***.

Step 3 : Determine Sourcing Strategy

There is no single sourcing strategy which can satisfy the requirements of all purchases. Because of this, the purchasing strategy adopted for a particular item or service will influence the approach adopted for supplier evaluation and selection process.

A commodity sourcing strategy provides direction on the overall objectives to be achieved for the commodity such as the number of suppliers that will be used (multiple sourcing), the type of contract (long term or short term) and the type of suppliers to be evaluated.

Some of the strategy options available are :

- Single versus multiple supply sources.
- Short-term versus long-term purchase contracts.
- Choosing suppliers who provide product design support versus those who lack design support capability.
- Developing a close working relationship versus traditional purchasing.

The strategy option selected has great influence on the supplier selection and evaluation process.

Step 4 : Identify Potential Supply Sources

Purchasers rely on various sources of information when identifying potential sources of supply. Several variables determine the degree to which a buyer must search for information about suppliers. *Exhibit 10.2* illustrates the intensity of an information search under various conditions.

Exhibit 10.2 : Information Search for Potential Sources of Supply

		Strategic importance of purchaser/ technical complexity requirement	
		High	Low
Capability of existing supply base to satisfy low cost, delivery, technology and service requirements	High	Minor-moderate information search	Minor information search
	Low	Major-moderate information search	Major information search

A major source of information comes from existing suppliers. Buyers often expect existing suppliers to satisfy a new purchase requirement. The advantage is that doing business with an already familiar supplier thereby saving time and resources required to evaluate a new supplier's capabilities. The disadvantage of using existing suppliers to supply new items is that the purchasing manager may never know whether better suppliers are available without information about other sources of supply.

Selecting an existing supplier for a new purchase requirement may be recommended if a list of **preferred suppliers** is maintained. A preferred supplier status conveys immediate information about the supplier's overall performance and competency.

Other sources of information are :

(a) Sales representatives

(b) Information data bases

(c) Experience of purchasing personnel by which they gain knowledge about potential suppliers

(d) Trade journals and trade directories

(*e*) Industrial trade shows or exhibitions

(*f*) Indirect information gathered from other suppliers

(*g*) Internal sources such as purchasing personnel of other units or divisions of the company

(*h*) Internet searches

Step 5 : Limit Suppliers in a Pool

Based on the information gathered, the purchaser may identify many potential supply sources from which to choose. Because the performance capabilities of suppliers vary widely and also because of limited resources available to the purchaser, an in-depth visit to all the potential suppliers or evaluation of all of them will not be possible. Hence, a preliminary evaluation of potential supplier is often used to narrow-down the choice before conducting an in-depth formal evaluation.

The various criteria used for making the preliminary evaluation are :

(*i*) Financial risk analysis

(*ii*) Evaluation of current and previous supplier performance and

(*iii*) Evaluation of information provided by suppliers

Step 6 : Determine the Method of Supplier Evaluation and Selection

Based on the preliminary evaluation, suppliers who are not capable are eliminated. The buyer or purchase team must then decide how to evaluate the remaining suppliers who may appear to be equally qualified. This requires an in-depth evaluation in more detailed manner than that used in the preliminary evaluation process. The way of in-depth evaluation and selection of suppliers include evaluation from supplier provided information, supplier visits and the use of preferred supplier lists.

Step 7 : Select Supplier

The final step of the evaluation and selection process is to select one supplier or more than one suppliers. The selection methods vary widely depending on the purchase item under consideration. For routine items, this may require notifying and awarding a purchase contract to a supplier. For major purchases, the process can be more complex. The buyer and the seller may have to conduct detailed negotiations to agree upon the specific details of the purchase agreement.

➤ KEY SUPPLIER EVALUATION CRITERIA

Most evaluations rate suppliers on three primary criteria: (*i*) **cost/price**, (*ii*) **quality** and (*iii*) **delivery**. These performance areas are generally the most obvious and most critical areas that affect the purchaser. For many items, purchasers will be concerned with only these three performance areas. But for critical items requiring in-depth analysis of supplier capabilities, a more detailed supplier evaluation study is necessary. An initial supplier evaluation will usually cover the following supplier performance categories to some extent :

(*a*) Supplier management capability

(*b*) Overall personnel capabilities

(*c*) Cost structure

(*d*) Total quality performance, systems and philosophy

(*e*) Process and technological capability (including supplier's design capability) (*f*) Environmental regulation compliance

(*g*) Financial capability and stability

(*h*) Production scheduling and control systems including supplier delivery performance

(*i*) Financial capability and stability

(*j*) Information systems capability (E commerce capability)

(*k*) Supplier purchasing strategies, policies and techniques

(*l*) Longer-term relationship potential.

➤ CHOOSING THE SUPPLIERS

When suppliers are chosen, a number of considerations arise. Even though *quality* of the products or services and **on-time delivery** are the most important considerations, there are many other factors that must be taken into account. *Exhibit 10.3* illustrates the factors that must be considered while choosing a supplier.

Exhibit 10.3 : Choosing a Supplier		
(*i*) **Lead Times and On-time Delivery**	(*a*)	What lead time can the supplier provide?
	(*b*)	What procedure does the supplier have for assuring on-time deliveries?
	(*c*)	What procedures does the supplier have for documenting and correcting delivery problems?
	(*d*)	Are there proper procedures?
(*ii*) **Quality and Quality Assurance**	(*a*)	What procedures does the supplier have for quality control and quality assurance?
	(*b*)	Are problems and corrective actions for quality documented?
	(*c*)	Are investigations conducted to determine and correct the causes of non-conforming materials?
(*iii*) **Flexibility**		How flexible is the supplier in handling changes in quantity, delivery schedules and product or service design changes?
(*iv*) **Location**		Is the supplier located nearby?
(*v*) **Price**	(*a*)	Are prices reasonable given the entire package the supplier will provide?
	(*b*)	Is the supplier willing to negotiate prices?
	(*c*)	Is the supplier willing to engage in a joint effort to reduce costs (and prices) by value analysis?
(*vi*) **Product or Service Changes**	(*a*)	How much advance notification does the supplier give when changes are made in products or services?
	(*b*)	To what extent does the buyer have inputs regarding changes?
(*vii*) **Reputation and Financial Stability**	(*a*)	What is the reputation of the supplier?
	(*b*)	How financially stable is the supplier?
(*viii*) **Other Accounts**		Is the supplier heavily dependent on other buyer or buyers causing the risk of giving priority to another buyer's needs over own?

➤ VENDOR EVALUATION AND VENDOR RATING

It is not easy to identify good suppliers. Records maintained or procured from some other sources about the vendors help in their evaluation and rating. Usually, a combination of **price, quality, quantity, delivery time** and **service** is used to rate the vendors, giving relevant weightages to those factors. In addition, a checklist is used to facilitate from the department standpoint. Some of the points are :

(i) **Reliability**

- Is the supplier reputed, stable and financially strong?
- Are the supplier's integrity and ability beyond doubt?
- Is the supplier going along with product development?
- Is the supplier's competitive strength as to price, quality etc., proved by past experience?

(ii) **Technical Capabilities**

- Can the supplier provide assistance as to application engineering?
- Can the supplier provide assistance as to analytical engineering?
- Can the supplier provide design assistance?
- Can the supplier handle special needs and contribute to improve product efficiency/basic processes?

(iii) **Convenience**

- Can the supplier help reducing acquisition cost?
- Can he/she offer other related products?
- Is he/she qualified to help in solving difficult problems?
- Does the supplier pack his product conveniently?

(iv) **Availability**

- Does the supplier assure delivery in time?
- Are his/her stocks locally available and/or at short notice?
- Can he/she plan his supply to minimise inventory?
- Can he/she be depended on for a steady supply of materials?

(v) **After-Sales Service**

- Does the supplier have a service organisation?
- Is an emergency service available?
- Are parts available when needed?

(vi) **Sales Assistance**

- Can the supplier help building mutual markets?
- Will he/she recommend our products?
- Does the use of supplier's product enhance appearance of our products?

➤ VENDOR EVALUATION

Recognising that there is a need for having a good, reliable vendor, it is essential that supplies are obtained from vendors after an evaluation of the supplier's capabilities. The buyer who has to do the evaluation, is faced with two different situations :

(i) Evaluating the performance before the vendor has delivered anything and

(ii) Evaluating the performance of the vendor after the deliveries have been made by the vendor.

The former is known as **Vendor Evaluation** and the latter **Vendor Monitoring** or **Vendor Rating**. In case of Vendor Evaluation, prior to the supply of materials from the vendor, the buyer lacks evidence on the results achieved by the vendor. Hence, the buyers must get the information by ways which induce general reputation of the vendor, data from other buyers and vendor surveys.

Factors to be Considered in Vendor Evaluation

After the list of potential suppliers (or vendors) has been compiled, a **qualitative** evaluation and elimination process is used. The process of evaluation compares vendors in terms of their ability to provide the desired quality, quantity, price and service.

In the context of purchasing, **quality** refers to the reliability of an item for its **intended purpose**. Therefore, the best quality need not necessarily be of highest quality, but must be evaluated in consideration of the intended use to which the product will be put. In purchasing parlance, **quantity** means not only the total amount required but also the time schedule according to which the goods have to be supplied to meet the buyer's requirements. The supplier must be able to supply the desired quantity during the time period specified by the buyer. The factor "**price**" is considered with regard to **desired quality** and **quantity** and also when accompanied by other useful services along with the goods supplied.

Service is an intangible factor in vendor evaluation and includes such issues as location, reserve capacity, technical capabilities, quality-control procedures, production assurance and labour and financial stability. These factors are discussed in detail in the following paragraphs.

Evaluating Sources of Supply : Choosing a vendor involves taking into account many of the same factors associated with making a major purchase such as a car or a stereosystem. A company considers factors such as **price, quality, the supplier's reputation, past experience with the supplier** and **after-sales-services**. This process is known as **vendor analysis**.

The main factors a company takes into account when it selects a vendor are :

(i) **Price :** This is the most obvious factor, along with any discount offer, although it may not be the most important. Because firms spend a large percentage of their total income on purchased items, finding suppliers who charge **low prices** is a key objective in vendor analysis.

(ii) **Quality :** Quality of a supplier's materials also is important because a company may be willing to spend more money to obtain materials of high quality. Also, hidden costs of poor quality can be high, particularly if defects are not detected until after considerable value has been added by subsequent operations. For a retailer, poor merchandise quality can mean loss of customers' goodwill and future sales.

(iii) **Delivery :** Shorter lead times and on-time delivery help the buying firm maintain acceptable customer service with less inventory. The benefits of fast, on-time deliveries apply to both service and manufacturing sectors. Many manufacturers demand quick, dependable deliveries from their suppliers to minimise inventory levels.

(iv) **Services :** Special services can sometimes be very important in choosing a supplier. Replacement of defective items supplied, instruction in the use of equipment, repair of equipment and other similar services can play a key role in preferring one supplier over another.

(v) **Location :** Location of a supplier can have impact on shipping time, transportation costs and response time for rush orders or emergency service. Local buying can create goodwill in the community by helping the local company.

(vi) **Inventory Policy of the Supplier :** If a supplier maintains an inventory policy of keeping spare parts on hand, this could be helpful in case of an emergency equipment break-down.

(vii) **Flexibility :** The willingness and ability of a supplier to respond to changes in demand and to accept design changes could be important considerations.

In addition to the above major factors, several other factors are also considered in supplier selection. They are :

(a) **Reserve Capacity :** A supplier with an adequate reserve of productive facilities can respond to increased requirements of customers.

(b) **Internal Facilities and Quality Control Procedures :** The stage of a supplier's technological development and its ability to keep up with current methods are also considerations affecting source. The technological capabilities provide the buyer with outstanding research and development. Buyers rely on vendors to suggest design and material changes as new concepts are perfected. The inspection and quality-control procedures maintained by the prospective supplier are also important in evaluating service.

(c) **Labour Relations :** A possible interference with the continuity of production in a supplier's plant may originate with the workers themselves. Strikes or production slow-down are directly related to the labour relations of the supplier.

(d) **Warranties :** Service may include the kind and form of warranties that accompany the supplier's products. Relevant considerations would include a vendor's capabilities to provide installation wherever necessary and to make available replacement parts as needed.

(e) **Vendor Sources :** Vendor relations also influence the supplier's service rating. A good supplier has well-developed sources of raw materials and components that will ensure continuity of production during periods of fluctuating business conditions.

(f) **Plant Visits :** Visits to the plants of suppliers constitute an important means of initial evaluation and periodic re-examination of existing vendors. It is often desirable for a representative of the production or engineering departments to accompany the buyer on such visits, especially if highly technical products are involved. The major areas of concern that should be observed and examined during the visits of the plants of suppliers are facilities, personnel, house-keeping, procedures and production specialisation of the supplier.

Credit and Financial Analysis

Another method of evaluations of suppliers is the analysis of credit reports of suppliers. The credit reports contain information about a supplier's facilities. These reports also provide information relative to the experience and management of the potential vendor.

A supplementary related procedure involves independent analysis of the vendor's financial statements. The purchasing officials can obtain information regarding financial stability, pricing cushion and general operating efficiency by applying tools of *ratio analysis* to the balance sheet and income statements of the vendor. Some of the popular ratios used are : **current ratio** (usual acceptable value of the ratio of current assets to current liabilities is 2 : 1), **acid test ratio** (usual accepted ratio of current assets less current inventories to current liabilities is 1 : 1), **sales-receivables ratio** (*i.e.,* sales divided by accounts receivable). **Net profit to sales ratio, cash flow** and Inventory turnover ratio (*i.e.,* cost of goods sold divided by average inventory).

➢ VENDOR RATING (OR SUPPLIER-EVALUATION) PLANS

Product quality submitted by vendors has always been evaluated and used as a factor in making purchasing decisions. Recently, the evaluation has been formalised by the use of vendor rating formulae which provide a quantitative measure of vendor quality. These ratings are primarily meant to provide an **overall quality rating** of a vendor for use in reviewing, comparing and selecting vendors.

Objectives of Vendor Rating

(i) To establish a procedure by which quality control, purchasing and user departments can fulfil the corporate objective of obtaining quality product at minimum cost.

(ii) To develop an effective tool for rectification of defects, improving the vendor's ability to serve more satisfactorily and as a basis for making future purchase decisions.

(iii) To periodically evaluate the written evaluation aspects relating to quality, quantity, price and service pertaining to the vendor.

Advantages of Vendor Rating

(i) An efficient vendor rating system obtains the best vendor for the buyer organisation which saves both time and money and also achieves the best value for money spent on purchases.

(ii) Provides a scientific vendor rating system, which if used improves the image of the purchasing executive.

(iii) Rates the entire performance of the vendors and is not guided by a narrow (tunnel) vision.

(iv) Provide the buyer additional information on the capabilities of the vendor with regard to know-how, testing, transport, contractual willingness etc.

(v) Objectively compares performance of vendors and improves the relationship with better performers (vendors).

(vi) Ratings can be used to provide a feedback to the vendors to improve their performance.

(vii) Decisions to disqualify, blacklist or discriminate the existing vendors can be arrived at on an objective basis.

(viii) Inculcates a competitive spirit among vendors.

(ix) Vendor rating can be used as an important mechanism to allocate the share of business amongst a large member of suppliers.

(x) Vendor rating not only enables the buyer organisation to know the performance of their suppliers, but also gives an idea as to how much they out-perform their competitors regarding price, quality, lead-time, split shipment, service, technical assistance, meeting in emergency, ad hoc requirements of buyers etc.

Parameters of Vendor Rating

A large number of factors usually grouped under **technical, financial, managerial** and **service factors** are considered for the purpose of an elaborate vendor rating scheme. The technical factors include past performance in quality, warranty, inspection plans, tool-room facilities, laboratory testing equipments, skill mix of supervisors of various departments, support document availability, testing equipments, design facilities, knowledge of cost reduction technique such as value analysis, quality consciousness at all levels, plant capacity, plant layout, maintenance policies, manufacturing experience and so on.

The financial parameters include volume discounts, credit terms, cash discounts, product price, real profit margin, return on total assets, current ratio, quick ratio, funds flow analysis, cash flow analysis, follow-up procedure for payment, guarantee of price protection against inflation and the like.

The management aspect includes number of employees and executives, ability of management, adaptability to change, reputation of board members, corporate image, integrity, length of time in business, industrial relations, staff morale, dynamism, nature of company, honesty, strength, weakness, opportunity, threat, strategies, structure, system, staff, skills and the like.

The service parameters based on experience include the delivery lead-time, reliability in delivery, willingness to accept small orders, width of production levels, depth of production line, management information system, guarantee, after-sales-services, ready availability of spare parts, ability to meet emergency requirements of buyer organisations and the like.

Usually vendors are rated on factors such as *quality, delivery, price* and *response,* which are discussed in various rating methods in the following paragraphs. Three popular techniques (methods) or plans used for vendor rating are :

(i) The categorical plan,

(ii) The weighted-point plan and

(iii) The cost-ratio plan.

The three vendor rating plans or methods mentioned above are discussed in the following paragraphs:

The Categorical Plan : This plan is the simplest and the least precise of the evaluation techniques. It relies heavily on the experience and judgement of the individual buyer. Essentially, it consists of a procedure whereby the buyer keeps a record of all vendors and their products. After establishing a list of factors for evaluation purpose, the buyer assigns a grade indicating performance in each area. A marking system of plus, minus or neutral is usually used. In addition, evaluation lists are given to all departments involved with the supplier's mechanisms, such as quality control, production and receiving departments. At periodic evaluation meetings, the buyer discusses ratings with representatives of these departments. Later, those suppliers with composite high or low rating many be notified and future business allocated accordingly. A list of factors can be established on the supplier's performance in each area based on the experience with the supplier over a period of time and each factor is given a grading as "never", "seldom", "usual", "always" etc. This system, though non-quantitative, provides a means of systematic record keeping on performance criteria. It is also inexpensive and requires a minimum of performance data. However, it relies heavily on the memory and judgement of individuals doing the rating and the possibility exists that ratings will become a routine chore performed with a minimum of critical thought.

The Weighted Point Plan : This plan provides for quantifying the evaluation criteria. Any number of evaluation factors can be included in the evaluation plan and their relative weights can be expressed in numerical terms so that a composite performance index can be determined and supplier comparisons made.

For example, the buyer decides to use the evaluation criteria which includes quality of shipments, accuracy of delivery promises, frequency of cost-reduction suggestions and price. Assuming that quality and delivery are the most significant, a point rating system such as the following might be used : quality = 40 points, delivery = 30 points, cost-reduction suggestions = 20 points and price = 10 points (note that the total points for all factors equals 100 points).

Exhibit 10.4 shows the composite rating schedule.

Exhibit 10.4 : Composite Rating Schedule

(a) Quality Rating	*Total Shipments Received*	*Percentage with Normal Rejects*	*Weighted Quality Rating*
Vendor A	100	90%	$\frac{90}{100} \times 40 = 36$
Vendor B	60	80%	$\frac{80}{100} \times 40 = 32$
Vendor C	50	70%	$\frac{70}{100} \times 40 = 28$

(b) Delivery Rating	*Percentage on Schedule*	*Weighted Delivery Rating*
Vendor A	80	$\frac{80}{100} \times 30 = 24$
Vendor B	90	$\frac{90}{100} \times 30 = 27$
Vendor C	100	$\frac{100}{100} \times 30 = 30$

(c) Cost-reduction Rating

Reduction	*Number of Cost-Reduction Suggestions*	*Percentage of Cost-Savings*	*Weighted cost Cost-Reduction Rating*
Vendor A	1	20	$\frac{20}{100} \times 20 = 4$
Vendor B	1	20	$\frac{20}{100} \times 20 = 4$
Vendor C	3	60	$\frac{60}{100} \times 20 = 12$

(d) Price Rating

	Average Price/ Unit	Lowest Price / Actual Price	Price Rating
Vendor A	Rs. 40/-	$\frac{40}{40} = 1$	$1 \times 10 = 10$
Vendor B	Rs. 50/-	$\frac{40}{50} = 0.8$	$0.8 \times 10 = 8$
Vendor C	Rs. 60/-	$\frac{40}{60} = 0.67$	$0.67 \times 10 = 6.7 \approx 7$

(e) Composite Rating

	Quality (max. 40 points)	Delivery (max. 30 points)	Cost Reduction (Max. 20 points)	Price (max. 10 point)	Composite Rating
Vendor A	36	24	4	10	74
Vendor B	32	27	4	8	71
Vendor C	28	30	12	7	77

The Cost-Ratio Plan : This plan relates all identifiable purchasing costs to the value of shipments received from respective suppliers. The higher the ratio of costs to shipments, the lower rating applied to that supplier.

The choice of the costs to be allocated depends somewhat on the product involved. However, quality, delivery, service and price are the usual categories. Costs associated with quality usually include costs of visits to vendor's plants and sample approval, inspection cost of incoming shipments and costs associated with defective products. *Exhibit 10.5* shows the various elements of quality costs.

The usual costs associated with delivery include expediting, telephone and telegram charges, emergency transportation (*e.g.,* air shipments) etc.

Exhibit 10.5 : Quality Costs

Vendor _______ **Month** _______ **Year** _______

		Rupees
(i)	Visits to vendor's plant	200/-
(ii)	Sample approval	300/-
(iii)	Incoming inspection	75/-
(iv)	Manufacturing losses	NIL
(v)	Reworking costs	NIL
(vi)	Value of rejected parts	425/-
(vii)	Other costs	NIL

Total costs = Rs. 1000/-

Total value of purchases = Rs. 1,00,000/

$$\text{Quality/cost ratio} = \frac{1000}{1{,}00{,}000} = 1\%$$

Delivery cost ratio is calculated as the ratio of total delivery costs to the total value of purchases, expressed as a percentage. Another costs-ratio used is service-cost ratio. The quality and delivery and service cost ratios are combined with the vendor's quoted prices to determine the net cost. Here, the vendor performance is reviewed periodically by an evaluation committee comprising the representatives from all departments involved with purchasing.

Supplier Audits : Buyers need to keep up to-date information regarding suppliers production capabilities, quality and delivery problems and resolutions as well as suppliers' performance on other buyer criteria. This is facilitated by means of periodic audit of suppliers. If an audit reveals problem areas, a buyer can address these and prevent the problems becoming serious. Supplier audit covers factors such as management style, quality assurance, materials management, the design process used for product design, process improvement policies and procedures for corrective action and follow up.

Supplier Certification : Supplier certification is a detailed examination of the policies and capabilities of a supplier. The supplier certification verifies that a supplier meets or exceeds the requirements of a buyer. Supplier certification is important in supplier relationships and facilitates establishment of long-term relationships with suppliers. Certified suppliers are sometimes referred to as *world class* suppliers. One advantage of using certified suppliers is that the buyer can eliminate much or all of the inspection and testing of delivered goods. Buying from certified suppliers has much less risk than with non-certified suppliers. The most widely used industry certification is ISO 9000 certification.

Supplier Partnerships : Of late the buying firms have realised the importance of building good relations with their suppliers instead of treating them as adversaries and dealing with them on that basis. Japanese are pioneers in applying the concept of supplier partnerships and deriving benefits of good supplier relations. These benefits include supplier flexibility in terms of accepting changes in delivery schedules, quality and quantities. Also, suppliers can help buyers to identify problems and offer suggestions for solving them. Hence, simply choosing and switching suppliers on the basis of price alone is not a good practice for buyers.

Many Japanese firms rely on one or a few suppliers whereas many US firms deal with numerous suppliers to remain flexible and have the advantage of playing one against the others.

Keeping good relations with suppliers is an important factor in maintaining a competitive edge. Hence, many buyer firms are adopting a view of suppliers as partners in their business. Such suppliers should be reliable and have the capability to provide high-quality supplies, maintain precise delivery schedules and offer flexibility with respect to changes in product specifications, quality, quantity and delivery schedules. Nine areas in which potential ideas from suppliers could lead to improved competitiveness of a buyer firm are :

(i) reduced cost of making the purchase,

(ii) reduced transportation costs,

(iii) reduced production costs,

(iv) improved product quality,

(v) improved product design,

(vi) reduced time to market (*i.e.,* time to get the product to the market),

(vii) improved customer satisfaction,

(viii) reduced inventory costs,

(ix) introduction of new products or processes.

Problems in Developing Supplier Relationships

(i) Because many of the benefits go to the buyer, suppliers may hesitate to enter into such relationships.

(ii) Suppliers may have to increase their investment in equipment which may put a strain on their cash flows.

(iii) Differences in the cultures of the buyer and supplier which may become a barrier for good supplier-buyer relationship between them.

Vendor Motivation

Two common approaches used in motivating vendors to perform satisfactorily are : *(i)* punishment and *(ii)* reward. A combination of both approaches may be used by many progressive buyers.

(i) **Punishment :** The greatest punishment for unsatisfactory performance is not to award contracts for future requirements. This is a powerful motivator especially when the buyers reduce the number of suppliers. Another approach known as "bill back" is used when dealing with a "partnership" supplier. Under this, incremental costs resulting from quality problems or late deliveries are billed back to the appropriate vendor.

(ii) **Rewards :** The biggest reward for satisfactory performance of vendors is repeat orders or follow-on business. Recognisition also is a powerful stimulant to future successful performance. High rating of vendors result in increased follow-on business for the vendors. Another kind of motivation to vendors is the **assistance** provided by the purchasers. Two types of assistances to vendors are : *(a)* **training** and *(b)* **problem solving**.

Training may be provided to vendors in the areas of statistical process control (SPC), just-in-time manufacturing and total quality commitment. The purchasers ensure that their vendors' quality systems and procurement systems operate effectively.

Problem Solving : Progressive firms provide technical and managerial assistance to their vendors when quality and related problems are encountered.

➤ MANAGING SUPPLIER RALATIONSHIPS

A key factor in achieving efficiency and effectiveness in the area of procurement is the development of successful supplier (or vendor) relationships. In today's global market place, developing strong supplier relationships becomes necessary to create and sustain a competitive advantage. When vendors are partners and/or stake holders, companies tend to rely more upon them to provide input into product design, engineering support, quality control and so on.

Procurement plays a key role in supply chain management and the supplier/vendor relationship are a vital part of successful procurement strategies, especially when companies reduce the total number of suppliers in conjunction with TQM programs or JIT Production and inventory systems.

The strategy to utilize a smaller number of suppliers/vendors means an alliance or **partnership** with suppliers/vendors. This is necessary because of the need to assure an adequate supply of quality materials over time at an optimum total acquired cost. Partnerships are being developed today throughout the supply chain. For example, partnership with transportation companies, third-party and fourth-party logistics providers and distribution channel members.

Supplier partnership is important because procurement contributes to the competitive advantage of a company. The advantage could be one of low cost, differentiation or a niche orientation. The procurement management program has to be consistant with the overall competitive advantage that a company is seeking to attain in the market place.

Supplier Partnership is defined as a tailor made business relationship based on mutual trust, openness, shared risk and shared rewards that yields a competitive advantage.

Types of relationships : Relationships between the buying firm and its suppliers or vendors can range from arm's length relationships to vertical integration of the two organizations.

Exhibit 10.6 illustrates the types of relationships.

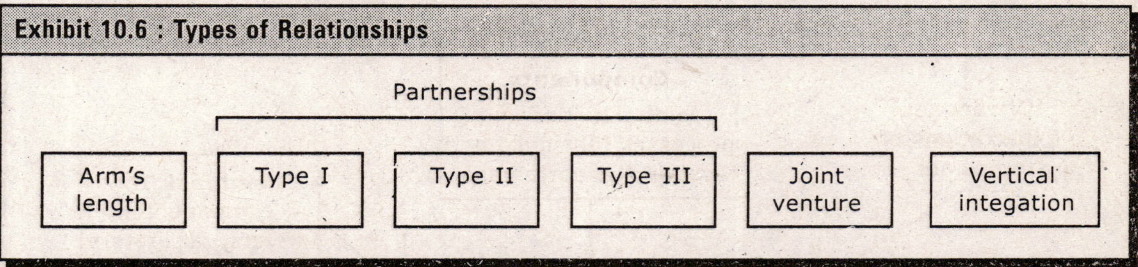

Most relationships between organizations have been at arm's length where the two organization conduct business with each other often over a long period of time and involving multiple exchanges. However there is no joint operations between the two companies. In arm's length relationship, a seller typically offers standard products/services to a wide range of customers who receive standard terms and conditions. The relationship ends when the exchange ends. Partnership is a more integrated relationship and would provide more significant benefits to both partners than arm's length relationship.

However, it may be noted that partnership relationship is not the same as joint venture or strategic alliance which entails some degree of shared ownership across the two partners. It is not the same as vertical integration. But a well managed partnership can provide benefits similar to joint ventures or vertical integration.

Three types of partnerships are:

(i) **Type I partnership** in which the firms involved recognize each other as partners and coordinate activities and planning to a limited extent. This kind of partnership has a short-term focus and involves only one functional area within each firm.

(ii) **Type II partnership** in which firms involved progress beyond coordination of activities to integration of activities. This kind of partnership has a long-term focus and involves multiple functions or divisions within the firms involved in the partnership.

(iii) **Type III partnership** in which the firms share a significant level of integration. Each firm views the other as an extension of their own firm. This kind of partnership does not have an end date for partnership. Normally, for a firm, the majority of its relationships will be of arm's length relationship. Of the partnership type of relationships, the largest percentage will be Type I and only a limited number will be Type III partnerships.

Type III partnership relationship is recommended for those suppliers or customers of a firm who are critical to the firm's long term success.

The Partnership Model : *Exhibit 10.7* shows the partnership model or partnering process.

Exhibit 10.7 : The Partnering Process

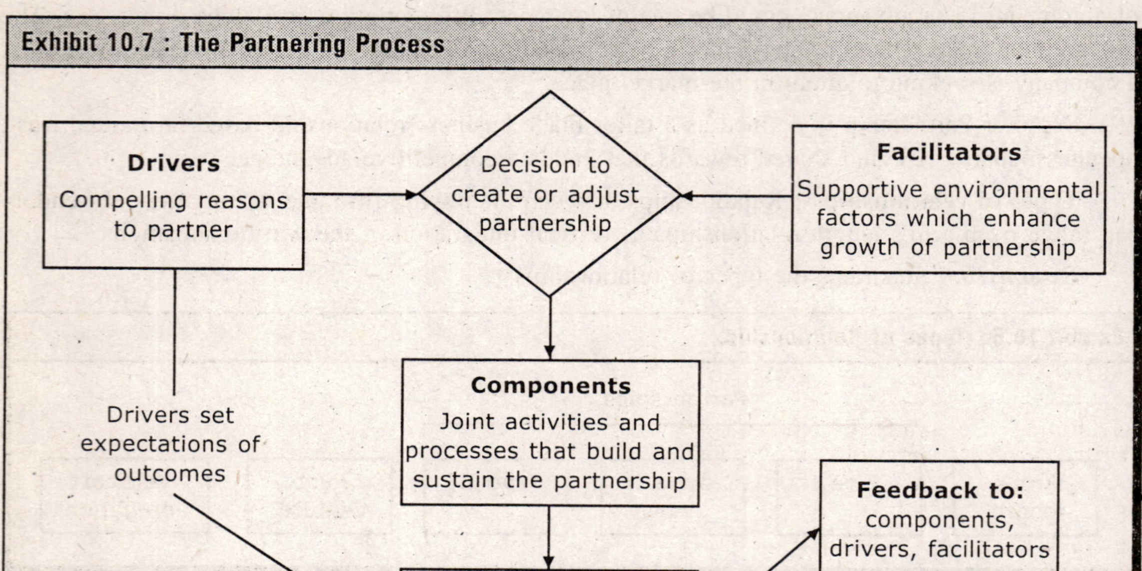

The major elements of the model are : *(i)* **drivers**, *(ii)* **facilitators** and *(iii)* **components**.

Drivers are compelling reasons to go for partnership relationship – **Facilitators** are supportive corporate environmental factors which enhance partnership growth and development. **Components** are joint activities and processes which are used to build and sustain the partnership relationship. All these three elements lead to **outcomes** which reflect the performance of the partnership.

Drivers : Four categories of drivers (or primary potential benefits that drive the desire to go for partnership) include *(i)* asset/cost efficiencies, *(ii)* customer service improvements, *(iii)* marketing advantage and *(iv)* profit stability/growth.

Facilitators : Four categories of facilitators are: *(i)* corporate compatibility, *(ii)* management philosophy and techniques, *(iii)* maturity and *(iv)* symmetry. Facilities apply to the combined environment of the two potential partners and therefore facilitators should be assessed jointly. The more positive the facilitators, the better the chance of partnership success.

Components : Components make the partnership relationship operational and help managers to create the benefits of partnering. Components include: *(i)* planning (style, level and content), *(ii)* joint operating controls (measurement and ability to make changes), *(iii)* communications (non-routine and day-to-day), *(iv)* risk/reward sharing, *(v)* trust and commitment to each other's success, *(vi)* contract style (time frame and coverage), *(vii)* scope (share of partner's business, value added and critical activities) and *(viii)* investment (financial, technology and people).

Partnership outcomes : The desired outcomes are:

(i) global performance outcomes (enhancement of profits, levelling of profits over time)

(ii) process outcomes (improved service, reduced costs)

(iii) competitive advantage (market positioning, market share, access to knowledge).

Feed back : Feed back can loop back to any step in the model. It can take the form of periodic updating of the status of drivers, facilitators and components.

Supplier/Vendor Selection Criteria

Even with a partnership or strategic alliance with a supplier/vendor, certain key criteria should be considered in any procurement situation. *Exhibit 10.8* provides an overview of the vendor selection criteria.

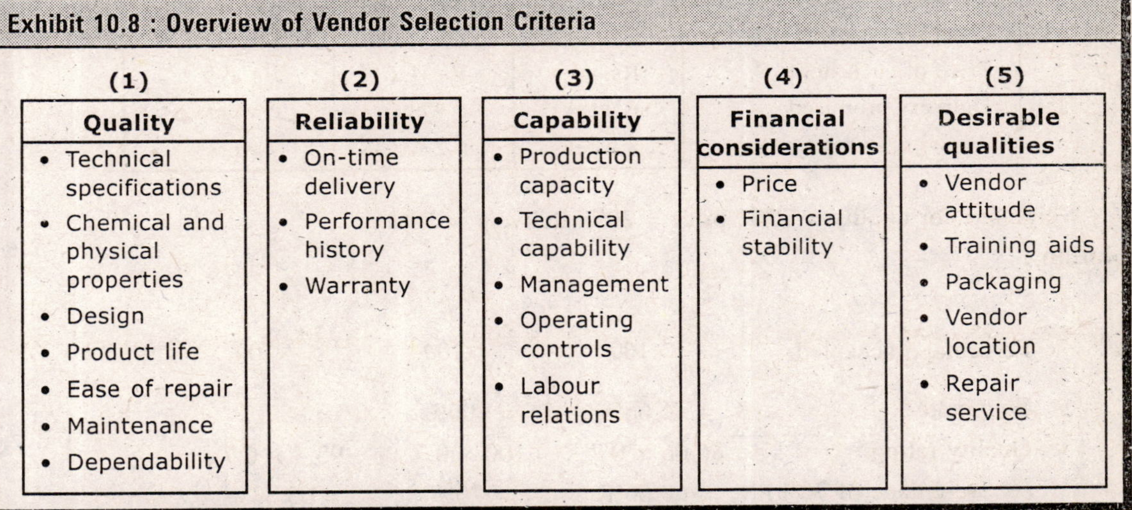

Exhibit 10.8 : Overview of Vendor Selection Criteria

(1) Quality	(2) Reliability	(3) Capability	(4) Financial considerations	(5) Desirable qualities
• Technical specifications • Chemical and physical properties • Design • Product life • Ease of repair • Maintenance • Dependability	• On-time delivery • Performance history • Warranty	• Production capacity • Technical capability • Management • Operating controls • Labour relations	• Price • Financial stability	• Vendor attitude • Training aids • Packaging • Vendor location • Repair service

Quality is the most important criterion in vendor selection. Quality refers to the specifications a user desires to have in a product which he/she wants to buy. In addition to specifications quality includes factors such as product life, ease of repair, maintenance requirements, ease of use and dependability.

Another criterion for vendor selection is **reliability** of the vendor in his supply performance. It comprises delivery and performance history. The buyer expects from the vendor consistent, on-time deliveries to prevent shut down of product line due to delayed deliveries of supplies from vendors.

Capability the third vendor selection criteria, considers the potential vendor's production facilities and production capacity, technical capability, management and organising capabilities and operating controls. These factors indicate the vendor's ability to provide the quality and quantity of materials desired by the buyer in a timely manner.

The fourth major vendor selection criterion is financial consideration including price of the product sold by the vendor and the vendor's financial position or financial stability to ensure long-term uhiterrupted supply of materials.

The remaining miscellaneous factors include vendor's attitude, training aids or support given to the user by the vendor, (*for example,* vendors supplying technical machinery, computers, robots etc., should provide training to the buyer/user) packaging, vendor's location, repair service (after-sales-support) etc. Vendor's geographical location affects the transportation cost. Other factors such as the ability to fill rush orders, meet delivery dates, provide shorter delivery times and utilise greater vendor/buyer cooperation, for the use of local suppliers.

➤ SOLVED PROBLEMS

1. *Calculate the vendor rating for the following. The item under consideration is the same from all suppliers.*

Supplier's data	*A*	*B*	*C*
Quantity supplied	90	80	75
Quantity accepted	78	80	70
Price of each item	Rs. 4	Rs. 4.2	Rs. 3.9
Delivery promised	6 weeks	6 weeks	6 weeks
Actual deliveries made in	8 weeks	6.2 weeks	7 weeks

Weightage for quality = 70%, price = 20%, delivery = 10%

Solution :

		A	*B*	*C*
(a)	Percentage accepted	$\frac{78}{90}\times 100$	$\frac{80}{80}\times 100$	$\frac{70}{75}\times 100$
	Weighted	= 86.66%	= 100%	= 93.3%
	Quality rating	86.66 × 0.7	100 × 0.7	93.3 × 0.7
	(@ weightage of 70%)	= 60.66%	= 70%	= 65.33%

(b) Price rating = $\frac{\text{Lowest price}}{\text{Net price}}\times 100$ Price rating = Price ratio × Weightage

	A	*B*	*C*
Price rating	$\frac{3.9}{4}\times 100$	$\frac{3.9}{4.2}\times 100$	$\frac{3.9}{3.9}\times 100$
Weighted	= 97.5%	= 92.85%	= 100%
Price rating	97.5 × 0.2	92.85 × 0.2	100 × 0.2
(@ 20% weightage)	= 19.5%	= 18.57%	= 20%

	A	*B*	*C*
(c) Delivery rating =	$\frac{6}{8}\times 100$	$\frac{6}{6.2}\times 100$	$\frac{6}{7}\times 100$
$\frac{\text{Delivery promise kept}}{\text{Actual delivery}}\times 100$	= 75%	= 96.77%	= 85.7%

Weighted			
Delivery rating	75 × 0.10	96.77 × 0.1	85.7 × 0.1
(@ weightage of 10%)	= 7.5%	= 9.68%	= 8.57%
Total vendor rating	87.66%	98.25%	93.87%

Vendor 'B' having the highest rating is chosen.

2. *Calculate the vendor rating for the following.*

Quality = 50; Delivery = 25; Price = 15; Response to suggestions = 10

Supplier's data	*A*	*B*	*C*
Quantity supplied	108	90	80
Equivalent quantity accepted	102	90	75
Price of item	Re. 1/-	Rs. 1.2	Rs. 1.1
Delivery promised	3 weeks	4 weeks	4 weeks
Actual deliveries	2.7 weeks	5 weeks	4.4 weeks
Response to suggestion	90%	85%	100%

Solution :

(a) Quality rating

	I	*II*	*III*
Percentage accepted	$\frac{102}{108} \times 100$	100%	$\frac{75}{80} \times 100$
Weighted	= 94.4%		= 93.75%
Quality rating	94.4 × 0.5	100 × 0.5	93.75 × 0.5
	= 47.2%	= 50%	= 46.875%

(b) Price rating = $\frac{\text{Lowest price}}{\text{Price of supplier}} \times 100$ Price rating = Price ratio × Weightage

	I	*II*	*III*
Price rating	$\frac{1.0}{1.0} \times 100$	$\frac{1.0}{1.2} \times 100$	$\frac{1.0}{1.1} \times 100$
Weighted	= 100%	= 83.33%	= 90.9%
Price rating	100 × 0.15	3.33 × 0.15	90.9 × 0.15
	= 15%	= 12.50%	= 13.63%

(c) Delivery rating

	I	*II*	*III*
$= \frac{\text{Delivery promise}}{\text{Actual delivery}}$	$\frac{3}{2.7} \times 100$	$\frac{4}{5} \times 100$	$\frac{4}{4.4} \times 100$
Weighted	= 111.11%	= 80%	= 90.99%
Delivery rating	111.11 × 0.25	80 × 0.25	90.99 × 0.25
	= 27.77%	= 20%	= 22.72%

	I	II	III
(*d*) Response to suggestion	90%	85%	100%
Weighted Response	90 × 0.10	85 × 0.1	100 × 0.1
Rating	= 9%	= 8.5%	= 10%
	I	II	III
Total vendor rating	98.97%	91.00%	93.23%

Since vendor I has highest rating, he is ranked number one, vendor III is rank number two and vendor II is rank number three.

➤ REVIEW QUESTIONS

1. Discuss the need for vendor development and vendor rating.
2. Discuss the four levels of vendor assessment.
3. Explain the various steps involved in vendor evaluation and selection process.
4. Discuss the criteria used for supplier evaluation.
5. Explain briefly the factors that must be considered while choosing a supplier.
6. Distinguish between "vendor evaluation" and "vendor rating".
7. Discuss the factors to be considered in vendor evaluation.
8. What is credit and financial analysis?
9. State the objectives of vendor rating.
10. Mention the advantages of vendor rating.
11. Discuss the parameters for vendor rating.
12. Describe the following vendor rating plans or methods. *(a)* The categorical plan, *(b)* The weighted point method, *(c)* The cost-ratio plan.
13. What is supplier audit? Why is it done?
14. What is supplier certification? What are its benefits?
15. Discuss the advantages and problems of supplier partnerships.
16. Explain how vendors can be motivated for better performance.

❖ ❖ ❖ ❖

CHAPTER 11

STORES MANAGEMENT

Receiving and storing are important flow control activities in the materials management chain. In industries, materials have to be stocked to meet the consumption requirements during lead time or during extension of lead time due to delays by suppliers or due to unexpected increase in the consumption rate. **Warehousing** is not the simple act of storing materials, but rather a package of services which enables the smooth flow of materials through the production departments without causing stoppage of production due to shortage of materials.

Storekeeping is primarily a *service function* in which the storekeeper acts as a custodian of all items carried in the store. Stores management should aim at providing this service as efficiently as possible with minimum possible cost. Store keeping may be defined as a function of receiving, storing and issue of raw materials, bought-out parts and components, spare parts, tools, consumables, supplies and stationery items etc. to the user departments which have indented for the same. It is the aspect of material control concerned with the physical storage of materials and goods.

Types of Materials Stored : Store is a building where materials and goods are kept and preserved. The word *"stores"* refers to the place where all kinds of materials and goods are held in stock and *storage* or *storekeeping* is defined as the act of storing the goods. The word *"stores"* is sometimes used to refer to anything which is stored.

Stores are generally classified as :

(i) Raw materials stores, *(ii)* Component stores, *(iii)* Consumable materials stores, *(iv)* Semi-finished goods stores, *(v)* Finished goods stores, *(vi)* Inwards goods stores or transit stores, *(vii)* Holding stores, *(viii)* Spare parts stores, *(ix)* Inflammable materials stores, *(x)* Tools stores, *(xi)* Stationery stores, *(xii)* Maintenance materials stores, *(xiii)* Rejected materials stores, *(xiv)* Scrap or disposal stores (Scrap yard), *(xv)* Stationery items stores, *(xvi)* Packing materials stores.

Importance of Storekeeping : The benefits of efficient storekeeping are :

(i) Ready accessibility of important materials which provides efficient service to users.
(ii) Efficient utilisation of cubic space in the storage area (stores).
(iii) Flexibility in arranging the storage of goods in stores.
(iv) Minimisation of deterioration and pilferage of materials stored.
(v) Ease of physical counting at the time of annual stock checking.

➤ OBJECTIVES OF STORES MANAGEMENT

(i) To facilitate a balanced and smooth flow of raw materials, components, tools and any other items necessary to meet production requirements.
(ii) To maintain optimum stock of materials to compensate for irregular supplies by suppliers.
(iii) To achieve efficient utilisation of storage space.
(iv) To reduce usage of materials handling equipments.
(v) To provide codification of stored items for easy recognition.
(vi) To enable flexibility in production schedules.
(vii) To facilitate quantity purchases at discount prices.
(viii) To keep the account of all goods kept in stores.
(ix) To prevent theft, damage, wastage and deterioration of stored materials.
(x) To maintain record of all incoming materials and issue of materials to user departments.

➤ FUNCTIONS OF STOREKEEPING

(i) To receive raw materials, components, tools, equipments and other items and account for them.
(ii) To provide adequate and proper storage and preservation of various kinds of materials.
(iii) To meet the demands of the user departments by proper issues and keeping account of items used by user departments.
(iv) To minimise obsolescence, surplus and scrap through proper codification, preservation and handling.
(v) To highlight accumulation of stocks, discrepancies and abnormal consumption and implement proper control measures.
(vi) To ensure good house-keeping to facilitate proper material handling, material preservation, receipt, stocking and issue of materials.
(vii) To assist material accounts department in stock verification and provide supporting information for effective purchasing.
(viii) To co-ordinate storekeeping with related production functions.

Problems due to Inefficient Storekeeping

(i) Failure to locate store rooms properly and the inefficient use of available storeroom space can increase the storage costs.
(ii) Excess handling of materials, need for more persons and equipments for materials handling.

(iii) Difficulty is locating materials.

(iv) Overstocking and the resulting costs.

(v) Problems in material control and time involved in supplying materials when needed because of improper store-room location and use.

(vi) Inventory carrying costs due to deterioration, damage and pilferage of materials and related indirect labour costs.

➢ PLANNING FOR STOREKEEPING

The stores department does not determine such factors as quantities of materials to be purchased, order periods, usage rates etc., but these data must be acquired and reviewed to plan for storage area required. In case of an existing store room, with fixed storage capacity, the present limitations of space and facilities are to be considered while planning the procurement of materials. When new factories are planned, much careful planning will have to be done for deciding the location and layout of stores to facilitate efficient storekeeping.

Planning for storekeeping involves collection of all the available data relating to the items to be stored, the space requirements, the store room equipments and facilities and probable flow paths into, through and out of stores. Allowances for variability in the data should be included. Finally, **alternative** layouts should be planned and cost analyses made before deciding on the final storekeeping plan.

The first stage of planning is to determine the overall **cubical space requirements** for store keeping the materials. These requirements should be estimated on both a short-term and long-term basis to anticipate present as well future requirements of storage space. It is necessary to determine the quantities of materials to be stored and their specifications such as *size* **(volume)**, **weight**, **fragility**, **susceptibility** *to* **pilferage** (costly items) and other factors which may require special handling or storage treatment. Also, data must be gathered covering the purchasing lead time, the delivery rates and usage rates of materials to be stored by stores department. This information must be translated into space requirements. It is necessary to project the space requirements over a longer period of time such as five years to twenty years depending on the type of industry.

The proper layout of stores results from the determination of the most effective utilisation of space. Consequently planning for storage and layout of stores (storage space) are **interdependent** activities and should either be done concurrently or separately.

Materials handling equipment selection is also directly related to the planning and layout of stores and therefore should be taken into account.

➢ LOCATION OF STORES

The determination of the location of stores area will depend on the needs of the plant and will vary from plant to plant. Certain basic factors to be taken into account to determine the best location for stores are:

(i) **Materials Classification :** Materials of the same classifications may be stored together regardless of differences in size, weight, and destination. *For example,* separate storage areas may be designated for raw materials, purchased parts, supplies, semiprocessed parts, finished products, packing materials, inflammable materials, spare parts for maintenance department etc.

(ii) **Similarity of Materials :** Items of similar size, shape, and weight may be stored together even though they may be classified differently or be required at different production locations. According to this approach, all *small parts* may be stored in one place, bar stocks in another, castings, forgings and bulky items in another place, raw materials such as steel, aluminium and brass sheets etc., in yet another place.

(iii) **Point of Use :** It is sometimes desirable to locate all materials to be used at each production centre as close as possible to that particular centre. This approach may result in decentralisation of stores, creating holding stores for each production division or centre.

(iv) **Materials Handling Consideration :** Materials which require similar handling equipment may be grouped together. *For example,* materials in the form of liquids may be stored together. Also, items which are to be frequently handled because of a greater frequency of requisition may be placed at more accessible locations than less frequently handled items.

(v) **Special Requirements :** Some items may be fragile, explosive, extremely valuable or may require special atmospheric conditions for storage. Such materials will have to be stored in locations which provide proper facilities.

Centralised Versus Decentralised Storing

The basic principle of stores location is to minimise handling of materials, rehandling and internal transportation, reducing the distance moved by the materials and avoiding back tracing.

In small plants, it is desirable to store the materials in a central store (centralised storing) controlled by a stores officer or stores manager. In such cases, the store is located very near to the place of use. (*i.e.,* production centre). If there are a number of production centres (in big plants) the stores department should be located in such a way it is in a **central place** having almost equal distance to all production centres. Such stores are referred to as centralised stores.

Advantages of centralised storing are as below :

(i) Fewer storekeepers.

(ii) All storekeepers will become familiar with all materials stored. Hence, stores function will not be affected if some storekeeper quits or is absent.

(iii) Better control of inventory.

(iv) All stores records will be kept in one place and hence easy to refer.

(v) Reduced duplication of items results in reduced total inventory.

(vi) Balanced load on storekeepers.

(vii) Less obsolete materials are held in stores.

(viii) Periodic inventory checks against balance-of-stores records are easier to take.

(ix) Less clerical costs.

The disadvantages of centralised storing are as below :

(i) The store room may be far away from some departments and hence the transportation cost will be more to move materials from the store room to these departments.

(ii) Centralised stores clerical staff are less familiar with the needs of each individual being served.

(*iii*) Longer waiting lines tend to form because a single store has to serve a number of user departments.

Decentralised Storing : Decentralised storing is preferred in large plants having different divisions or departments using different kind of materials. *For example,* electrical stores is located near electrical maintenance section, tools and equipment stores near tool room, spare parts stores near maintenance department and so on. *Similarly,* raw materials such as sand, limestone, coke, iron ore and pig iron should be stored near the foundry shop. Items such as stationery, lubricating oils, cotton waste etc., which are used by all departments are stored in a central store.

Advantages of decentralised storing are as below :

(*i*) Reduced material handling distance and costs.

(*ii*) Reduced bottlenecks or waiting lines for collection of materials from stores.

(*iii*) Less risk of loss by theft or fire.

(*iv*) Convenient for all departments to draw materials as store rooms are located nearby.

Disadvantages of decentralised stores are as below :

(*i*) Duplication of orders for materials from the supplier and also small order quantities from each user department.

(*ii*) More manpower is required.

(*iii*) More storage space is required.

(*iv*) Standardisation of materials is not possible.

(*v*) Higher chances of pilferage or theft of materials.

➤ STORES ORGANISATION

To achieve the objectives of stores management, the receiving and storekeeping functions must be properly organised to facilitate both service and control functions. Stores managers generally organise and control the flow of materials into production, operations. Further, the stores organisation acts as a custodial and controlling agency. It is responsible for the safety and physical control of a firm's current assets. Also, the existence of storage function enables purchase department to go for quantity buying to take advantages in price, paper work and material handling.

The specific responsibilities of stores organisation include:

(*i*) receipt, identification and general inspection of incoming materials by the receiving department.

(*ii*) physical storage of all production materials, including in-process inventory, spare parts, maintenance, repair and operating supplies and finished goods.

To discharge the above responsibilities satisfactorily, the stores manager must develop a system for classifying, identifying (marking) and locating all materials so that they are readily accessible and at the same time they are protected against pilferage, spoilage, unauthorised usage, damage or deterioration. In addition the stores department must also control physical issue of materials and provide effective service for the production departments and service departments, such as maintenance, quality control, testing etc.

Organising Stores : Traditionally stores department has been attached to production department or production planning and control department. Such stores are classified as **holding stores** and

work-in-progress stores. Finished goods stores were usually attached to sales department or shipping department. But the modern approach is to delink stores from production and sales departments and place the stores under materials department headed by the materials manager, who has a status equal to that of managers of production, production planning and control, finance, marketing/sales departments. Stores organisation involves systematic co-ordination of efforts in such a manner which would result in optimum efficiency with minimum expenditure. Organising the stores function requires proper guidance, regulation and control to ensure that materials are arranged in a way that will permit easy storage, minimum pilferage, proper identification, and quick retrieval, with minimum waste of time and effort.

A typical stores organisation chart for a large manufacturing firm is illustrated in *Exhibit 11.1* below:

Exhibit 11.1 : A Typical Stores Organisation Chart

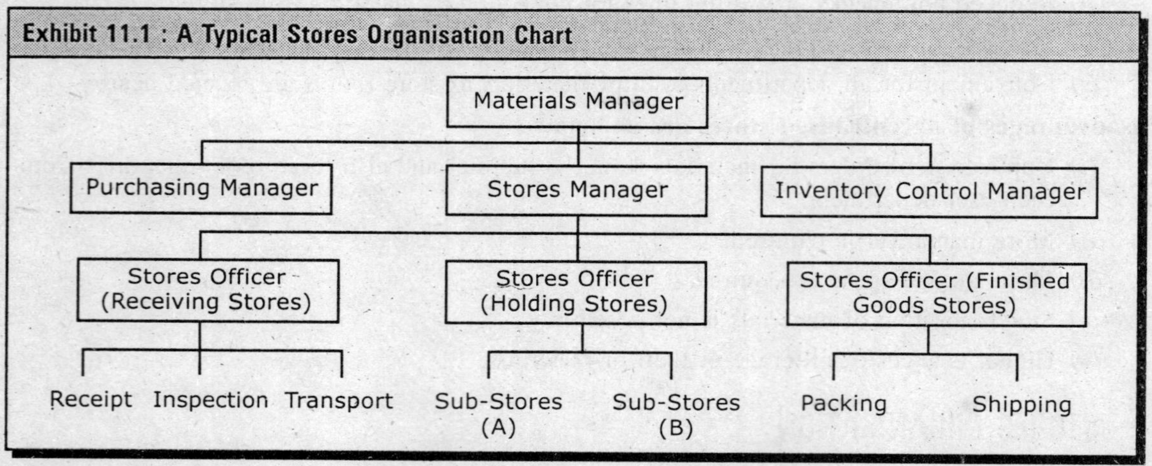

Types of Stores

Stores are broadly categorised as :

(i) **Functional Stores** depending on the use of materials stored. *For example*, raw material stores, finished goods stores, chemical stores, tools stores, maintenance stores (for spare parts) and the like.

(ii) **Physical Stores** depending on the size and location of stores, *for example*, central stores, transit stores or inwards-goods stores, site stores, sub-stores, holding stores and the like.

The types of stores mentioned above are briefly described in the following paragraphs:

1. Functional Stores

(i) **Raw Material Stores :** This is a place where raw materials used for production are stored. Depending on the nature of raw materials used, the store could be an open yard, a shed with a roofed structure without walls, and it could be near a railway line, road or river depending on the mode of transport used for transporting the materials from the supplier to the purchasing organisation. If raw materials are inflammable or explosive, such materials should be stored in an isolated place of storage.

(ii) **Production Stores :** This is a store storing production materials such as consumables, cutting oils, jigs and fixtures, cutting tools and the like.

(iii) **General Stores :** This is a place where various kinds of miscellaneous items such as paints, painting brushes, cleaning materials, spirit etc., are stored.

(iv) **Tools Stores :** This is a place where all kinds of cutting tools, measuring instruments, cutting pliers, hammers, and special tools are stored.

(v) **Salvage Stores :** This is a store where materials which have been rejected during production are stored either to salvage them by rework or to dispose them as scrap. Metal scraps, old machinery etc., are stored in disposal stores or scrap yard.

(vi) **Packing Stores :** Packing materials are stored here. *For example,* wood, card board cartons, bottles, empty cylinders etc., which are used for the packing the finished goods and despatching the same.

(vii) **Receiving Stores :** This is a place where goods supplied by vendors are received and inspected for quality and quantity before these goods are sent to the departmental holding stores. This stores is also referred to as *inwards goods stores* or *transit stores*.

(viii) **Work-in-progress Stores :** It is an intermediate storage place where semi-processed parts are stored for some time before they are moved to next stages of operation.

(ix) **Finished Goods Stores :** This is a place where finished products meant for despatch to customers are stored. These finished goods may be despatched to regional warehouses or to wholesalers/ distributors or to end customers.

(x) **Stationery Stores :** This is a place where all kinds of stationery items required for office use of various departments are stored.

(xi) **Bonded Stores :** This is a store where goods subjected to customs duty are stored and for goods which are debonded (*i.e.,* removed out of the bonded store) when needed for production, customs duty is paid.

(xii) **Refrigerated Stores :** This kind of stores is used for storing perishable items such as vegetables, fruits, medicines, meat, chemicals, etc.

(xiii) **Inflammable Materials Stores :** This is the stores where materials such as oil, paints, acids etc., which are prone to fire hazards are stored with adequate arrangements for protection again fire hazards.

2. Physical Stores

The various types of stores classified under this category are :

(i) **Central Stores :** A centralised store which serves many divisions or units in a large manufacturing organisation or a centralised warehouse where finished goods of several units are stored. Common items used by several production units are stored in central stores.

(ii) **Sub-Stores :** This type of store serves the requirement of a particular production unit and is located nearer the manufacturing shop of that unit.

(iii) **Departmental Stores:** This store serves the need of a particular department. *For example,* in a textile factory each department such as spinning, weaving, bleaching, and printing has its own departmental store to store the required materials for each department.

(iv) **Group Stores :** This kind of stores keeps the materials required for a number of production units belonging to the same industrial group (say *for example,* Godrej industry or J.K. group of industry) located in one location in an industrial estate or industrial area. The group stores serves all the industrial units belonging to a group of industries.

(v) **Site Stores :** This is a stores used to store construction materials like steel, cement, tools etc., required for large construction projects such as construction of dams, high ways, bridges, railway lines, factories, housing complexes, shopping complexes etc.

➢ LAYOUT OF STORES

Physical arrangement of storage facilities for efficient receiving, storing and issuing materials is referred to as *stores layout.* A properly laid out store will result in proper and orderly storing of materials, minimum handling of materials and optimum utilisation of storage space.

Factors to be considered while planning the layout of stores are as below :

(i) **Type of Materials Stored :** The prior knowledge of the nature of various types of materials to be stored is essential for planning the layout of stores. It helps in determining the nature, size, quantity of equipment and material to be stored and type of storage facility needed.

(ii) **Volume of Materials Stored :** The volume and weight of the materials to be stored have a major role in layout of stores and in deciding the kind of materials handling equipment needed in stores department. Sufficient passages (gangways or aisles) should be provided for free movement of materials handling equipments inside the stores. Also, the storage space depends on the volume of materials to be stored.

(iii) **Availability of Space :** Lack of adequate space causes congestion of materials in stores. It also limits the quantity of materials that can be stored. Both too much of space and too little space lead to storing of materials haphazardly and higher handling costs.

(iv) **Physical Factors :** Physical environmental factors such as good lighting, ventilation, controlled noise and temperature etc. protects the materials from damage, deterioration and hazard during storage. It also increases efficiency of stores personnel.

Principles of Stores Layout

(i) Provision for easy receipt, storage and disbursement of materials and nearness to point of use.

(ii) Minimum handling and transportation of materials.

(iii) Good accessibility of materials for handling equipment and personnel.

(iv) Optimum utilisation of floor space and cubic space.

(v) Clear identification of materials, quick location of items and ease of physical counting.

(vi) Flexibility to suit the changing storage requirements of the future.

(vii) Protection against waste deterioration, damage, pilferage and fire.

(viii) Good lighting to prevent thefts, damage to materials and errors in storing.

(ix) Easy shelf-life rotation to permit first-in-first out issue control.

(x) Periodic house-keeping and rearrangement.

(xi) Isolated storage of inflammable materials like oil, wood, paint, cotton waste, kerosene etc.

(xii) Incorporation of safety in the layout plan.

➢ STORAGE SYSTEM

Stores layout is a fundamental factor in determining the efficient performance of the stores department. The following factors deserve serious consideration, while planning for stores layout :

1. Provisions for easy receipt, storage and disbursement of materials, and nearness to point of use.
2. Minimum handling and transportation of materials, good accessibility for handling equipment, and personnel.
3. Adequate capacity provision for flexibility for future expansion.
4. Efficient utilisation of floor space and height.
5. Clear identification of materials, quick location of items and ease of physical counting.
6. Protecting against waste, deterioration, damage and pilferage.
7. Design the buildings' physical appearance to create goodwill and to invite business.
8. Arrange storage for fast and easy customer order processing.
9. Use compatible storage or display equipment to create good interior appearances.
10. Install good lighting to prevent theft, parts damage and errors in stocking.
11. Plan storage for easy shelf-life rotation to permit first-in-first-out control.
12. Segregate rebuilt, remanufactured, used and new merchandise.
13. Include safety as a part of the facility plan.
14. Maintain a periodic house-keeping and rearrangement plan.

Two aspects of stores layout are significant, *viz.,* 1. storage system and 2. type of stores layout.

Storage System

Choosing the most suitable storage system means **dealing with a number of interacting and often conflicting factors**. Inevitably, the degree of mechanisation affects layout while scarcity of space affects the height to which, racking is erected. The need for rapid, intensive order packing means a need for rapid and easy access to stock. But accessibility weighs against space economy. A satisfactory storage system is, therefore, a compromise between the **use of space** and the **use of time**. The way in which stock is located helps make the compromise a satisfactory one.

There are three basic ways of locating stock: fixed location, random location and zoned location.

Fixed location means that goods of a particular type have a position in the store assigned to them exclusively. It means that while stock can be found immediately without a complex system for recording its position, there can be considerable waste of space, because when stocks of any one item are low, the space left vacant cannot be filled.

The assignment of fixed position to a particular type of goods is made on any one of the following basis :

1. On the basis of supplier.
2. On the basis of similarity of the items.
3. On the basis of the joint issue of the items.
4. On the basis of the size and frequency of use.

Random location means that items can be stored in any storage position which is available. Space is thus better utilised but, particularly where there are a large number of product lines, a record has to be kept of where goods are and frequency of when they entered the storage area.

Zoned location means that, goods of a particular product group are kept in a given area. They may be randomly stored in a zoned location or stored according to fixed locations.

Type of Stores Layout

Whatever the location followed, stock may be kept on one side of the aisle in which case it is called **comb type** layout (*Exhibit 11.2*) or goods may be placed on either side of the aisle in which case, the method is called *tree type* layout (*Exhibit 11.3*). Selecting a particular type depends on the availability of space and the layout of the building.

Exhibit 11.2 : Comb Type Layout

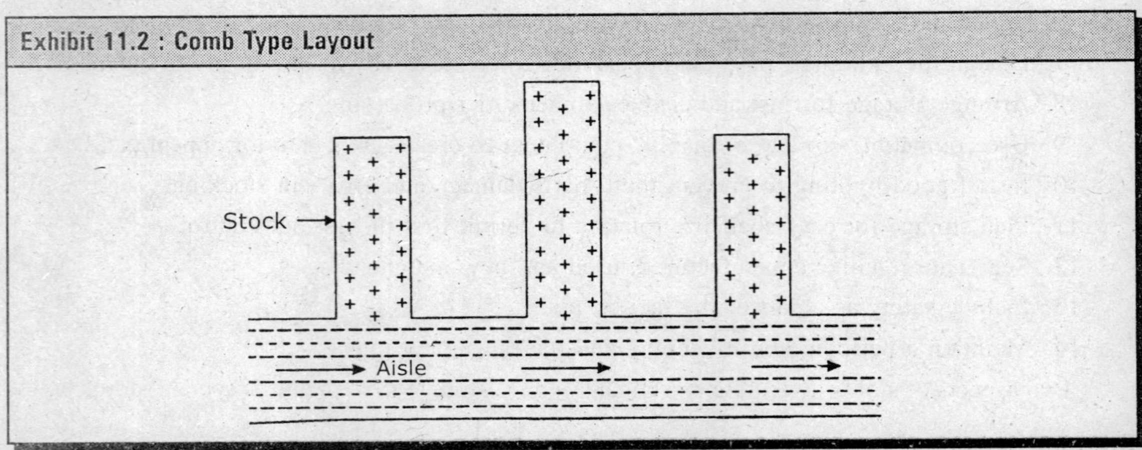

Exhibit 11.3 : Tree Type Layout

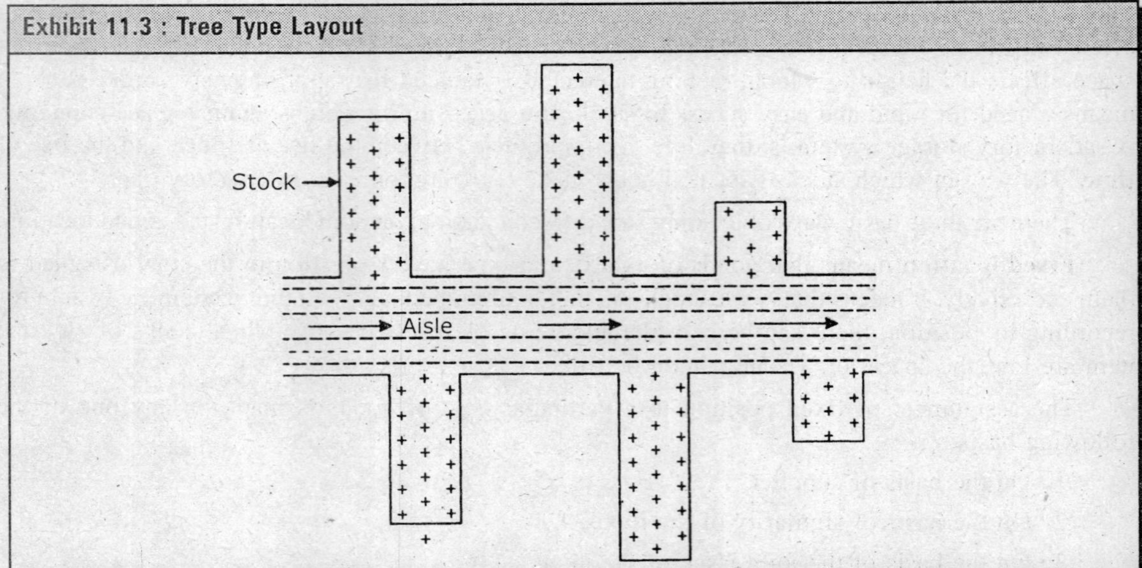

Stores Manual

Manual is a written statement of policies and procedures. A manual has several advantages such as spelling out responsibilities and authority of storekeeping, standardising storekeeping activities and stimulating new ideas and suggestions for improving and streamlining storage operations.

➢ MEASUREMENT OF STORES EFFICIENCY

Like any other department dealing with materials, stores needs evaluation of its performance. Stores is the **repository of inventory worth crores of rupees**. How well the materials and other items of stock are handled should be judged by measuring the performance of the storekeeper.

The storekeeper's performance can be measured objectively through quantitative techniques. It may be done through qualitative aspects also, though the measurement is subjective. A few quantitative techniques normally used are :

(a) Stores efficiency index = $\dfrac{\text{No. of requisitions delivered on time}}{\text{Total number of requisitions}}$

(b) Storage loss index = $\dfrac{\text{Value of inventory lost due to deterioration, obsolescences and pilferage}}{\text{Average value of inventory}}$

(c) Obsolescence index = $\dfrac{\text{Value of non - moving items}}{\text{Total inventory value}}$

(d) Space utilisation index = $\dfrac{\text{Area used for storage}}{\text{Total storage area available}}$

Subjective measurement is done through such factors as stock-out situation, reducing non-moving items, checking of records maintained, house-keeping, handling, and the like.

➢ STORES MANAGEMENT FUNCTIONS

The major functions involved in stores management are :

1. Receiving of materials
2. Storing of materials
3. Controlling of issue of materials
4. Stock verification and valuation

These functions are discussed briefly in the following section.

1. Receiving of Materials

Receiving of materials is the first major function in stores management. Even though receiving is a clerical operation, it is important because at this stage the physical materials supplied by the vendors are verified with purchase orders regarding both quantity ordered and quality specifications indicated in the purchase order. Most problems or errors in a purchasing transaction can be detected during receiving operation. If the problems such as quantity shortage, damaged materials, incorrect items shipped, and the like are not detected at the receiving stage, it would be costly to correct the mistake later.

The *receiving report* (often termed inspection cum receiving report) prepared upon receipt of a shipment details the materials actually received. It also contains information such as delivery timing, shipment damage, rejection percentage, split shipments and so on. This document forms the basis for invoice payment, for continued negotiation with supplier and also for closing the purchase order. Hence receiving operation at the receiving stage in the inwards goods or receiving stores should be efficiently supervised by sufficiently experienced and competent stores executives who are familiar with physical characteristics of materials and have ability to coordinate with inspectors and capable to make sound judgements in situations where a choice of alternatives must be made (*for example*, whether to return the defective item to the supplier, asking for replacement or whether to rework the item to salvage the same and charge the rework expenses to the supplier after obtaining the supplier's consent for the same).

Receiving Procedure : The steps involved in the receiving procedure are :

(i) **Unloading and checking the consignment received :** The containers or packages received are checked against the freight bill to ensure that the full containers or packages are received as per invoice.

(ii) **Unpacking and inspecting the material :** The receiving clerk or stores person checks the materials received against the supplier's packing slip and against a copy of the purchase order to verify the correctness of items received. Next, the quantity of the shipment is verified in the same manner. Finally the receiving stores person inspects the general condition of the materials to determine whether any external damage was incurred during shipment.

(iii) **Completing the receiving report :** The receiving stores person completes inspection or gets the items inspected by the inspector of inspection department. The inspection cum receiving report is prepared in which the quantity of items received, the quantity accepted after inspection, the defects observed in the items that are rejected etc., are recorded. The copies of inspection cum receiving report are sent to the indenting department, purchasing department, accounts department (*i.e.,* Bills payable section) and the inspection department if further technical inspection is required.

(iv) **Delivering the material to the holding stores :** For non-stock materials, the receiving department is usually responsible for delivering the item to the indenting department directly. For materials which have to be stored in centralised stores, the materials may be delivered to stores by an internal material handling service or the storekeepers may pick up their own materials from the receiving stores. The receiving stores person obtains the signature of the recipient on the copy of inspection cum receiving report or obtains a separate delivery receipt from the recipient (either the indenting department or the central or holding stores person).

It may be noted that, in firms practising JIT procurement, the materials are delivered by the suppliers directly to the point of use by-passing receiving.

2. Storing of Materials

(i) **Identification of Materials :** Stores operation involves the physical aspects of materials handling and storage. To facilitate this a proper system for effective identification of materials carried in stores should be developed. Although all standard purchased items can be identified by supplier's part numbers, different suppliers use different numbering systems and descriptions. Hence the purchasing firm should develop its own identification system for its materials using its own part numbers with cross-reference to supplier's part numbers for each purchased item.

(ii) **Identification Systems :** Firms use two types of material identification systems – *(a)* for external use and *(b)* for internal use. The system designed for external use facilitates sales transactions in international trade. The internal system is designed to communicate the identification and description of materials to all departments within the organisations – from engineering to production to purchasing and accounting department. Most firms follow their own internal system for identification of materials.

(iii) **Physical Identification :** Even though a satisfactory identification system is developed, physical identification of materials in store room may pose some problem. This is minimised by recording the storage location (bin or rack) of all items in the inventory record or catalog. The storage location is given a numerical designation, *for example,* bin number or rack number. Each inventory item is assigned a specific storage location and then locations are noted in the inventory catalog or a storage locator index so that any person can locate any material with ease. Each storage bin is labelled with the part number of the item stored in the bin. For materials such as forging, casting, steel plate, bars, rods, and the like, standard identification markings (colour coded strips using paints of different colours) are used.

(iv) **Stores Systems :** Two basic stores systems are : *(a)* a closed stores system and *(b)* an open store system. A **closed stores system** is one in which all materials are physically stored in a closed or controlled storage area or store room which can be locked to maintain physical control. This system affords maximum physical security and tight accounting control for costly inventory materials. The **open stores system** represents a storage system where no store room as such exists. Each material is stored as close to its point of use as possible. Materials are stored in bins, racks or shelves near the work station or assembly line by making use of available space. Storage facilities are completely open and accessible to any person (worker or planner or store keeper). The open system is designed to expedite production activities and places little emphasis on physical security of materials and suitable for firms practising JIT procurement.

(v) **Storing of Materials :** The benefits of good stores lay out and storage methods are: *(a)* ready accessibility, *(b)* efficient space utilisation, *(c)* flexibility of arrangement, *(d)* reduced need for materials handling equipment, *(e)* minimisation of deterioration and pilferage of materials, *(f)* ease of physical counting.

(vi) **Methods of Storing :** Where large quantities of materials are to be stocked, block stocking is most effective. **Block stocking** involves stocking of pallets or containers in rows such that each row contacts the adjacent row. For small quantities, row stocking is preferable. **Row stocking** involves stocking of materials in rows with sufficient spaces between rows. Row stocking is more flexible than block stocking, but require more aisle space.

A large number of items stored are best kept in storage **bins**, **shelves** or **racks**. The type of bin, shelf or rack selected is important in determining the most efficient use of the store room or storage area.

(vii) **Store room equipments:** The general types of equipment commonly used in storing materials are: *(a)* Pallets and skids, *(b)* Open and closed shelves, *(c)* Cabinets, *(d)* Bins, *(e)* Stacking boxes, *(f)* Special storage racks, *(g)* Gravity feed racks, *(h)* Out door platforms and racks.

(viii) Automated warehousing: Highly sophisticated automated storage and retrieval systems with computer control system are used in modern stores. The storage facility is a high-rise structure (10 to 20 metre high), constructed of open steel columns, configured into storage cubicles of different sizes and utilises various types of standardised pallets and containers for storage.

By linking the production planning computer system with the automated warehousing systems, required production materials are automatically located and mechanically picked from storage by a computer command initiated by a computerised production schedule in the production planning department.

3. Controlling of Issue of Materials

The materials issued out of stores can be : *(a)* issues to internal consuming departments and *(b)* issues to outside suppliers (subcontractors) for processing and conversion to finished parts or products. In either case, there is a need to have control over the issue of materials from the stores. The issues of materials are based on production programs which form the basis for preparation of bill of materials, work orders etc. The bill of materials indicate the quantity of each item to be issued for carrying out production activities against a work order for the product to be produced. Any material requirement over and above the quantity indicated in the work order amounts to excessive wastage. Stores persons are not authorised to issue materials beyond the work order quantities.

In addition, proper delegation of authority to stores officers limiting the value of materials which can be issued by certain level of stores officers provide adequate control over issue of materials from stores. The stores requisitions presented by the user department must be duly authorised by the competent stores officer before the materials are issued from stores.

4. Stock Verification and Valuation

Two aspects of stores accounting or materials accounting are : *(i)* Physical stock verification of materials stored and *(ii)* Valuation of materials stocked in stores. These two aspects are briefly discussed in the following section:

(i) Stock Verification

No matter how diligently a storekeeper performs the custodial job or how carefully a ledger clerk maintains records (computerised or manual) some discrepancy between the actual and book balances of inventory is bound to occur. The system is operated by people, and people do commit mistakes. For this reason, every inventory item should be physically counted and checked against its book balance at least once in a year. The books are subsequently adjusted to match the actual count. Most companies create an 'inventory discrepancy' or 'inventory short and over' account to absorb such discrepancies. This account is eventually closed by transferring the balance to manufacturing overhead account.

Stock verification can be conducted in one of the three ways :

1. Periodic verification or fixed annual inventory.
2. Perpetual or continuous inventory.
3. Low point inventory.

Under **low point inventory** method companies take physical inventory when the stock is the lowest, irrespective of the period. Stock taking is naturally irregular. The low point approach minimises the time required for actual inventory work because of the small quantities of materials involved. However, it has the disadvantage of producing an irregular inventory schedule which tends to peak the work load for stores personnel.

In the **continuous inventory** approach, at the beginning of each year some firms divide their inventory into 52 equal groups and assign one of them to be physically counted each week. Thus, the physical inventory operation goes on without interrupting production operation or upsetting store room activities. This approach has three advantages. It can be planned and worked into scheduled activities without a shutdown. It can be conducted in an orderly and relaxed manner; these conditions are also conducive to accurate work. Secondly, there is the possibility of detecting and eliminating causes for discrepancies without allowing them to continue throughout the year. Finally, this approach facilitates efficient utilisation of stores personnel. In many storerooms, withdrawals are heavy early in the day and are much lighter later on. Thus, when the issue clerk's busy work slacks off, he will have backlog of inventory work to do.

In some companies separate staff are appointed for the purpose of continuous stock taking. This approach involves extra cost and only very large companies can afford it.

In the **fixed or periodic inventory**, inventory is taken once a year, generally coinciding with the financial year. This necessitates shutting down the production operation and organising a special crew for the inventory job. This approach is ideal for seasonal businesses. It is troublesome because it is a major task which must be accomplished in a short time, interrupting production operation.

Classification and Codification

Good storekeeping requires proper classification and codification of various items stored in stock. Proper classification and codification offer several advantages such as the following :

1. Systematic grouping of similar items for correct identification of each and every item.
2. The usage of long descriptions is simplified and possible confusion avoided.
3. Avoids duplicate stocks of same item being held under different names, descriptions, brand names, part number and different stores.
4. Enables reduction in sizes and varieties.
5. Helps in standardisation of materials and helps in finding substitutes.
6. Can be used as a basis for setting up different stores.
7. To arrange bin cards and records in stores, accounts and inventory control sections in the same uniform manner.
8. Ensures accuracy in correspondence, records and posting of receipts and issues in appropriate records.

Principles of Classification and Codification

The following principles should be observed while establishing an effective classification and codification system :

1. There must be a **consistency** in the point of view so that the basis of classification should remain unchanged for all items.
2. The system of classification must cover the entire range of items for which it is devised and at the same time, allow reasonable scope for extension. This principle is that of **comprehensiveness**.
3. The third principle is that of **mutual exclusiveness** which means, that there must be only one code number possible for any item.
4. The system developed should be **simple** enough to be understood and **easily adopted** by non-specialist personnel. This also means that the codification basis when once understood, the code numbers should be self-explanatory to a certain possible extent.

Methods of Classification and Codification

Stores are generally classified on the basis of their nature or usage, the former being the most common method used. Based on nature, stores are classified into specific groups as shown below:

Raw materials	Components	Consumable stores
Spare parts	Tools	Packing materials
Work-in-process	Finished goods	Hardware
Motors	Gearbox	CKD - Completely knocked down items.

(ii) **Stock Valuation**

Valuation of materials stocked in stores as inventory and of materials issued for production is necessary because of two reasons They are :

(a) **Inventory valuation** of converting physical quantities of materials into monetary value (rupees) is necessary to judge the performance of materials management function in terms of **inventory turnover ratio** and to control inventory to satisfy the norms set for inventory by top management.

(b) **Materials costing** in terms of the valuation of the cost of materials consumed by the user departments in order to estimate the **cost of the products** produced which forms the basis for *pricing decisions.*

Costing the Receipt of Materials : The factors to be considered in the cost of the materials received are calculating : *(i)* materials price, *(ii)* freight charges, *(iii)* insurance, *(iv)* taxes, *(v)* customs duty if any, *(vi)* packing charges, *(vii)* discounts availed, if any, *(viii)* duty-draw backs against export orders etc.

Valuation of stocks has to be done on two occasions :

(i) While issuing the materials to the consuming departments to enable the costing of production and

(ii) When preparing periodic performance statements in terms of value of inventory on hand from time to time.

Methods of Valuation of Stocks

The process of valuation of the material in the industry varies from conservative practice of considering the **market price** *or* **cost of procurement** whichever is less, on hand to modern method such as **replacement cost** or **current value method.**

The choice of a method should be based on the nature of the material and the type of business.

Some of the methods of pricing (or valuation) of materials issued are as below :

(i) "First-in, First-out" method (FIFO).

(ii) "Last-in, First out" method (LIFO).

(iii) Average price method and weighted average method.

(iv) Actual price method.

(v) Replacement price or current value method or market value method.

(vi) Standard price or standard cost method.

(vii) Inflated price method.

For income tax purposes, only one of the following methods *i.e., FIFO* or *standard price* or *actual price* or *market value,* whichever is lower is accepted. However, for internal control purposes the organisations can choose any of the above methods mentioned.

These methods are discussed in detail in the following paragraphs.

1. First-In, First-Out (FIFO) Method

As the name suggests, this method assumes that the oldest stock is issued first *i.e.,* materials are issued in strict chronological order – *i.e.,* whatever is received first is consumed first. Hence, this method ensures that the materials are issued at **actual cost** and stocks are valued as per the latest price paid. The limitations are that the process becomes cumbersome when too many changes in price levels occur.

Table 11.1 illustrates an example of FIFO method.

Exhibit 11.4 : FIFO Method

Date	Receipt			Issue			Stock		
	Qty. (units)	*Rate (Rs.)*	*Value (Rs.)*	*Qty. (units)*	*Rate (Rs.)*	*Value (Rs.)*	*Qty. (units)*	*Rate (Rs.)*	*Value (Rs.)*
5th June									
6th May	200	2.0	400				200	2.0	400
10th June	300	2.4	720				200 300	2.0 2.4	1120
12th June				100	2.0	200	100 300	2.0 2.4	920
14th June				100 150	2.0 2.4	200 360	150	2.0	360

2. Last-in, First-out (LIFO) Method

This method assumes that the materials coming in last are issued first. The advantage of this method is that production is charged at the latest price, reflecting market conditions, if materials are received recently. Hence, pricing charging decisions can be taken realistically under the LIFO system, in a period of rising prices, latest prices are charged to the issues, thereby leading to lower reported profits and savings in taxes, when the price levels are fluctuating, LIFO tends to minimise unrealised gains or losses in inventory. But, LIFO system has the same limitations as that of FIFO system. *Table 11.2* illustrates LIFO method.

3. Average Price Method

In this method, the issues are valued on the basis of a simple average price. The prices of purchases prior to any issues are added and the average price is calculated by dividing the total value by the number of purchase prices used. The simple average price in the example illustrated in *Table 11.3* is Rs. 2.20 (*i.e.,* $\frac{2.0+2.4}{2} = 2.2$ Rs.). The issues as well as stocks are valued on the basis of Rs. 2.20 per unit. The calculations are shown in *Table 11.3.*

Table 11.2 : LIFO Method

Date	Receipt			Issue			Stock		
	Qty. (units)	Rate (Rs.)	Value (Rs.)	Qty. (units)	Rate (Rs.)	Value (Rs.)	Qty. (units)	Rate (Rs.)	Value (Rs.)
5th June	–								
6th May	200	2.0	400				200	2.0	400
10th June	300	2.4	720				200 300	2.0 2.4	1120
12th June				100	2.4	240	200 200	2.0 2.4	400 480 880
14th June				100 100 050	2.4 2.4 2.0	240 240 100 580	150	2.0	300

Table 11.3: Average Price Method

Date	Receipt			Issue			Stock		
	Qty. (units)	Rate (Rs.)	Value (Rs.)	Qty. (units)	Rate (Rs.)	Value (Rs.)	Qty. (units)	Rate (Rs.)	Value (Rs.)
5th June									
6th May	200	2.0	400				200	2.0	400
10th June	300	2.4	720				200 300	2.0 2.4	1120
12th June				100	2.2	220	400	2.2	880
14th June				100 150	2.2 2.2	220 330 550	150	2.2	330

This method is very simple to use and gives reasonably valid estimates. But this method is not accurate because the prices are not weighed by the quantities purchased and hence the average price calculated does not give a true picture of the facts unless the price changes are not much and the quantities purchased in each lot are the same.

3*(a)* Weighted Average Method

In this method the issues to the production department are split into equal batches from each shipment at stock. It is a realistic method as it reflects the price levels resulting in stabilisation of cost figures. The rate is calculated by dividing the total cost by the number of items and this rate is applied to issues in production. As more purchases are made, a new average rate is calculated and this new rate is applied to the subsequent issues.

Table 11.4 illustrates the weighted average method.

Table 11.4 : Weighted Average Cost Method

Date	Receipt			Issue			Stock		
	Qty. (units)	Rate (Rs.)	Value (Rs.)	Qty. (units)	Rate (Rs.)	Value (Rs.)	Qty. (units)	Rate (Rs.)	Value (Rs.)
5th June									
6th May	200	2.0	400						
10th June	300	2.4	720				500	*2.24	1120
12th June				100	*2.24	224	400	*2.24	896
14th June			-	250	*2.24	560	150	*2.24	336

$$\text{Average rate as on 10th June} = \frac{(200 \times 2.0) + (300 \times 2.4)}{500} = \frac{400 + 720}{500}$$

$$= \frac{1120}{500} = 2.24 \text{ Rs.}$$

4. Actual Price Method

In this method actual cost is charged for the materials to be issued from the store. This method is used where the purchases are made for the specific purposes such as spare parts, special dies, jigs and fixtures and other special equipments. Each material receipt is recorded in a separate stores ledger and the material issues are costed at the actual purchase cost. This method is used where few costly items or non-standard materials are purchased to meet production requirements against specific customer orders (in jobbing industries).

5. Replacement Price or Current Value Method or Market Value Method

In this method, the material issues are priced at the prevailing market price on the date of issue. The principle is that materials issued for production of any job on a particular date should be charged at the rate at which these materials could be replaced immediately from the new purchases on the same date. This method is used for materials of standard grades which are traded at commodity exchanges, such as cotton, cereals, certain metals for which the prices are quoted in newspapers and hence, it is easy to ascertain the current market price.

Advantages : (i) It considers the current market price for materials, which is more relevant for pricing the product made out of these materials. *(ii)* It enables comparison of operating efficiencies with those of competitors.

Disadvantages : (i) It is difficult for finding out actual market price at every issue from the stores. *(ii)* Since the costing of material issues are done at market prevailing at the time of issue, the stock on hand is continuously **under-estimated** when prices increase, because the costing according to receipts are done at actuals and issues at higher rates. On the other hand, when prices are falling, the stock on hand is **overestimated** resulting in writing-off huge amounts to make it realistic.

6. Standard Price or Standard Cost Method

In this method, a forecasted unit price for a specific period of six months or one year or more is used to evaluate the issues. The forecasted price (standard price) is computed after considering the market conditions, usage rates, storage conditions, current market price, trend of the price etc., so that a fairly correct average standard price may be determined. After the stipulated period for which a standard price is fixed is again reviewed. The material receipts are recorded at the actual price while the material issues are costed at the pre-determined standard price. In this method, the efficient use of materials is truly reflected because the accounting is divorced from fluctuation in rates. The limitation is that stock is under estimated in the context of rising prices and overestimated at the time of falling prices.

7. Inflated Price Method

In this method, the cost of material charged is slightly inflated (raised) by a small percentage of the actual purchased price. This is because there may be certain types of material wastages incidental to material usage (*i.e.,* loss, breakage, evaporation etc.,) and the resulting loss should be uniformly spread on the residual units (remaining stocks). *For example,* if 100 units were purchased at Rs. 25 per unit, and if the material is subjected to 10 per cent normal wastages then the total cost (Rs. 2500) will be spread over to 90 units (good units) and the issue of materials will be charged at an inflated price of Rs. 2500 ÷ 90 units *i.e.,* Rs. 27.77 instead of Rs. 25.

➤ STANDARDISATION AND SIMPLIFICATION IN STORES MANAGEMENT

Classification and codification of various items stored reveal that a large variety of items similar in nature would have been stored. A large variety of materials stored increases the inventory costs. Hence there arises a need for **rationalisation** through standardisation, variety reduction and simplification. These three concepts are discussed briefly in the following section:

Standardisation : Standardisation is defined as the process of formulating and applying rules for an orderly approach to a specific activity, for the benefit and with the cooperation of all concerned and in particular for the promotion of the overall economy, taking due account of functional performance and safety requirements (according to International Standards Organisation).

The Indian Standards Institution (ISI), now referred to as Bureau of Indian Standards, is the national body which deals with the standardisation at the national level in India. Four levels of standards used are **international standards, national standards, industrial standards** and **company standards**. One area of standardisation is standardisation of products through the use of standard specifications which limits the sizes and types of products to the minimum. The Bureau of Indian Standards has laid down specifications for a wide range of materials and products.

Advantages of Standardisation

(i) Purchasing standard products (*i.e.,* products of standard specification meeting national or international standards) saves considerable time and money because such items are readily available at lower costs (due to economies of scale for manufacture) and with better quality than products which are made against customer orders (manufactured as per company standards).

(ii) Use of standard products of standard sizes facilitate interchangeability. *For example,* bolts and nuts, screws, bearings, and the like.

(iii) Standardisation reduces variety of products and thereby improves quality and reduces costs.

(iv) Procurement costs will reduce due to bulk purchasing.

(v) Inventory carrying cost can be reduced due to variety reduction.

(vi) Storage space can be saved.

(vii) Chances of obsolescence can be reduced.

How Standardisation in Purchasing Reduces Costs?

The use of standard parts in the product design enables purchase of fewer items, in larger quantities, and at lower prices. Fewer items are processed and stocked. This reduces costs of purchasing, receiving, inspection, storing and payment of bills. Stocking fewer items makes controlling inventories easier and less costly. The use of standard items reduces the number of defects in incoming materials because the supplier adheres to standard specifications while manufacturing. The purchase of standardised materials and component parts saves money because of lower prices, lower processing costs, lower inventory carrying costs and fewer quality problems.

Simplification : Simplification is a corollary of standardisation. Simplification means reducing the number of standard items a firm has in its product design and carries in its inventory. Simplification is not synonymous with standardisation. Standardisation is creative but simplification is selective and deliberate variety reduction. For instance, by reducing the variety of standardised products, the number of parts held in inventory can be reduced further. But simplification aims at deliberate reduction of variety of items used in the product, taking care at the design stage itself and thereby bringing economy in manufacture. Simplification is beneficial to manufacturers, suppliers and consumers.

➢ REVIEW QUESTIONS

1. What is store keeping? How does it differ from warehousing?
2. List the various types of materials stored in a manufacturing firm.
3. State the importance of store keeping.
4. State the objectives of stores management.
5. List the functions of storekeeping.
6. Mention the problems that arise due to inefficient storekeeping.
7. Explain what is meant by planning for storekeeping.
8. What is meant by "location of stores"? Discuss the basic factors that must be taken into account to determine the best location for stores.
9. Discuss the advantages and disadvantages of centralised and decentralised storing.
10. What is meant by stores organisation?
11. Explain how stores are organised, using a typical stores organisation chart.
12. Discuss the various types of stores under the category
    (i) Functional stores and *(ii)* Physical stores
13. What is meant by layout of stores? Discuss the factors to be considered while planning layout of stores.
14. Discuss the various types of stores layout.
15. State how stores efficiency is measured.
16. Discuss briefly the various major functions involved in stores management.

17. How is stock verification conducted?
18. What do you mean by classification and codification. What are their benefits?
19. Why is stock evaluation necessary?
20. Describe the various methods of valuation of stocks.
21. Discuss the role of standardisation and simplification in stores management.
22. How standardisation in purchasing reduces costs?

STANDARDISATION AND CODIFICATION

For a balanced growth and efficient functioning of an enterprise, it is necessary to control the material cost, material supply and material utilisation in such a manner that these efforts lead to: *(i)* maximisation of production, *(ii)* reduction in the cost of production and distribution and *(iii)* maximisation of profits. Efficient purchasing and inventory management strategies lead to reduction of material costs and inventory costs. But in order to facilitate this, efficiency in receiving and storing of materials is also important as flow control activities. Ware-housing is a package of services which not only includes efficient storage of materials, but also enables the smooth flow of materials through the conversion processes without causing stoppage of production due to shortage of materials.

To contribute effectively to the profit centre concept, the materials management constantly strive to identify the areas where high costs are incurred and to reduce the costs to the maximum possible extent. The starting point of any cost reduction programme is to identify the individual material associated with the unique problem. To facilitate a systematic identification of materials in storage, store keeping requires proper ***classification*** and ***codification*** of materials stored. This is followed by further attempts at cost reduction namely ***standardisation***, ***simplification*** and ***variety reduction***.

➤ CLASSIFICATION AND CODIFICATION

The materials procured by a firm must be classified and coded (or identified with name, part number or colour codes) before the materials are inspected, accounted in stores ledgers and binned. Hence, materials are broadly classified according to their nature, use and service before the job of codification is taken up.

Codification is the system adopted for accurate identification of materials by allotting a **numerical number** (referred to as **part number**) for each item procured and stored. It is the process of representing each item by a part number, the digits of which indicate the classification, the group, the sub-group, the type and the dimension, or size or specification of the item coded.

Advantages of Classification and Codification

Proper classification and codification offer several advantages such as the following:

(i) Systematic grouping of similar items for correct identification (name and part number) of each and every item.

(ii) The usage of long descriptions is simplified and possible confusion is avoided.

(iii) Avoids duplicate stocks of same item being stored under different names, descriptions, brand names, part number and different storage locations and stores

(iv) Enables reduction in sizes (standardisation) and varieties (simplification and variety reduction).

(v) Helps in standardisation of materials (preferred sizes and specifications of materials) and helps in finding substitutes.

(vi) Can be used as a basis for setting up of different stores suitable for storing different types or categories of materials.

(vii) To arrange bin cards and records in stores, accounts and inventory control departments in the same uniform manner.

(viii) Ensures accuracy in correspondence, records and postings of receipts and issues in appropriate records.

Principles of Classification and Codification

The following principles should be observed while establishing an effective classification and codification system.

(i) There must be ***consistency*** in the point of view so that the basis of classification should remain unchanged for all items

(ii) The system of classification must cover the entire range of items for which it is devised and at the same time, allow reasonable scope for extension. This is known as principle of ***comprehensiveness***.

(iii) The third principle is that of ***mutual exclusiveness*** which means that there must be only one code number possible for any item.

(iv) The system developed should be ***simple*** enough to be understood and ***easily adopted*** by nonspecialist personnel. This also means that the codification basis when once understood, the code numbers should be self-explanatory to a certain possible extent.

Nature and process of codification: Since a large number of different types of materials are stored and used by the manufacturing firms or large super retail stores, the common practice of identifying the items by their mere descriptions may lead to lot of confusion. This is because the description may be sometimes vague and may be confusing or may be too long and may vary for the same item. *For example,* a "dust bin" may also be described as "waste paper basket", "scrap container", "refuse container", "rubbish box", "dust container" and the like. These different names or descriptions for the same item may result in confusion and tend to duplicate ordering and result in overstocking.

On-the-other hand, accurate identification of an article some times necessitates lengthy descriptions to distinguish one article from the other belonging to the same category. *For example,* a simple description of a chair by the name "chair" may not be accurate and enough to represent any type of chair such as wooden chair, plastic chair, or steel chair, chair with arms, chair without arms, chair with caned back rest, revolving chair, chair with foam cushion or without cushion and the like. Hence a lengthy disruption may be required to correctly specify the type of chair to be purchased, stored and accounted in the stores.

The **process of codification** involves representing each item by a number, the digits of which indicate the group, the subgroup, the type, dimension and specification of the item. Many organisations have evolved their own system of codification using six, eight, ten or twelve digit numbers or with a combination of alphabetic letters and numerals. In a numerical codification, the first two digits normally represent the major category or group to which the item belongs (such as raw material, spare part, hardware item, chemical, packing material, tool, stationary, electronic component, fastenings etc.) The next two digits indicate the sub-groups (such as ferrous or non-ferrous in case of industrial metals used as raw material). Dimensional characteristics such as length, breadth, thickness, diameter etc. may be represented by the next three digits and the remaining digits may indicate minor variations.

Methods of Classification and Codification

Stores (materials) are generally classified based on their nature or usage, the former being the most common basis. Based on nature, materials are classified into specific groups as below:

(i) Raw materials, *(ii)* Components, *(iii)* Consumables, *(iv)* Spare parts *(v)* Supplies, *(vi)* Tools, *(vii)* Packing materials, *(viii)* Work-in-progress items *(ix)* Finished goods, *(x)* Completely knocked down items (CKD), *(xi)* Hard ware items, *(xii)* Fasteners, *(xiii)* Subcontracted items, *(xiv)* Wires and cables, *(xv)* Paints and Chemicals and so on.

Systems of Codification: The common codification systems in use are:

(i) Alphabetic system, *(ii)* Simple numeric system, *(iii)* Alpha-Numeric System or Combination System, *(iv)* Block System, *(v)* Decimal system, *(vi)* Numeric System, *(vii)* Mnemonic System.

These systems are briefly discussed in the following paragraphs:

(i) **Alphabetic System:** In this system, alphabetic letters are used to represent a particular classification. The English alphabet has 26 letters. Hence there can be 26 different classifications each preceded by an alphabet (A to Z).

(ii) **Simple Numeric System:** In this, numbers are assigned for classification instead of alphabets. The disadvantage of this system is that considerable time is wasted in searching for code numbers in the material code books since there are no memory *adds* incorporated in this system.

(iii) **Alpha-Numeric system or Combination system:** In this system, alphabetic letters and numbers are combined to have certain advantages of the alphabetic and simple Numeric Systems.

(iv) **Block System:** In this, blocks of numbers are reserved for specified classifications such as a specific block of numbers (say 1000 to 1100 for raw materials, 2000 to 2100 for components etc.) are used to represent certain category of items. The advantage of this system is that new block of numbers can be assigned to new category of items to be classified as and when required.

(*v*) **Decimal System:** In this system, numbers are assigned in such a way that each digit represents a sub-group or sub-account of the previous digit. The advantage of this system is its flexibility to accommodate a new item.

(*vi*) **Numeric System:** In this system a 6 digit, or 8 or 10 or 12 digit number is used to represent the item. The first few digits indicate specific classes or groups with subsequent digits used to indicate further sub-classifications or sub-groups in the specific classification or group.

(*vii*) **Mnemonic System:** It is an alphabetic system in which the alphabets which are easy to be memorised are used for classification.

Objectives of Codification

(*i*) To bring all similar items together under one classification or group.

(*ii*) To enable accommodation of any new item in the proper classification or group in thefuture.

(*iii*) To classify an item according to its nature or characteristics.

(*iv*) To give a unique code number to each item to avoid duplication and confusion.

(*v*) To expose excessive varieties being used so as to promote standardisation and variety reduction.

(*vi*) To establish a common language to identify an item.

(*vii*) To fix essential parameters to specify an item.

(*viii*) To specify an item as per national and international standards.

(*ix*) To facilitate computerisation of material data which is helpful in inventory analysis and accounting.

Major Steps Involved in Codification System

Codification is based on a simple system having the following steps:

Step 1: The large number of items of different varieties comprising the inventory needs to be classified under major groups known as *"Generic groups"*. The basis for classification of raw materials may be either *composition of materials* e.g., ferrous metal, non-ferrous metal, rubber, plastics, lubricants, chemicals, textiles etc. or *based on usage wise e.g.,* electrical, mechanical, electronic, chemical etc.

Step 2: Items under each generic group should be further divided into distinct subgroups according to the type of the material. *For example,* under the generic group non-ferrous metals, the specific group may be aluminium which will cover all alloys of aluminium.

Step 3: In this step, all the items in the subgroup are further listed in alphabetical order and then according to the size. Each item thus listed should be allotted consecutive numerals as codes. While allotting numbers, some serial numbers should be left vacant so that the same can be used for allotment to new items added to the inventory in the future as and when needed.

Some Important Codification Systems

The coding structure for materials should be designed taking into account the estimated number of items, their end uses and their type. In addition, the specific requirements listed below should be considered while designing the structure:

(*a*) The coding should be governed by logical, simple and easy rules.

(*b*) The code allocated to an item must be unique and with no likelihood of its being duplicated for another item.

(c) Similar items should be grouped together, say all types of resistors or all sizes of bolts or nuts, so that it should be possible to retrieve a group of items as a whole.

(d) The code should facilitate identifying major categories of items such as raw materials, chemicals, spare parts, fasteners, electronic components, packing materials, tools, office supplies, consumables etc.

(e) Codes should also identify machinery, equipments, accessories and maintenance spares.

(f) The retrieval of the code of an item should be simple and easy.

(g) The code should have the flexibility for the accommodation of new items that may be introduced from time to time.

A nine-digit coding structure is shown below:

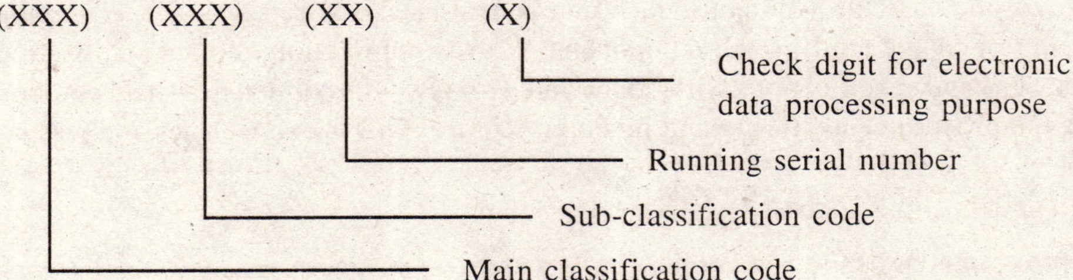

Two Codification Systems are discussed in the following section:

1. The Kodak System and 2. The Brisch System.

These two systems described below give an indication to the procedure used in codification.

1. The Kodak System: This system was developed in the US- by Eastern Kodak Company of New York. It consists of 10 digits numeric code with 100 basic classifications and each class is further subdivided into 10 subclasses. The classification is based on procurement considerations. *For example,* a bolt is listed as a hardware item if it is listed in hardware catalogues and available as hardware supplies. However, if this bolt is available as a sparepart of a machine, it will be listed under maintenance category.

2. The Brisch System: This system was introduced by a consulting British engineer by name Brisch in UK. It consists of seven digits applied in three phases. The first two digits represent a broad classification of all materials as primary materials, subassemblies, assemblies, components, plant and machinery, tools etc. Each of these classes are then broken into subclasses represented by the third digit. The fourth and fifth digit represent the type of the item and the last two digits denote the size of the item. *For example*, a hand punch is coded as 10 3 05 15 in which, the number 10 denotes the category as hand tool, the number 3 denotes "punch", the number 05 represents "shank type" and the last two digits - '15' denotes the dimension of the punch. One more digit (8th digit) may be introduced as a cheek digit which is computed for use in electronic data processing.

➤ STANDARDISATION

Standardisation is the process of establishing basic specifications for a set of commonly used characteristics of size, shape and performance for products. *For example,* light bulbs and bulb holders are standardised which means any electric light bulb can be fixed in any electric bulb holder whatever is the brand of the bulb and whoever is the manufacturer of the holder.

Simplification is a closely related concept or process which refers to the reduction in the number of different sizes and shapes of items produced or stocked.

Standardisation including simplification is an important economic concept in product design. The use of standard components and materials is more economical than the use of non-standard items. Standardisation may occur in the product line itself, in the product design as well as in the choice of components and materials used in the production processes.

The standardisation and simplification can reduce the total costs to the firm of its products over the life cycle. In ***simplification*** a product is designed to have as few parts and components as are necessary to perform its intended function. Because there are few parts to fail, one of the indirect benefit of simplification may be to increase the reliability of the product. In ***standardisation***, less variety is used in more than one type of product. The use of common components in a variety of end products will increase the volume of each component used and can result in ***economies of scale*** in purchasing or manufacturing the component. With simplification and standardisation the number of part designs and specifications will reduce and with few types of materials and components to be purchased, the procurement, storing and inventory control will become easier and less costly.

➤ TWO AREAS OF STANDARDISATION

The concept of standardisation is applied in two areas of business practice – *(i)* ***Industrial standardisation*** concerned with the standardisation of physical things *viz.*, raw materials, components, parts, tools and the like – their size, shape, colour, physical properties, chemical properties, performance characteristics and so on and *(ii)* ***Managerial standardisation*** concerned with the managerial aspects of business activity – standardising things like operating practices, methods, procedures, processes and systems.

This study on inventory management deals with industrial standardisation which deals with reducing the variety of materials and component parts held in inventory and thereby help reduce costs.

Industrial standardisation is defined as "the process of establishing agreement on uniform identifications for definite characteristics of quality, design, performance, quantity, service and the like." A uniform identification that is agreed on is referred to as ***"Standard"***.

Broad Implications of Standardisation

In manufacturing organisations, there can be three basic systems of production – *(i)* **job-shop production**, *(ii)* **batch/mass production** and *(iii)* **process production**. These systems themselves can represent degrees of industrial progress and each system can have its own applications and benefits. Right from the days of industrial revolution, the production systems were heavily influenced by standardisation. Eli Whitney, one of the pioneers of industrial revolution, discovered that by standardising parts, the skills of labour can be transferred to machines that could be operated by less skilled labour; which in turn would reduce the labour cost. He also applied standardisation to improve **inter-changeability of parts** in mass production. While Eli Whitney introduced standardisation in the US, Henry Ford made it universal. However, Ford visualised mass production to mean a standard product produced in an assembly line. This misinterpretation of the relationship of standardisation to mass production was reflected in Ford's statement **"The customer can have any colour car he wants as long as it is black"**. But mass production is the production of many diverse products, assembled from standardised parts which themselves have been mass produced.

How standardisation reduces costs? The use of standards enables a firm to purchase fewer items, in large quantities and at lower prices. Thus fewer items are processed and stocked. This reduces purchasing, receiving, inspection and payment costs. Inventory control becomes easier and less costly because of stocking of fewer items.

The use of standardised approved items greatly reduces the defectives in the materials purchased. Thus, purchase of standardised materials will result in ***lower prices, lower processing costs, lower inventory carrying costs and fewer quality problems*** – all of which will save money (due to cost reduction) for the firm. In the US, billions of dollars are saved by firms through standardisation. *For example*, a survey of American National Standards Institute (ANSI) lists the following:

(i) A manufacturer of business machines spends about $ 90,000 a year on standardisation. The firm estimates annual savings at $ 500,000.

(ii) A manufacturer of electronic equipments spends $ 24,000 annually on standards to save $ 1,25,000.

(iii) An engineering firm saves $ 25,000 per year, mostly on engineering and drafting time through standards at a cost of $ 2000 per year.

In Japan, an engineer of Nissan Motor Company has reduced the variety of 6000 fasteners by 50 percent resulting in enormous savings through saving of time in the assembly line (a saving of 50 seconds per car and one second equals one yen). Using standard parts in a product or throughout many products saves design time, tooling costs and production problems (say quality problems). Standardisation facilitates the ***interchangeability*** of parts among products, which will result in higher – volume production and purchasing, lower investments in inventory, easier purchasing and materials handling, fewer quality inspection and fewer problems in production. Some popular standardised products are light bulbs, dry cells, VCR tapes etc. But standardisation reduces competitive advantage as all brands of the same product are equally good without any differentiation. Then the question is "**how to gain the cost benefits of standardisation without losing the market advantage of variety and uniqueness**". One solution to this problem is **modulerisation**. Modular design consists of combining the modules (*i.e.*, standardised building blocks) in a variety of ways to create unique finished products. This approach is common in the automobile industry and electronics industry.

Component Standardisation: Not only end products are standardised, but component parts and raw materials that go into the products also need standardisation. In designing end products, standard components should be used whenever possible. Standardisation throughout the system reduces the kinds, types and sizes of raw materials, and component parts which have to be purchased. Thus, larger quantities of the required sizes or types can be purchased at lower prices – standardisation also reduces manufacturing costs by allowing larger production batches (longer production runs) on the smaller number of products and component parts. Set up costs and change-over costs are reduced and special purpose machinery can be utilised. It also results in requirement of fewer blueprints, processing instructions, tools etc.

Objectives of Standardisation

(i) To achieve maximum overall economy in terms of cost, human effort and materials.

(ii) To ensure maximum convenience in use. This approach leads to simplification, rationalisation and interchangeability of parts

(iii) To ensure uniformity and reduction in variety

(iv) To help in quality assurance by improving quality in every activity

(v) To achieve simplification and variety reduction by focusing on standardisation of materials specifications.

Levels of standards: A *standard* is the description of an acceptable level of quantity, design and composition of a particular item, that evolves as a result of study and experience by organisations. There are five levels of standards determined by the group of interests creating and using the standard in its day-to-day operations.

These five levels of standards are:

(i) **Individual standard:** An individual standard is laid down by an individual user, manufacturer or a department to suit the specific needs such as specification for a design or for a purchased item.

(ii) **Company standard:** It is a standard (*i.e.,* an in-plant standard) prepared by common agreement between various departments of a company for guiding its operations *viz.*, design, purchase, production, quality assurance, testing etc.

(iii) **Industry Standard:** It is a standard prepared by an organised group of related interests in a given industry (say automobile industry, steel industry, machine-tool industry, electronic industry etc.) or within a given trade or profession (association level).

(iv) **National Standard:** It is a standard established after consulting all interested organisations within a nation. The national standards are established by a government department (Bureau of Indian Standards) or a non-government body.

(v) **International Standard:** It is an international recommendation for standardisation resulting from agreement between independent sovereign nations having common interests.

Advantages and Disadvantages of Standardisation:

Standardisation has a number of benefits as well as certain disadvantages. The advantages are:

(i) Fewer parts to deal with inventory and in manufacturing

(ii) Simpler and more routine purchasing, handling and inspection procedures

(iii) Facilitates longer production runs (mass production) and automation

(iv) Helps in better understanding of customer requirements

(v) Examines all aspects of quality

(vi) Cost of producing a standard item is always lesser than that of producing a non-standard item

(vii) Reduces the work-load of design and drafting staff as fewer drawings and fewer designs are required

(viii) Procurement of standard items takes lesser time as there are many suppliers who can supply off-the-shelf.

The disadvantages are:

(i) Decreased variety of end products results in less consumer appeal and thereby affecting the competitive advantage for the firm.

(ii) Designs may be frozen with too many imperfections remaining

(iii) Design changes involve high costs which will increase resistance to improvements in design.

(iv) Standard products may not always exactly suit the customer needs who may reluctantly accept the same without any alternative. This may create a risk that a competitor will introduce a better product or a greater variety and gain a competitive advantage.

Preferred Number System: When the end products are standardised, a system of preferred numbers is often used to determine sizes. Products such as light bulbs, electrical switches, electrical motors, oil sold in tins, packaged food, shoes, hosiery, readymade garments, electrical cables, fasteners etc., are examples of products for which sizes and weights and other specifications are selected based on a preferred number system. These products can be made in a continuous series of sizes from very small to very large size. Since this would be impractical from both a production and sales point of view, manufacturers of such products must focus on certain particular sizes in order to permit economic manufacture and sales. The size chosen usually follow a **geometric progression** from small size to large size with each size in the series being proportionally, rather than absolutely, larger than the preceding size. To determine proper proportion to use, the product designer must specify the largest and the smallest size and the number of sizes in between. Then the proportionality factor is calculated as $\text{P.F.} = \sqrt[n-1]{\frac{\text{Largest size}}{\text{Smallest size}}}$ where 'n' is the total number of sizes to be made. *For example,* if the computed ratio is 1.5 it means that each size is 50 percent larger than the previous smaller size.

Some of the examples of products with their preferred sizes are given in table below :

Table 12.1

Item	Size	Increase in %age
Electric bulb	10 W	
	15 W	+ 50%
	25 W	+ 66.6%
	40 W	+ 60%
	60 W	+ 50%
	100 W	+ 66.6%
Oil Tins	1 kg	–
	2 kgs	+ 100%
	5 kgs	+ 150%
	10 kgs	+ 100%
Electrical switches	5 Amperes	–
	10 Amperes	+ 100%
	15 Amperes	+ 50%
	23 Amperes	+ 43.5%
	33 Amperes	+ 91%

➤ ORGANISING STANDARDISATION PROGRAM

Organisations have a standardisation program, which is carried out by a standards department or by a standardisation committee which comprises of representative of various departments *viz.*, Production, Research and Development, Marketing, Purchase and Stores, Maintenance etc. The materials management division which comprises purchasing and stores departments plays an important role in the standardisation program.

The objectives of the standardisation program are:

(i) To standardise the materials used in the firm (company standards).

(ii) To bring the company standards in line with the industry standards.

(iii) To reduce the varities of raw materials and components used.

(iv) To establish the specifications of materials to be purchased.

In large firms, a standards department headed by a manager who directly reports to the unit head may be made responsible for an effective standardisation and simplification program. While the particular organisational arrangement may vary among firms, it is important that a continual effort to implement standardisation and simplification be made instead of having such programs on a **crash basis** only. A consistent, continual standardisation program requires cooperation among a number of organisational entities. The sales department must regularly analyse the sales volume of products and periodically drop products that fail to generate sufficient sales. Inventory control should furnish engineering design department with information on slow moving materials and components which may be examined for elimination. Finally the responsibility lies with engineering design. It uses the information from other sources, but it is here that standardisation must be implemented. As each new product is designed, a continual effort to use standardised parts must be maintained. Also, a continual review of existing designs must be made not only to ensure that sizes and models do not increase but also to ensure that existing products are continually improved.

Types of Standards

The various types of standards are :

(i) ***Product standards*** refer to established ingredients, physical characteristics, quality and performance of a particular product. They include a set of technical description for the information of the buyers. Standard products ensure uniform quality and performance to the customers.

(ii) ***Engineering standards*** are concerned with the parts and components that constitute a product. A manufacturing firm producing a range of similar products may standardise the products to reduce the varieties of products.

(iii) ***Material standards*** refer to materials of preferred sizes and specifications (quality and other physical aspects) recommended for use by the firm's standards department.

(iv) ***Quality standards*** refer to the procedures to be adhered to ensuring quality of operations, processes and outputs.

(v) ***Process standards*** refer to methods of carrying out an operation or process or a procedure to ensure efficient and economic processes.

(vi) ***Equipment standards*** refer to types of equipments used for manufacturing, materials handling, packaging etc.

(vii) ***Safety standards*** refer to rules and regulations to be adhered to ensure safety of workers and machines at the workplace.

(viii) ***Administrative standards*** refer to methods and procedures to be followed to ensure efficient and effective working.

➤ SIMPLIFICATION

Simplification of product design refers to the elimination of the complex features and undesirable or marginal features of a product to eliminate waste and to achieve economy. Simplification results in product designs which achieve intended function of products with reduced costs, higher quality and better customer satisfaction.

Simplification is defined as the elimination of superfluous varieties, sizes, dimensions, features etc., making the design, assembly or product simpler, less complex and less difficult to use. Usually simplification precedes standardisation. It is deliberate reduction of variety of product design about which the sales department may not be happy.

Advantages of Simplification

(i) Reduces inventories and results in higher inventory turnover.

(ii) By simplification of operations, the efficiency of the production process increases and this leads to higher productivity.

(iii) Customer satisfaction may be increased by making a product easier to recognise, buy, install, maintain or use.

(iv) Reduced product cost per unit through easier assembly, eliminated operations, less expensive substitute materials and reduced scrap (wastage of material).

(v) Simpler production planning and control due to reduced number of parts and simplified manufacturing operations.

(vi) Faster delivery of products to customer due to shorter production cycle time.

Standardisation Versus Simplification

These two terms are often used interchangeably even though they are different. Simplification refers to deliberate reduction of varieties of products in a product line and the number of parts used to make up a product. Standardisation incidentally results in reduction of varieties of products, components or materials. Simplification also aims at elimination of unnecessary varieties, sizes and grades of products, whereas standardisation aims at optimum number of sizes (known as preferred sizes), varieties or grades of products. Standardisation is *technical* in nature where as simplification is *commercial* in nature.

➤ SPECIFICATION

A specification is a detailed description of a material, component part or a product, including physical measures such as dimensions, volume, weight, surface finish etc. These specifications also indicate ***tolerances*** on physical measures which provide production department with precise information about the characteristics of products to be produced and the process and production equipments to be used to achieve the specified tolerances (*i.e.*, acceptable variations). Specifications are made up of detailed description or listing of the characteristics of a particular item. Compiling specifications is a time consuming activity and may be quite costly. Nevertheless, buying based on specifications is common because a majority of business purchases required its use.

The various kinds of specifications are:

(i) Dimensional and material specifications and *(ii)* Performance specifications.

Dimensions and material specifications may involve a listing of the physical or chemical properties desired in a product or an item. The dimensional specifications express the desired properties in measurable terms. *For example,* metallic raw materials, oil, paint etc., are typical items for which this type of specification is used.

Another form of specification is the precise prescription of both material and its method of manufacture (mostly used in defence purchases)

Performance specifications may detail the performance or use of the bought-out item. The buyer indicates the use or application that the product will have and tests the product for appropriate performance. The vendor, while accepting the performance specifications, assumes the responsibility for supplying a satisfactory product. Performance specifications are the simplest specifications to formulate and are especially suitable when the purchaser has little technical knowledge.

Use of design drawings or blue prints: Use of engineering drawings or blue prints or specifications sheet (dimension sheet) is a corollary of many specifications. The blue print usually accompanies some descriptive text in the purchase order. It is the most precise and most accurate form of description of the product or item and is applicable where close tolerances or a high degree of mechanical perfection is required. *For example*, for items that call for high degree of accuracy, such as castings, forgings, machine parts etc., the blue print is the most feasible method of description and specification. Blue prints also facilitate accurate check with specifications by the inspection department when the material or the item is received at the buyer's premises.

Specifications should be revised as conditions change. In cases of long-term purchase contracts, there should be a clause regarding the supplier's compliance for any modifications in the specifications as and when necessary (demanded by the buyer/user).

Advantages and Disadvantages of Specifications

Advantages of buying based on specifications are as follows:

(i) The specifications are drawn after careful thought and review of the buyer's needs. This often results in simplification of the variety of products purchased and often reveals the possibility of using less costly items.

(ii) Buying according to specifications frequently induces more suppliers to bid or quote because all suppliers have identical terms. This increased competition will result in lower prices and hence beneficial to the buyer.

(iii) Specifications ensure uniformity in the nature of items bought from several sources.

(iv) Purchasing according to specifications provides an exact standard against which the incoming materials/items can be checked. This results in accurate inspection and a uniform quality of materials.

(v) Buying to specifications in a necessary step toward industry-wide standardisation with associated economies.

Disadvantages of Specification Buying are as follows:

(i) Preparing specifications for small lot purchases may be expensive

(ii) Specification buying increases the responsibilities of the buyer. The supplier is having the obligation of only complying with the specifications. If the product doesnot perform satisfactorily, the responsibility rests with the buyer.

(iii) Specifications may be too rigid and hence more costly than necessary

(iv) Once specifications are established, it is difficult to revise them. Specifications should be periodically reviewed to avoid the chance of overlooking product improvements.

(v) In case of some complex products which require unique skill of the manufacturer, the specifications are inappropriate.

➤ KINDS AND SOURCES OF INDUSTRIAL STANDARDS

In industry, there are three basic kinds of material standards:

(i) International standards

(ii) Industry or national standards and

(iii) Company standards.

If a designer or user can not adopt a national or international standard, for his/her purpose, then the alternative is to use a company standard. **Where one can get standard specifications?**

Specifications for items that have been standardised can be obtained from national or international standards organisations. *For example*, the Indian Standards Institution, now known as Bureau of Indian Standards has the main objective of preparing and promoting the general adoption of standards on national and international basis (over 15,000 Indian Standards have been issued so far). Standards for over 1000 new items are being issued every year by the Bureau of Indian Standards. All these standards are the result of agreement reached in their technical contents between the producers, consumers, technical experts, testing authorities and others concerned with the effort of standardisation.

International Standards facilitate increased international trade and prosperity. The ISO 9000 series of quality standards are used voluntarily world wide. All the industrially advanced countries have their own national standards but they strive to meet the international standards or specifications issued by International Standards Organisation (ISO) head quartered at Geneva, Switzerland. For any country to export its goods it is mandatory that their goods meet the specifications as per international standards established by ISO. Countries around the world currently have widely different standards for virtually everything from safety to ecology. Therefore there is a need for the nations to conform to common standards which are agreed upon by majority of the industrialised and advanced countries. Hence the development of international standards has become very vital for the development of international trade and commerce.

➤ VARIETY REDUCTION

The process of standardisation logically leads to simplification and variety reduction. While **standardisation** refers to the design activity that reduces variety among a group of parts or products (by producing preferred sizes) and to the process of establishing basic **specifications** for a set of commonly used characteristics of size, shape and performance of products, **simplification** of product design refers to the elimination of the complex features and undesirable marginal features of a product to eliminate waste and to achieve economy. Simplification refers to the elimination of superfluous varieties, sizes, dimensions, features etc. making the design, assembly or product simplex, less complex and less difficult to use. **Usually simplification precedes standardisation**.

While simplification results in variety reduction also, variety reduction as such is more than mere simplification. It is a deliberate activity aimed at cost reduction. Variety management or variety control is a company wide programme which is implemented on a continuous basis. ***Variety reduction*** *may be defined as a form of standardisation consisting of the reduction of the number of types of products, or materials or parts within a definite range to a lesser number which is adequate to meet prevailing needs at a given time.* When we speak of the term **"variety"**, it means we refer to functionally similar materials, components designed for a particular requirement. A variety reduction programme is deliberately carried out with the aim of minimising *(a)* variety of products and services, *(b)* variety of parts, *(c)* variety of materials, *(d)* variety of processes and *(e)* variety of people/skills.

Why should the variety be controlled?

Within any organisation, we find varieties of products made and services offered, methods and procedures used, materials and documentation employed and the processes and operations used. As varieties increase, organisational problems and costs will also increase. *For example*, an increase in the variety of materials stored will increase the storage space needed, increase in the difficulty of recording of stocks and maintaining stores records, increase in the number of purchase order processed and so on. While variety is inevitable to a certain extent, as variety increases, controlling costs becomes more and more difficult. Therefore, control of variety is essential in any type of organisation. Some of the major adverse effects of undue variety are:

(i) Shorter production runs (*i.e.*, smaller batch sizes) resulting in higher production costs per unit produced.

(ii) Frequent production change overs involving idle time on machines due to change overs, retooling and more setups.

(iii) Higher stocks of materials, components, parts etc., requiring larger capital outlay and storage space.

While greater variety of finished products or services offered can provide significant competitive advantage (marketing advantage with higher customer appeal), it has an adverse effect in the areas of procurement and production.

Why does the variety tend to increase?

The various reasons for the tendency to increase varieties are:

(i) Use of non-standard materials and components.

(ii) Use of many sizes of similar materials which are not much different from each other.

(iii) Concealed identity due to trade/proprietary names of items of same specification produced by different manufacturing firms.

(iv) Different systems of classification of materials/components followed by different divisions of the same firm.

How to control the variety?

Variety control can be carried out in three ways:

(i) By ***Simplification*** – the reduction of unnecessary variety

(ii) By ***Standardisation*** – the control of necessary variety and

(iii) By ***Specialisation*** – the concentration of effort on undertakings where special knowledge is available.

System of preferred numbers is one of the greatest contributions made by standardisation. Adoption of preferred numbers (sizes) helps in variety reduction by reducing the choice of customers to a definite pattern following geometric progression.

Value analysis is another approach to variety control and thereby cost reduction. In this approach two simple considerations used are:

(i) Can we eliminate the item altogether? and

(ii) Should we modify or change the item to another standard item of better value.

➤ BENEFITS OF VARIETY CONTROL

Three areas in which benefits of variety control can be realised are: *(i)* Marketing, *(ii)* Design and *(iii)* Production Operations.

Benefits in the area of marketing include:

(a) intensification of selling effort and

(b) better after-sales service

Benefits in the area of product design includes:

(a) greater technical productivity and

(b) better understanding of technical problems

Benefits in the area of production/operations include:

(a) larger production runs

(b) lesser setup times

(c) fewer operation aides such as accessories and tools

(d) higher equipment utilisation

(e) reduction in inventory

(f) easier inventory control

(g) better use of storage space

(h) quicker stock-checking

(i) simplified production planning and control

(j) reduction in purchasing effort.

➤ REVIEW QUESTIONS

1. What is meant by classification and codification of materials?
2. Discuss the advantages of classification and codification.
3. State the principles of classification and codification.
4. Describe the nature and process of codification.
5. Describe the methods of classification and codification.
6. State the objectives of codification.
7. Describe the major steps involved in a codification system.

8. Discuss some important codification systems.
9. Define the term "standardisation".
10. What is meant by "simplification"?
11. What are the two areas of standardisation? Elaborate.
12. Discuss the broad implications of standardisation.
13. Explain how standardisation reduces costs?
14. What is meant by "Component standardisation"?
15. State the objectives of standardisation? What is a standard?
16. Discuss the various levels of standards.
17. State the advantages and disadvantages of standardisation.
18. What is meant by "preferred number system"? Elaborate with examples.
19. What is meant by "organising standardisation program"? – Explain.
20. Discuss the various types of standards.
21. State the advantages of simplification.
22. Distinguish between standardisation and simplification.
23. What is meant by "specification"?
24. Discuss the various kinds of specification.
25. Discuss the advantages and disadvantages of specification.
26. Discuss the kinds and sources of industrial standards.
27. What is meant by "Variety reduction"? Explain how it is different from standardisation and simplification.
28. Why should the variety be controlled?
29. Why does the variety tend to increase?
30. How would you control variety?
31. What is value analysis? How it is useful for variety control?
32. State the benefits of variety control.

VALUE ANALYSIS/ VALUE ENGINEERING

Companies are continually examining ways to reduce manufacturing and/ or purchasing costs and value engineering or value analysis has this ultimate objective. **Value engineering or value analysis** – the two words which are used almost interchangeably involve a study of the function of manufactured parts or purchased materials and components to see whether specifications can be modified, in order to reduce cost without impairing use or performance.

The concept of value analysis was developed during World War II by Lawrence D. Miles of General Electric Company. Under war time conditions, studies were continually made to see whether alternative materials could be used for components and assemblies because those specified were either expensive or difficult to obtain.

Value analysis is an important and powerful approach for improvement in the performance of products, systems or procedures and reduction in costs without jeoparding their function. (*i.e.,* **equivalent performance at lower costs**). Lawrence D. Miles defined value analysis in his book, **"Techniques of Value Analysis and Engineering"** as an organised creative approach which has for its purpose the efficient identification of unnecessary cost *i.e.,* cost which provides neither quality, nor use, nor life, nor appearance, nor customer features.

Meaning of the Term 'Value'

It is not enough for a firm simply to meet the expectations of the customer. To succeed, firms must exceed these expectations. They must learn how to profitably delight the customers. Different customers desire different characteristics in goods and services they buy. Some customers view *cost* (price) as less important than **speed** (delivery). Some other customers rate **quality** as the most important factor in their purchase decisions, some others may be interested in **flexibility**. These various views of what makes a good or service acceptable or highly desirable to the customer fall together under the umbrella of **value**. Value is the customer's subjective evaluation, adjusted for cost, of how well a product meets or exceeds expectations. Operations managers help their firms to win new customers and retain existing customers, providing products that offer the highest level of value to customers.

However, certain realities about value must be recognised in accepting the need for value-driven functions in a firm :

(i) Value of a good or service is ultimately defined and assessed by the customer. Hence, the firm must always keep in touch with the customers to know their specific needs. (*i.e.*, what customers value).

(ii) Value is dynamic. Perceptions of value may change as a result of many factors : competitor's actions, government regulations or changing customer preferences.

(iii) Any action that does not contribute to value may add to waste.

Characteristics of Value

(i) Value links the customers, the firm and the operations management system.

(ii) Effective operations management systems are value driven.

(iii) Value is customer specific, not market or product specific.

(iv) Value combines four major attributes: cost, quality, speed and flexibility.

(v) The importance of attributes of value differ for different customers.

(vi) Value is dynamic, value today may not be value tomorrow.

Every firm faces two 'critical tasks'. First, it must create customers, then it must keep the customers it creates. To create and keep customers, a firm cannot simply provide a good or service, it must offer those customers something that they value. It can do this by giving customers an **existing product for a lower price or offer a better quality product for the same price**. It can also attract customers by faster product development or delivery or flexibility. All these approaches amount to an attempt to offer customers a product that is something that they value.

Value Defined : "**Value**" is easy to understand but difficult to define. It is easy to understand because people know what they value and what they don't. Value is what customers are demanding – **the right combination of product quality, fair price and goods and services**.

What Value is Not?

Value does not mean high quality, if it is only available at even higher prices. It doesn't necessarily mean cheap. It doesn't mean high prestige if prestige is viewed as snobbish.

Value is difficult to define because it is subjective. Value is defined as the customer's subjective evaluation of a product (good or service), adjusted for cost, of how well a good or service meets or exceeds expectations of the customer.

Customers do not care about the firm's maximising its *cost effectiveness* or *profit;* rather they want to maximise value for themselves. They buy products that offer the highest levels of value. The firms must design, build and deliver goods and services that customers perceive as offering more value than competitor's products.

Traits or **attributes** that shape value are :

(i) Value is ultimately defined by the customer.

(ii) Value is dynamic.

(iii) Value is best understood through a value equation.

(iv) Value combines four major traits : speed, cost, quality and flexibility.

(v) Value changes the way in which managers view and structure the delivery process.

Value and the Value Equation

The value equation offers one convenient way of approaching the task of defining value for an identified customer and determining how the operations management function can affect the perceived value of the firm's goods and services.

The value equation is written as :

$$\text{Value} = \frac{\text{Performance}}{\text{Cost}} \text{ or } \frac{\text{Function}}{\text{Cost}}$$

The value equation expresses value as a comparison of what a product can do for the customer against what it costs to him. **Performance** describes what the good or service does for the customer. Performance is described in terms of **quality, speed** and **flexibility**. ***Quality*** represents how well the good or service meets or exceeds the expectations of the customer at the time of purchase. **Speed** describes the time needed to deliver the good or service to the customer or the time that the firm needs to design and produce the good or service. **Flexibility** reflects how easily the firm can change the product to more closely match the needs of the customer.

Performance presupposes the notion of the function of the product. The product must satisfy a real need, it must perform as promised and it must offer the features that the customer wants. Value-based competition must always create or enhance functionality by improving the other elements of value.

The three components of performance need not always carry equal weights. When different weights are assigned to the components of performance, namely quality, speed and flexibility, the performance is expressed as a weighted sum of these variables (components of performance) based on subjective weights that reflect customer priorities.

$$\textbf{Performance} = \beta_1 \times \textbf{quality} + \beta_2 \times \textbf{speed} + \beta_3 \times \textbf{flexibility}$$

The denominator in the value equation *i.e., cost* represents all costs (objective or subjective) that the customer incurs, acquire to, use and dispose off the good or service.

Box 13.1 shows the influence of value equation on a set of guidelines to effective value marketing.

Importance of Value Equation

(i) It identifies the four components of value, *i.e.,* cost, quality, speed and flexibility against which all operations managers must evaluate their systems.

(ii) It identifies the various ways in which the firm can create value for customers and compete in the market place.

(iii) The components of the value equation can change in many different ways to enhance value for the customer.

Box 13.1 : How to be a Value Marketer

(i) **Offer products that perform :** Customers who are unhappy with shoddy goods/ service won't distract by fashion. They expect the products they buy to perform to meet their expectations.

(ii) **Give more than the customer expects :** In addition to offering products that meet customer expectation and achieve customer satisfaction, the goods or service provider must ensure that he or she offers more than what the customer expects. This means achieving more than customer satisfaction by delighting the customer by offering pleasant and useful goods/services. (*For example,* providing environmentally sound packaging or including airconditioners in a car's standard price). Surprises will win customer loyalty and help in retaining such customers.

(iii) **Give guarantees :** Offering an enhanced warranty or guarantee and refunding fully when problems arise for customers regarding goods/services offered can help to justify higher prices.

(iv) **Avoid unreasonable pricing :** Avoid pricing the good or service to a premium pricing if the basic product (good or service) offered could not justify.

(v) **Give the customer the facts :** Use advertising to provide the kind of detailed information that today's sophisticated customer demands.

(vi) **Build relationships :** Build long term relationships with customers to help to bind the consumer to the product offered.

Approach to Value-Driven Competition

The five major approaches are : *(i)* **Any time,** *(ii)* **Any place**, *(iii)* **No Matter**, *(iv)* **Mass Customisation**, *(v)* **Risk Reduction**. These five strategies are discussed in the following paragraphs.

(i) **Any Time :** This strategy option focusses on time to create value for the customer. Time influences the actions of the customer as a resource, not a constraint. The firm offering the product can enhance value by reducing lead time for the customer in many different ways :

- Reducing means and variances.
- Managing both design and delivery lead times.
- Reducing total system lead times.
- Focussing on lead times for specific activities that interest the customer.

(ii) **Any Place :** This strategy option attempts to reduce the distance between the customer and supplier. This can be done in several different ways.

- Increasing the amount of product that takes place at the customer's location.
- Involving customers actively in the design, manufacturing and delivery activities.
- Bringing together suppliers and customers to reduce the number of stages between them.
- Changing the basic customer-supplier relationship from **competition** to **cooperation**.

(iii) **No Matter :** This strategy option describes a change in the way that customers view the firm's product as they use it. Sellers no longer sell and customers no larger buy strictly tangible goods. Intangible product characteristics such as security, goodwill, safety, information and services are beginning to play more important roles in company-customer relationships.

(iv) **Mass Customisation :** This strategy option describes a system that can customise the products on a mass scale. Instead of building products for markets, mass customisers build products for

individual customers. They must be able to deliver acceptable products to these customers at prices not much higher than they would pay for standard products.

(v) **Risk Reduction :** This strategy attracts customers by offering to eliminate or greatly reduce the risks of doing business. Risk reduction may focus on conversion process itself. Companies increasingly move towards systems that rely on less inventory and short lead times. These systems are designed to instill customer confidence by demonstrating control that assumes on-time delivery of products that satisfy customer's quality and quantity needs.

Risk reduction efforts may also focus on products. A firm may try to provide a product that is easy to maintain, easy to use and easy to repair. This approach to risk reduction tries to convince the customer that the firm can substantially reduce any risks associated with a purchase.

Dynamic Nature of Value

Customer's definition of value change continually. Yesterday's thrilling innovation is considered simply acceptable today and may become insignificant or inadequate tomorrow. These changes often result from changes in customer expectations and affect the various parameters of performance in the value equation (*i.e.,* quality, speed and flexibility).

Customer expectations and values may change at any time for any of the several reasons :

(i) **Familiarity :** This is the notion that exposure to something leads people to take it for granted. As a result, familiarity reduces the effect of a product trait or attribute as an order winner. Familiarity changes a unique order winner to a basic expectation that the customer expects in every product.

For instance, customers have become so much familiar with quality products that they have become less sensitive to the whole issue of improved quality. Instead, they now look for **faster delivery, easier product customisation** and **quicker introduction of new and better products** as new sources of value.

(ii) **Income/Education :** As income levels increase, customers can afford to consider products that cost more, but also offer far higher levels of performance. *Similarly,* higher levels of education increase customers' expectations. Education also tends to make customers more aware of the importance of performance.

(iii) **Economic conditions :** Changes in economic conditions affect people's perceptions of value. During recession (depressed economic conditions), people find themselves with less money or with less secure economic features. As a result, they buy at lower cost, more practical products. Value becomes especially critical in tough economic times.

(iv) **Competitor's action and corporate strategies :** Competitor's action or changes in their corporate strategies can change customer expectations. Every firm tries to develop and maintain sustainable competitive advantage for itself by offering its customers something that its competitors do not. This will often result in a series of moves and countermoves each of which influences customer expectations and ultimately value.

Competitive sparring makes order winners to order qualifiers. As order winners become order qualifiers, firms and managers search for new order winners, especially in areas where their systems excel but competitors' systems do not. Many of these order winners involve time and flexibility.

(v) **Government Actions :** Government actions establish standards for adequate performance. They set minimum performance levels that firm's goods and services must meet, helping to

shape order qualifiers for many customers. These actions can take the form of new regulations or certification procedures.

Kinds of Value

Economic value (or simply value) may be classified into four kinds:

(i) **Use value :** The properties, features and qualities which accomplish the use, the work or the service – causing the item to perform or serve an end.

(ii) **Esteem value (or need value) :** The properties, features or attractiveness which cause us to yearn to possess it, causing the item to be sold.

(iii) **Exchange value :** The properties or qualities which enable us to exchange an item for something else we want and

(iv) **Cost value :** The total of material, labour and other costs that have to be incurred to produce an item.

Use value, being derived from the delivered function and representing the properties and qualities which perform the function, can be quantified, while other values are difficult to quantify. Value can be improved by :

(i) By improving the function (or performance) for the same cost.

(ii) By reducing the cost for the same function (or performance) and

(iii) By combination of *(i)* and *(ii)* but by large improvement in function for a smaller increase in cost.

➤ VALUE ANALYSIS (OR VALUE ENGINEERING)

Value analysis involves systematised techniques for reducing costs and improving the performance of materials, components and manufacturing processes. Value analysis is defined as "**an intensive appraisal of all the elements of the design, manufacture or construction, procurement, inspection, installation and maintenance of a product and its components including the applicable specifications and operational requirements in order to achieve the necessary performance, maintainability and reliability of the item at minimum cost.**"

Value Analysis may also be defined as follows :

(i) Value Analysis is the **study of the relationship of design, function and cost** of any product, material or service with the objective to *reduce cost* through modifications of design or material or specification or the manufacturing process, changing source of supply (external or internal) or possible elimination of parts or their incorporation into a related item.

(ii) Value Analysis is the **investigation of the performance** of a material or a component in terms of its function and its unit price to develop the most effective specification at the lowest ultimate cost.

(iii) Value Analysis is an **organised creative approach** which has for its purpose, the **efficient identification of unnecessary cost**, *i.e.*, cost which does not add to quality, use, life, appearance or other customer features.

Exhibit 13.1 illustrates the concepts involved in the above three definitions.

Value Analysis should not be treated as a mere cost reduction technique which makes the product become cheaper in price. It is more comprehensive and the improvement in value is attained without any sacrifice in quality, reliability, maintainability, availability, aesthetics and the like. The basic objective of value analysis is to achieve **equivalent or better performance at a lower cost while maintaining all functional and quality requirements**.

Box 13.2 gives various definitions of value analysis.

Exhibit 13.1 : Concepts Involved in Value Analysis

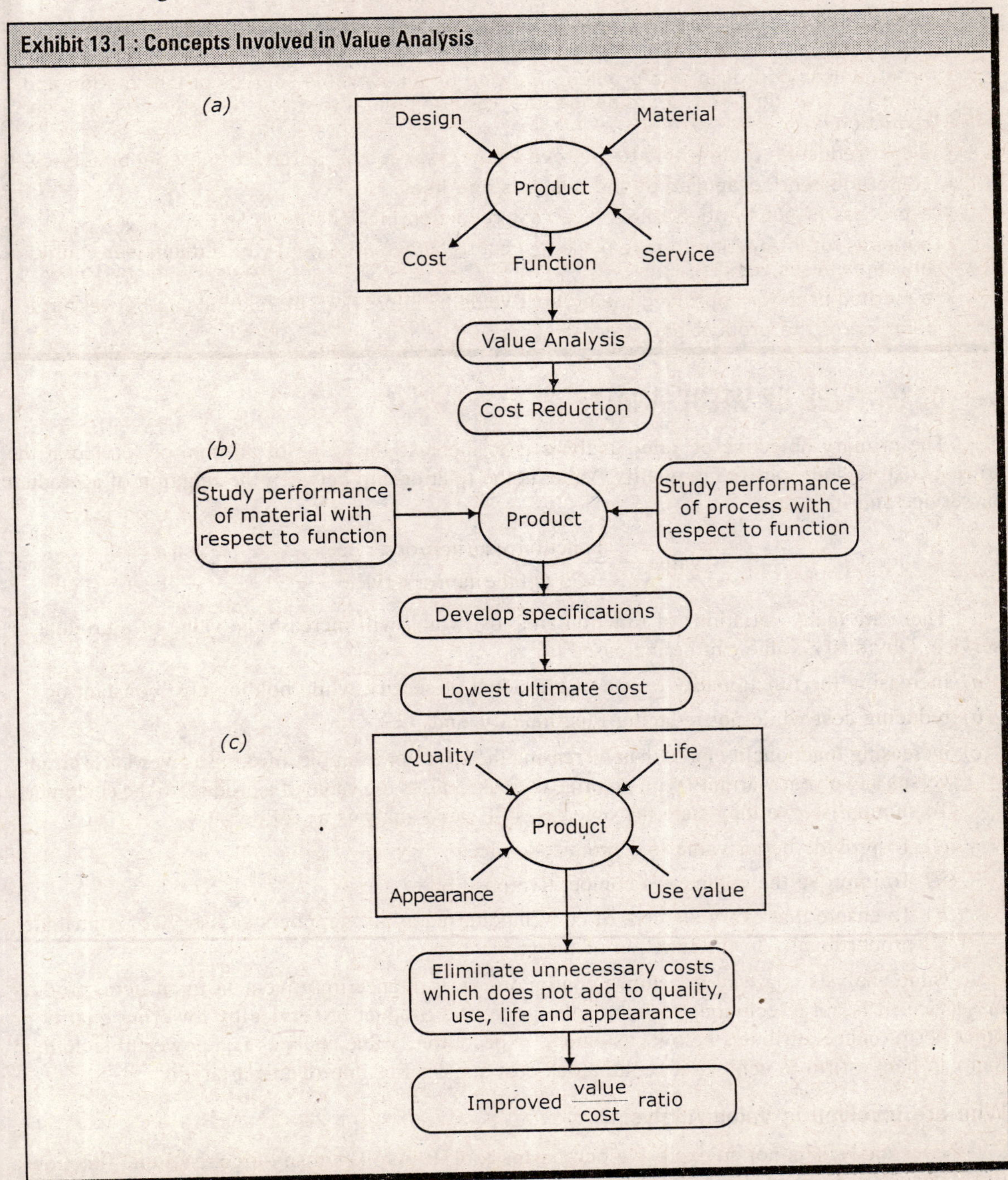

Box 13.2 : What is Value Analysis?

Value Analysis is :

- a task of finding a more economical way of making or buying a product.
- a systematic, organised approach for attaining the same performance at lower cost (equivalent performance at reduced cost).
- an organised approach to a problem, drawing on all available sources of information and expert knowledge and coordinating the resulting data towards the objective of cost reduction.
- a cost reduction programme to improve value/cost ratio of a product, material or service.
- value engineering applied at the design stage itself.
- a process of substitution to achieve cost reduction incidentally.
- a means for interaction to take place in a controlled environment which minimises conflict and maximises results.
- a method used for improving the product value by improving the relationship between the function of the product and its cost.

OBJECTIVES OF VALUE ANALYSIS

The primary objective of value analysis is to increase the value of an item or service at the lowest cost without sacrificing quality. Value is the relationship between the function of a product or service and its cost:

$$\text{Value} = \frac{\text{Function of an item or service}}{\text{Cost of the item or service}}$$

There are many variations of function and cost which will increase the value of a product or service. Obviously, value can be increased by:

(*a*) increasing the functionality or use of a product or service while holding cost constant or

(*b*) reducing cost while not reducing functionality, and

(*c*) increasing functionality more than increasing the cost. For example, offering a five year warranty versus a two year warranty with no price increase, raises the value of a product to the customers.

To summarise, we may state the objectives of value analysis as follows:

(*i*) To provide better value to a product/service.

(*ii*) To improve the company's competitive position.

(*iii*) To ensure that every element of cost (labour, materials, suppliers and service) contributes proportionally to the function of the product.

Value analysis is a way to achieve continuous performance improvement in an item, product or service. It is not a technique to reduce the price of a product or service by lowering quality or other performance attributes below customers' expectation. Value analysis is a powerful technique that can help a firm to achieve its continuous cost and quality improvement targets.

Who are Involved in Value Analysis?

Value analysis is not an exclusive purchasing tool. It involves many organisational functions. But, because most products and services require major inputs from suppliers, purchasing should take an active role in co-ordinating value analysis activities. A **value analysis team** (VA team) composed of professionals having knowledge about a product or service is made responsible to use value analysis. The various functional groups which can contribute to the value analysis team are:

(i) **Executive management :** Executive/top management provides overall guidance and support to the value analysis process. Executive management can provide support to functional groups by providing the time, budget and personnel to work in value analysis projects.

(ii) **Suppliers :** Suppliers can propose alternative materials, and identify low-cost production methods. Buyers motivate suppliers to participate in the process in many ways. Suppliers may provide cost reduction ideas if they can share in the savings resulting from their ideas or suggestions.

(iii) **Purchasing :** Purchasing takes a primary role in organising value analysis effort by co-ordinating and disseminating relevant information. Purchasing may bring suppliers directly into the process.

(iv) **Design engineering :** Design engineers evaluate any proposed changes in the design of an item. They also help in defining product function, establishing quality and engineering standards and evaluate the effect of value analysis changes on other parts within the product.

(v) **Marketing :** The marketing group provides insight about the impact of value analysis changes on customers. Marketing may involve customers in the value analysis process just as purchasing involves suppliers. In addition, marketing can help establish price ranges and provide information about competitor actions and responses.

(vi) **Production :** The production group is responsible to produce the finished items or products and hence can propose better ways to produce an item or service to achieve higher quality and/ or lower total cost.

(vii) **Industrial/process engineering :** This group can evaluate proposed manufacturing methods, materials handling and flow, the effect of alternative materials on the production process and packaging requirements.

(viii) **Quality control :** Quality control can evaluate the impact on quality that proposed changes may have. Quality control can also establish how and where to evaluate quality performance levels for proposed production method. This group can also co-ordinate with purchasing to support quality control efforts at supplier firms.

Value analysis works best where the process involves different functional groups.

Test for Determining Value in a Product or Service

The questions which value analysis teams ask to determine whether opportunities exist for item, product or service improvement are listed below:

1. Does the use of this product contribute value to our customers?
2. Is the cost of the final product proportionate to its usefulness?
3. Are there additional uses for this product?
4. Does the product need all its features or internal parts?
5. Are product weight reductions possible?
6. Is there anything else available to our customers given the intended use of the product?
7. Is there a better production method to produce the item or product?
8. Can a lower cost standard part replace a customised part?

9. Are we using the proper tooling considering the quantities required?
10. Will another dependable supplier provide material, components or sub-assemblies for less?
11. Is any one currently purchasing required materials, components or sub-assemblies for less?
12. Are there equally effective but lower-cost materials available?
13. Do material, labour, over head and profit equal the product's cost?
14. Are packaging cost reduction possible?
15. Is the item properly classified for shipping purposes to receive the lowest transportation rates?
16. Are design or quality specifications too tight given customer requirements?
17. If we are making an item now, can we buy it for less and vice versa?

The most likely value analysis improvement areas include modifying product design and material specifications, using standardised components in place of custom components, substituting lower-cost for higher-cost materials, reducing the number of parts that a product contains and developing better production or assembly methods.

Barriers or Road Blocks for Value Analysis

The following statements indicate the attitude of people towards value analysis which act as road blocks for value analysis.

(i) We have done it this way for 15 years. Why change now?
(ii) Our business is different.
(iii) We don't do things that way in our firm.
(iv) It is jolly good idea. Let somebody else try it first.
(v) It has been tried before – in fact, we do it all the times.

Selecting Items for Value Analysis

The products or items that provide most of a firm's revenue can have the greatest impact resulting from a formal value analysis. Other key items include products that are complex in design, and items that are not currently competitive because of changing market conditions. Other selection criteria include items, parts or products with *(a)* high scrap or rework costs, *(b)* large purchased quantities from suppliers, *(c)* many non standard parts and *(d)* relatively difficult production requirements.

Difference Between Value Analysis and Value Engineering

The term *value analysis* and *value engineering* are often used interchangeably but they do not mean the same. While the concepts are similar, there is a basic difference between the two. Value analysis is a technique which is applied to existing items or products, usually after introducing them to the market place. It is an after-the-fact activity.

Value engineering is the application of value analysis techniques during product design and development. Value engineering techniques are applied during new-product development, whereas value analysis is emphasised as a way of achieving continuous improvement. The only way to maintain customers and demonstrate market leadership is to offer improved products and services on a continuous basis.

➤ AREAS OF APPLICATION OF VALUE ANALYSIS

(i) **Value Analysis in Production :** There is a need not only to meet customer requirement but also to ensure that product is manufacturable. **Design for manufacturing** (DFM) is an approach that consists of two things :

(i) simplification of products and

(ii) manufacture of multiple products using common parts, processes and modules (standardisation and variety reduction).

Simplification of products based on value analysis (or value engineering) is preferably conducted before the product is produced (*i.e.,* at the product design stage itself).

Value analysis attacks two aspects of the product :

(i) the use function or the ability of the product to perform according to specifications.

(ii) the aesthetic function, appearance or style of the product.

Value Analysis is easier to apply to industrial products because the client is principally interested in the product performing correctly rather than its appearance. In contrast consumer products are often purchased according to their appearance, where the aesthetic appearance is also an important consideration in addition to performance.

In value analysis, the following terms are used :

(i) **Objective :** the primary purpose of the product

(ii) **Basic Function :** a function if eliminated, would render the product useless in terms of its stated objective.

(iii) **Secondary Function :** a function that is the result of the way the product is designed and permits accomplishment of the basic function.

For example, the task of accessing the contents of a sealed tin can might include the following:

- **Objective :** remove the contents of the can,
- **Basic Function :** open the can,
- **Secondary Function :** cut the lid.

Value Analysis is the process of examining the secondary function to see whether an alternative function can be identified that will improve the value ratio *i.e.,* the ratio of usefulness to cost (*i.e.,* usefulness / cost). This is done by first identifying the cost of the current secondary function. Then the costs of alternative secondary functions are calculated. If these alternatives have lower costs without sacrificing the usefulness of the product or service to the customer, then value is improved. Also, the usefulness may be improved at the same cost, which would also increase the value to the customers.

Value analysis is frequently related to manufacturability, since the product designed for manufacturability has the lowest cost and highest value. **Design for manufacturability** removes unnecessary parts and makes the product easier to produce. This approach will reduce cost or improve the usefulness of the products or both.

Exhibit 13.2 illustrates the example of product simplification that improved manufacturability and value.

Exhibit 13.2 : Value analysis (Evolution of a DFM study that resulted in reducing the design part count from 20 to 2 parts)

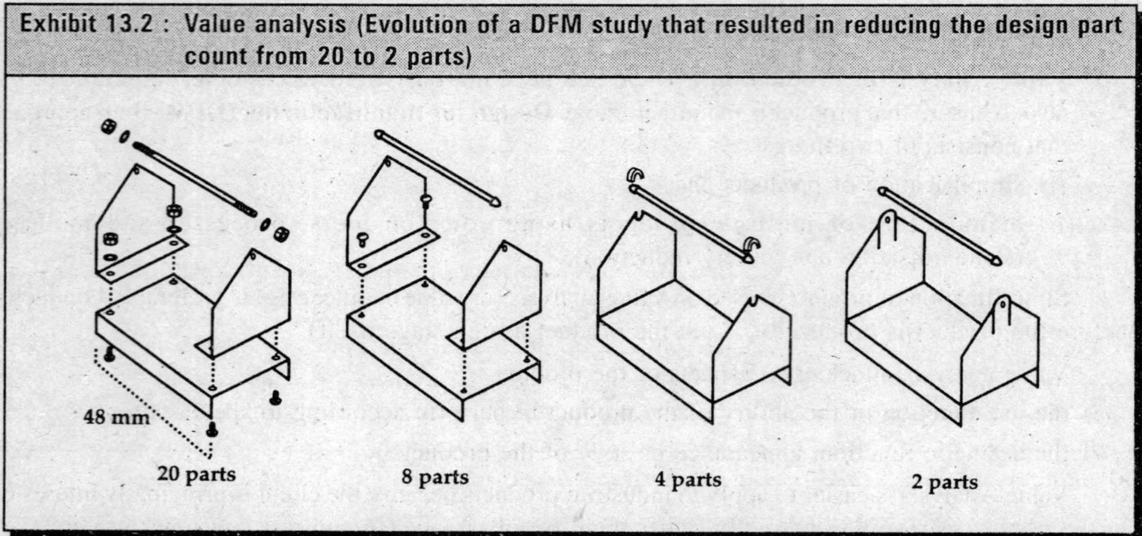

(ii) **Value Analysis in Purchasing :** Value Analysis refers to an examination of the function of purchased parts and materials in an effort to reduce the cost and/or improve the performance of those items. From a purchasing viewpoint, value analysis represents a relatively recent change from concentrating on finding the best price for a certain item to finding the lowest cost for any item that will satisfy an intended function. The analysis answers such questions as :

(i) Could a less expensive material serve the same function?

(ii) Is the function necessary?

(iii) Could it be eliminated?

(iv) Could other items serve the same function?

(v) Can they be simplified?

(vi) Could the supplier reduce the price by a cooperative redesign or revised specifications?

(vii) Could the product specification be relaxed and would it result in a lower price?

(viii) Could standard parts be substituted for non-standard parts?

Naturally, purchasing cannot perform an investigation each time materials are ordered. However, it should conduct value analysis periodically on large value items because of potential savings.

Purchasing does not ordinarily have the authority to substitute or modify materials designated by the operating units. It does have the responsibilities to question requisitions and to suggest alternatives that would lead to better prices (lower prices). It can make suggestions to operating units, designers and suppliers, which may lead to improved performance of purchased goods and/or reduction of the cost of those goods. Also, when originators of purchase requisitions know their requisitions are going to be scrutinised, more attention is normally devoted to their preparation.

Purchasing can offer a different perspective to the analysis and purchasing people because of their association with suppliers, possess information not known to others within the organisation. If a fair amount of technical knowledge is required to review a part or product, a team can be formed with representatives from design and/or operations to work with purchasing in conducting value analysis.

Box 13.3 provides a checklist of questions that can guide a value analysis exercise in purchasing.

Box 13.3 : Value Analysis Checklist

(i) Select an item that has a high annual rupee volume. This can be a purchased part or material or a service.

(ii) Identify the function of the item.

(iii) Obtain answers to questions such as these :

(a) Is the item necessary, does it add value or can it be eliminated?

(b) Are there alternative sources for the item?

(c) Can the item be provided internally? (*i.e.,* manufactured in house)

(d) What are the advantages of the present arrangement?

(e) What are the disadvantages of the present arrangement?

(f) Could another part, material or service be used instead?

(g) Can specifications be made less stringent to save cost or time?

(h) Can two or more parts be combined?

(i) Can more (less) processing be done on them to save on cost.

(j) Does suppliers/providers have suggestions for improvements?

(k) Do employees have suggestions for improvement?

(l) Can packaging be improved or made less costly?

(iv) Analyse the answers obtained plus answers to other questions that arise and make recommendations.

In purchasing, the value equation that guides purchasing is

Use Value + Esteem Value = Exchange Value

Box 13.4 : Six "Whats of Value Analysis"

(i) What is it?

(ii) What does it do?

(iii) What does it cost?

(iv) What is it worth?

(v) What else will do the job?

(vi) What does that cost?

Considerations in Value Analysis

Exhibit 13.3 illustrates the points to be considered in value analysis in purchasing.

Exhibit 13.3 : Value Analysis in Purchasing

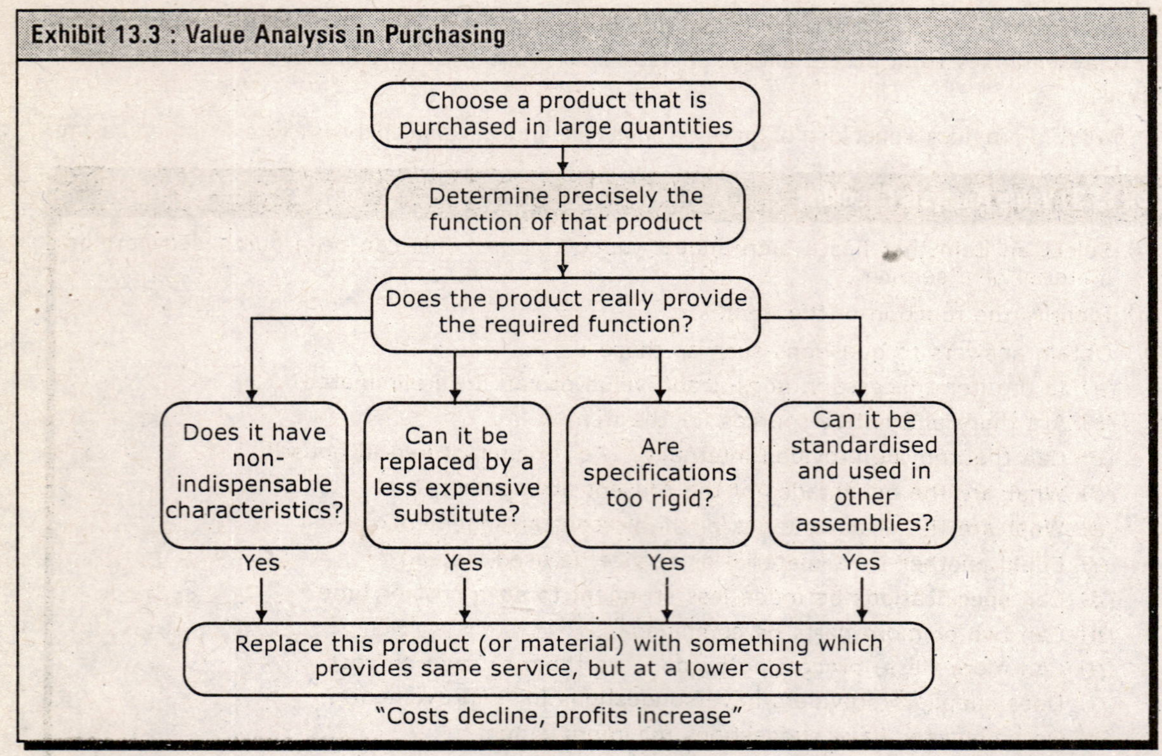

➤ STEPS IN CARRYING OUT A VALUE ANALYSIS EXERCISE

Conducting a value analysis would proceed as follows :

(i) Establish the objectives (*e.g.,* reduction of cost).

(ii) Consider a multi-disciplinary team from marketing, sales, production, cost control, suppliers and purchasing (the team leader).

(iii) Analyse the production process of the supplier company. This would include decoupling the cost price at each step of the production process.

(iv) Analyse the use of the product at the purchaser's firm, phase by phase.

(v) Decompose and analyse the various characteristics of the purchased product, applying a weighting coefficient to each according to its importance. Characteristics would include physical (size, shapes, form), chemical composition, use and preparation.

(vi) Hold a creative brainstorming session to explore all alternative possibilities, with the team having no preconceived ideas.

(vii) Sort the ideas to establish the cost of each.

(viii) Select the best alternative.

(ix) Develop a plan for implementing the change.

Value Tests

Value engineering or value analysis is essentially a questioning attitude looking at all the functions and costs. Lawrence D. Miles designed a set of value tests to ascertain whether there is scope for value improvement. Some of these questions which can work as thought-starters for developing better value alternatives could be as follows :

(i) Can the design be changed to eliminate the part?

(ii) Can you purchase it at a lower cost?

(iii) Does it need all its features?

(iv) Is there anything better for the intended use?

(v) Can a usable part be made by a lower-cost method (cheaper method)?

(vi) Can a standard part be used?

(vii) Is it made on proper tooling considering the quantities involved?

(viii) Are there any newly developed materials that can be used?

(ix) Can two or more parts be combined into one?

(x) Can any specification be changed to effect cost reduction?

By applying the value tests, we may come across poor value areas which are responsible for unnecessary costs. These could be in the design of the product, procurement, handling and storage of materials, production processes, packaging and distribution of the final product. Once we identify poor value areas, we can focus our attention on these so that these unnecessary features can be eliminated.

Value Analysis Process (or Value Engineering Process)

The value analysis or value engineering process is a systematic and organised approach that examines all aspects of a problem, employing a questioning attitude. Thus, a formal approach has to be adopted for value analysis process which is called **"value engineering job plan"**. These job plans have various steps and phases with their associated value engineering techniques at each phase. The **seven steps** involved are:

(i) General phase, *(ii)* Information phase, *(iii)* Function phase, *(iv)* Creation phase, *(v)* Evaluation phase, *(vi)* Investigation phase and *(vii)* Recommendation phase.

Each of these phases comprise or is supported by one or more techniques. Brief description of each phase together with associated value engineering techniques are discussed in the following paragraphs:

(i) **General Phase :** Throughout the application of the entire job plan, the techniques of this phase must be meticulously applied to create the right environment for value engineering job plans to be effective. The five techniques associated with this phase are :

(a) **Use good human relations :** Considerable degree of personal contact is essential throughout the value analysis project. Use of good human relations means assistance in place of resistance.

(b) **Inspire team work :** Good teamwork calls for subordinating personal prominence or ego in the interest of the group as a whole.

(c) **Work on specifics :** Avoid generalities and work on specifics. Secure concrete data and information on specific problems.

(d) **Overcome road blocks :** In every organisation, we can find a group of dissenters who knowingly or unknowingly use every means at their command to resist change. Recognise road blocks and then take suitable steps to overcome them.

(e) **Apply good business judgement :** Business decisions and judgements must be based on facts rather than on personal opinions and feelings. One must be resourceful, able to think and pursue new knowledge in order to apply good judgement.

(ii) **Information Phase :** The objective of this phase is to gain an understanding of the project being studied and to obtain all essential facts relating to the project as also to estimate the potential value improvement. Three techniques involved in this phase are :

(a) **Secure facts :** Information gathered must be authentic; it is one of the most arduous tasks. The types of information required are :

(i) Technical specification – dimensions, grades, tolerances, quality, appearance and the like.

(ii) Environmental specifications – severity, test conditions.

(iii) Engineering drawings (design drawings).

(iv) Production sample – actual working model or dummy model.

(v) Production data – operations, speed, rates of output and stock levels.

(vi) Cost data – material, labour and overload costs.

(vii) Work specifications – work place lay-out, standard times.

(viii) Features preferred by customers.

(ix) Development, testing and service records.

(x) Quantities involved and

(xi) Scrap rates.

(b) **Determine costs :** Complete and accurate costs must be determined in order to direct efforts and time towards those areas of activities promising the greatest return on the value of efforts put and time spent.

(c) **Fix costs on specifications and requirements :** By establishing a relationship between the costs and the specifications and requirements, a means is presented by which the latter two can be quantitatively evaluated.

(iii) **Function Phase :** The objectives of this phase are to define the functions that a product actually performs and is required to perform as well as to relate these functions to the cost and work of providing them. Two techniques of this phase are :

(a) **Define function :** The method of functional analysis requires functions to be described in terms of a verb and a noun. By this, it is possible to describe the functions clearly. The rules of function description are :

(i) Determine user's need for a product or service.

(ii) Use only passive or indirect verb.

(iii) Avoid goal like words or phrases, such as improve, maximise, minimise, optimise and the like.

(iv) List a large number of two-word pairs and then select the best pair.

(b) **Evaluate function relationship :** This technique attempts to determine relative importance of various functions. A descending order of important functions is established along with relative value of their importance.

(iv) **Creation Phase :** The objective of this phase is to create ideas for valuable alternatives to accomplish the functions defined in the previous phase. The first step is to try to answer the question "What also will do?" which requires **creativity**. **Brainstorming** is a very effective way of promoting creativity. Two powerful techniques to promote creativity are :

(a) **Establish positive thinking :** The judicial part of the mind is separated from the creative part of the mind. This means that we do not attempt to judge an idea simultaneously when it is being created.

(b) **Develop creative ideas :** This is done by cultivating uninhibited thinking and developing a multitude of ideas and approaches for accomplishing the defined functions.

(v) **Evaluation Phase :** The objective of this phase is to select for further analysis the most promising of the ideas generated during the creative phase and to subject the ideas to a preliminary screening to identify those which satisfy the following criteria:

- Will it work?
- Is it less costly than the present design?
- Is it feasible to implement?

The judicial part of the mind is actively used in this phase. There are four techniques associated with this phase. They are :

(a) **Refine and combine ideas :** The ideas must be practicable and to make them so, we may have to refine an idea or combine two or more than two ideas.

(b) **Establish cost on all ideas :** As an idea or a combination of ideas is being refined, an estimated cost should be calculated. The questions to be answered are : *(i)* What are the potential costs of implementing the idea and *(ii)* What are the resultant savings implied?

(c) **Develop function alternatives :** This makes further use of the information developed in the valuation of functional relationships to mould the individual functional solutions into total solutions.

(d) **Evaluate by comparison :** When these rough total solutions and their related estimates of costs have been established, they are compared to determine which one will provide the greatest *value advantage.*

(vi) **Investigation Phase :** The selected ideas are further refined into workable and acceptable solutions providing lower cost methods for performing the desired function by some techniques. They are:

(a) Use company and individual standards to the extent possible.

(b) Consult vendors and specialists to get cost-reducing and quality improving ideas.

(vii) **Recommendation Phase :** This is the final phase of the job plan in which the finally selected value alternative is recommended for acceptance and implementation. The entire project of conducting value analysis would succeed only if the recommendation is accepted.

Two techniques associated with this phase are : *(a)* Present facts and *(b)* Motivate positive action. The presentation of facts can be either verbal or written in standard format or in combined form. The combined strategy is the best.

Value Analysis Techniques : Value analysis techniques aim at cost reduction through a critical examination of the relationship of **design**, **function** and **cost** of any product, material or service with the objective of cost reduction. This is achieved through the following techniques :

(i) Modification of the design.

(ii) Standardisation of parts/components.

(iii) Variety reduction and simplification.

(iv) Use of alternative (cheaper) materials without affecting quality/performance.

(v) Changing sources of supply.

(vi) Elimination of parts/components.

(vii) Modification of manufacturing processes.

(viii) Design and cost analysis.

(ix) Waste reduction.

(x) Better utilisation of resources (materials, men and machines).

Benefits to be Achieved by Value Analysis

Value analysis helps to achieve better value for a product through :

- Better purchasing techniques.
- Design re-evaluation and design modification.
- Lower operating costs.
- Substitution.
- Better materials handling.
- Lower cost of maintenance and
- Better suppliers.
- Better manufacturing methods.
- Standardisation.
- Better packaging.
- Better inventory control.
- Lower overhead expenses.

Guiding Principles for Value Analysis

(i) Avoid accepting general negative statements, without going into cause and their remedies.

(ii) Collect all the available cost data.

(iii) Use only the best source of information.

(iv) Screen data thoroughly.

(v) Give importance to creativity.

(vi) Spot and remove obstacles.

(vii) Use specialists for advice.

(viii) Evaluate **use value** of tolerance.

(ix) Use available functional products.

(x) Reward suppliers for their contributions to knowledge and skills.

(xi) Apply specialised processes.

(xii) If possible, utilise existing standards and

(xiii) Evaluate your money-spending in detail.

The techniques of value analysis are discussed in detail in the following paragraphs.

➤ TECHNIQUES OF VALUE ANALYSIS

The basic question involved in value analysis is "What is this part worth?" To answer this question, function must be related to price. *For example,* a fastener function can be performed by welding, rivetting, fastening with bolt and nut or gluing. The most desirable alternative for a given application depends on the use to which the product will be put and the attendant conditions of use. The best product is the one that will perform satisfactorily at the lowest cost. Value analysis procedures essentially follow the same pattern in all cases. First, there is an analysis of the design of the item and its uses and then the application of price analysis to the alternatives.

Design Analysis : To start with, it is helpful to visualise the total functional product and its components. During initial design and development, components are often developed by designers working individually. Then, a value analysis team with members representing different backgrounds view each of the sub-assemblies in relation to each other and to the total product. These results may include suggestions in relation to each other and to the total product. The results may also include suggestions for an entirely different method of manufacture, a new material, or possible elimination of the component altogether as a result of a regrouping of other components.

Check Lists : The value analysis procedure usually includes the use of a detailed checklist to ensure that every pertinent question is asked about each component. Check lists vary in detail, but their basic purpose is to assure that a careful investigation is made. The following questions are indicative of those usually included in value analysis checklists:

(i) What is the precise function of the item?

(ii) Can the item be eliminated?

(iii) If the item is not a standard item, can a standard item be substituted?

(iv) Are there any similar items used by the company that can be substituted?

(v) Can the item be redesigned to allow greater tolerances?

(vi) Will a design change permit the item to be made from a lower cost process or a lower cost material?

(vii) Could the item be produced within the firm at a lesser cost?

(viii) Are the finishing requirements greater than necessary?

(ix) If different sizes of the item are stocked, can some of these be combined to reduce inventory and take advantage of quantity buying?

(x) Is there difficulty in obtaining the part at present?

(xi) Are there any possible economies available in packing or shipping techniques.

Brain-Storming : Brainstorming is a process in which members of value analysis team throw out ideas as they occur during the group sessions known as brain-storming sessions. It attempts to elicit **creative thinking**. Suggestions are not evaluated as they are presented, but are written down as fast as they are made. The emphasis is on stimulation or "hitch-hiking" - that is, using one person's ideas as a spring board for a completely different idea from others. After the free wheeling brainstorming sessions, the resulting ideas are evaluated as to their possible contribution in reducing cost. This technique is still being used by some companies even though it has lost its popularity.

Price Analysis : Although cost is related to all phases of value analysis procedures, it is advisable to have intensive price analysis as a distinct phase of the procedures. Essentially, the question to be asked is "under optimal conditions, what is the cost to the producers of the item being purchased and in the view of the estimated cost, how much should the company pay for the item?" The cost of producing the item is established on the assumption that the supplier is thoroughly efficient, equipped with modern facilities and allowed to make a reasonable return on his investment.

Price analysis must include a thorough study of methods of manufacturer as well as the business conditions prevailing in the industry. In order to arrive at a realistic figure, factors such as the following must be considered: *(i)* Industry wage rates, *(ii)* Rates of operation of suppliers, *(iii)* Excess capacity and its effect on overhead costs, *(iv)* Amount of engineering services required, *(v)* Degree of competition in the industry, *(vi)* Rate of profits in the industry, *(vii)* Age and condition of industry facilities, *(viii)* Changes in productivity and methods of manufacture that may reduce cost.

If the conclusion of the price analysis study is that the price being asked for the item is too high, the company may decide to make the items instead of buying it. In other cases the company may decide that it would be preferable to show the supplier how the item might be preferably produced at a lower price. Larger companies that have expert engineering and administrative talent often find that it is possible for them to counsel smaller suppliers along these lines to the advantage of both parties.

To conclude, we can say that benefits of value analysis include reduced production costs, materials and distribution costs, improved profit margins and increased customer satisfaction. Also, because teams involving purchasing, production and engineering personnel from both the firm and its major suppliers play a key role in value analysis; another potential benefit is higher employee morale. Hence, value analysis should be part of a continual effort to improve the performance of the supply chain and increase the value of the item to the customer.

➤ REVIEW QUESTIONS

1. What does the term "value" mean?
2. What is value analysis or value engineering?
3. Mention the characteristics of value.
4. What is value equation? What is its importance?
5. Discuss the five major approaches to value-driven competition.
6. Discuss the reasons for changes in customer expectations and value.
7. Mention the four kinds of value.
8. State the objectives of value analysis.
9. Mention the roadblocks to value analysis.
10. Discuss the ròle of value analysis in purchasing.
11. Who are all involved in value analysis? Elaborate.
12. Enumerate the tests for determining value in a product or service.
13. How do you select items for value analysis?
14. Differentiate between value analysis and value engineering.
15. Mention the steps involved in carrying out a value analysis exercise.
16. Mention the value tests designed by Lawrence D. Miles.
17. Explain the various phases involved in value analysis.
18. Mention the various value analysis techniques used for cost reduction.
19. Mention the benefits that can be achieved by value analysis.
20. State the guiding principles for value analysis.
21. Explain the following :

    (a) Design analysis, (b) Check lists, (c) Brain storming, (d) Price analysis.

MATERIALS HANDLING

Handling of materials is an integral part of the production process and the procurement, storing and packing and shipping functions and hence, it is an important area of production and materials management. The term "materials" in this context includes raw materials, bought-out parts and components, sub assemblies, semi finished goods, equipments, jigs and fixtures, tools, supplies, packaging materials, consumables, scrap and wastage. Material handling includes all such movement of materials from the stage of receipt at inwards goods stores to the stage of packing and shipping of finished goods. These materials being handled are of various size, shape, volume, weight and other specific features (*for example,* fragile, inflammable, etc.) while the nature and characteristics of the materials to be used in production are largely determined by **product design** and **process design**. The plant layout and shop layout including the stores layout are directly affected by the nature and characteristics of the materials being used. *For example,* large and bulky materials, heavy materials, solids, fluids, flexible and rigid materials, fragile materials which are susceptible for breakage while handling, and materials requiring special handling to protect them from heat, cold, humidity, light, dust, flame, vibration etc., affect the layout of physical facilities and the facilities for handling, storing and processing these materials.

Definitions of Materials Handling : The Materials Handling Division of the American Society of Mechanical Engineers has approved the following definition : **"Materials handling is the art and science involving the moving, packaging, and storing of substance in any form".**

Other definitions include :

(i) Creation of time and place utility.

(ii) Movement and storage of material at the lowest possible cost through the use of proper methods and equipments.

(iii) Lifting, shifting and placing of materials, which effect a saving in money, time and place.

(iv) Art and science of conveying, elevating, positioning, transporting, packaging and storing of materials.

➤ FUNCTIONS OF MATERIALS HANDLING

The most important functions of materials handling are :

(i) the movement of bought-out materials, tools, spare parts, supplies, consumables and positioning them for the purpose of storage.

(ii) the internal movement of materials from stores to the production shops for processing.

(iii) the movement of semi-finished goods from one machine to another for carrying out the manufacturing operation, from the work centres to inspection areas and from one production department to another until all operations are carried out and then moving the finished items to assembly lines.

(iv) the movement of finished products from the production departments to finished goods stores.

(v) unloading materials from transport carriers at the inwards goods stores and moving them to the receiving bay in the stores and then to the inwards goods inspection area.

(vi) moving finished goods from finished goods stores to the packing and shipping and then transporting the packed goods to their destinations (warehouses or customers premises).

Relevance of Materials Handling to Materials Management Function

The buying process in any industry can be thought of as a series of steps in materials handling. These steps are :

(i) packaging carried out at suppliers' premises.

(ii) loading and transportation by suppliers.

(iii) unloading at buyers' premises.

(iv) inspection of incoming materials.

(v) warehousing and binning in stores (*i.e.,* storing the materials in appropriate locations in stores department).

(vi) issue of materials to production shops.

(vii) in-process handling at various stages of production.

(viii) handling materials at various stages of inspection.

(ix) packing finished goods.

(x) warehousing the finished goods (packed).

(xi) loading on transport carries.

(xii) shipping to customers premises or to wholesalers' warehouses.

It has been found by research that about 50 per cent of production cycle time in some industries is spent on materials handling and the materials handling cost can be as high as 30 per cent of the total product cost particularly in heavy engineering, mining and process industries.

➤ SCOPE OF MATERIALS HANDLING

The scope of materials handling activity within an organization depends on the type of the product manufactured, the size of the organization, the value of the product and the value of the activity being performed and the relative importance of materials handling to the enterprise.

There are three perspectives about materials handling, *viz.*,

(a) The traditional point of view.

(b) Plant-wide concern for overall flow of materials.

(c) The systems point of view.

In the **traditional point of view** of materials handling, the emphasis is on the movement of materials from one location to another within the confines of the individual plant. The concern is to find the best way to move the materials from one place to another within the plant.

Plant wide concern focuses the attention on the overall flow of material in the plant. The main concern is the inter-relationships between all handling problems and the possibility of establishing an overall materials handling plan.

The systems point of view of materials handling requires visualization of materials handling problems, the physical distribution activities and all closely related functions as one, an all - encompassing system. This point of view involves a much broader consideration of all materials handling activities involving the movement of materials from all sources of supply (vendors), all handling activities within and around the plant and the handling activities involved in the distribution of finished goods to all customers of the firm.

The subject of materials handling as discussed in this chapter is concerned only with handling of materials within the plant.

➤ IMPORTANCE OF MATERIALS HANDLING

1. Efficient materials handling is important to manufacturing operations. Materials sent by vendors must be unloaded, moved through inspections and production operations to stores and finally to the shipping department. These movements do not add **value** to the product but they do add to the **cost**.
2. Materials handling analysis is a subset of plant layout. Method study, plant layout and materials handling are all part of the design of a production facility and can hardly be treated as separate. Materials handling system and plant layout enhance effectiveness of each other. A good plant layout enables an operation to use the most efficient handling method. Efficient operation of appropriate materials handling methods reduces costs and enables maximum capabilities to be derived from a given production facility.
3. Materials handling in manufacturing organisations in our country accounts for approximately thirty to forty per cent of the cost of production.
4. Nearly 50 per cent of the production cycle time is spent on handling materials in heavy engineering, mining and process industries.
5. The material procurement process in any industry can be viewed as a series of steps involving handling of materials. These steps are : *(a)* packaging of materials at the supplier's premises, *(b)* loading and transportation of materials by suppliers, *(c)* unloading of materials at the buyer's premises, *(d)* inspection of incoming materials at the receiving stores of buyers' organisation, *(e)* storing and binning the materials in holding stores, *(f)* issue of materials to the user departments, *(g)* handling of materials in the form of work-in-progress at various stages of production, *(h)* handling of materials at various stages of inspection, *(i)* packaging of

finished goods, *(j)* storing finish goods in warehouses, *(k)* loading finished goods on transport vehicles (lorries, goods trains, ships or aircrafts), *(l)* shipping and transporting finished goods to customer's premises, *(m)* unloading finished goods at customer's premises.

Hence, any industrial activity can be viewed as an integrated materials handling activity which accounts for about 50 per cent of the total cycle time from procurement of materials to the delivery of finished goods to the customers.

➤ OBJECTIVES OF MATERIALS HANDLING

Even though the best solution to the materials handling problem is *no handling,* it is hardly practicable in a manufacturing process. Hence, the **main objective** of materials handling is to reduce the number of handlings as well as the overall cost of material handling equipments and reducing the distances through which the materials are handled.

The following may be considered as other objectives of materials handling :

1. Lower unit materials handling costs.
2. Reduction in manufacturing cycle time through faster movement of materials and by reducing the distance through which the materials are moved. Reduction in manufacturing cycle time results in reduced work-in-progress inventory costs.
3. Contribution towards a better control of the flow of materials through the manufacturing facility.
4. Improved working conditions and greater safety in the movement of materials.
5. Contribute to better quality by avoiding damage to products by inefficient handling.
6. Increased storage capacity through better utilization of storage areas.
7. Higher productivity at lower manufacturing cost.

➤ MATERIALS HANDLING PRINCIPLES

Certain principles have evolved to guide facility layout to ensure efficient handling of materials. Although there are no hard and fast rules, they do provide effective guidelines for the efficient movement of materials in most facility layouts.

Exhibit 14.1 lists the materials handling principles which provide a frame-work for selecting specific materials handling devices/equipments which are the core of the materials handling system.

Exhibit 14.1 : Materials Handling Principles

Sl. No.	*Principles*
1.	Materials should move through the facility in direct flow patterns, minimizing zig-zagging or backtracking.
2.	Related production processes should be arranged to provide for direct material flows.
3.	Mechanized materials handling devices should be designed and located so that human effort is minimized.
4.	Heavy and bulk materials should be moved the shortest distance during processing.
5.	The number of times each material is handled should be minimised.
6.	Systems flexibility should allow for unexpected breakdowns of materials handling equipments, changes in production system technology, etc.
7.	Mobile equipments should carry full loads all the times.

The seven principles can be summarized in the form of the following guide lines :

1. **Eliminate handling :** If not, make the handling distance as short as possible.
2. **Keep moving :** If not, reduce the time spent at the terminal points of a route as short as possible.
3. **Use simple patterns of material flow** (the simplest path is a straight line path of flow which minimizes the handling distance between two points). If not, reduce backtracking, crossovers and other congestion producing patterns as much as possible.
4. **Carry pay loads both ways :** If not, minimize the time spent in 'transport empty' by speed changes and route relocations.
5. **Carry full loads :** If not, consider increasing the size of unit loads, decreasing carrying capacity, lowering speed, or acquiring more versatile equipment.
6. **Use gravity :** If not, try to find another source of power that is reliable and inexpensive.

In addition to the above guidelines, there are certain other very important aspects of materials handling, such as the following :

(a) Materials handling consideration should include the movement of men, machine, tools and information.

(b) The flow system must support the objectives of receiving, sorting, inspecting, inventorying, accounting, packaging and assembling.

Since the considerations and objectives do conflict, it is essential to take a systems decision followed by delicate diplomacy to establish a material movement plan that meets service requirement without sub-ordinating safety and economy.

➤ MATERIALS HANDLING COSTS

The costs of materials handling arise from two sources: *the cost of owning and maintaining equipment* and *the cost of operating the system.* While the costs of owning the equipment are generally known since entries are available in the books of accounts, the costs of operating the handling system are elusive as records are not generally maintained.

Every effort should be made to reduce materials handling costs, particularly because they do not add any value to a product. The product will not be worth any more to the consumer simply because it was moved, but it will cost the customer more.

How to reduce handling costs? There are three fundamental ways of minimising the costs :

(a) Eliminating the handling itself whenever and wherever possible.

(b) Mechanising, largely by conveyors and power driven trucks, whatever handling still remains.

(c) Making the necessary handling more efficient.

Primary requisite for any action to be taken towards minimising handling costs is to have a record maintained for them. It is here that majority of the companies are not doing the right thing.

➤ FACTORS INFLUENCING MATERIALS HANDLING SYSTEM

Many factors such as plant layout, manufacturing process, nature of raw materials processed and products manufactured – all influence the materials handling system.

The materiasl handling activities encompass suppliers, stores, inspection, manufacturing, packaging, warehousing and transportation of finished goods to consumers. Many important decisions will have to be taken to achieve maximum overall effectiveness in materials handling. Some of these decisions are :

(i) Layout decisions – both plant layout and stores layout decisions taken based on technological considerations in consultation with materials management and materials handling departments. The objective is to reduce investment on handling equipments and also to reduce the production cycle time. Movement of materials right from the receipt of incoming raw materials to the dispatch of finished goods to warehouses or customers.

(ii) Decisions regarding selection of handling equipments, number of equipments and maximum utilisation of floor space.

Guidelines for Design and Cost Reduction of Materials Handling System

1. Eliminate materials handling wherever possible because handling adds no value to materials but increases production cycle time. No handling is ideal.
2. Sequence the operations in a logical manner so that materials handling is unidirectional and smooth.
3. Use gravity wherever possible to save power and fuel costs.
4. Standardise the handling equipments to the extent possible.
5. Install a preventive maintenance programme for materials handling equipments to minimise down time.
6. Select general purpose materials handling equipments to the extent possible and keep investment in special purpose handling equipments at a minimum.
7. Eliminate unnecessary movement and consider combination of processes while installing a materials handling system.
8. Minimise non-productive operation in handling through appropriate design of handling equipment.
9. Locate the stores close to the production centre which uses the materials to minimise materials handling.
10. Ensure that the handling equipments have inbuilt safety provisions and are safe to operate.
11. Train operators to handle the equipments properly.

➤ ORGANISATION FOR MATERIALS HANDLING

Materials handling is a job that directly affects each area in a plant, and as such requires a carefully planned organisational structure. The structure varies with the industry, the type of manufacturing process, the product manufactured, its bulk, and its value. Emphasis depends on the amount of handling required in the manufacturing process. In small firms, *for example,* the materials handling function may be one of several duties assigned to the plant engineer, the purchasing manager, or the production manager. As firms grow in size, however, an increase in specialisation is usually manifest in this area until a stage is reached where a separate department is developed to study procedures and devise better materials handling techniques. When thus organised, materials handling is a function and is often a part of the industrial engineering section. In some organisations, however, materials handling is subordinated to materials management, production, purchasing, storing or maintenance. Irrespective of which department it is subordinated to, materials handling should be centralised under one head so that an overall co-ordinated approach is possible.

➤ UNIT LOAD CONCEPT

One of the basic requirements of efficient materials handling is observance of the unit load principle, which implies that the larger the load handled, the lower the cost per unit handled.

A **unit load i**s understood as a number of items, or bulk material, so arranged that the mass can be picked up and moved as a single object, too large for manual handling. It is implied that any single object too large for manual handling is a unit load.

Simply stated, the unit load principle means that it is quicker to move a lot of items as a unit than it is to move each one of them individually. With handling equipments at our disposal, these units can be made for handling equipment size rather than man size.

In grouping materials into units many companies use skids, or pallets so that mechanical trucks can be employed to lift and move the unit. Not only do skids and pallets save time in handling materials, but goods so handled are more compact and require less floor space because they can be stacked.

The use of the principle of unit load has been so effective that many firms today are insisting that materials which they buy be supplied on a unit load basis (palletised, for example) rather than in individual units or packages.

Despite the obvious advantages, unit load has specific disadvantages which should not be ignored.

The disadvantages are :

1. Cost of unitising and de-unitising.
2. Equipment and space requirements.
3. Bare weight of unitising medium.
4. Problem of returning empty pallets or containers.
5. Transfer equipment often not available on both ends of the move.

➤ FLOW PATTERN

Another basic requirement of effective materials handling is the **planned material flow**. When drawn on paper the flow pattern becomes a flow chart which will help locate needless, crisscrossing and backtracking of materials movements. Once areas of unwanted movement are known, steps can be taken to eliminate or reduce such moves. A typical flow chart is shown in *Exhibit 14.2*.

A well conceived and carefully planned materials flow pattern will have many advantages. Some of the advantages are as follows :

1. Increased efficiency of production.
2. Better utilisation of floor space.
3. Simplified handling activities.
4. Better equipment utilisation, less idle time.
5. Reduced in-process time.
6. Reduced in-process inventory.
7. More efficient utilisation of work force.
8. Reduced product damage.

9. Reduced walking distances.
10. Minimal accident hazards.
11. Basis for an efficient layout.
12. Faster supervision.
13. Simplified production control.
14. Minimal back tracking.
15. Smooth production flow.
16. Improved scheduling process.
17. Reduced crowded conditions.
18. Better housekeeping.
19. Logical work sequence.

Exhibit 14.2 : Typical Flow Pattern of Materials

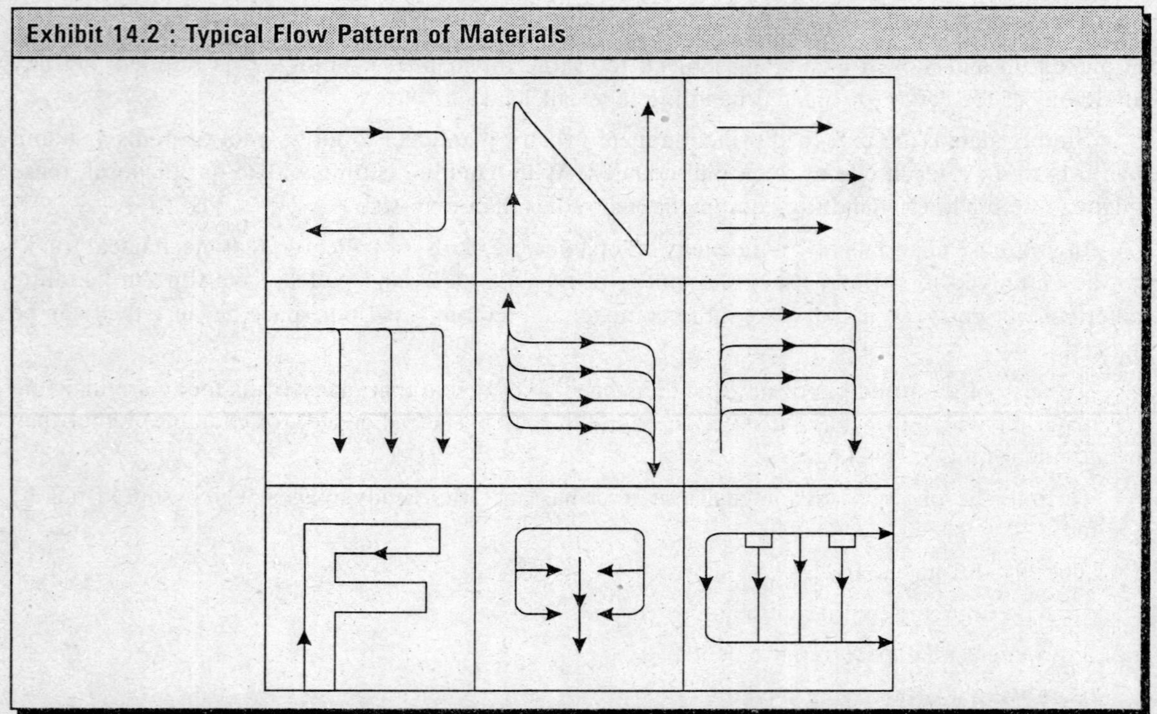

➤ PROBLEMS IN MATERIALS HANDLING

Symptoms of bad material handling are :

(i) Frequent stoppage of production for want of materials (raw materials or semiprocessed parts) due to delay in handling and moving the required materials to the point of use.

(ii) Waste of labour skills by using skilled workers to do materials handling functions such as loading, unloading, moving and storing materials.

(iv) Damages caused to materials which are handled due to negligence or use of improper handling boxes and handling equipments.

(v) Accumulation of materials of all kinds at all places waiting for movement.

(vi) Bad handling causes damages to the materials handled, thereby necessitating re-work or resulting in scrap (rejected materials due to defects caused by negligence in handling).

(vii) Congestion of floor space near the machines and work centers and near the gangways or aisles.

(viii) Congestion of space at receiving stores, holding stores, production and inspection areas.

(ix) Materials are kept waiting for a long period for want of material handling equipments to pick up and move the materials to their destinations.

➢ FACTORS AFFECTING SELECTION OF MATERIALS HANDLING EQUIPMENTS

The selection of materials handling equipment requires consideration of and attaining of proper balance between the following factors :

(i) Production problem,

(ii) The capabilities of the handling equipment available,

(iii) The human element involved.

The ultimate aim is to arrive at the lowest cost per unit of material handled.

(i) The production problem factors are :

(a) Volume of production to be attained.

(b) Class of materials to be handled.

(c) The layout of plant and building facilities.

For example, the handling equipment that can be economically justified for the manufacture of 1000 TV sets per day would be entirely different from the handling equipment needed in a plant manufacturing 20 steam turbine generators a year because the production rate, weight and class of materials needed are different.

(ii) Equipment factors to be taken into consideration include the following:

1. **Adaptability :** The load-carrying and movement characteristics of the equipment should fit the material handling problem.
2. **Flexibility :** Wherever possible, the equipment should have flexibility to handle more than one material (class or size).
3. **Load Capacity :** Equipment selected should have enough load-carrying characteristics to do the job effectively.
4. **Power :** The equipment should have enough power available to do the job.
5. **Speed :** The speed of movement of the handling equipment should be as high as possible, within the limits of production process and plant safety.
6. **Space Requirements :** The space required to instal or operate materials handling equipment is also an important consideration.
7. **Supervision Required :** The degree of automation in the handling equipment decides the amount of supervision required.
8. **Ease of Maintenance :** Equipment selected should be capable of easy maintenance at reasonable cost.
9. **Environment :** Equipment selected must conform to any environmental regulations.
10. **Cost :** The cost of the equipment (capital investment) is an obvious factor in the selection. The various kinds of costs to be considered in addition to the initial purchase price of the handling equipment are :

    (i) Operating costs

    (ii) Installation costs

    (iii) Maintenance costs

    (iv) Power requirements

(v) Insurance requirements
(vi) Space cost
(vii) Depreciation charges
(viii) Salvage value
(ix) Time value of money invested
(x) Opportunity cost.

(iii) ***The human factors cannot be overlooked in the selection of materials handling equipment. They are :***

(a) The capabilities of the available manpower to operate the equipment.
(b) Safety of personnel (those who operate it or come into contact with it).

➤ TYPES OF MATERIALS HANDLING SYSTEMS

The materials handling systems can be classified according to the type of handling equipment used, type of material handled and the methods, need or functions performed.

These classifications are :

1. *Equipment oriented systems* depending upon the type of equipment used. They are :
   (a) Overhead systems
   (b) Conveyor systems
   (c) Tractor-transfer system
   (d) Fork-lift truck and pallet truck systems
   (e) Industrial truck systems
   (f) Underground systems
2. *Material oriented systems* consisting of following types :
   (a) Unit handling systems
   (b) Bulk handling systems
   (c) Liquid handling systems.
3. *Method oriented systems* can be of the following types :
   (a) Manual systems
   (b) Mechanised or automated systems
   (c) Job-shop handling systems
   (d) Mass-production handling systems.
4. *Function oriented systems* such as
   (a) Transportation systems
   (b) Conveying systems
   (c) Transferring systems
   (d) Elevating systems

➤ SELECTION AND DESIGN OF HANDLING SYSTEM

Materials handling systems are expensive to purchase and operate. The expenses are those of initial costs, labour cost for operating the material handling equipments and maintenance and repair costs. The indirect expenses are those resulting from damaged or lost materials, delays in material deliveries and accidents. Since these expenses are quite substantial, greater attention of management is needed to the design and selection of materials handling systems.

Since the pattern of flow of materials in a plant definitely affects the material handling costs, it is vital that the design and layout of buildings must be integrated with the design of the materials-handling system. Hence, the selection and design of the material handling system should be done along with the development of the layout as each one affects the other.

For example, if overhead cranes are to be used, the structure of the building must be strong enough to support the operation of these services. If heavy loads are to be transported on trucks, floors must have adequate support to withstand these loads. Aisles or gangways must be wide enough to accommodate fork lift trucks that will travel through the areas carrying the loads. Adequate floor space has to be provided in the layout for fixed positions handling devices such as *conveyors.*

Steps to be followed in the selection and design of material handling systems are :

1. Identification of the appropriate systems.
2. Review of design criteria and objectives of the handling system.
3. Collection of data regarding flow pattern and flow requirements.
4. Identification of activity relationships between departments.
5. Determination of space requirement and establishment of material flow pattern.
6. Analysis of material and building characteristics.
7. Preliminary selection of basic handling system and generation of alternative systems considering feasibility of mechanisation and equipment capabilities.
8. Evaluation of alternatives with respect to optimal material flow, utilising gravity, minimum cost, flexibility, ease of maintenance, and capacity utilization.
9. Selection of the best suitable alternative system and checking it for compatibility with the layout.
10. Specification of the system.
11. Procurement of the equipment and installation of the system.

➤ TYPES OF MATERIALS HANDLING EQUIPMENTS

The materials handling equipments are classified into four basic types, *viz.*, conveyors, cranes and hoists, trucks and auxiliary equipment.

Conveyers

These are gravity or powered devices. Commonly used for moving loads from point to point over fixed paths. The various types of conveyors are :

(a) **Belt conveyor** – Motor driven belt, usually made of rubberised fabric or metal fabric on a rigid frame.

(b) **Chain conveyor** – Motor driven chain that drags materials along a metal slide base.

(c) **Roller conveyor** – Boxes, large parts or unit loads roll on top of a series of rollers mounted on a rigid frame. The rollers may be powered or unpowered.

(d) **Pneumatic conveyor** – High volume of air flows through a tube, carrying materials along with the air flow. The other types of conveyors are bucket conveyor, screw conveyor, pipe line conveyor, vibratory conveyor, tube conveyor, trolley conveyor and chute or gravity conveyors. Advantages of conveyors are that they do not require operators, will move a large volume of products and are inexpensive to operate. [Refer to *Exhibit 14.3*].

Cranes, Elevators and Hoists

These are overhead devices used for moving varying loads intermittently between points within an area, fixed by supporting and binding rails :

(a) *Cranes* are devices mounted on overhead rails or ground level wheels or rails. They lift, swing and transport large and heavy materials. Examples are Gantry Crane, Jib Crane and Electrically Operated Overhead Crane (E.O.T).

(b) *Elevators* are a type of cranes that lift materials - usually between floors of buildings.

(c) *Hoists* are devices which move materials vertically and horizontally in a limited area. They are used primarily when materials must be lifted prior to being moved from one point to another. Example of hoists are air hoist, electric hoist and chain hoists.

Other devices under these categories are winches, monorail and the like. [Refer to *Exhibit 14.4*].

Exhibit'14.3 : Some Conveyors in Use for Materials Handling

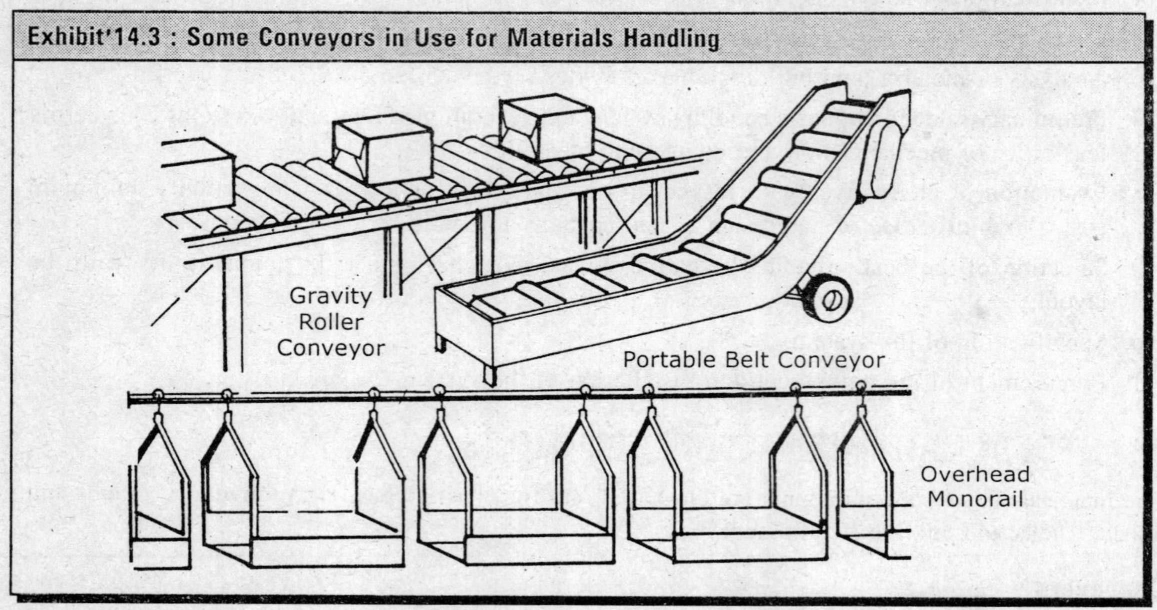

Exhibit 14.4 : Some Types of Cranes and Hoists

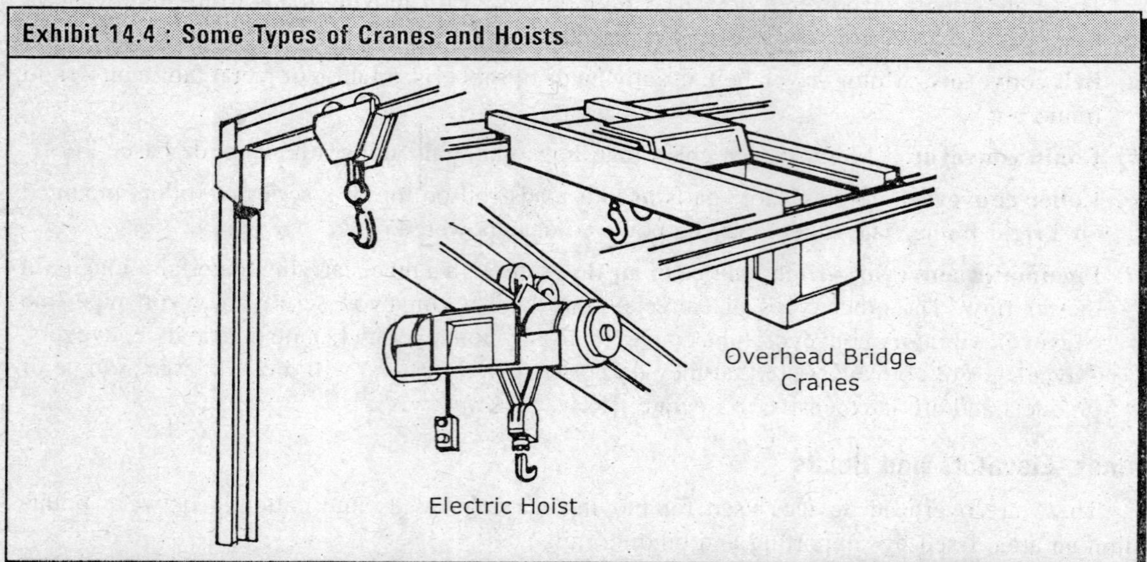

Industrial Trucks

These devices are used for moving mixed or uniform loads intermittently over variable paths. They are electric, diesel, gasoline or liquefied petroleum, gas powered vehicles equipped with beds, forks, arms or other holding devices. Examples are fork-lift trucks, pallet trucks, tractor with trailors, hand trucks and power trolleys. (Refer *Exhibit 14.5*).

Exhibit 14.5 : Trucks

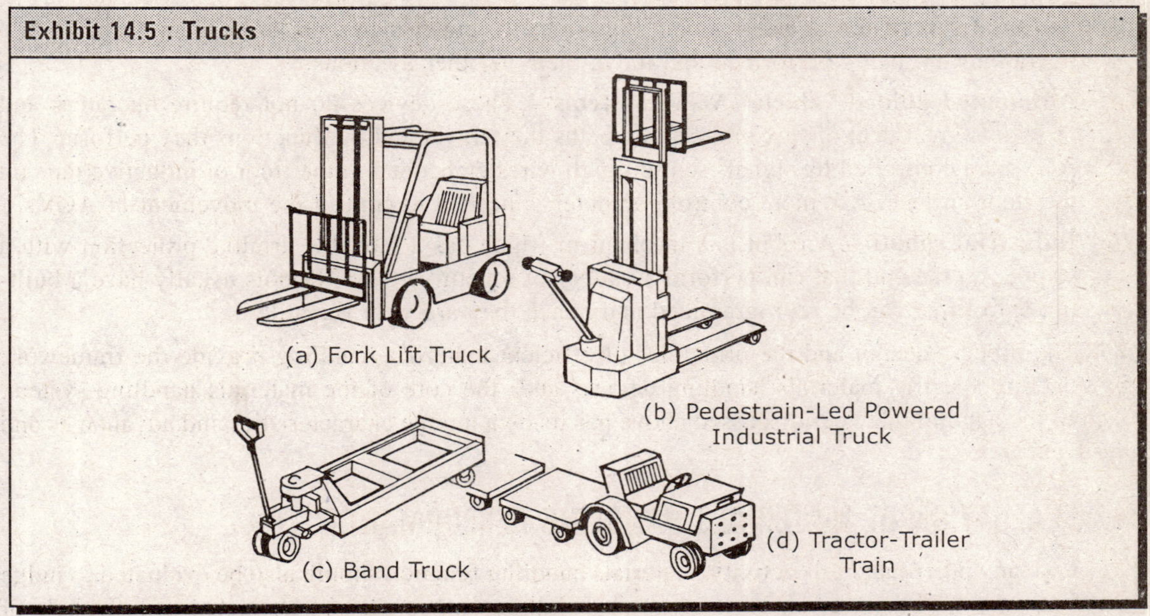

Auxiliary Equipments

These are devices or attachments used with handling equipment to make their use more effective and versatile. Examples are ramps, positioners, pallets, containers and turn tables. (Refer *Exhibit 14.6*).

Exhibit 14.6 : Auxiliary Equipments

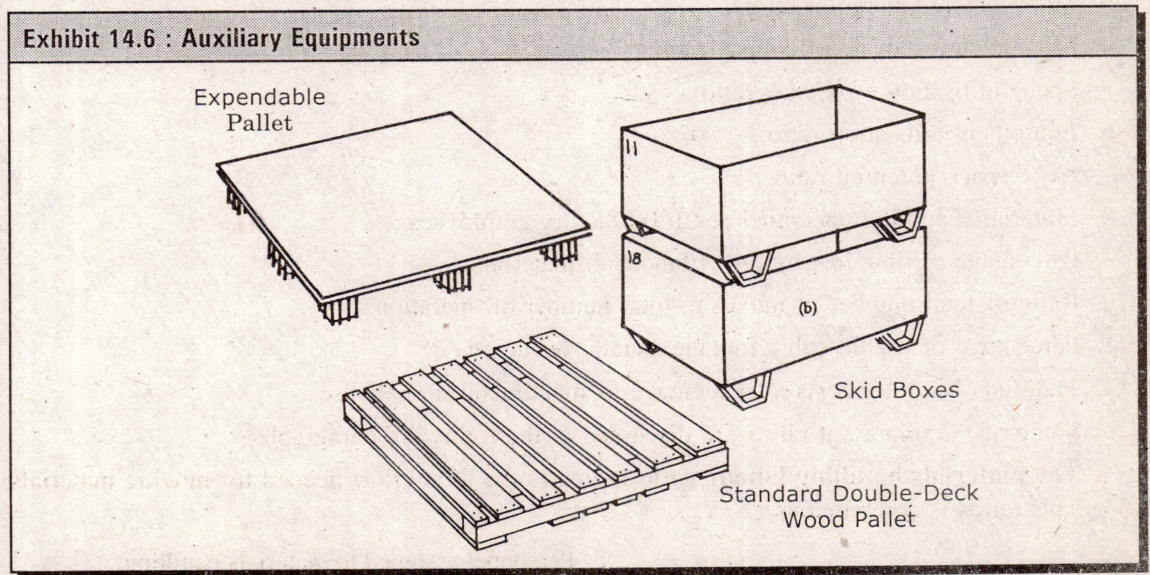

➤ MISCELLANEOUS HANDLING EQUIPMENTS

(i) **Pipe lines** which are closed tubes that transport liquids by means of pumps or gravity.

(ii) **Automatic transfer** *devices* which automatically grasp materials, hold them firmly while operations are being performed and move them to other locations.

(iii) **Automated guided vehicle (AGV) systems** – These devices do not require operators and provide a great deal of flexibility in the paths they travel and the functions they perform. The AGVs are controlled by signals sent through wires embedded in the floor or inductive tape on the floor surface. A remote control computer is needed to control the movement of AGVs.

(iv) **Industrial robots** – A robot is a mechanism which has a movable armlike projection with a gripper on the end that can perform a variety of repetitive tasks. Robots usually have a built-in control that can be reprogrammed and hence they are very versatile.

The process design and the principles of efficient materials handling provide the framework for selecting specific materials handling devices and the core of the materials handling system. Each of the handling devices discussed above has its own unique characteristics and advantages and disadvantages.

➤ EVALUATION OF MATERIALS HANDLING PERFORMANCE

Like any other materials activity, materials handling function should also be evaluated to judge its effectiveness. The performance of materials handling function can be evaluated with the help of several ratios such as the following :

1. Materials handling labour ratio.
2. Direct labour handling ratio.
3. Management/Operation ratio.
4. Manufacturing cycle efficiency ratio.
5. Space utilisation efficiency ratio.
6. Equipment utilisation ratio.
7. Aisle space potential ratio.
8. Materials handling personnel per 1000 factory employees.
9. Percentage of time lost by direct labour in materials.
10. Ratio of total number of moves to total number of operations.
11. Percentage of usable cubic footage usually occupied.
12. Materials handling costs as percentage of manufacturing expenses.

Some of the important ratios are discussed in the following paragraphs :

(i) **The materials handling labour ratio** indicates the total effort needed for moving materials. This ratios is computed as :

$$\text{Materials handling labour ratio (MHL)} = \frac{\text{Personnel assigned to materials handling}}{\text{Total opreating work force}}$$

(ii) **Direct labour handling loss ratio** helps to ascertain whether the handling system delivers materials to work centres with maximum efficiency. This ratio is calculated as :

$$\text{Direct labour handling loss ratio} = \frac{\text{Materials handling time lost by direct labour}}{\text{Total direct labour time}}$$

(iii) The equipment utilisation ratio is computed and compared with similar firms or in the same firm over a period of time. It is an important indicator to judge the effectiveness of materials handling system.

(iv) The ratio of total number of moves to total number of operations (referred to as movement's operations ratio) indicates whether the workers are executing too many motions (or movements) because of poor routing.

(v) The ratio of materials handling personnel to total operating force indicates the extent of labour cost expended for handling of materials.

➤ EFFICIENCY IN HANDLING MATERIALS

Materials handling is a necessary evil. It adds to the *cost* of the product and not much to the *value* of the product. The cost of materials handling is quite considerable and affects the efficiency and cost of production. Hence, materials handling is an important area for reducing costs and improving productivity. For this, the materials handling system should be designed to maximise efficiency in handling and minimise handling costs. The movement of materials should be kept to the minimum possible. In addition to the elimination of unnecessary handling and rehandling of materials, the essential movements should be mechanised or automated to the extent possible in order to increase the efficiency of handling materials.

The efficiency of materials handling system depends upon : *(i)* efficiency of handling methods employed for a unit weight through a unit distance, *(ii)* efficiency of the shop layout and plant layout which determines the distance through which the materials have to be moved, *(iii)* utilisation of handling equipments, *(iv)* efficiency of the speed of handling.

The efficiency of the handling system is judged by the costs of handling materials. The material handling costs can be classified into :

(i) labour cost – direct labour, purchasing and maintenance employees.

(ii) space cost – storage, production, offices, gangways.

(iii) handling equipments – interest on capital, depreciation and maintenance spares.

(iv) storage equipments – bins, racks, pallets etc.

Efficiency in materials handling can be achieved by minimisation of : *(i)* bottlenecks and breakdowns, *(ii)* misuse of space, *(iii)* under utilisation of labour (materials handling equipment operators), *(iv)* poor customer service and *(v)* breakage and spoilage of materials.

Steps that may be taken to improve efficiency in material handling are as below :

(i) **Mechanisation :** Use of mechanical devices helps to reduce materials handling costs. But, to be cost effective, the savings in handling costs should cover the cost of owning and maintaining the handling equipments.

(ii) **Better Systems Design :** The production system comprising the plant layout and materials handling system can be designed well by using method study techniques to minimise materials handling distance and time.

(iii) **Effective Organisation Structure :** An efficient organisational structure facilitates co-ordination between production department personnel, materials handling personnel and materials management personnel.

Further to the above, careful and mechanical handling (instead of manual handling), use of existing handling facilities and speed in handling materials-all help to improve efficiency in materials handling.

➤ RELATIONSHIP BETWEEN PLANT LAYOUT AND MATERIALS HANDLING

Materials handling and plant layout are very closely related to each other. The materials handling system is an integral part of the plant layout and shop layout. The materials handling method has a direct influence on the shop layout, plant layout and design of factory buildings. A good materials handling system should ensure smooth flow of materials, preferably in a straight line path and the total materials handling distance and time should be kept as low as possible. This is facilitated by judicial arrangement of machines and equipments, proper location of various departments related to one another, a logical sequence of operations within the department, the location of stores and tool cribs at convenient places. While designing the shop layout and plant layout, adequate provisions should be made for aisles, storage space near the machines and equipments for intermittent storage of semiprocessed goods, storage space at the inspection area, receiving and shipping of materials etc. The overhead space must be provided for installation of electrically operated overhead travelling cranes (EOT crane), Gantry cranes etc. Also, adequate space should be provided near machines for the installation of jib cranes for loading heavy jobs, on the machines and unloading the same. In assembly shops or paint shops, conveyors may be installed for handling the materials. For multi storey buildings elevators or lifts must be provided. Because of all these requirements we can say that **materials handling system is an integral part of the production system**.

Materials Handling System in Process Layouts

The materials handling system used in process layouts should have high degree of flexibility *i.e.,* flexibility of path of movement of materials and flexibility of size, weight and volume of the load being handled. In general, tractor with trailer, power trolleys, fork lift trucks, pallet trucks, cranes are the handling equipments which are used in process layouts. Overhead cranes are used to transport and position large, heavy jobs within a fixed area in the manufacturing shops. Jib cranes are used for loading and unloading of heavy jobs while carrying out the operations on the machines. However, it may be noted that in a process layout, since the route or path of flow of materials depend on the sequence of operations and as the equipments are not laid out as per the sequence of operation, the materials handling distance, time and cost will be higher than that in the product or line layout.

Materials Handling in Product or Line Layouts

In product layouts usually special purpose machines and equipments are used and these are laid out as per the sequence of operations adjacent to each other. Materials usually flow in straight ine paths. The type of materials handling equipments used are different types of conveyors. Sometimes operations can be combined with movement (*for example,* spray painting and stoving in the furnace ater).

SAFETY IN MATERIALS HANDLING

Since about two-thirds of the general causes of accidents are directly related to materials handling, safety in materials handling is a major concern of production managers and safety engineers. The considerations for safe handling of materials are as follows :

(i) Instal adequate guards and safety devices on handling equipments.

(ii) Keep handling equipments in good operating conditions.

(iii) Replace manual handling by mechanised handling for difficult, hazarduous handling activities.

(iv) Do not permit the handling equipments to be overloaded or operated beyond rated capacity.

(v) Keep aisles clear and uncluttered.

(vi) Avoid congestion of materials.

(vii) Maintain adequate lighting.

(viii) Maintain floors in good condition.

(ix) Provide good house keeping.

(x) Stack materials carefully.

(xi) Train operators in properly operating the handling equipments.

(xii) Highlight handling hazard or danger zones.

REVIEW QUESTIONS

1. Define the term "materials handling".
2. State the functions of materials handling.
3. Discuss the relevance of materials handling to materials management function.
4. Discuss the scope of materials handling.
5. State the importance of materials handling.
6. State the objectives of materials handling.
7. State the principles of materials handling.
8. Discuss the various kinds of costs associated with materials handling.
9. What is "unit load" concept? What are its advantages and disadvantages?
10. "A well conceived and carefully planned materials flow pattern will have many advantages"? Elaborate.
11. Discuss the factors affecting the selection of materials handling equipments.
12. Explain briefly the various types of materials handling systems and equipments used.
13. Explain the steps involved in the selection and design of materials handling systems.
14. How do you evaluate the efficiency of materials handling performance?

15. Explain what is meant by efficiency in handling materials.
16. Discuss the relationship between plant layout and materials handling.
17. Explain the special features of materials handling equipments used in process layouts and product layouts.
18. Explain what is meant by safety in materials handling.

ANNEXURES

ANNEXURE I

SNAPSHOTS OF MATERIALS AND LOGISTICS MANAGEMENT

1. MATERIALS MANAGEMENT IN A NATIONAL RETAIL STATIONERY ORGANISATION

ABC Inc. has several hundred retail shops through out the country. Each shop sells stationary items, toys and some confectionary, but mainly books and magazines. The company maintains a central national materials administration directorate operating from the corporate head quarters. The director-materials management and his staff are responsible for the acquisition of all products sold through the retail branches, their delivery to the three warehouses, their stocking in the warehouses, subsequent distribution to the shops, retail stock at shops; point-of-sale display and local promotion of items. All the retail shops offer the same stock lines and all shops must obtain their entire supplies from the company's warehouses. A catalog is available offering a limited part of this range on mail orders to customers. Mail orders are met directly from one of the warehouses through a mail order distribution function, which is also the responsibility of the director-materials management.

The regional staff of the director-materials management liase with retail branches in various areas. These staff operate from the warehouse locations. They are primarily responsible to advice local retail shop managers of merchandising policy, new product lines which are to be introduced, local and point-of-sale promotion requirements.

A centralized computer-based system for materials records is established. Point-of-sale return are made directly from check-out counters to retail branch stock records and from there to warehouse records on a weekly basis. Deliveries are made to retail shops on a weekly basis.

(*Source:* Ray Wild – *Operations Management*, p. 547, Thomson Asia Pvt. Ltd. Singapore)

2. INVENTORY MANAGEMENT ALONG IBM'S SUPPLY CHAIN

IBM is the largest producer of computer software, hardware and services in the world. Its supply chain is made up of manufacturing locations linked with tens of thousands of suppliers and distribution channels around the world. A single product line of IBM may involve thousands of parts and components with varied lead times and costs and upto hundreds of manufacturing and distribution sites connected by different modes of transportation. In the year 1994, faced with increasing competition and rapid technological advances, IBM began a reengineering program to stream line its global supply chain in order to improve the flow of material and information. The focus of the reengineering effort was on improving customer satisfaction and IBM's competitiveness by increasing the speed, reliability and efficiency with which it delivers its products to the market place. The key objectives related to inventory management were *(i)* to set strategic inventory and customer – service targets *(ii)* to optimize inventory allocation and placement and *(iii)* to reduce inventory while meeting customer targets.

The IBM personal systems group (PSG) which is responsible for the development, manufacture, sale and service of personal computers, employs 18,500 workers with manufacturing plants in the US, Latin America, Europe and Asia. In 1998, PSG sold approximately 7.7 million computers. Faced with stiff competition from PC manufacturers like Dell and Gateway, which sells computers to customers direct and built-to-order, PSG felt the need to redesign its supply chain. One of the objectives was to determine the safety stock inventory for each product at each locations in the supply chain in order to minimize the investment in total inventory. By redesigning the supply chain, PSG was able to reduce its overall inventory by 50 percent from 1998 to 1999 without affecting customer service. This resulted with savings of more than 100 million dollars. The other improvements achieved by IBM were *(i)* reduction of time between parts procurement and actual sales by 4 to 6 weeks which resulted in additional annual cost savings of 650 million dollars, *(ii)* as a result of the system implementation, IBM was able to determine the level of service it should promise to customers based on the accuracy of their forecasts.

(*Source:* Roberta S. Russel, Bernard W. Taylor III, *Operations Management*, 4th Edn., Pearson Education)

3. INVENTORY MANAGEMENT AT WAL-MART

Wal-Mart manages its inventory with precision on a grand scale and many other companies both domestic and foreign seek Wal-Mart's advice on inventory taking.

For Wal-Mart, preparation to check its inventory takes four to six weeks. Wal-Mart's internal audit department sends a preparation kit to each store forty five days in advance. It contains detailed instructions, including 13 schedules.

The team involved in inventory taking consists of 18 to 40 independent auditors and representatives of the company's operations divisions and departments of loss prevention and internal audit.

At randomly selected stores, employees of internal auditors for Wal-Mart are present to test accuracy by recounting.

An inventory is taken between 8 am and 6 pm while the store is open to customers, Immediately after the inventory checking is completed the physical count team reconciles its finding with the book inventory. The results are reviewed later by the internal audit department.

Inventory checking is undertaken every 11 to 13 months and mostly from March through September. The job can be made no easier by the fact that Wal-Mart's inventory turns over 4.5 times a year (competitors average about 2.8 turns) and its stores carry between 60,000 to 90,000 specific types of merchandise.

Between physical counts, Wal-Mart employs a perpetual system that records, at the time of sale, the cost and quantity of goods sold. This reveals the cost and/or quantity of goods sold since the beginning of the current period and of goods that are on hand at any given time.

(*Source:* Richard B. Chase, F. Robert Jacobs, Nicholas J. Aquilano, Nitin. K Agarwal. *Operations Management*, 11th Edition, Tata Mc-Graw Hill Publishing Company Limited).

4. REDUCING THE NEED FOR SAFETY STOCKS IN THE FASHION APPAREL INDUSTRY

"Hi-Fi" fashion apparels design and manufactures fashion skiwear that is sold by more than 800 retailers throughout the U.S. Recurring problems in this business are *(i)* running out of stock in the 'hot' items and *(ii)* having an excess stock in the slow-moving items at the end of the selling season. Because the garments produced by 'Hi-Fi' are fashion items, they can not be profitably carried from one year to the next. As a result, 95 percent of its products are new each year and the company is under pressure to do anything it can do to reduce the need for safety stocks.

"Hi-Fi" used two levers to reduce the need for safety stocks:

(i) It reduced the uncertainty in its forecast by inviting 25 of its largest retailers each February to its manufacturing site to evaluate its new line of garments. Early orders from these key retailers enabled "Hi-Fi" to forecast national demand for each product with a margin of error of only 10 percent.

(ii) "Hi-Fi" launched an effort to reduce its lead times in purchasing materials and manufacturing the garments. Long lead times forced "Hi-Fi" to commit to products well before February so that it could ship them to retailers by end September. However the forecast were not ready until February. "Hi-Fi" found that shipping products from Asian factories at the end of September to retail stores by early October on a rush basis costs Rs. 25,000 per day. Hence each day saved in the lead time of products was worth Rs. 25,000. Employees were asked to find ways to reduce lead time and they responded with many ideas. One idea involved using express-mail at a cost of Rs. 250/- to get design information to a plant manager in Hong Kong rather than using standard mail service, saving many days in lead time. Shortening lead time offered "Hi-Fi" the luxuary of delaying orders until better demand forecast were available.

(*Source:* Lee J. Krajewski, Larry P. Ritzman, *"Operations Management"*, 5th Edn., Addison-Welsley)

5. MRP HELPS PLASCO INC REDUCE COSTS AND IMPROVE SERVICE

Plasco Inc, a firm of 170 employees, produces plastic components and products for the health-care industry that require radio frequency sealing of plastic film. The products include a variety of drainage bags and other medical devices sold under contract to about 100 different original equipment manufacturers. The company produces 150 different products each month, each with an average of 30 different components. Plasco had installed a small main-frame computer to run its accounting operations. This computer system was inadequate for manufacturing purposes and could not be used for tracking of individual products through the shop. All costs such as labour and raw materials were computed on a company-wide basis. Consequently, determining the cost of each product and its contribution to profits was difficult. Also forecasting labour needs was problematic. It was difficult to estimate the length of time required for processing an order. Production schedules based on estimate of processing time might require more or less employees than the company had on the pay roll, often leading to an imbalance of work loads between departments. Finally, maintaining an appropriate level of inventory was difficult because estimating future requirements was erratic. Consequently, high levels of inventory and stock-outs were common. There was too much inventory of some items and not enough of others.

Therefore, the management of Plasco decided to establish a comprehensive manufacturing management system to enable the company remain competitive and grow, Thus Plasco installed an

MRP system which helped the company to realize some benefits. When an order for a finished product is scheduled into production, the MRP system automatically produces orders for all the needed components and schedules the people and equipment to meet e realistic due date. The system tracks each order through the shop. The system allows management to assign high priority to some orders to facilitate the processing of the 'hot' ones. By knowing the requirement for materials with greater accurracy Plasco was able to reduce raw materials inventories by 25 percent and labour requirements by 10 percent. In addition customer relations improved because of the company's ability to provide delivery dates with more reliability

6. STANDARDISATION HELPS FORD MOTORS TO CUT COSTS

The Ford Motor Company exceeded its original goal of cutting out one billion dollars in costs in 1997. One major chunk of savings resulted from worker suggestions for improving productivity. Another major chunk came from the use of standard parts – using the same parts in different models. Not only did this reduce design and assembly costs, it reduced the number of different parts held in inventory and simplified record keeping. At the same time it increased production flexibility, Beyond that, standard parts help reduce the chance of experiencing stock-out situations which can result in costly shutdowns at assembly plants and also standard parts mean dealers don't have to carry as many different replacement parts

(*Source:* William J. Stevenson, *Operations Management*, 8th Edn., Tata McGraw-Hill Edition)

7. XEROX'S EUROPEAN LOGISTICS SUCCESS

In Europe, Xerox meets its customers' needs for new product, suppliers and maintenance through a central distribution centre in Venray, the Netherlands. Including older machines, Xerox estimates it must maintain a 1,00,000 – item catalog to meet customer requirements. The company uses air transport for priority shipments. To meet the needs of a more unified Europe, Xerox has entered into long-term alliances with surface carriers which transport copiers and replacement parts. These contracts include provisions for a common tracking system for inventory management. Xerox estimates that 80 percent of all repairs and parts deliveries can be performed within one day, 98 percent by the second day and 100 percent by the third day. The company's goal is to improve its performance to 98 percent within one day.

Xerox sees its European logistics systems as a model for those in the US and eventually in all its markets around the globe. The company aims to establish a new manufacturing plant near its Venray distribution centre. Its benchmarking approach focuses on qualitative measurements of logistics and over-all corporate performance, including responsiveness to customers, profitability and return on assets. Plans call for establishing a build-to-order/direct delivery system for manufacturing and transportation and linking this electronically with Xerox management, suppliers, shippers and customers. The company estimates that its progress toward this goal has reduced its inventory from 25 percent to 14 percent of sales revenue.

As a large and complex multinational firm, Xerox has shown the value of combining **integrated logistics, advanced information technology** and **customer-responsive management** to prosper in a fast changing global market place, The Company appears well positioned to meet the challenges of a unified Europe.

(Source: Douglas M. Lambert, James R. Stock, Lisa M. Ellram, *"Fundamentals of Logistics Management"*, International Edition, 1998, Irwin McGraw-Hill)

8. SUPPLY CHAIN MANAGEMENT AT DELL COMPUTER CORPORATION

The Dell Computer Corporation, a mass customiser of personal computers, is experiencing phenomenal growth and profitability in an industry that traditionally has low profit margins. In 1996 sales increased by 71 percent and because of Dell's low-cost style manufacturing and marketing operations, profits shot up by 91 percent. With this success Dell rose to 3rd position among P.C. makers ahead of Packard-Bell, NEC and Apple Computer. What is Dell's secret? In a single word – **'speed'** . A customer order for a customized computer can be on a delivery truck in 36 hours. This capability allows Dell to keep parts costs and inventories low – 13 days of sales versus 25 for Compaq – thereby enabling it to sell at prices 10 to 15 percent below those of competitors.

A primary factor in filling customers' orders is Dell's **manufacturing operations** and the **performance of its suppliers**. Dell's manufacturing process is flexible enough to delay the ordering of components and the assembly of components until an order is booked. In addition, Dells' warehousing plan calls for the bulk of its components to be warehoused within 15 minutes of its Austin (Texas), Limerick (Ireland) and Penang (Malaysia) Plants. To accomplish this feat. Dell selected suppliers who were committed to the warehousing plan, now numbering 74 companies, down from 204 companies in 1992. At its Austin plant, Dell doesn't really have to order the components because the suppliers restock the warehouse and manage their own inventories. Dell uses these components as needed and is not billed for them until they leave the warehouse. This system of suppliers and manufacturing operations has proven to be a great advantage for Dell over competitors. For example if Compaq suddenly needed a supply of components from its warehouse, 12 to 18 hours would be required to get them, at IBM two days would be needed. For Dell, only few minutes are required.

Dell's efficient operations carry over to service providers who also are used to lower costs and reduced lead time. For example Dell might send an e-mail message to UPS requesting that a computer monitor be sent to a particular customer as part of a purchased computer system. UPS pulls a monitor from the monitor supplier's stock and schedules it to arrive with the PC, saving Dell shipping and inventory costs.

Such careful management of the materials and services from the suppliers through production to the customers lets Dell operate more efficiently than any other computer manufacturer.

(*Source:* Lee J. Krajewski, Larry P. Ritzman, *'Operations Management'*, 5th Edn., Addison-Wesley)

9. E-PROCUREMENT AT LAMINATED PRODUCTS

For Laminated products, a manufacturer of laminated counter tops and other fixtures, machine uptime is a critical factor in the company's performance. This outs pressure on the plant's maintenance department to have the right parts available when needed.

To keep the facility at peak , laminated products has an inventory of $80,000 worth of spare parts. Before using "**i Procure**" there was no system in place for monitoring parts inventory levels.

Tracking inventory used to be a big problem to the supervisor of maintenance department of laminated products. There was no system at all. The company needed an integrated system to track inventory in order to reduce the risk of running out of crucial parts and delaying production.

With the installation of "**i Procure**", Laminated Products achieved a unified purchasing system. Budgeting became easier and more accurate. The easier practice was to process purchase orders in batches (as many as 10 to 12 orders per batch) and to fax these purchase orders to suppliers, which used to take a lot of time. Now to purchase electronically through "**i Procure**" takes only a few seconds.

Other benefits of "**i Procure**" are lower prices and a solid list of suppliers. The maintenance supervisor is pleased with the suppliers available through "**i Procure**" and their willingness to sell at competitive prices and to search for parts they do not regularly carry. The suppliers are very flexible. They are willing to work with Laminated Products to get the right part when needed.

(*Source:* Ray Wild, *Operations Management*, 6th Edn., Thomson Asia Pvt. Ltd., Singapore)

10. INDIA'S 21-DAY DISADVANTAGE

The conference room has a busy, workman's look about it, with a long table in the centre. Around, on the two of the walls hang shirts with premium labels; Abercrombie and Fitch, Nordstrom, Tommy Hilfiger and Hugo Boss. Through the large, sealed window, is the familiar Shanghai Sprawl of skyscrapers stretching across. It's raining outside.

We are in the China sales offices of the $500 million Esquel, a Hong Kong-headquartered shirt maker, among the world's largest. Rebecca, a young merchandiser of Taiwanese origin, is taking my friend Vijay through a corporate presentation .She mentions, by the way, that her founder, Marjorie Yang, was voted one of the most powerful women business leaders in the world by Fortune. Yang is also MIT and Harvard educated.

The next slide is on Esquel's production (60 million shirts) facilities. I notice their largest manufacturing plant is in Gaoming, near Guangzhou, on the east coast. The plant employs some 21,000 workers. The rest are in Malaysia, Vietnam, Mauritus and even Sri Lanka. "I can understand they are big in China but how come they are not in India", I ask Vijay, who wants to import Esquel's yarn –dyed (a specialty) fabric for Indian garment makers.

The next day we visit Syed, a GAP Inc "converter" or fabric source, in another Shanghai office block. Right next to one of the city's six elevated roads. Translated, It's a 14-km, six-lane flyover that runs above the city. Syed hails interestingly, from one-time textile city Davangere in Karnataka. Trained as an engineer, he went to Dubai 14 years ago but wandered into textiles and fabrics.

Syed says only 20 percent of his fabric consignments head for India. The rest go all over the region, including Bangladesh and Sri Lanka. "Why is India not a bigger buyer, particularly in this post quota world,: I ask him. Syed takes a pen and paper. "We work mostly with the big brands. Their lead times are small and orders big. And a garment manufacturer in India will find it tough. Assuming he has the capacity," he says.

Why is that, I ask, "Compounded delays," says Syed. A consignment of fabric can take up to 25 days to reach the manufacturer in India, particularly in Mumbai or Delhi, compared to 15 in Sri Lanka. Customs clearance can be tricky. IT might be three days in Chennai but upwards of 10 days in Mumbai. Depending on whether you have a full container or not. And then comes the long march; negotiating inter-state barriers, octroi check points, and bad roads.

Moreover, Syed says the containers don't come straight to India. Mostly, they are trans-shipped (transferred from one vessel to another) in Singapore or Colombo. Like I was on my Singapore Airlines flight back to Mumbai. "But why Colombo," I ask, "Well, they have a bigger and more efficient port, he explains. Anyway, that's another two-three days lost. And additional costs. And it's the same story on the outbound, though time at the customs is less".

So that's one reason companies like Esquel are in Colombo and not in India. And Syed is exporting there. Customs clearance is brisk both ways, the garment factories are close by and labour, like the rest of the region, is cheap. Not to mention flexible. "But we are managing, aren't we, "I ask Syed, thinking of all the IPO-fuelled expansion plans of the Indian garment makers.

"Of course," he replies, But then it is about the opportunity lost. China exports almost ten times as many garments as India. But lost opportunity is only part of the problem. Says Syed," you have to remember the supply chain is always getting shorter and tighter". Deliveries are usually expected with 120 to 150 days of placing an order. Some-times less. Depending upon the kind of fabric and whether it's in stock. And the order size.

Syed says that increasingly, big brands in the US and Europe are creating "fast track" segments. Like demanding that 15 percent of the total order must be delivered within 60 days. "That's not possible for an Indian garment maker to match, even with locally sourced fabric." Though a garment maker based out of Sri Lanka could potentially deliver, he says.

As we leave Syed's office and proceed for an Indian lunch, I collect my thoughts. **An Indian garment exporter will almost always be at a 15 to 21 day logistics disadvantage**. Come to think of it, it's the same reason Intel has to think so much before investing in an Indian chip fab. It's one thing to invest for local growth, another **to create a cog in a smoothly turning global supply chain wheel**.

A multi-location garment maker, like Esquel, will hesitate to put India on its global manufacturing map. Not surprisingly, there is little or no foreign direct investment in this sector. And thus more jobs. As long as it takes weeks to clear customs and days to transport the product from the ports to the factories. So, the bad news is that customs and procedures are one of the key causes for the delays. That's the good news as well. Revamping should be simpler than building infrastructure.

(*Source:* Govindraj Ethiraj, Business Standard, dated 2nd May 2006)

ANNEXURE II

CASE STUDIES

1. TOUGH TYRE COMPANY

Ganesh has realized that his distribution operation is consistently carrying too much inventory. He is considering seriously implementing some sort of inventory system to reduce inventory.

Tough Tyre Company is a small distributor of radial tyres. It is composed of three retail outlets and one warehouse. The warehouse buys its supply of tyres directly from the factory and supplies only the three retail outlets. Also the three dealers buy only from tough tyre company's warehouse.

Table *(1)* below shows last year's demand for tyres by month for the three dealers. The demand has remained fairly constant over the last three years. The variations in demand are random rather than seasonal or part of a trend.

Table *(2)* shows the result of a study done last year to determine inventory costs for the dealers and the warehouse.

Table (1) : Demand for Tyres of Tough Tyre Company			
Month	Dealer		
	A	B	C
January	4000	6000	5000
February	3000	8000	4000
March	2000	4000	9000
April	6000	3000	6000
May	8000	5000	2000
June	6000	3000	6000
July	3000	4000	8000
August	2000	5000	8000
September	4000	6000	5000
October	3500	6500	5000
November	2500	3500	9000
December	6000	6000	3000

Table (2) : Inventory costs (Tough Tyre Company)			
Dealer	Ordering cost/ Order	Inventory carrying cost per tyre/year	Lead time (months)
A	Rs. 90	Rs. 1.60	1
B	Rs. 45	Rs. 2.20	1
C	Rs. 60	Rs. 0.90	1
Warehouse	Rs. 150	Rs. 0.75	2

Ganesh expects that the demand and cost estimates shown in these two tables are representative of what will happen in the future.

Questions

1. Discuss the nature of the problem faced by Ganesh in his distribution operations.
2. What would you recommend that Ganesh do to develop a new inventory system for the dealers and the warehouse, assuming that the existing system is based on just an educated guess

2. 'XYZ' MANUFACTURING. INC

XYZ Manufacturing Inc produces a range of health-care appliances for hospital as well as for home use. The company has experienced a steady demand for its products, which are highly regarded in the health-care field.

Recently the company has undertaken a review of its inventory ordering procedures as part of a large effort to reduce costs.

One of the company's products is a blood sugar testing kit. XYZ manufactures all of the components for the kit in-house except for the digital display unit. The display units are ordered at six-week intervals from the supplier. The ordering cost is Rs. 50 per order. The company assembles 100 kits a week. Also the carrying cost is the Rs. 8 for each display unit.

The supplier has been quite reliable with deliveries, orders are received in five working days after they are faxed to the supplier. There is no variation in the lead time.

Questions

1. Would using another order interval other than every six weeks reduce costs? If so what order interval would be the best, and what order size would that involve?
2. Would you recommend changing to the optimal order interval? Explain.

3. INVENTORY CONTROL AT WHEELED COACH

Controlling inventory was one of the toughest problem faced by Wheeled Coach. Its management operated according to a strategy of *mass customization* and *quick response* and knew that the success of their strategy depends on strict inventory control. Lack of tight inventory control would result in an inability to deliver promptly, problems on the assembly line and huge inventory investment. It was found that almost 50 percent of the cost of the vehicle is bought-out materials. A major portion of that 50 percent is in chassis (purchased from Ford), aluminium (from Reynolds Metal) and plywood used for flooring and cabinet construction (from local suppliers) These 'A' category items were tracked carefully, maintaining tight security/control and ordering carefully so as to maximize quantity discounts while minimizing on-hand inventory.

Aluminium has to be ordered as much as 8 months in advance because of the long lead time and scheduling needs of Reynolds Metal.

Wheeled Coach is the only giant in the ambulance industry and its 45 competitors do not have the purchasing power to draw the same discounts as Wheeled Coach. But Wheeled Coach resorts to cycle counting in their stores. All items must appear in the bill of materials before issuing them to production.

Accurate bill of materials are a must for products to be built on time. Further, because of the custom nature of each vehicle, most orders are won only after a bidding process. Accurate bill of materials are critical to cost estimation and the resulting bid. Therefore Wheeled Coach maintains outstanding inventory control.

Questions

1. Explain how Wheeled Coach implements ABC analysis.
2. If you were to take over as inventory control manager at Wheeled Coach, what additional policies and techniques would you initiate to ensure accurate inventory records?
3. How would you go about implementing these suggestions?

(Source: Jay Heizer, Barry Render, *Operations Management*, 8th Edn., Pearson Education)

4. G.R. GRILLS' INVENTORY PROBLEM

G.R.Grills is an old-line company which has recently switched over to a new product line-electric barbecue grills, with five models of grills it sells nationally. For many years the company maintained a single warehouse from which it supplied to its distributors.

The plant where the company produces the grills is located in a small town and employs many workers for many years.

During the company's transition to the new product line, many loyal employees worked on week end holidays without pay to help with changing over the plant and learning the new skills they would need. Therefore, the president of the company took a decision not to lay-off any workers and maintain steady rate of output with the current level of human resources.

But as the demand for grills was seasonal, steady rate of output would result in excess inventories at times even though on an annual basis, output matches sales.

Inventory is handled by a system of four warehouses. There is a central warehouse located near the plant which supplies some customers directly and the three regional warehouses.

The director of sales is not happy with the current inventory system. He refers to the increasing complaints firm regional sales managers about poor customer service, orders going unfilled or getting delayed to be filled, apparently due to shortages at the regional warehouses. Regional warehouse managers have responded to these complaints by increasing their order sizes from the central warehouse and maintaining larger amounts of safety stock. This has resulted in inventory holding costs but it has not eliminated the problem.

The regional warehouse managers complain that their orders to the central warehouse are not being shipped in time or smaller quantities are shipped against the quantities requested by them. The central warehouse manager gives preference to filling direct orders from actual customers rather than warehouse orders which are viewed as mainly replenishment orders to maintain safety stock levels in regional warehouses. But the regional warehouse managers feel that their orders are neglected even though they are the biggest customers of the central warehouse.

The sales director observed that items that were out of stock at one regional warehouse are in ample supply in at least one other regional warehouse.

Questions

1. Analyse the problems faced by G.R.Grills in the area of inventory management.
2. Assuming that you are a consultant hired by the CEO of the company, what recommendations can you make to over come the problems the company is encountering.

5. TASTY-FOOD PRODUCTS

Tasty-Food Products established in 1980, distributes a 100 item product line of canned vegetables, fruits, condiments and speciality items (such as pappads, fruit jams and pickles) to wholesalers in several states of South India.

Tasty-food products introduced a new customer-order policy to improve its service to its wholesalers and also the effectiveness of its sales representatives. Two important features of this program are *(i)* sales people are free from the work of order taking and *(ii)* orders received from wholesalers on a predetermined schedule.

The company's sales representatives are no longer to process customer orders. Earlier practice was to accumulate wholesale orders until they had enough volume to make up a truck load and then send the orders to the head office. Under the new program, wholesalers are to e-mail their orders directly to the head-office as per a fixed schedule (say once in a month or so). If the wholesalers miss their fixed date they have to wait for the next fixed date as per schedule.

These procedures are designed to increase the number of sales calls the sales people could make to their customers. The assumption is that sales people would spend more time determining the sales patterns and the effect of sales promotions if they are relieved of the task of order taking and transmitting the consolidated orders to head office. By this, each sales person could do more of a sales job rather than the order taking job.

But, unfortunately many wholesalers failed to follow a predetermined order schedule. They were not used to the system where some one would have to tell them when to order. Some wholesalers complain against fixed schedules and lack of flexibility. Others were so much dependent on sales persons to determine what their requirements are and felt that the new program meant more work for them.

If the orders do not reach the head office according to the schedule, the wholesaler has to wait for two weeks to place the next order. If a wholesaler misses a fixed scheduled date for ordering, he would run the risk of having a stockout which would cause a loss of 20 to 30 percent of sales of tasty-food's products. But due to this only tasty-food products company suffered because the wholesalers and retailers carried several product lines of competitors and when Tasty-Food's brands were out-of-stock, they sold other brands.

Tasty-Food Products has no integrated logistics department to deal with its distribution activities. In the past, three salespersons were made responsible for arranging transportation. When they accumulated orders worth rupees 3 lakhs (nearly a truck load) they would send the orders to the headoffice for shipment. To expedite shipment for wholesalers who have urgent need, a sales person in one area would try to combine his orders with another sales person of the adjoining area to meet the requirement of a full truck load. However, in the new practice, the head office would ship according to a fixed schedule and arrange the shipment with the wholesalers even if the order totaled to less than rupees 3 lakhs.

Questions

1. What are benefits and limitations of the new system of Tasty-Food Products for taking orders?
2. What are the advantages and disadvantages of the new system to *(a)* sales representatives, *(b)* wholesalers/retailers?
3. Suggest a system that would provide better service to customers of Tasty-Food Products company, to improve sales and build closer ties between the company and the wholesalers.

6. DILEMMA AT "COOL AIR" AIR CONDITIONERS

"Cool Air" Airconditioners is a manufacturer of commercial airconditioning units which are exclusively used on the roof of malls or restaurants. Nearly 80 percent of its sales are replacement models which means that the company relies heavily or repeat customers.

An air conditioner usually breaks down with little or no warning. Often the customer is under pressure on finding a replacement within a day or two to run his business. Therefore, the customer is mainly concerned with supplier response no matter who the supplier is—

"Cool Air" Airconditioners hired "Reliable Logistics", a logistics consulting company to help optimise their distribution network and revive sales. At that time, they had 20 distribution centres and warehouses around the country, stocking 40 different models.

"Reliable Logistics" first thought of shrinking the distribution network to four or five strategically located warehouses, each with extensive inventory. This strategy would have reduced 25 percent of "Cool Air" Airconditioners' costs, but would have made rapid delivery tough. The marketing manager of "Cool Air" Airconditioners suggested that the company should go in the opposite direction and expand to 30 locations with a full range of products. But that would have been prohibitively expensive.

Questions

1. What do you think are the problems faced by "Cool Air" Airconditioners?
2. Comment on the idea of "Reliable Logistics" to reduce the distribution centres/warehouses from 20 to 4 or 5 strategic locations.
3. What would you suggest to ensure local availability with minimum inventory for "Cool Air" Airconditioners in their distribution network?

7. SUPPLY CHAIN MANAGEMENT AT BOSE CORPORATION

Bose Corporation manufactures audio premium speakers used in automobiles, high-fidelity systems and consumer and commercial broad-casting systems. Head quartered in Framingham, Massachusetts, Bose Corporation has plants in Massachusetts and Michigan as well as in Canada, Mexico and Ireland. Bose speakers are the best sellers in Japan, the world leader in consumer electronics. Bose's competence is in its electronic engineering skills, but the company attributes much of its business success to its **tightly controlled materials management and excellent integrated supply chain management**.

Bose purchases most of its electronic and other components from independent suppliers scattered around North America, the Far East and Europe. About 50 percent of its purchases are from foreign suppliers, the majority of them are from the Far East. Its purchasing organisation while decentralized has some overlap that requires coordination between sides. Bose attempts to coordinate its globally dispersed supply chain so that material holding and transportation costs are minimised. This requires component parts to arrive at Bose's Massachusetts assembly plant just in time to enter the production process. But because Bose must remain responsive to its customers, it sometimes must respond quickly to increases in customer demand for certain speakers so as to remain competitive. Since Bose does not want to hold extensive inventories at its Massachusetts plant, this need for responsiveness requires Bose's globally dispersed supply chain to respond rapidly to increased demand for component parts.

Bose's materials management function is responsible for coordinating the supply chain to meet both objectives – minimising transportation and inventory holding costs and yet responding quickly to customer demands. This function achieves coordination through a sophisticated logistics operation. Most of Bose's imports from the Far East come via ships to the West coast and then across North America to its Massachusetts plant via train. Most of the company's export also move by ocean freight. Bose does not hesitate to use airfreight when goods are needed urgently.

Bose has a long standing relationship with W.N. Procter, a Boston based freight forwarder and customs broker. Procter handles customs clearance and shipping from suppliers to Bose. Procter provides Bose with up-to-the minute electronic data interchange (EDI) capabilities which enable

Bose to track parts as they move through its global supply chain. Procter provides several other services to Bose such as selecting overseas agents who can help move goods out of the Far East.

Procter's well-established network of overseas contacts is especially useful when shipments must be expedited through foreign customs. Procter also is electronically linked into the US customs system, which allows it to clear freight electronically as much as five days before a ship arrives at a US port or hours before an international airfreight shipment arrives - This helps to get goods to Bose's manufacturing plant several days sooner.

Bose has developed a detailed supplier performance system that measures on-time delivery, quality performance, technical improvements and supplier suggestions. A report is generated twice a month from this system to be sent to the suppliers providing feed-back about supplier performance.

Bose has written contracts with suppliers. After six months of delivery without rejects, Bose certifies the suppliers as qualified suppliers.

Bose uses a sophisticated transportation system which is the best EDI system in the US. This system operates close to real time and allows two-way communication between every one of the freight-handlers' 230 terminals and Bose. Information is updated several times daily. This state-of-the art system helps Bose's managers to proactively manage logistics time elements in pursuit of better customer service.

Perhaps one of the most unique features of Bose's procurement and logistics system is the development of JIT II. The basic premise of JIT II is: "the person who can do the best job of ordering and managing inventory of a particular item is the supplier itself" Bose negotiated with each supplier to provide a full-time employee at the Bose plant who was responsible for ordering, shipping and receiving materials from that plant, as well as managing on-site inventories of the items. This was facilitated through an EDI connection between Bose's plant and the supplier's facility.

Questions

1. Briefly present the salient features of the integrated supply chain management system at Bose.
2. Discuss how the strategy development process might work at a company like Bose.
3. What should be the relationship between Bose's supply management strategy and the development of its performance measurement system?
4. Discuss the importance of quality of purchased components to Bose.

8. SKF BEARING'S BEST PRACTICES

"SKF'S outbound logistics outsourcing is characterised by strong control over quality norms and delivery schedules by SKF personnel"

SKF Bearings is one of the world's biggest ball bearing manufacturing units, and they have a sizeable presence in India. As part of its supply chain management practice, SKF Bearings handles the training, implementation and quality control activities themselves, while outsourcing the actual operations to logistic solution providers. Outbound warehousing and transportation practices are outsourced to logistic solution providers and national transporters.

(A) **Inbound transportation and warehousing :** Complete vendor outsourced, *i.e.*, transportation and warehousing managed and handled by vendors.

(B) **Outbound transportation :** Handled predominantly by national fleet operators, with some responsibilities of contingency transportation outsourced to organised players.

(C) **Outbound warehousing :** Completely outsourced to organised players with five players handling different warehouses of the company.

SKF's outbound logistics outsourcing is characterized by strong control over quality norms and delivery schedules by SKF personnel. Outbound warehousing which is a completely outsourced activity is controlled by SKF personnel by integrating the warehouses through their in-house developed ERP software platform.

Training of logistics company personnel to load/unload goods, assemble and disassemble and for integrating scheduling and supply orders is imparted by SKF. Through this, they have managed to achieve 100 percent order cycle fulfillment, bring down damaged/short/over delivery instances to almost 0.25 percent of total annual order and train logistic personnel to meet all in-house developed quality norms.

Even though majority of their logistics partners have IT capabilities of their own, SKF Bearings doesn't use them as they have integrated their own IT platform to schedule orders, keep track of consignments and to manage both effective and efficient distribution. Their warehousing costs are higher than their outbound transportation costs because of the extensive warehousing practices, but they have achieved gains through the application of internal control over implementation of quality norms, strict adherence to Standard Operating Procedures (SOPs) and a robust system of IT implementation throughout their supply chain.

Future Plans: Moving slowly towards Vendor Managed Inventory (VMI) for inbound sourcing and also looking at outsourcing more warehouse management responsibilities. Looking to implement more definitive 3PL solutions for outbound activities of the supply chain, but will still keep operational control in its own hands..

Questions

1. Discuss the activities involved in the supply chain of SKF Bearings.
2. Explain how SKF establishes strong control over its outbound logistics.
3. What is meant by vendor managed inventory (VMI)?
4. What is meant by third party (3PL) logistics solutions? Explain how SKF will be able to implement the same.

9. STAR SOUND SYSTEMS

Star Sound Systems manufactures and sells sound systems for both home and automobiles. All parts of the sound systems, with the exception of DVD players are produced in the Rourkela (Orissa) plant. DVD players used in the assembly of Star Sound Systems are purchased from Mangala Electronics of Vishakapatnam (Andra Pradesh)

Star Sound Systems purchase manager Madan Kumar submits a purchase requisition for DVD players once every 4 weeks. The company"s annual requirement total 5000 units (20 per working day, 250 working days per year) and the cost per unit is Rs. 6000. (The company does not purchase in higher quantities because Mangala Electronics does not offer quantity discounts). The supplier of DVD players promises delivery within one week following the receipt of a purchase requisition, and rarely there is a shortage of DVD players (Total time between date of order and date of receipt is 5 days)

Procurement costs are estimated as Rs. 200 per order including the costs of preparing the requisition, inspecting and storing the delivered goods, up dating inventory records and issuing a voucher and a cheque for payment. In addition to the procurement costs, Star Sound Systems incurs inventory carrying costs that include insurance, storage, handling, taxes *etc.*, These costs are estimated as Rs. 60 per unit per year.

Beginning in April of this year, Star Sound Systems will embark on a company-wide cost-control drive in an attempt to improve its profits. One area to be closely scrutinized for possible cost savings is inventory procurement.

Questions

1. Compute the optimal order quantity of DVD players.
2. Determine the appropriate re order point.
3. Compute the cost savings that the company will realize if it implements the optimal inventory procurement decision.
4. Should procurement costs be considered a linear function of the number of orders?

10. MRP AT COMFORT COACH

Comfort coach, the worlds largest manufacturer of luxury buses builds thousands of different and constantly changing configurations of its products. The custom nature of its business means lots of options and special designs and a potential scheduling and inventory night mare for the company. Comfort coach succeeded in solving its problems with an MRP system. But as with most MRP implementations, however solving one set of problems incovers a new set.

One of the new issues that had to be addressed by plant manager was newly discovered excess inventory. Managers discovered a substantial amount of inventory that was not called for in any finished products. Excess inventory was evident because of the new level of inventory accuracy required by the MRP system.

The other reason was a new series of inventory report generated by the MRP system software purchased by the company.

One of these reports indicate where items are used and is known as "where used" report. Many items found in the inventory were not called out on bills-of-materials (BOM) for any current products.

The discovering of this excess inventory led to renewed efforts to ensure that the BOMs were accurate. With significant effort it was possible to increase the accuracy of BOMs and consequently the number of engineering change notices decreased. Also, it was possible to improve the purchase-order accuracy with regard to both part numbers and quantities ordered. Additionally, receiving department and stock-room accuracy improved all helping to maintain schedule, costs, and ultimately shipping dates and quality.

Eventually, the plant manager concluded that the residual amounts of excess inventory were the result of rapid changes in luxury coach design and technology. Another source was customer changes made after specifications had been determined and materials ordered. This excess occurs because even though the throughput time is only 20 days, many of the items that the company purchases require much longer lead times.

Questions

1. Why is accurate inventory such an important issue at Comfort Coach?
2. What kind of a plan would you suggest for dealing with excess inventory at Comfort Coach?
3. Be specific in your suggestions for reducing inventory and how to implement them.

REFERENCES

1. K. Shridhara Bhat, *"Materials Management"*, 1st Edition, 2004, Himalaya Publishing House.
2. K. Shridhara Bhat, *"Logistics Management"*, 1st Edition, 2005, Himalaya Publishing House.
3. K. Shridhara Bhat, *"Inventory Management"*, 1st Edition, 2007, Himalaya Publishing House.
4. K. Shridhara Bhat, *"Essentials of Logistics and Supply Chain Management"*, 1st Edition, 2007, Himalaya Publishing House.
5. K. Shridhara Bhat, *"Logistics and Supply Chain Management"*, 1st Edition, 2007, Himalaya Publishing House.

INDEX

[A]

A-B-C analysis, 139
Action bucket, 169
Action planning, 225
Actual price method, 275
Allocated inventory, 168
Allocation method, 121
Alphabetic system, 281
Alpha-numeric system , 281
Ancillary development, 211
Anticipation inventory, 126
Attack strategies, 48
Auxiliary equipments, 327
Available inventory, 168
Average price method, 273
Average usage, 121

[B]

Bar coding, 76
Basic EOQ model, 128
Benefits of variety control, 293
Bill of material file, 148, 167
Bill of materials explosion, 120
Bill of materials implosion, 120
Bill of materials, 119, 168
Blanket order, 216
Block system, 281
Brain-storming, 313
Brisch system, 283
Buffer stock, 136
Business logistics, 17

[C]

Capability, 253
Capacity requirement planning, 170
Capital reduction strategy, 48
Carrying (holding) costs, 127
Cash purchasing, 216
Categorical plan, 246
Centralised purchasing, 219
Centralised versus decentralized storing, 260
Centralised-decentralised purchasing, 219
Channel power, 2
Channel-based strategy, 49
Characteristics of value, 296
Check lists, 313
Classification of inventories, 125
Classification, codification, 271, 279
Closed loop MRP, 182
Codification, 279
Common costs, 232
Company standard, 286
Competitive environment, 45
Competitive pressures, 22
Component standardization, 285
Concept of consolidation, 55
Continuous review system ("Q" system), 135
Contract purchasing, 215
Conveyers, 325
Corporate mission statement, 36
Cost reduction strategy, 48
Cost value, 300
Customer service explosion, 46
Customer service policies, 39
Customer service, 53
Cycle counting, 170, 178

Cycle inventory decision, 83
Cycle view, 66
Cycles, 102

[D]

Decentralised purchasing, 219
Decimal system, 282
Demand and supply methods, 121
Demand forecasts, 98
Demand, 53
Dependent demand, 170
Design analysis, 313
Desired inventory level (DIL), 137
Deterministic inventory models, 128
Differentiated distribution concept, 54
Distribution requirement planning, 77
Drivers, 252

[E]

Economic forecasts, 97
Economic order quantity (EOQ) model, 128
Economic order quantity, 122
Effectiveness of inventory management, 144
Efficiency in handling materials, 329
Electronic data interchange, 76
Enterprise resources planning, 183
EOQ model system, 128
Esteem value, 300
Event logistics, 18
Exchange value, 300
Exponential smoothing method, 104
External interfaces, 13

[F]

Facilitators, 252
Feasible optimal quantity, 134
Financial planning, 96
Finished goods inventories, 125
First-in, first-out (FIFO) method, 273
Fixed order system, 121
Fixed-order quantity system (Q system), 128
Flexibility advantage, 118
Flexible budget, 114
Flow pattern, 321
Fluctuation inventory, 126
Forecasting approaches, 100
Forecasting process, 99
Forecasting time horizons, 96
Forecasting, 95
Forecasts, 95
Forward buying, 215
Fourth-party logistics, 56
Frozen MPS, 170
F-S-N analysis, 143
Functional stores, 262
Functions of inventory, 126
Functions of materials handling, 316

[G]

Generic logistics strategies, 49
Global sourcing, 228
G-O-L-F analysis, 143
Gross requirements, 169
Group purchasing, 215

[H]

Hedging, 215
Hierarchy of planning, 36
H-M-L analysis, 143

[I]

Impulse response, 105
Independent demand, 170
Individual standard, 286
Industrial standardization, 284
Industry standard, 286
Inflated price method, 276
Information flow, 33

Information technology, 2
Innovations in logistics, 75
In-process inventories, 125
Integrated concept, 10
Integrated data model, 186
Integrated logistics management, 29
Integrated logistics model, 31
Integrated logistics, 1
Integrated management information, 184
Integrated supply chain management, 62
Interchangeability, 285
Internal interfaces, 12
International standard, 286, 291
International transaction costs, 232
Inventory costs, 127
Inventory decisions, 128
Inventory flow, 32
Inventory status file, 148, 167, 168
Inventory, 124

[J]

JIT deliveries, 77
JIT purchasing, 71
Judgemental methods (Delphi method), 101
Jury of executive opinion, 100
Just-in-time purchasing, 217
Just-in-time systems (JIT), 187

[K]

Key supplier evaluation criteria, 240
Kodak system, 283

[L]

Last-in, first-out (LIFO) method, 273
Layout of stores, 264
Lead time, 121
Levels of standards, 286
Levels of vendor assessment, 237
Life-cycle support, 45
Load schedules, 170
Location of stores, 259
Logistical activities, 23
Logistical competency, 20
Logistical mission, 21
Logistical objectives, 44
Logistical operations, 33
Logistics audit, 40
Logistics costs, 27, 54
Logistics environment, 35
Logistics environment, 45
Logistics management, 14, 18
Logistics mission statement, 43
Logistics outsourcing, 56
Logistics plan, 41
Logistics planning, 42
Logistics strategic plan, 35
Logistics strategic planning, 37
Logistics strategies, 47
Logistics supply chain, 25
Logistics, 16, 17, 74
Long-range forecast, 97
Lot-for-lot ordering, 170, 176
Lot-sizing decisions, 169
Lot-sizing, 175
Low-level coding, 169
Lumpy demand, 170

[M]

Make or buy decisions, 226
Make-or-buy, 211
Manufacturing resource planning or MRP-II, 146, 165
Manufacturing support, 34
Market research method, 101
Market-based strategy, 49
Mass customization, 298
Master production schedule (MPS), 148, 167, 168
Material requirements planning, 163
Materials budgeting, 113
Materials classification, 259

Materials control cycle, 118
Materials handling costs, 319
Materials handling equipments, 325
Materials handling principles, 318
Materials handling system, 324
Materials handling, 315
Materials management, 3, 4
Materials planning, 110
Materials requirements planning (MRP-I), 145
Materials utilization, 118
Mechanisation, 329
Medium or long-range objectives, 99
Medium-range forecast, 97
Military logistics, 18
Minimum inventory, 44
Minimum variance, 44
Mixed strategy concept, 55
Mnemonic system, 282
Model of supply chain management, 77
Movement consolidation, 45
Moving averages method, 103
MRO inventories, 125
MRP computer program, 168
MRP system inputs, 148
Multilevel bills of materials, 119

[N]

Naïve approach, 103
National standard, 286
Net change MRP, 170
Net requirements, 169
New facility planning, 96
Noise dampening, 105
Noise, 102
Numeric system, 282

[O]

Objectives of materials handling, 318
Objectives of MRP, 145
Objectives of standardization, 285
Objectives of stores management, 258
Objectives of value analysis, 302
On-hand inventory, 169
Operational planning, 37
Optimum stock requirements, 118
Ordering costs (acquisition costs), 127
Ordering system, 213
Organisational planning process, 37
Outsourcing, 70
Overall inventory, 144

[P]

Pareto analysis, 139
Pareto's law, 139
Pegging, 170, 177
Periodic review system ("P" system), 137
Period-order quantity (POQ) method, 170
Physical distribution, 34
Physical stores, 262, 263
Pipe-line inventory, 126
Place utility, 26
Planned order receipts, 169
Planned order releases, 169
Planning horizon, 169
Post-purchase system, 214
Preferred number system, 287
Pre-purchase system, 213
Price advantage, 118
Price analysis, 313
Pricing policy, 54
Principle of postponement, 55
Principles of classification and codification, 271, 280
Principles of stores layout, 264
Proactive logistics strategy, 48
Procedure manual, 212, 222
Process of codification, 281
Process view of a supply chain, 66
Process-based strategy, 49
Procurement, 34, 197

Product explosion, 170
Product structure, 168
Production characteristics, 54
Production inventories, 125
Production planning, 96
Production stores, 262
Profit centre concept, 10
Profit leverage, 23
Purchase parameters, 200
Purchase requisitions, 122
Purchasing cycle, 69, 207
Purchasing ethics, 212
Purchasing management process, 223
Purchasing management, 202
Purchasing manual, 212
Purchasing methods, 214
Purchasing organizations, 217
Purchasing policies, 211, 220
Purchasing procedures, 222
Purchasing systems, 213
Purchasing, 197
Push/pull boundary, 67
Push/pull view of supply chain process, 67

[Q]

Quality, 45, 253
Quantity discounts for EOQ model, 133

[R]

Random variations, 102
Rapid response, 44
Rationalisation, 276
Raw material stores, 262
Reciprocal purchasing, 217
Reciprocity, 6, 212
Regenerative MRP, 170
Reliability, 253
Re-order level, re-order point, 128
Reorder point, 121
Reserve stock, 121
Resource management, 186
Resource requirement planning system, 162
Resource requirement planning, 161
Review period, 137
Right contract, 202
Right place of delivery, 202
Right price, 200
Right procedure, 202
Right quality, 201
Right quantity, 201
Right source, 201
Right time, 201
Right transportation, 201
Rough-cut capacity planning, 161

[S]

Safety stock inventory, 125
Safety stock, 133, 176
Sales composite method, 100
Scheduled receipts, 169
Scheduled purchasing, 216
Scrap allowances, 177
S-D-E analysis, 143
Seamless integration, 184
Seasonal purchasing, 217
Seasonality, 102
Selective inventory control, 139
Service improvement strategies, 48
Service level constant, 136
Service level, 136
Service logistics, 18
Shortage costs, 127
Short-range forecast, 96
Simple moving average method, 103
Simple numeric system, 281
Simplification, 277, 284, 289
S-O-S analysis, 143
Specification, 289
Speculative buying, 211

Speculative purchasing, 215
Standard price (standard cost) method, 275
Standard, 284
Standardisation, 6, 276, 283
Stock verification, 270
Storage system, 264
Storekeeping, 257
Stores management functions, 267
Stores manual, 266
Stores organization, 261
Stores record method, 121
Strandardisation, 56
Strategic decisions, 226
Strategic logistics plan, 39, 40
Strategic plan, 36
Strategic planning process, 35
Strategic planning, 36
Strategy formulation, 52
Subcontracting, 217
Supplier audits, 73, 249
Supplier certification, 73, 249
Supplier partnership, 73, 205, 249
Supplier selection, 208
Supplier/vendor selection criteria, 253
Supply chain drivers, 81
Supply chain management, 13, 14, 58, 61, 184
Supply chain operations, 65
Supply chain planning, 65
Supply chain strategy, 65
Supply chain thinking, 60
Supply chain, 13, 58, 64 59, 204
Supply management, 202
System of preferred numbers, 293
Systems approach, 30
Systems contracting, 215
Systems of codification, 281

[T]

Tactical decisions, 226
Tactical planning, 36
Techniques for averaging, 102
Techniques of value analysis, 312
Technological forecasts, 97
Tender buying, 216
The purchasing cycle, 222
Third party logistics services, 92
Third-party logistics, 56
Time compression, 46
Time fence, 170, 178
Time series, 102
Time utility, 26
Total cost concept, 54
Tracking signal, 106
Traffic management, 75
Trend, 102
Turnover ratio, 144
Type I partnership, 251
Type II partnership, 251
Type III partnership, 251
Types of logistics, 17
Types of standards, 288
Types of stores layout, 266
Types of stores, 262

[U]

Unit load concept, 321
Use value, 300

[V]

Valuation of stocks, 272
Value analysis process (value engineering process), 309
Value analysis techniques, 311
Value analysis, 70, 212, 293, 364
Value equation, 297
Value tests, 308
Value, 295
Value-driven competition, 298
Variety reduction, 291
V-E-D analysis, 142
Vendor analysis, 73

Vendor development, 236
Vendor evaluation and selection process, 237
Vendor evaluation, 243
Vendor motivation, 250
Vendor rating, 211, 242

[W]

Warehousing, 76, 257
Weighted average method, 274
Weighted moving average method, 103
Weighted point plan, 247
Workforce scheduling, 96

[X]

X-Y-Z analysis, 142